WESTERN INDIA
IN THE NINETEENTH CENTURY

STUDIES IN SOCIAL HISTORY

edited by

HAROLD PERKIN

Professor of Social History, University of Lancaster

WESTERN INDIA IN THE NINETEENTH CENTURY

*A Study in the Social History
of Maharashtra*

by
Ravinder Kumar

LONDON: Routledge & Kegan Paul
TORONTO: University of Toronto Press
1968

First published 1968
in Great Britain by
Routledge & Kegan Paul Limited
and in Canada by
University of Toronto Press

Printed in Great Britain by
Richard Clay (The Chaucer Press) Ltd.,
Bungay, Suffolk

SBN 7100 4568 9

Acknowledgements

THIS book is based on a thesis which I presented to the Australian National University for the award of a Ph.D. degree in 1964. I am, therefore, deeply indebted to the Australian National University for providing me with the financial assistance which enabled me to look into material at archival repositories in New Delhi, Bombay and Poona. I am also indebted to the Director of the National Archives of India at New Delhi, and to the Director of the Maharashtra State Archives at Bombay, for permitting me to consult the material located in the offices under their charge.

As a student of history I owe a great intellectual debt to Professor Anthony Low, who supervised my work in Canberra; and to Professor P. H. Partridge, whose seminars on the sociology of power opened up a new horizon before me. Among those who read the thesis and made valuable suggestions are: Shri V. C. Joshi; Shri B. R. Nanda; Professor T. Raychaudhri; Dr. Eric Stokes; Professor P. M. Joshi; Professor N. R. Pathak; Dr. Bruce Graham; Professor T. R. Metcalfe and Dr. Eleanor Searle.

I am obliged to Miss Pamela Griffiths for preparing the index, and for assistance in checking the proof copies. Last but not the least, I would like to thank Mrs. May Richardson and Mrs. B. A. Gallina for typing out the manuscript, and also to thank Mr. H. E. Gunther for preparing at very short notice a most useful map of Maharashtra.

RAVINDER KUMAR

Canberra, February 1967

to ASHA

Contents

A Select Glossary of Indian Terms

Abhangas	The songs composed by the folk saints of Maharashtra.
Adawlut	A court of justice.
Advaita	A monistic school of philosophy founded by the Indian philosopher Sankaracharya.
Beegah	A unit of area, approximately ½ acre.
Bhayachara	A term which indicates a relationship of brotherhood.
Bhowbund	A brotherhood.
Bullotedars	The Marathi term for village artisans.
Camvisdar	A subordinate native revenue officer.
Carcoon	A servant.
Chamar	The caste of leather-workers.
Chowar	A unit of area, approximately 120 acres.
Chowrie	The municipal hall in a village.
Cowl	A contract or engagement.
Cusbah	A substantial village or township.
Daftar	An office or Secretariat.
Daftardar	The ranking native officer in a District Office.
Dakshina	(*Lit.* a gift) The prize awarded annually to brahmans by the Peshwas.
Deshmukh	A Marathi term for a landed aristocrat.
Dharamsala	A rest house for travellers.
Enam	(*Lit.* a gift) A term designating a grant to a feudal dependent.
Ghutcool	(*Lit.* Past families) A Marathi term which refers to land belonging to extinct families.
Huzoor Cutcherry	(*Lit.* Principal Office) A term which refers to the office of a District or Settlement Officer.

Jathas   A group of families.

Julaha   A weaver.

Jyotish   The art of astrology.

Kamal   The revenue survey conducted in Maharashtra under Madhav Rao Peshwa.

Khatik   The caste of butchers.

Kulkarni   The village accountant.

Kunbis   The caste of cultivators in Maharashtra.

Mahar   A caste of untouchables which provides watchmen in the villages.

Mamlatdar   A revenue officer who was in charge of a *taluka* under the Marathas. The term also refers to a native officer responsible for the collection of tax in a *taluka* under the British Government.

Mauzewar   A term which refers to a village or a revenue estate.

Meeras   A form of tenure which confers 'proprietary' rights upon a cultivator.

Meerasdar   A cultivator who holds land on the *meeras* tenure.

Mohturfa   A tax on urban incomes.

Nazarana   The presents given by a feudal dependent to his lord.

Nyaya   A school of Hindu philosophy.

Panchayat   A council of five persons.

Pathshala   A school.

Patil   The headman of a village.

Puntoji   A brahman, usually a teacher.

Puttah   A title deed.

Rivaj   (*Lit.* custom) A term which refers to the traditional rates of assessment.

Ryot   A peasant.

Ryotwari   A form of settlement in which the peasants pay their land-tax directly to the State.

Sadar Adawlat   The Principal Court.

Shastras   The sacred books of Hinduism.

Shastri   A brahman versed in the *Shastras*.

Sillahdar   A soldier of cavalry.

Sowcar   A financier who resides in a city.

Sthul	An estate.
Taluka	A territorial unit smaller than a district.
Tankha	A settlement introduced by Malik Amber in Maharashtra.
Thulwaheeks	Cultivators descended from the founding families of a village.
Tukseem	(*Lit.* a fraction) A branch of a family.
Uprees	Cultivators who do not possess any prescriptive rights in the land.
Vani	A village moneylender.
Vedanta	A system of philosophy which seeks to interpret the Vedas. The term normally refers to Sankara's *advaitavada*.
Vyakaran	Grammar.
Vydic	A term which refers to the medical profession.
Watan	A grant in land or a right in office.
Watandar	One who holds a *watan*.

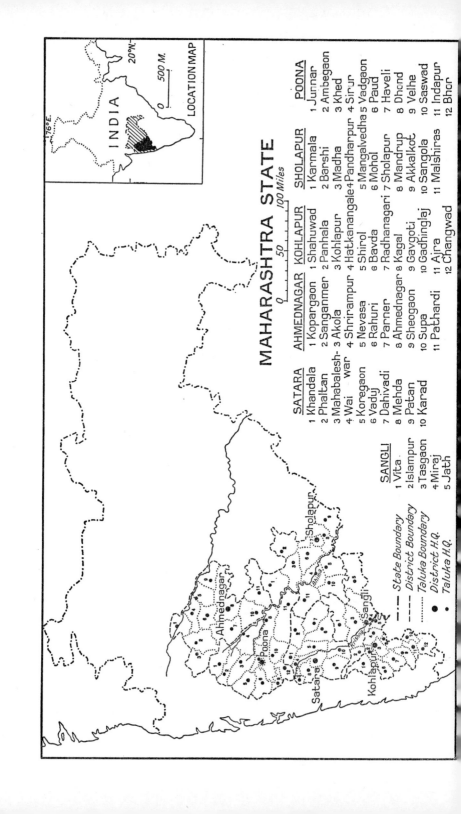

MAHARASHTRA STATE

INDIA

LOCATION MAP

0 500 M.

0 50 100 Miles

SATARA
1 Khandala
2 Phaltan
3 Mahabalesh-war
4 Wai
5 Koregaon
6 Vaduj
7 Dahivadi
8 Mehda
9 Patan
10 Karad

SANGLI
1 Vita
2 Islampur
3 Tasgaon
4 Miraj
5 Jath

AHMEDNAGAR
1 Kopargaon
2 Sanganmer
3 Akola
4 Shrirampur
5 Nevasa
6 Rahuri
7 Parner
8 Ahmednagar
9 Sheogaon
10 Supa
11 Pathardi

KOHLAPUR
1 Shahuwad
2 Panhala
3 Kohlapur
4 Hatkanangale
5 Shirol
6 Bavda
7 Radhanagari
8 Kagal
9 Gavgoti
10 Gadhinglaj
11 Ajra
12 Changwad

SHOLAPUR
1 Karmala
2 Barshi
3 Madha
4 Pandharpur
5 Mangalvedha
6 Mohol
7 Sholapur
8 Mandrup
9 Akkalkot
10 Sangola
11 Malshiras

POONA
1 Junnar
2 Ambegaon
3 Khed
4 Sirur
5 Vadgaon
6 Paud
7 Haveli
8 Dhond
9 Velhe
10 Saswad
11 Indapur
12 Bhor

State Boundary
District Boundary
Taluka Boundary
● District H.Q.
• Taluka H.Q.

Ahmednagar

Poona

Sholapur

Satara

Sangli

Kohlapur

I

The Poona Districts in 1818

MAHARASHTRA, literally the great country, lies in central and western India. It is inhabited by a people who speak the Marathi language, and who possess a distinct historical and cultural tradition, which sets them apart from the rest of the subcontinent of India. Maharashtra covers an area which is bounded by the Arabian Sea on the west, the rivers Narbada and Tapti on the north, and the Malaprabha on the south, while its eastern boundary is defined by geographical characteristics which demarcate the western limits of the Telugu region. Apart from the narrow Concan coast, which lies between the Arabian Sea and the Ghats, Maharashtra comprises a plateau which slopes gradually to the east, but descends precipitously to the west towards the coastal plain and the Arabian Sea. From the Ghats, which stretch roughly north to south, long tongues of higher ground run east and divide the plateau into compartments like the plains of Berar and Nagpur, the basin of the upper Godavri, and of the Bhima between Poona and Sholapur.

The location of Maharashtra has conferred certain advantages upon her people which are reflected in their history and in their political and cultural traditions. The Narbada and Tapti, which define the northern boundary of Maharashtra, act as formidable barriers in the path of any invader who proceeds towards the Deccan from the north. Besides such obstacles, the terrain of Maharashtra offers ideal conditions for sustained

I

resistance against an alien authority. Both the Ghats, which run parallel to the coast, and the tongues of higher ground, which branch off eastwards from the Ghats, are flanked by rich valleys and plains in which are located many towns and villages. The uplands of Maharashtra therefore constitute an ideal base for armed resistance against an invader, since they possess abundant sources of supply, and numerous sites for military strongholds, where power can be organised both for aggression and for defence. The region is considered to be one of the most inaccessible parts of India by military strategists.

Because of the location of Maharashtra and the identity of her people, the region possesses a political and an historical tradition which distinguishes it from other parts of the subcontinent of India. In referring to these unique qualities of Maharashtra Spate, for instance, has summed up the land and the people with remarkable acumen and perception. 'The entire region,' he points out, 'bears the imprint of the Marathas: a tough, hard-working, and cheerful peasantry, ably served by an adroit Brahmin élite which maintained close touch with the people.'[1] The unique qualities of Maharashtra were equally apparent to Sir Richard Temple, the Governor of Bombay in the 1870s. Speaking of the extent to which the high culture of Hinduism had influenced the religious traditions of the region, Sir Richard Temple observed: 'But despite (the values which they share with the rest of India) the Mahrattas have always formed a separate people or nation, and still regard themselves as such.'[2] The qualities which struck Spate and Temple could hardly have failed to make an impression on indigenous scholars, who have consequently devoted considerable time and attention to scholarly studies of the history and culture of the region.[3]

[1] O. H. K. Spate, *India and Pakistan* (London, 1954), p. 654.
[2] R. Temple, 'The Maratha Nationality' in *Shivaji and the Rise of the Marathas* (Calcutta, 1953), p. 1.
[3] The history of Maharashtra has been investigated in detail by Maharashtrian scholars who have published their findings both in English and in Marathi, though mainly in the latter. The pioneer in this field was M. G. Ranade, who wrote a series of essays attempting to unravel the reason behind the rise of Maharashtra in the 17th and 18th centuries. The scholar who has exercised the greatest influence on the historians of Maharashtra, however, is V. K. Rajwade. He collected and published twenty-two volumes of original documents dealing with the history of the region, and he touched upon all the important problems of the history of the region in

I

Behind the unique qualities of the people of Maharashtra lies an historical tradition which stretches into the beginnings of the Christian era. During the three centuries which followed the birth of Christ, the region was ruled by the Satvahana kings from Paithan on the Godavri. Besides being the capital of a powerful kingdom, Paithan under the Satvahanas was a well-known centre of culture and commerce, and its architectural remains speak of a thriving and prosperous city. The decline of the Satvahanas was followed by a time of troubles in Maharashtra. But the Chalukyas, who established their sway over the region in the 6th century, and ruled over it for the next century and a half, were powerful enough to inflict a defeat on Harsha of Kanauj, who controlled the whole of India north of the Narbada. The Chalukyas were displaced in A.D. 780 by the Rashtrakutas, who dominated Maharashtra till the end of the 10th century, and were the most powerful rulers of the region before the Peshwas, of whom more later. The Rashtrakutas were in turn overthrown by a cadet branch of the Chalukyas, but political control over the region passed into the hands of a Yadava clan, which was overwhelmed by Alauddin Khilji in the closing years of the 13th century.[1]

Though the Yadavas were vanquished by Alauddin Khilji, the intrusion of Islam in the Deccan weakened rather than destroyed the power of the landed chiefs of Maharashtra, whom we shall presently discuss in greater detail. The inaccessibility of their mountain strongholds bestowed considerable independence on these landed chiefs even when Muslim kingdoms were established south of the Narbada. But while they enjoyed a substantial measure of local autonomy, the landed chiefs of Maharashtra never presented any serious threat to the political dominance of Islam, partly because they were unable to

the introductions he wrote to these volumes. Rajwade's example influenced and inspired V. S. Khare, D. B. Parasnis and G. S. Sardesai, all of whom have made significant contributions to historical scholarship. The tradition set by these scholars is being maintained in our own times by Professor P. M. Joshi of Poona, and Professor N. R. Pathak of Bombay. The work of these historians reflects a sensitive awareness of the regional identity of Maharashtra.

[1] C. A. Kincaid and D. B. Parasnis, *A History of the Maratha People* (Oxford, 1918), Vol. 1, Chaps. I to VI.

unite in opposition to the Muslim rulers, and partly also because their interests were in no way seriously threatened by them.

Shivaji, the national hero of Maharashtra, who organised a movement against the Muslim rulers of the Deccan, belonged to an upstart family whose fortunes had been founded by his father. Shivaji saw his great opportunity when the Mughal Emperor Aurangzeb vanquished the Muslim kingdoms of the Deccan; and he exploited the political vacuum created by Aurangzeb to set up an independent State, which was inspired and sustained by the principles of resurgent Hinduism and Maratha dominance. Shivaji and his soldiers were Marathas of lowly caste, but his ministers and administrators were recruited almost exclusively from high-caste brahmans. Shivaji had many achievements to his credit. He inculcated self-confidence in his people; he organised them into a formidable military power; and he laid the foundations of an enduring political society. The State established by Shivaji was visited by various vicissitudes after his death. But despite the enormous resources which he controlled, Aurangzeb was unable to vanquish that spirit of independence which was Shivaji's greatest boon to his people, and he weakened the foundations of the Mughal Empire in an attempt to annihilate a State which rested on the support of the common people of Maharashtra.[1]

After the successors of Shivaji had consolidated their position in the Deccan, the Mughal Emperors were obliged to acquiesce in their independence, and to grant them formal recognition. The instrument of recognition was negotiated on behalf of Shivaji's grandson by his brahman minister, whose official designation was the Peshwa. The office of the Peshwa grew in importance as the Marathas gained in strength, and eventually be-

[1] A considerable amount of biographical literature is available about Shivaji. Sir Jadunath Sarker's *Shivaji and His Times* (4th edn, Calcutta, 1961) is still the best general survey of the life and times of the Maratha statesman. J. Grant-Duff devotes a considerable portion of the first volume of his *History of the Marathas* (4th edn, Bombay, 1876) to Shivaji's career. Most Maharashtrian scholars, however, find Grant-Duff's account of Shivaji lacking in sympathy, and they feel that he pays inadequate attention to the religious changes which were sweeping across Maharashtra contemporaneously, and which created a favourable climate for the political unification of the region. See, for instance, M. G. Ranade's essays on the *Rise of the Maratha Power* (Bombay, 1961), and Chapter III of G. S. Sardesai's *The Main Currents of Maratha History* (Bombay, 1949).

came hereditary, while the descendants of Shivaji sank into a position of insignificance. By the middle of the 18th century the political system founded by Shivaji became dominant throughout Maharashtra, with the Peshwas controlling authority from their seat at Poona, while the titular kings clung to the shadow of power at Satara.

While the Peshwas established their authority over Maharashtra, some of the Maratha chiefs busied themselves in carving out independent principalities from the outlying provinces of the Mughal Empire. Prominent among these chiefs were the Bhonsles who established themselves in Nagpur; the Scindhias who gained control of Gwalior; the Gaekwads who set themselves up in Baroda; and the Holkars who seized hold of Indore. Between the Peshwas and the Maratha chiefs there subsisted a relationship which it is most difficult to define. The chiefs were to all intents and purposes independent, yet they recognised the Peshwa as the head of the Maratha polity. But while they accepted the Peshwa as their suzerain, they reserved to themselves considerable freedom of action. The political system of Maharashtra therefore resembled a Confederacy. The Peshwa, who was the head of this Confederacy, ruled the Marathi speaking territories from his seat at Poona, while the subordinate Maratha chiefs controlled extensive provinces in central and western India. Despite its loosely knit structure, the Maratha Confederacy became the dominant power in India under the leadership of Balaji Baji Rao, who occupied the office of Peshwa from 1740 to 1761.

The growth of Maratha power was first checked at the battle of Panipat, which was fought in 1761. The débâcle of Panipat shook the political edifice headed by the Peshwas to its very foundations, and seriously weakened Maratha power. But while the Marathas were able to recover from the defeat of Panipat, and applied themselves with renewed vigour to a policy of expansion, they met their Nemesis in the British East India Company. The first Anglo-Maratha War, which was fought in the 1780s, proved inconclusive. But within a decade dissensions in the Confederacy created a serious rift between the Peshwa and the Maratha chiefs, and forced the former to seek British protection. Whereupon the East India Company, acting on behalf of the Peshwa, inflicted in 1803 a series of military reverses on the Maratha chiefs, and obliged them to cede large chunks of territory and to accept British political supremacy.

Though the events of 1803 destroyed the Maratha Confederacy by placing the Peshwa under British tutelage, he refused to accept the verdict of the Second Anglo-Maratha War as final. The initiative for the third and final round of hostilities came from the Peshwa, despite the fact that in 1802 he had placed himself voluntarily under British protection. Spurred by memories of past glory, the Peshwa placed himself at the head of a combination which sought to rid the country of British control. However, his desperate attempt to reassert his independence ended in military disaster at Kirki near Poona in 1818. Under the terms of a peace settlement, the Peshwa retired as a state prisoner to Bithur near Kanpur, while the territories under his control were taken over by the British Government.[1]

II

The geographical factors which enabled the political leaders of Maharashtra to offer effective opposition to Islam, and which also enabled them to dominate the subcontinent of India, have received considerable attention at the hands of the historians of the region. It would be foolish to deny that the inaccessibility of Maharashtra played a significant part in moulding the resistance which her leaders offered to Islam. But it would be equally foolish to maintain that factors of geography alone explain the resistance which the people of Maharashtra offered to the spread of Islam in the Deccan. To explain this resistance, and to explain the striking political vitality of the region, we have to look in other directions.

The key to the vigour of Maharashtra lay in the secular and spiritual values which inspired the people of the region. These values stemmed from a religious upsurge which coincided with the advent of Islam in the Deccan, and which affiliated the

[1] The events leading to the dissolution of the Maratha Empire can be gleaned from a number of works, of which the most important are: (i) J. Grant-Duff, *History of the Marathas* (4th edn, Bombay, 1876), Vol. II; (ii) Sir Jadunath Sarker, *Fall of the Mughal Empire* (2nd edn, Calcutta, 1950), Vol. II; and (iii) G. S. Sardesai, *New History of the Marathas* (Bombay, 1957), Vols. I and II. The career of the last Peshwa is sketched out in detail by P. C. Gupta in his *Baji Rao II and the East India Company* (Oxford, 1939). Also see *Poona Residency Records*, ed. by G. S. Sardesai, Vol. XII Bombay, 1950), and Vol. XIII (Bombay, 1953).

élite castes, like the brahmans, and the lower and middle castes, like the *kunbis* and *mahars*, to a common corpus of religious ideas. By resolving the tension between the élite and the plebeian castes, Maharashtra was able to bridge a gulf which bedevilled Hindu society elsewhere, and prevented it from offering effective resistance to Islam. The resolution of caste tensions released a flood of creative energy which expressed itself in the political genius of Shivaji and the imperial vision of Baji Rao I.

The seminal intellectual influence upon the brahman castes of Maharashtra was the *advaita* philosophy of Sankara, who lived in the 8th century.[1] Like other exponents of orthodox Hinduism, Sankara sought to initiate the individual into a state called *moksha*, which represents complete spiritual realisation, and which liberates the individual from the trials and tribulations of the secular world. Also like other exponents of orthodox Hinduism, Sankara looked upon his system as the only valid interpretation of the sacred texts of Hinduism, namely, the Upanishads, the Bhagavada Gita and the Vedanta Sutras. The basic postulates of *advaita* were set out in a few simple propositions; that the ultimate reality was a principle called *Brahman*; that the individual soul was a part and parcel of *Brahman*; and finally, that the phenomenal world or *maya* was a reflection of *Brahman* upon the centres of human consciousness. But Sankara expounded these propositions with a skill and subtlety which made him the most distinguished figure in Hindu philosophy.

The vitality of Sankara's ideas lay partly in their intellectual sophistication and logical rigorousness, and partly in the monastical order which he organised to provide a firm institutional basis for his philosophy. However, the concepts advanced by Sankara were directed exclusively to the brahmans, with the result that the values of Hindu orthodoxy did not in the first instance influence the middle and lower castes. Indeed, the activities of Sankara actually divided the Hindu community into a small brahman élite, whose values were firmly anchored to *advaita*, and a host of lesser castes, which were only marginally influenced by the high culture of Hinduism. The integration of the lower castes with the brahmans was a task to which a

---

[1] F. Warden, 'On the Customs of the Gosavees' in A. Steele, *Summary of the Laws and Customs of Hindu Castes Within the Dekhun Provinces Subject to the Bombay Provinces* (Bombay, 1827). Hereinafter referred to as Steel's *Summary of Hindu Laws*.

7

remarkable coterie of religious leaders, the so-called Saints of
Maharashtra, addressed themselves in the centuries following
the spread of Sankara's ideas among the brahmans. The earliest
figures in this movement were Mukundraj and Jnaneshwar, who
lived in the 12th and 13th centuries.[1] Mukundraj was a brahman by caste, a devotee of Shiva, and he wrote a number of
philosophical works in which he expressed in simple Marathi
poetry the *advaita* philosophy of Sankara. In choosing Marathi,
the language of the common folk, instead of Sanskrit, the language of the brahmans, for his philosophical writings Mukundraj
initiated a movement which aimed at influencing the lower and
middle castes of Hindu society. The significance of this transi-
tion is eloquently brought out in an account of the reaction of
the plebeian castes of Paithan when Eknath, a brahman saint in
the populist tradition, acquiesced in the desire of his son, Hari
Pandit, to perform the *kirtan* in Sanskrit instead of Marathi:

> The news spread in the city that Eknath had abandoned the read-
> ing of the *Prakrit* books, and the Hari *kirtans*. . . . The pious took
> this very seriously to heart. 'Our good fortune is broken and lost,'
> they said, 'and therefore Eknath has given up reading the Prakrit
> books, and he himself listens to the *Puranas* in Sanskrit.' The
> women, sudras and those of other castes (than the Brahmans)
> could not understand the Sanskrit, and so while the Purana was
> being read they would get up and leave, abandoning the habit of
> regularly listening. When Sri Nath (Eknath) used to read the
> *Purana* the *wada* (house) was more than filled. Five or ten had to
> remain outside regularly. The place simply swarmed with men.
> Eknath understood the inner feelings of all, and said to himself,
> 'There has been a great falling off in bhakti. . . .'[2]

[1] A wealth of documentary and analytical material is available for the *bhakti* movement in Maharashtra. Attention was first focused on this movement by M. G.
Ranade in his essay entitled 'The Saints and Prophets of Maharashtra'. Ranade
compares the *bhakti* upsurge to the Reformation in Europe, and attributes to it the
creativity of Maharashtra. His interpretation is completely repudiated by a
marxist scholar like D. D. Kosambi (see his *Myth and Reality* (Bombay, 1962), pp.
31–36), and partly repudiated by R. V. Oturkar (see his introduction to *Rise of the
Maratha Power* (Bombay, 1961), p. vi), yet his views find wide if somewhat un-
critical acceptance with most of the historians of Maharashtra. I believe that the
most sophisticated account of the Saints of Maharashtra is to be found in a series
of lectures given by Professor N. R. Pathak before the Bombay *Prarthana Samaj* in
1935. These lectures were subsequently reproduced in the weekly *Subodh Patrika*
between 29 September 1935 and 10 November 1935.
[2] J. E. Abbott, *The Poet-Saints of Maharashtra*, Vol. 2, p. 216. This series, twelve in
number, consists of translations by J. E. Abbott of the account by the Marathi poet,

The most significant figure among the Saints of Maharashtra was Jnaneshwar, who was a brahman like Mukundraj, and who wrote a commentary on the Bhagavada Gita in Marathi called the Jnaneshwari. In expounding the Gita for the common man Jnaneshwar took as his principal theme *bhakti*, or devotion to God, and he is therefore regarded as the founder of the *bhakti* school of Marathi poetry. He was the coryphaeus of the devotional movement, which honoured without distinction Shiva and Vishnu, the two principal Gods of the Hindu pantheon, and which was inspired by the philosophy of Sankara. Since Jnaneshwar was initially a devotee of Shiva, and since he was also an *advaitin*, his conversion to the Vaishnava belief in *bhakti* as an instrument of salvation was probably due to the influence of Ramanuja, a Vaishnava philosopher of the 11th century. It is likely that Jnaneshwar belonged to the Bhagawata cult, which attaches equal importance to Shiva and Vishnu, and that the *bhakti* movement was heavily influenced by the beliefs of the Bhagawatas.[1]

Though it was initiated by brahmans of high caste, the *bhakti* movement soon passed into the hands of plebeians like Namadeva the *shimpi*, or Tukarama the *vani*, who expressed religious and philosophical ideas through poetry which appealed to the emotions rather than the intellect, and which exercised great influence over the common people of Maharashtra. The poetry reflecting the movement glorified *bhakti*, and it laid emphasis on the facility with which it provided access to God. Besides preaching the superiority of devotional as opposed to intellectual realisation, of God the *bhakti* saints tried to undermine the obstacles which stood between high and low castes, and prevented the latter from gaining access to spiritual salvation. But although they advocated the novel doctrine of the spiritual equality of different castes, the *bhakti* saints desisted from attacking secular distinctions of caste, partly in the interests of social harmony, and partly out of indifference to the material world. Eknath the brahman saint, for instance, assured Ranya the *mahar* that

Mahipati, of the life and teachings of the Saints of Maharashtra. Besides providing the reader with an insight into the religious values which sustained the people of Maharashtra, Abbott's work presents a fascinating picture of the social and economic conditions which prevailed in that period.

[1] Vide S. M. Edward's introduction to J. Grant-Duff, *History of the Marathas* (Oxford, 1921), p. lxi.

9

an outcaste could become 'very acceptable to God' through *bhakti*; he even accepted an invitation to dine at Ranya's home, much to the disgust of his caste-fellows. But it was Vithala who assumed Eknath's form, so runs the myth, and dined in his stead at Ranya's home, thus preventing Eknath from being ostracised by the brahmans of Paithan.[1]

The attitude of the Saints of Maharashtra towards God, and towards the institution of caste, was vividly reflected in the poetry of Namadeva and Tukarama, the two most popular figures in the movement, who wrote with such compassion and feeling that they inspired a whole group of minor poets from the plebeian castes. The most important of these minor poets were Samvatya the *mali*, Chokamela the *mahar*, Goa the potter and Narharid the goldsmith. In their attempt to establish a spiritual democracy, the Saints of Maharashtra rejected the values of orthodox Hinduism, and they advocated the idea of salvation for every individual, whatever be his station in the scale of caste, and howsoever humble be his status in life:

> One and all have a right to benefit from my teachings [wrote one of the *bhakti* poets]. . . . There is no restriction here. All the varnas can benefit from it. Brahmins, Shudras, Vaishyas, Kshtriyas and even Chandalas have an equal right here. Vaishnavas feel that all distinction and discrimination is a delusion, i.e., inauspicious. One who describes the caste of the Vaishnavas will fall in the worst of hails. . . . He is no Brahmin to whom God's name is not dear. . . . One who straight away on uttering the name of Rama-Krishna has before him his image, though born an untouchable, is a Brahmin indeed. . . .[2]

By proclaiming the spiritual equality of high and low castes, the Saints of Maharashtra were able to spread the values of Hinduism among the plebeian castes, and as a result of their proselytisation different castes and classes were drawn close together in the pursuit of common spiritual and secular objectives.

The first phase of the *bhakti* movement ended with Namadeva and his associates. During the period which followed no outstanding religious literature was produced, and the creative

[1] J. E. Abbott, *The Poet-Saints of Maharashtra*, Vol. 2; pp. 139–40.
[2] Quotation from Professor D. K. Garde's unpublished doctoral dissertation entitled: 'Social and Political Thought of the Saints of Maharashtra', Allahabad University, 1956.

legacy of the time is negligible. The reason for this decline in creativity is foreshadowed in the *abhangas* of Namadeva, which speak of a foreign invasion, and of a *Padshah* or a Muslim ruler. The Muslim invasion of the Deccan disturbed the smooth flow of life in Maharashtra, and created social chaos and political disorder. The sentiment of solidarity generated by the Saints of Maharashtra helped the community in meeting the challenge of Islam. But since Namadeva and his associates were concerned with the spiritual rather than with the secular world, they did not stimulate any active response to Islam. Because of the passivity of the *bhakti* movement in its first phase, the Hindu community acquiesced tamely in the political supremacy of Islam, and its energies were entirely absorbed in maintaining its religious and cultural identity.

But even during the centuries of Muslim predominance, the political apathy of the Hindu community as a whole was not shared by some of its leaders, whose ancestors had bequeathed to them traditions of daring and initiative. Such leaders recognised the weak foundations of Muslim power over Maharashtra. They also recognised that the sentiment of religious solidarity between high and low castes could form the basis of a vigorous political society resting upon resurgent Hinduism. The bigotry of the Muslim rulers assisted such leaders by creating a climate which bestowed upon the *bhakti* movement a militancy, and a concern for the secular world, that was conspicuous by its absence in the teachings of Jnaneshwar, Namadeva and Tukarama. The outstanding exponent of militant *bhakti* was Ramdasa, who spent the most creative period of his life in the villages around Poona and Satara, preaching the ethic of involvement to the common people, and establishing *maths* and temples for the dissemination of his ideas.

Ramdasa substituted the sword for the cymbals as the symbol of the *bhakti* movement. In doing so he created suitable conditions for the emergence of a political leader seeking to unite Maharashtra on the basis of resurgent Hinduism. Such a leader was Shivaji, who laid the foundations of Maratha power.[1]

[1] Vide S. S. Apte, *Samarth Ramdas: Life and Mission* (Bombay, 1965). Also see J. E. Abbott, *The Poet-Saints of Maharashtra*, Vol. 5, Chaps. XVI to XVII, and R. D. Ranade, *Pathway to God in Marathi Literature* (Bombay, 1961), pp. 284–333.

My interpretation of the *bhakti* movement is based partly on the available literature on the subject, and partly on discussions with Irawati Karve, Professor of

III

The political system established by Shivaji on the foundations prepared by the Saints of Maharashtra was characterised by several interesting features. The task confronting the Saints of Maharashtra consisted in bridging the gulf in values between the élite castes and the plebeian castes. They bridged this gulf through disseminating the high culture of Hinduism by means of a religious literature which was specially created for the unsophisticated sections of the community. But even though the *bhakti* movement generated values which brought the *kunbi* and the brahman close together, it still required political leadership of a high quality to knit the conflicting elements of Maharashtra into an integrated society.

There flourished under the Hindu rulers of Maharashtra a class of landed chiefs, or *deshmukhs*, who exercised extensive powers over the territories under their control. Such were the Naik Nimbalkars of Phaltan, who belonged to one of the most ancient families in Maharashtra. Such also were the Jadavs of Jindkheir; the Shirkes of Mahabaleshwar; the Savants of Waree; the Ghatgays of Maun; and last but not the least, the Ghorpades of Kapsi and Mudhol.[1] The *deshmukhs* were either petty rajas who had accepted the suzerainty of the rulers of the region, or they were administrators who had usurped hereditary status over the period of time. But whatever be their origin, when the Muslims conquered the Deccan they found the *deshmukhs* firmly entrenched in their estates and their authority was accepted without question both by the Hindu rulers whom the Muslims displaced, and by the village communities of Maharashtra. Indeed, the *deshmukhs* possessed so firm a hold over rural society that when the Muslim rulers appointed collectors of revenue to administer the land-tax on their behalf, the peasants

Sociology, Deccan College, Poona; D. K. Garde, Professor of Political Science, Poona University; S. V. Dandekar, Professor of Sanskrit, Poona University; and N. R. Pathak, formerly Professor of Marathi in Bombay University. Responsibility for the shortcomings of this interpretation, needless to say, rest exclusively on me. The extent to which the tradition of *bhakti* has bridged the gulf between the masses and the intellectuals in Maharashtra was vividly illustrated by Professor Karve's remark that 'because of the Saints of Maharashtra one could get a better exposition of *advaita* from an illiterate peasant woman, than one could from the Professor of Philosophy at Poona!'
[1] J. Grant-Duff, *History of the Marathas* (Bombay, 1878), Vol. I, pp. 71-4.

refused to accept the authority of these collectors, and rallied around their traditional leaders, namely, the *deshmukhs*. The Muslim rulers were consequently obliged to purchase the co-operation of the *deshmukhs* by granting them a proportion of the land-tax. As a result of such a compromise, the *deshmukhs* remained a powerful social group in Maharashtra, both under the Bahmani rulers, and under the successor states of Ahmednagar, Bijapur and Golconda.[1]

The conflict between the *deshmukhs* who represented local autonomy, and the Muslim rulers who sought to centralise authority in their hands, became the principal feature of politics in Maharashtra after the Muslim conquest. This conflict resulted in the eclipse of some of the old landed families; but it also created new ones, like the Mores of Jaoli, who owed their rise to the rulers of Bijapur. So long as power was vested in a competent ruler, the *deshmukhs* acquiesced in his authority. But the moment the control of the ruler weakened, the *deshmukhs* tried to set themselves up as independent chiefs. Their interests conflicted with the interests of a powerful ruler, and led them to oppose any attempt at the creation of a centralised State, whether the attempt was made by a Muslim king under the inspiration of Islam, or by a co-religionist under the aegis of resurgent Hinduism.

The *deshmukhs* of Maharashtra, therefore, opposed the attempt of Shivaji to create a centralised State.[2] Baronial families like the Ghorpades of Mudhol and the Mores of Jaoli lent their services readily to the kings of Bijapur in order to crush Shivaji, whom they regarded as an upstart who threatened their position in a way it was not threatened by the Muslim rulers. Shivaji, on his part, recognised the reasons which inspired the hostility of the old *deshmukh* families, and he realised how important it was for him to be surrounded by men who owed their position to his generosity and were therefore bound to him by ties of interest and sentiment. As the area under his control widened, he installed in the administration, as a counterpoise to the

---

[1] See Memoranda by J. Briggs and H. Pottinger enclosed in Report by W. Chaplin, Commissioner of Deccan, dated 20 August 1822: *Papers from the Records of the East India House Relating to the Administration of Revenue, Police and Civil and Criminal Justice* (London, 1826), Vol. IV. Hereinafter referred to as *East India Papers*.

[2] G. S. Sardesai, *The Main Currents of Maratha History* (Bombay, 1949), pp. 74-7. Also see Grant-Duff, *op.cit.*, pp. 196-7.

deshmukhs, deshasth brahmans trained in the art of government by his astute minister, Dada Kondev. The role of a subservient administration was equally apparent to the Peshwas. Consequently, when Balaji Vishwananth assumed control of the Poona Government he displaced the deshasth brahmans in the administration by chitpavan brahmans, who were his caste-fellows and therefore served his interests with unflinching loyalty.[1]

To strengthen their authority the rulers of Maharashtra not only recruited administrators from castes on whose loyalty they could depend in all circumstances but they also created new landed groups which had a vested interest in their régimes. As a result, by the time the British conquered Maharashtra in 1818, two groups of landlords had been superimposed upon the old *deshmukh* families whom Shivaji had subjugated in the first instance: namely, those who held grants from the Rajas of Satara, issued when the Marathas were engaged in a war of survival against the Muslim rulers, and those whom the Peshwas had ennobled in order to consolidate their position. To the first group belonged chiefs like the Naik of Sunda; while the second group was represented by landlords like the Patwardhans, who had risen under the Peshwas from comparative obscurity to the ownership of the most substantial landed estates in Maharashtra.[2]

The system of administration created by the Peshwas, to control the *deshmukhs,* and to collect the tax on land, rested on simple principles. The provinces of Maharashtra were divided into revenue divisions, each one of which was placed under an officer called the *mamlatdar,* who supervised the collection of the land-tax, and attended to police and judicial duties. The *mamlatdar* was appointed by the central government, but he was permitted to select for himself the subordinate officers who assisted him in discharging his responsibilities. In the districts surrounding Poona the *mamlatdar* received his orders direct from the central government. But in the peripheral districts an officer called the *Sirsubedhar* was interposed between Poona and the *mamlatdars.* The functions of the *Sirsubedhar* were ill-defined, and

[1] R. E. Enthoven, *The Tribes and Castes of Bombay* (Bombay, 1920). Vol. I, p. 242.
[2] For a detailed account of the Patwardhans see letter from M. Elphinstone to the Government of India dated 26 October 1911: *Poona Residency Correspondence,* Vol. XII, pp. 81–4. Also see Sardesai, *op. cit.,* p. 80.

his prerogatives and responsibilities varied from place to place. In the Carnatic he possessed extensive powers, appointing his own *mamlatdars*, and bearing personal responsibility for the collection of the land-tax. In Kandesh the *mamlatdars* conducted their business under the direct control of Poona, and the *Sirsubedhar* merely performed a supervisory function.[1]

The *mamlatdar* was the most important member of the administration, and he was consequently chosen from families of proven loyalty, whose antecedents were known to the Peshwa or to a distinguished member of his court. When a new *mamlatdar* was appointed to a district, he first acquainted himself with the *deshmukhs* and the landed chiefs of the region, whose knowledge of the condition of the peasants, and the tax which they could pay, supplemented the information with which he equipped himself from the revenue records in the *daftar*. In apportioning the land-tax on the villages under his charge the *mamlatdar's* negotiations with the *patils*, or headmen of villages, were always conducted through the *deshmukhs*, whose local knowledge was most useful in ensuring a fair distribution of the burden of tax. Since he represented the interests of the government the *mamlatdar* tried to procure the maximum return to the State by way of the land-tax; the *patils*, of course, represented the peasants, and tried to defend their interests to the best of their ability. In the conflict between the *patils* and the *mamlatdars* the latter could easily have imposed a ruinous tax on the peasants because they were not restrained by any legal or rational principles, and also because they were backed by the superior authority of the State. But the interposition of the *deshmukhs*, who were looked upon as their patrons and protectors by the peasants, ensured an equitable settlement of the land-tax. If, however, a *mamlatdar* persisted in demanding an excessive tax, then the *patils* appealed to the central government through the *deshmukh*. The existence of an alternative channel of communication between the central government and the villages restrained the *mamlatdars*, and prevented them from oppressing the peasants.[2]

[1] Report on the Maratha States by M. Elphinstone dated 25 October 1819: *East India Papers*, Vol. IV.
[2] Report on the Revenue Administration of the Peshwa's Territories during the Administration of Nana Farnavis by J. McLeod dated nil: *East India Papers*, Vol. IV.

While the delicate balance of authority and responsibility between the *deshmukhs* and the *mamlatdars* ensured the efficiency of the administration under a competent ruler, the tensions latent within the system flared into the open the moment a weakening of the controlling hand at Poona undermined the power of the *mamlatdars*. Whenever this happened, it was at the peripheries rather than in the districts surrounding Poona that the worst symptoms of disorder manifested themselves. In Thana on the Concan coast, for instance, a British official discovered that the peasants were being made to pay substantial sums of money over and above the standard land-revenue by way of illicit taxes.[1] Most of these illicit taxes originated in the time of troubles which followed the defeat of Panipat, and the death of Balaji Baji Rao. The Peshwa was succeeded by Madhav Rao, who was a minor, and whose ministers thought it expedient to farm out villages to individuals who took upon themselves the responsibility of collecting the land-tax. These farmers of revenue behaved with complete irresponsibility, and made quick profits for themselves by taxing [the peasants in excess of the customary rates. The practice of farming villages was revived by Baji Rao II, and it inflicted great misery and suffering upon the *kunbis* during the twilight of the Peshwas.

IV

The elements of instability in the administration would suggest that the villages of Maharashtra were subject to frequent fluctuations in fortune as a result of political changes in Poona. But despite this instability the rural communities were not seriously affected by changes in the capital of Maharashtra because of the restricted role played by the administration in the day-to-day life of the peasants, and also because of the existence in the villages of institutions of self-government which bestowed self-sufficiency on rural society.

The very appearance of a village in Maharashtra set it apart as a miniature world, self-sufficient in itself, and geared to a style of life calling for a minimum of contact with the world

---

[1] *NAI* (National Archives of India): Report by J. M. Davies on Illicit Taxes in Thana dated 8 October 1836: Home Department, Revenue Branch, Consultation No. 14 dated 27 February 1837.

outside.[1] It would be located on a smoothly rolling mound, in close proximity to a stream, and it would be surrounded by the fields cultivated by the *kunbis*. From a distance it had the appearance of a mass of crumbling grey walls, with a few stunted trees growing out among them, and with a few structures more conspicuous than the rest. All this was enclosed by a mud wall of irregular shape, and pierced by rude gates of wood at two or more points. On entering such a village appearances were no more prepossessing than from the outside. There was a complete lack of design in the layout of dwellings and streets. The crumbling walls would turn out to be the homes of the cultivators, which were made of calcareous earth, with terraced tops of the same material. These dwellings were devoid of any aesthetic pretensions. They had narrow and crooked lanes winding among them, and dividing them into groups of two or three. While conforming to a basic design, the homes of the substantial cultivators were slightly larger in size, and a little different in outward appearance, from the homes of the poor cultivators. But the most conspicuous structures in the village were the *chowrie*, or the municipal hall, where the public affairs of the village were debated; and the temple, built either by a rich and repentant *patil*, or by a philanthropic *deshmukh*, in the hope of commuting their earthly signs. Conspicuous, too, were the dwellings of untouchables like the *mahars* and the *mangs*, whose status in the scale of caste prevented them from coming into physical contact with the *kunbis*, and who consequently resided in little hamlets outside the walls of the village.

The vast majority of the villagers were cultivators of the *kunbi* caste, and they were subdivided into *thulwaheeks*, or hereditary cultivators, and *uprees*, or cultivators without any prescriptive rights in the soil. The *thulwaheeks* were descended from the first settlers of the village, who had in periods of remote antiquity migrated in *jathas*, or family groups, to new sites and had apportioned the available arable land between themselves. A *bakhar* setting out the circumstances which led to the establishment of the village of Muruda illustrates the ties which linked the *thulwaheeks* of a rural community to each other, and

[1] T. Coats, 'Account of the Present State of the Township of Lony' in *Transactions of the Literary Society of Bombay* (London, 1823), III, pp. 183–250. Hereinafter referred to as Coats' *Account of Lony*.

determined their property rights in the soil.[1] The site of Muruda was originally a jungle, and it served as the *rudrabhumi*, or burial ground, of the neighbouring hamlet of Asuda. To Asuda in the 16th century came an enterprising brahman called Gangadharbhatta, with two disciples in tow, and he decided to establish a new settlement in the neighbourhood of the village. With this end in view, Gangadharbhatta first asked the permission of the cultivators of Asuda to clear the jungle which served as their *rudrabhumi*. He next approached the raja of the region, a prince of the Sekara dynasty called Jalandhra, for a grant of the land surrounding the proposed village. The land gifted away by Jalandhra was then distributed by Gangadharbhatta among the thirteen *jathas* whom he had persuaded to migrate to the new settlement. The property of each *jatha* was marked off by stones called *Gadudus*, and *Kshetrapalas*, or tutelary deities, were appointed as divine witnesses to the allocation of fields. Besides providing them with holdings in land, the shrewd brahman Gangadharbhatta also defined the obligations and the prerogatives of the founding families of Muruda.

The *jathas* of a village like Muruda originally held their estates in joint ownership, and they were collectively responsible for the payment of the land-tax on the village. If the owner of one of the shares in a joint estate let his land fall waste, the family assumed responsibility for his share of the tax, and took over his fields for cultivation. Similarly, if the member of a *jatha* died without an heir, then his field was divided among the surviving members of the family. He was also free to dispose of his *baproti*, or patronymic, but his share was not permitted to pass out of the *jatha* if a co-sharer was willing to buy it. Only if no member of the *jatha* wanted to purchase the field was it sold to an outsider, who then entered the *jatha* on the same terms as the original incumbent, but was still designated *birader bhaus*, or legal-brother, instead of *ghar bhaus*, or brother-of-the-same-house. The institution of *jathas* was of great help in the collection of tax. In each village a representative of the eldest branch in a *jatha* accepted responsibility for the entire family, and collected the dues from its various members. Finally, the patriarch of the seniormost *jatha* served as the *patil* or the headman of the village,

[1] See 'Account of the Founding of the village of Muruda in the South Concan' in *Writings and Speeches of Vishwanath Narayan Mandlik* (Bombay, 1916).

and was required to collect the land-tax of the whole village by the *mamlatdar*.[1]

By the time Baji Rao Peshwa surrendered the Poona territories to the Government of Bombay in 1818, the *jathas* had lost some of their cohesion, partly through inbuilt tensions, but partly also through the attempt of the Poona Government to undermine their autonomy in the distribution and collection of the land-tax in the village. Prior to the 1760s, once the tax to be paid by a village had been settled through negotiations between the *patil* and the *mamlatdar*, the internal distribution of this tax was left to the *jathas* of the village, and was accomplished on the basis of the *rivaj* or customary rates of the community. After the disastrous defeat of Panipat, however, since the revenues of Maharashtra stood in desperate need of augmentation, Madhav Rao Peshwa introduced the *kamal* survey, which anticipated the *ryotwari* survey of Sir Thomas Munro, and attempted to undermine the autonomy of the *jathas* by replacing the *rivaj* rates with a new scale of assessment, and by obliging the *kunbis* to pay their dues directly to the State, instead of paying them through the agency of the *jathas*. But the *jathas* were so powerful in the villages of Maharashtra that the *kamal* survey was unable to undermine their authority, and even after its execution the *kunbis* continued to pay their taxes on the basis of the *rivaj* instead of the *kamal* rates.[2]

Despite the great influence which they had exercised over the villages of Maharashtra, and despite the success with which they had frustrated the objectives of the *kamal* survey, the *jathas* no longer flourished in full vigour at the time of the British conquest. The *kunbis* remembered the institution only to the extent

[1] BA (Bombay State Archives): H. R. D. Robertson to W. Chaplin dated 17 October 1820: R.D. (Revenue Department), Vol. 26/5 of 1822.

[2] *BA*: R. K. Pringle to H. R. D. Robertson dated 20 November 1823: R.D., Vol. 10/94 of 1823. The substitution of the *rivaj* for the *kamal* rates is open to the interpretation that the *kamal* survey only aimed at gaining for the State an accurate idea of the productive capacity of individual holdings. But this hypothesis is difficult to maintain since the *kamal* survey showed that the traditional rates were full of the most glaring inconsistencies. All this can be illustrated by comparing the *kamal* and *rivaj* rates for a village. In the hamlet of Oswaree Khuro in the Collectorate of Poona, for instance, the fields Pandru and Wursola contained a chowar of land each, and were therefore taxed an equal amount by the *rivaj* system. Yet these fields were found to possess different productive capacities by the *kamal* survey. A comparison of the fields Dhuljote and Amberket in the same village confirms the arbitrary nature of the *rivaj* rates.

of entrusting the oldest family in the community with the responsibility of collecting the land-tax from the entire village. But
joint responsibility for the payment of the land-tax was no
longer rigidly enforced. The members of the oldest family in the
village, who represented it in its dealings with *mamlatdars* and
other outsiders were called *patils*, and the seniormost among
them was called the *mukaddam patil*. Long after the founding of
a village, cultivators descended from the family of *patils* considered themselves to be superior in status to other cultivators,
even though their pretensions to superiority were not buttressed
by any social privileges, or by any accumulations of wealth. The
crucial difference within the cultivators of a village lay between
the *thulwaheeks* and the *uprees*. The former could not be dispossessed of their holdings so long as they paid their taxes; they
could also sell or mortgage their property with the consent of
other members of the *jatha*. In contrast, the *uprees'* connection
with the village was tenuous. They leased the deserted holdings
or the arable waste of the village on an annual basis, or on a
lease which ran concurrently for a number of years.

While the differences between the *thulwaheeks* and the *uprees*
were quite significant, they found expression in social rather
than in economic distinctions, and they were related to contrasting styles of life rather than to sharp differences in incomes. In
a typical village like Ambola, for instance, the holdings of *uprees*
like Suntojee Scindiah and Kundojee Scindiah were comparable in area and productivity to the holdings of the majority of
the *thulwaheeks* of the community.[1] Besides, *thulwaheeks* like
Beerjee Scindiah and Ambajee Scindiah, whose fields possessed
the same productivity as the holdings of Suntojee and Kundojee, paid a heavier tax as their share of the village rental. They
did so because the *uprees* could only be attracted to the villages
through low rents. In contrast to the *uprees*, who wandered from
one village to another in search of better leases, the *thulwaheeks*
were deeply attached to their holdings, and they never migrated
to a new village so long as they could make a bare living on their
ancestral lands. Their attachment to their holdings did not flow
exclusively from acquisitiveness. It was equally a result of the

---

[1] *BA:* 'Tabular View of the Distribution of Village Lands In the Village of Ambola,
Poona Collectorate': Appendix to Major Sykes' Report on Poona District dated nil:
R.D. Vol. 154B of 1826. Hereinafter referred to as Sykes' *Account of Ambola*.

social privileges which the possession of a *watan*, or a prescriptive right in land, bestowed on its owner in a society whose values were predominantly rural. The *thulwaheek* was a member of the council which debated the political affairs of the village; he had the right to pasture his cattle in the village common; he did not pay any house-tax so long as he had only one dwelling in the village; he was exempted from a tax paid by others on the occasion of marriage; and last but not the least, he was entitled to preference over the *uprees* on all social ceremonies in the village.

The absence of sharp differences in incomes in the villages of Maharashtra created a social climate which was devoid of serious conflict and strife, and which exercised a decisive influence on the behaviour of the *kunbis*. The *kunbis* possessed a mild and unobtrusive disposition, and they abhorred a want of gentleness in others. Yet for all their mildness, they had a latent warmth of temper, and if oppressed beyond a point, they could turn fiercely on their tormentors, as indeed they did during the disturbances of 1875 in the Deccan. A perceptive traveller in the villages around Poona would have found the peasants surprisingly well informed about agriculture, and the concerns of their village would immediately hold their interest. 'On the whole they are far better informed than the lower classes of our own population,' a British official observed, 'and they certainly far surpass them in propriety and orderliness of demeanour.'[1] That such a portrayal is not overdrawn is clear from the account we have of the distribution of holdings in the village of Ambola. Of the cultivators of Ambola, more than half possessed fields which ranged between 15 and 30 *beeghas* in area. Holdings of this size yielded a reasonable income by the standards of the time, although they did not provide any insurance against involvement in debt. The three substantial cultivators in Ambola were the *patil*, Babu Ram Scindiah, and the *kunbis*, Marojee Scindiah and Bapujee Scindiah, each one of whom had a holding that was 60 *beeghas* in extent, and thrice as large as the average holding in the village. In contrast to the three substantial cultivators of Ambola stood *kunbis* like Amruta Scindiah and Hykunt Scindiah, who found it impossible to keep body and soul together on

[1] *BA:* Vide Major Sykes' Report on Poona District dated nil: R.D., Vol. 153B of 1826.

the profits which they derived from their holdings. But such glaring contrasts were rare. For the rural scene was dominated by a mass of *kunbis* who lived at the level of subsistence, and who held the balance between the few substantial cultivators, on the one hand, and the fringe of hopelessly impoverished peasants, on the other.

The size of a *kunbi*'s holdings, however, did not provide a reliable index to his income because of the depressed conditions which characterised agriculture. Indeed, the investigations conducted into the profits of agriculture in 1825 in the villages around Poona by Colonel Sykes, an officer of the Revenue Department, indicated that irrespective of their size and fertility few holdings yielded any substantial profits to their owners. For instance, Bheema *mali*, who cultivated sweet potatoes on 4 *pands* of garden land in the village of Mahlunga sustained a loss of Rs. 9 as. 8 (Table A, Example 1). Similarly, a peasant who cultivated *bajra* on 60 acres of land of medium quality in Serur incurred a loss of Rs. 270; while a *kunbi* who grew *jowar* on a field of comparable size and quality lost Rs. 188 in his agricultural operations (Table A, Examples 2 and 3). This is not to imply that all those who were engaged in agriculture sustained losses instead of making profits. Thus a *kunbi* who cultivated sugar-cane on 1 *beegah* of land of the first quality at Chakun realised a profit of Rs. 46 as. 12; while the *mali* who cultivated vegetables on four *pands* of garden land at Mahlunga secured a return of Rs. 4 as. 9 (Table A, Examples 4 and 5). Indeed, it is highly likely that even those *kunbis* who told Colonel Sykes that they sustained losses in their operations were guilty of giving incorrect returns for produce, or inflated figures for

TABLE A: EXAMPLE I

Showing Account for the Cultivation of Sweet Potatoes by Bheema *mali* on 4 *pands* of Garden Land in the Village of Mahlunga in Poona District

	Rs.	as.	p.
Investment:			
Total cost of cultivating sweet potatoes on 4 pands of garden land	15	8	⅔
Return:			
Cash value of a crop of 85½ seers of sweet potatoes at 4 pies per seer	4	8	0
Half price of cuttings of vines of sweet potatoes provided by owner of the field	1	8	0
Loss sustained by Bheema *mali*	9	8	⅔

TABLE A: EXAMPLE 2

Showing Account of Cultivation of *Bajra* in 60 Acres of Land of Middling Quality in the Village of Serur in Poona District

	Rs.	as.	p.
Investment:			
Total cost of cultivating *bajra* in 60 acres o middling-quality land	595	9	$\frac{1}{4}$
Return:			
Cash value of 60 maunds of *bajra* at $13\frac{50}{70}$ seers per rupee	210	0	0
Returns from various secondary products	115	5	$\frac{1}{4}$
Loss sustained	270	4	0

TABLE A: EXAMPLE 3

Showing Account of Cultivation of *Jowar* in 60 Acres of Land of Middling Quality in the Village of Serur in Poona District

	Rs.	as.	p.
Investment:			
Total cost of cultivating *jowar* in 60 acres of land	596	6	$\frac{1}{4}$
Return:			
Cash value of 96 maunds of *jowar* at 16 seers per rupee	288	0	0
Returns for secondary products	120	0	0
Loss sustained	188	6	$\frac{1}{4}$

TABLE A: EXAMPLE 4

Showing Account of Cultivation of Sugar-Cane in 1 *Beegah* of First-quality Land at Chakun in Poona District

	Rs.	as.	p.
Investment:			
Total cost of cultivating sugar-cane in 1 *beegah* of first-rate land	98	12	0
Return:			
Cash value of the crop	145	8	0
Profit realised	46	12	0

TABLE A: EXAMPLE 5

Showing Account of Cultivation of Bringals in 4 *Pands* of Garden Land by Bheema *mali* in the Village of Mahlunga in Poona District

	Rs.	as.	p.
Investment:			
Cost of cultivating *bringals* in 4 *pands* of garden land	23	11	0
Return:			
Cash value of 580 seers of *bringals*	28	4	$\frac{2}{3}$
Profit realised	4	9	$\frac{2}{3}$

labour costs. Otherwise, to quote Sykes, 'their lands must have been abandoned long since, with the yearly loss described.'[1] Yet it would be legitimate to infer that the size of a *kunbi*'s holdings provided no reliable guide to his profits. It would also be legitimate to infer that irrespective of the size of their holdings, the majority of the peasants lived on the margin of subsistence.

[1] ibid.

The condition of the great proportion of the *kunbis* was, in fact, far from satisfactory. A stranger to the rural scene would have emerged with a mistaken impression of the lack of prosperity in the villages, since the cultivators were quick to suspect in any inquiry concerning their assets a possible increase in the burden of tax, and therefore presented an exaggerated picture of their poverty. Even the children were initiated into the skilful art of evasion, as one revenue officer discovered when he tried to gain an impression of the true state of affairs through them. 'I have often asked boys of eight or ten years old,' he wrote to his superior, 'whom I have seen perched on a little scaffold in a field, throwing stones from a sling to frighten the birds, how many bushels they expected when the corn was cut. The answer always was—"There is nothing in our house now to eat. The birds will eat all this, and we shall be starved."'[1] But even if the *kunbis*' account of their poverty be discounted, they were by no means rolling in affluence. While conducting his survey of the villages around Poona Sykes, for instance, gained the distinct impression that the cultivators were in great pecuniary difficulties:

> In my numerous inquiries from the families [he states] with respect to their affairs, inquiries conducted indirectly and tactfully, in only one instance could I get at an acknowledgement of freedom from debt, and this was in the case of an upree of the name of Ramjee Cudum of Nowsae Oombreh, who was assisted by his two stout sons with their wives in his cultivation. No doubt this melancholy state of the cultivators' affairs is much exaggerated, but the multiplied instances that have come under my observation of . . . persons selling themselves to serve others for a limited period for a sum of money, and in the very numerous instances of abandonment of land from distress, do not leave me the option of doing otherwise than place very considerable credit on their assertions with respect to their affairs.[2]

We can gain a quantitative idea of the condition of the rural districts from a close look into Lony, a largish village atypical only because it stood close to Poona. Of the eighty-four cultivators of Lony, as many as seventy-nine were indebted to the four

[1] Quoted in T. H. Beaglehole, *Thomas Munro and the Development of Administration in Madras 1792–1818* (Cambridge, 1966), p. 50.
[2] *BA:* Major Sykes' Report on Poona District dated nil: R.D., Vol. 154B of 1826.

jain and two marwari *vanis*, or moneylenders, who resided in the village. The total indebtedness of the *kunbis* of Lony amounted to the very considerable sum of Rs. 14,532, but this sum was split into small loans ranging from Rs. 50 to Rs. 500. All this, however, does not take into consideration the debts of Rs. 5,000 and more which had been contracted by the three respectable landed families which resided in Lony.[1]

The *kunbis* of Lony had contracted debts either to purchase seed, food or stock, or to defray expenses contracted on occasions of marriages or rituals connected with caste or religion. Each *kunbi* kept a running account with the *vani*, and he took a receipt for the sums which he paid from time to time in redemption of his debts. According to *dam dupat*, a principle which found wide acceptance, certainly among the *kunbis*, the interest on a loan accumulated only to the extent of the capital, and never beyond it. Relations between the *kunbi* and the *vani* were, therefore, conducted on an equitable basis, though it would be legitimate to have reservations about the rigorousness with which such principles were observed in practice. For despite a natural liveliness of the mind, the *kunbis* were not very shrewd in the handling of money. Besides, in their role as borrowers they were pitted against individuals who were acquisitive and grasping, and who specialised in the unlovely business of moneylending. Despite all this, however, to portray the relationship between the *kunbi* and the *vani* as a relationship of tension and strife would be untrue to the social temper of the times. The operations of agriculture involved co-operation between two social groups: the *kunbis*, who provided land and labour, and the *vanis*, who assisted with seed and capital. As a result of such a partnership, most of the surplus produce became the property of the *vanis* even before the crop was harvested. But while they expropriated the surplus produce of the *kunbis*, the *vanis* lacked the means to appropriate their holdings.

What prevented the appropriation of the *kunbis*' holdings by the *vanis* was the manner in which social power was distributed in the villages of Maharashtra. The two key concentrations of power in the village were the office of the *patil*, and the institution for dispensing justice known as the *panchayat*. The *patil*, as we have already pointed out, was the head of the senior

[1] Vide Coats' *Account of Lony*.

jatha and consequently the leader of the village. But his position as a leader was simultaneously endorsed by the officers of the State.[1] The *patil*, therefore, combined in his person facets of legal and traditional domination which made him the most important person in the village, and invested him with sweeping powers of initiative. Like Babu Rao Scindiah of Ambola, most *patils* were substantial landholders in their villages, besides which they enjoyed some freehold land as renumeration for their services. The *patil's* office was so important, and the maintenance of its dignity so heavy a responsibility, that many an incumbent who had fallen upon evil days was obliged to sell his prerogatives. However, the rights attached to the *patil*ship were considered so personal, that often only a part of the prerogatives of the office were sold. Such transactions created two or even more *patils* in a village, and although they were all equally powerful in questions affecting the administration, the senior among them retained rights of precedence in social and religious ceremonies.

The *patil* played his key role in representing the rural community in those crucial negotiations with the *mamlatdar* and the *deshmukh* in which the amount of tax to be paid by the village was settled. But in his dual capacity as a traditional leader of the community, and an officer of the administration, the *patil* was also entrusted with the task of promoting the prosperity of the village. He did so by encouraging improvements in agriculture, and by attracting *uprees* to the village. The *uprees* were induced to settle in a village through being offered leases on preferential rates, either on the basis of the *cowl* tenure, or through the *muckta* tenure.[2] Most significant of all, however, was the *patil's* prerogative to grant the rights of ownership to those who wanted to purchase, and not just rent, land in the village. But in bestowing such a right the *patil* had to consult all the *kunbis* who had a permanent stake in the village. Any request for the purchase of land was, therefore, debated in the *chowrie* by the *patil* and the

---

[1] R. N. Goodine, 'Report on the Village Communities of the Deccan', dated 10 October 1845: *Selections from the Records of the Bombay Government*, No. IV. Hereinafter referred to as Goodine's *Report on the Village Communities*.

[2] According to the *cowl* tenure, an *upree* paid a fraction of the rent in the first year, with annual increases leading to the full rent in the sixth year. The *muckta* rates enabled an *upree* to clear the arable waste of a village on the payment of a very nominal rent.

cultivators of the community. A document recording the grant
of land in ownership to a *kunbi* called Kosajee by the *patil* and
the cultivators of Multan vividly evokes the temper of such
deliberations:

> We [the *patil* and the *thulwaheeks* of the village of Multan] being
> present, you Kosajee, son of Kosajee patil Taruh of Sowkee, came
> and presented a petition, if a letter of inheritance (*meeras puttah*)
> were granted for lands in the above village that you would labour
> and secure their prosperity. Having approved of your petition we
> give you . . . the field called San. . . .
> We the village authorities have granted you this of our free will
> and pleasure. . . . You and your children's children are to enjoy
> this right. . . .[1]

The grant of a holding to Kosajee was clearly a collective decision of the *patil* and the cultivators of Multan. Since the *patil*'s
position rested on the acceptance of his authority and leadership by the community, we can infer that similar consultations
lay behind every important decision taken by the village,
whether it concerned the admission of a new member to the
community, or the erection of a temple or *chowrie*, or the additional levy of a tax in an emergency. In the village of Ambola,
for instance, it was virtually obligatory for *patil* Babu Rao
Scindiah to consult Madjee Scindiah and Raja Rao Scindiah
on all issues affecting the interests of the community, since their
lands were just as extensive as his, and their voice in the village
was consequently just as influential as his voice. This is not to
deny the special privileges which the *patil* enjoyed by virtue of
his position. For instance, although the decision to admit Kosajee into Multan was taken collectively, the new member was
still required to pay a special cess called *meeras puttah* to the *patil*
of the village. Nevertheless, the *patil* did not exercise any arbitrary authority over the village, and he was guided in his decisions by the interests of all the cultivators who had a permanent
stake in the community.

Indicative, too, of the manner in which the collective voice
of the community was brought to bear upon the problems of
administration was the constitution of the *panchayat*, or the

---

[1] *BA*: Translation of a Sale Deed granted by the *Patil* of Multan in 1814: Appendix
II to Major Sykes' Report on the Poona District dated nil: R.D., Vol. 154B of 1826.

village court.¹ Since the *patil* was the most influential person in the village, he was invariably approached by the individuals concerned when a dispute broke out in a rural community. The *patil* tried, in the first instance, to resolve the dispute through personal arbitration. But if he failed, which he often did, then the disputants were referred to a *panchayat*, or *ad hoc* council, of the most intelligent and influential *kunbis* in the village. The *panchayat* was an informal institution, and it was governed by very flexible rules of procedure. Its members, generally five in number, met in the open to hear the disputants argue their cases, and to examine the witnesses which they produced in defence of their respective positions. Next, the *panchayat* debated the issue, and then drew up an award which was communicated to the *patil* for execution. The *panchayat*'s chief advantage over formal judicial institutions lay in the identity of values between its members and the *kunbis* who brought their disputes before it. Since the *panchayat*'s decisions were inspired by values which were shared by the cultivators, they accepted its awards as equitable. Yet the *panchayat* was by no means free of defects. Indeed, it encouraged dilatoriness in the administration of justice, more particularly because it did not possess the means to execute its awards, and was in this respect completely dependent upon the *patil*. Besides, it was not designed to resolve complicated disputes, and when confronted with such disputes its members procrastinated to an extent which relieved them of the necessity of coming to any decision whatsoever.

Since the *panchayat* was the only judicial institution in the village, and because it was completely dominated by the *kunbis*, the *vanis* were unable to exploit the cultivators, despite the important role they played in the rural economy, and despite the extent to which the cultivators were dependent upon them for capital. It was, of course, open to the *vanis* to refer a recalcitrant debtor to a *panchayat*. But since the *panchayat* was recruited from the *kunbis* of the village, it was inclined to give awards which showed more than legitimate concern for the interests of the debtor. This was particularly true if the debtor happened to be a *patil* or a substantial peasant. But even otherwise the *vani* had no chance of recovering his debt unless he could persuade some powerful landed chief to intervene on his behalf. More

¹ Borrodaile's note on the *Panchayats* dated nil: *East India Papers*, Vol. IV.

frequently, he took recourse to incessant importunity, and by throwing himself on the threshhold of the debtor, and refusing to budge till the debt was settled, he sometimes gained his objective. So often were the *vanis* of Maharashtra obliged to dun the *kunbis* into repaying their debts that they had raised the practice of dunning to a fine art.

If offices like the *patil*ship, and institutions like the *panchayat*, served to make the villages autonomous in their administration, then the *bullotedars* played an equally vital role in bestowing self-sufficiency on the rural communities. The *bullotedars* were artisans hailing from different castes who possessed hereditary rights of service in the village, and who were renumerated by the villagers according to well-recognised scales for performing these services.[1] The most important *bullotedars* were those who assisted the *kunbis* in the operations of agriculture: the *sootar*, who fabricated the plough of the cultivator, and kept it in a state of good repair; the *lohar*, who fashioned the portions of the plough which were made of iron, but who could also press his skills to the tiring of a cart, or the shoeing of a horse; and the *chamar*, who made the leather holders, whips, ropes and bands required by the cultivator. Also ranked as *bullotedars*, though they were not artisans, were the *mahars* or the untouchable watchmen of the village. Every village contained a dozen or more *mahar* families, which had an important voice in the affairs of the village despite their lowly status in the scale of caste, since they were responsible for preventing encroachments upon the boundaries of the village, of which they possessed an accurate knowledge handed down to them by their forebears. The *mahars* also served as the ears and eyes of the community, and they were required to be on the lookout for unusual occurrences which might spell danger for the village.

Though our account of the *bullotedars* does not exhaust the list of artisans who lived in the village, and contributed their skills to its economy, we have indicated how the services required for agriculture were to be found within the community, making it self-sufficient to a remarkable degree. But how were these artisans ranked? And how were they remunerated for their services? The answers to these questions throw interesting light on the sentiment of solidarity which prevailed in the village. They

[1] Goodine's *Report on the Village Communities*.

simultaneously reveal the gulf between the formal rank of a caste, and the actual status which it occupied in secular society. Instead of being paid individually by the cultivators for the services which they performed, the *bullotedars* were collectively allocated one-eighth of the gross produce of the village. The fraction of this share received by an artisan was determined by the utility of the services which he performed, and bore no relation to his status in the scale of caste. Thus *bullotedars* of the first category, who received the maximum renumeration, included artisans like the *sootar*, the *lohar* and the *mahar*, whose services were of great importance in the operations of agriculture. But while low-caste artisans received high remuneration, the brahman astrologer who belonged to a superior caste was ranked as a *bullotedar* of the third and lowest category, and found it difficult to keep body and soul together on the income which he received from the village. By and large, however, the *bullotedars* lived reasonably by the standards of the age. The artisans of Kurmalla in Sholapur District, for instance, were paid Rs. 24 annually, which enabled them to live as well as the vast majority of the *kunbis* of the village.[1]

v

Besides the *kunbis* who cultivated the land, and the *vanis* and *bullotedars* who assisted them in the operations of agriculture, the villages of Maharashtra contained a number of brahman families which contributed in an important way to the spiritual and secular life of rural society. The brahmans were clearly distinguishable from other castes in the village, since they were 'fairer, better dressed, and more virtuous in their manners'.[2] They also monopolised the hereditary offices of the *joshi*, or the village astrologer, and the *kulkarni*, or the village accountant. These offices admirably suited the natural propensities of the brahmans, and conferred considerable power on them. The *kulkarni* was second only to the *patil* in the influence which he exercised over the village, since he kept a record of the holdings of the cultivators; the rents they paid to the State; and the conditions on which they held their land. Being in most cases the

[1] *BA*: Report on the Bullote Taxes by T. W. Langford dated 30 March 1840: R.D., Vol. 98/1182 of 1840.
[2] Vide Coats' *Account of Lony*.

only person in the village who could read and write, the *kulkarni* often acquired an importance in its affairs which was hardly justified by the responsibilities of his office. He was also known to inspire a split between the cultivators of a community, and lead a group of *kunbis* in opposition to the *patil* of the village. The influence of the brahmans in rural society also stemmed from the fact that the *joshi*, who forecast the events and the festivals of the year for the benefit of the *kunbis*, represented the only link between the *kunbis* and the great tradition of Hinduism.

Yet the *joshi* did not rank as high in society as his status in the scale of caste would lead us to expect. The *kunbis'* cavalier attitude towards the *joshis* is reflected in the fact that they permitted *guravs*, or non-brahman priests, to perform the ritual prescribed by Hinduism. The great tradition of Hinduism, and the *joshis* who claimed to represent this tradition in the villages in fact exercised very little direct influence over the *kunbis*. But while the *kunbis* submitted mechanically to the ritual prescribed by orthodox Hinduism, they discerned order and meaning in their world exclusively through the spiritual insights which the *bhakti* movement placed at their disposal. The peasants were, therefore, drawn to the values of Hinduism through the *abhangas* of popular saints like Namadeva and Tukarama; they were also drawn to the values of Hinduism through the shrines of *bhakti* gods like Vithala of Pandharpur, to whose temple thousands of devotees flocked every year. The pilgrimage to Pandharpur, the spiritual capital of Maharashtra, brought together high and low castes, and peasants from remote villages, and it served as an institution for the transmission of religious values, and the spread of social cohesion. On the road to Pandharpur the chaste brahman from Wai rubbed shoulders in plebeian intimacy with the humble *kunbi* from the Satara territories, while even the substantial *patil* for once desisted from avoiding physical contact with the *mahar* bound for the temple of Vithala. But whether brahman or *mahar*, or *kunbi* or *patil*, on the pilgrimage to Pandharpur everyone recited the same *abhangas* in praise of the *bhakti* gods:

So I was getting to know my Maharashtra anew every day [writes a contemporary sociologist, Irawati Karve, of the pilgrimage to Pandharpur even today]. *I found a new definition of Maharashtra: the land whose people go to Pandharpur for pilgrimage.* When the pilgrimage started from Poona there were people from Poona Junnar, Satara, etc. Everyday people were joining the pilgrimage from Khandesh, Sholapur, Nasik, Berar. All were Marathi-speaking people—coming from different castes, but singing the same song, the same verses of the varkari cult. . . . (Emphasis added)[1]

However the pilgrimage to Pandharpur was not a necessary condition for initiation into *bhakti*. All over the countryside there flourished groups of devotees, led by a *guru* or spiritual leader, which met in the village *chowrie* to recite their favourite *abhangas*, and to ponder over the meaning of earthly existence or the fate which lay beyond.[2] Often, too, a wandering mendicant who had dedicated his life to Vithala would visit the village, and hold a *harikirtan*, to which all the villagers would flock, for the gods of *bhakti* made no distinction between rich and poor, and brahman and shudra, and welcomed everybody to their fold. In this fashion the values and institutions of *bhakti* enveloped the people of Maharashtra in a finely woven fabric which held together different castes and classes, and formed the basis of a popular culture flowing out of the great tradition of Hinduism.

But even if the insights of *bhakti* enabled the *kunbis* to discern order and meaning in their harsh world, and even if *bhakti* provided them with the strength to withstand the calamities, *asmani* or *sultani*, which so frequently afflicted rural society, it would be a serious mistake to imagine that the activities of the *kunbis* were confined to the chanting of *abhangas*, or to making pilgrimages to Pandharpur. Indeed, the scepticism of the peasants, and their preoccupation with secular as opposed to spiritual activities, is reflected all too vividly in folk myths concerning the Saints of Maharashtra. The farmer who insisted upon exacting his pound of flesh from Tukarama for neglecting his fields; the *vani*'s assistant who lived next door to Eknatha, yet had never attended a *harikatha;* and the village urchins who buried Ramdasa alive under the impression that he was dead, all speak of a society that was more concerned with mundane questions of the flesh than with transcendental problems of the spirit.[3] Perhaps

---

[1] I. Karve, 'On the Road' in *Journal of Asian Studies*, Vol. XXII, No. 1, p. 22.

[2] Information concerning the organisation of the *bhakti* cult has been obtained from Professor S. V. Dandekar in an interview dated 22 December 1962.

[3] The three incidents are taken from J. E. Abbott's *The Poet-Saints of Maharashtra* in the following order: (i) Vol. 7, pp. 95–104; (ii) Vol. 2, pp. 208–10; and (iii) Vol. 8, pp. 68–74.

the most eloquent expression of popular irreverence is to be found in the utterances of Avali, Tukarama's shrewish yet likeable wife, who endured, although not without grumbling, a husband whose lack of worldly wisdom prevented him from providing his children with the necessities of life:

> I do not want to see that black fellow (Vithala) [Avali once stated in sheer disgust]. It was our ancestor, Vishambar, who brought that enemy here. That great demon is persecuting our whole family line. The wife and many children make a large family, and they cannot get food or clothing. He (Tukarama) has thrown on to me all our domestic concerns, and he goes and sits there on the mountain. When the night has advanced four *ghatikas*, he comes stealing into the temple. There he dances before that Black fellow (Vithala), having gathered together other vagabonds. In some or or other of his former births, he (Tukarama) became a debtor of God's and is now paying back what he borrowed. . . .[1]

But just as divine grace convinced Avali of the glory and compassion of Vithala, so did the *kunbis* and the *vanis* make their peace with the Gods of Pandharpur, since they depended upon their protection in a world which was cruel and pitiless, and which confronted them with situations beyond their comprehension and outside their control.

VI

The villages of Maharashtra, it is clear from the foregoing account, possessed a large measure of autonomy and self-sufficiency, despite a system of administration which linked them to Poona, and despite the popularity of values which tied them in bonds of spiritual allegiance to the Gods of Pandharpur. Yet it would be a mistake to look upon the villages of Maharashtra as isolated communities, if only for the reason that there flourished in the region cities as substantial as Poona, and also for the reason that there flourished in the region *petahs* or markets which served the needs of clusters of surrounding villages.

How the need for *petahs* to stimulate the exchange of goods and services served to integrate rural society can be illustrated through a close look at the market which assembled weekly at Goreh in Poona District.[2] To this *petah* there came, on 6 January

[1] J. E. Abbott, *The Poet-Saints of Maharashtra*, Vol. 7, p. 111.
[2] *BA:* Sykes' Report on Poona District dated nil: R.D., Vol. 154B of 1826.

1826, a dozen peasant women from the village of Goreh with food-grains for sale. Also to this market there came peasant women from surrounding villages like Chinchal, Pepulgaon and Gangapur, which lay within a radius of ten miles, to sell the surplus produce of their fields. Besides food-grains, the *petah* offered a wide variety of consumer goods to the prospective customer. There were more than a dozen weavers from Goreh, and from the surrounding villages, who offered coarse *saris* for women, and turbans for men; there were pedlars selling groceries and knick-knacks; there were cobblers who displayed shoes, and *malis* who offered vegetables; and last but not the least, there were *shroffs* who changed coins of one denomination into coins of another denomination at a high rate of discount. The *patil* of Goreh, not to be outdone by anyone, charged a fee of one pice from every peasant woman or pedlar who did not belong to the village of Goreh. Such markets were distributed all over the region, and they provided the *kunbis* with opportunities to sell the surplus produce of their fields, and to purchase the consumer goods and the little luxuries which they required for their daily needs.

The bonds between rural and urban society were reinforced through the flow of credit from the city to the village. This flow was geared to the distribution of certain castes like the marwari and the gujerati *vanis* in the towns and villages of Maharashtra. The gujerati *vanis*, who were concentrated in the township of Supa near Poona, had migrated to Maharashtra in the first quarter of the 17th century, when Surat was the chief centre of trade in western India. They arrived in the region as itinerant dealers in foreign spices, but after a time they settled down, and took to moneylending, and became rich and influential. Two centuries later, they were still regarded by the local peasants as aliens, and for their own part went back to Gujerat to contract marriages, or to perform important religious ceremonies. With the exception of a few rich *sowcars*, *vanis* from Gujerat were to be found mostly in the villages.[1]

The élite among the commercial classes were the marwari *vanis*, who had come to Maharashtra after the gujerati *vanis*. The marwaris, too, were regarded as aliens by the *kunbis*, prob-

[1] *Gazetteer of the Bombay Presidency*, Vol. XVIII, Pt. II, Poona District (Bombay, 1885), pp. 99–100.

ably with more justification than the gujerati *vanis*, since they owed allegiance to Jainism. The township of Vambori in Ahmednagar District was the seat of a large marwari community, and the centre of its business dealings. From Vambori individual marwaris migrated to the *petahs*, and from the *petahs* they spread into the villages, where they soon established a monopoly for themselves over the operations of moneylending. A marwari invariably started his career in a humble capacity as a clerk to an established caste-fellow. But the moment he had put aside some capital, he moved to a new *petah* or village, and soon established his control over its economy. The dominant trait of the marwari *vanis* was acquisitiveness, which was made all the more disagreeable by their disregard for local opinion and local sentiment. They could always outwit the *kunbis* who were dependent upon them for the supply of capital in their agricultural operations. But despite the hold which the *vanis* possessed over the rural economy, they were unable to exploit the *kunbis* because of the manner in which social power was distributed in rural society, and the control which the cultivators exercised over the judicial institutions within the village. In the *petahs* which served as centres for the sale of surplus agricultural produce, and in cities like Ahmednagar and Poona, however, the marwari's position was quite different. If a *patil* was unable to collect the tax which he had contracted to pay to the *mamlatdar*, which happened quite frequently, he turned to a marwari *sowcar* in the nearest *petah* for assistance in meeting his obligations, and pledged the joint credit of the village for a loan. The debt contracted by the *patil* in such circumstances is to be distinguished from transactions between the *kunbi* and the *vani* within the village, since the *patil*'s debt did not fall within the jurisdiction of the village *panchayat*, and because it enabled the *sowcar* to control the surplus of the village without involving himself in the operations of agriculture. Besides, the *sowcar* was quite a different person from the *vani*, both in the scale of his financial dealings and in the magnitude of his capital resources. Even obscure little *petahs* like Nandoobar and Sultanpur near Dhulia could boast of *sowcars* who had lent Rs. 200,000 to the *patils* of the surrounding villages. Most of these loans came from substantial marwaris like Ganput Moorar, who had lent Rs. 27,500 in all, of which a typical item was the sum of Rs. 4,000 which he had advanced to the *patil* of Dehwali. Yet there also flourished relatively small *sowcars* like Sambhaldas Dharamdas, whose resources of capital amounted to Rs. 4,000, and who was quite willing to give small loans like the sum of Rs. 400 which he had advanced to the *patil* of Bullair.[1]

The marwari *sowcars* commanded considerable influence in the cities despite their lowly status in the scale of caste, because of their financial standing and the important role they played in the economy. Quite the reverse was true of the artisans, who were engaged in production as opposed to commerce. The gulf between the artisans and the *sowcars* was almost impossible to bridge. This was so for several reasons. While there was a considerable concentration of artisans in urban society, a medium-sized town like Mulligaum boasting of 42 weavers, 32 goldsmiths, 44 oil-pressers and 31 dyers, these artisans fabricated goods in very small units of production, often their homes, and they consequently worked on a scale, and with resources of capital, which made technical improvement improbable if not impossible. The factors of scale and organisation that stood in the way of improvement were reinforced by a system of taxation which prevented the accumulation of capital in the hands of individual craftsmen through trenching heavily into their profits. Since the tax paid by a craftsman was determined by his caste rather than by an officer of the State, we can infer that the prevailing system of taxation stemmed from social values which frowned upon economic progress and social mobility, and which favoured a condition of primitive egalitarianism.

The popularity of social values which favoured equality at the cost of progress is best reflected in the *mohturfa* tax, which was levied on the artisan and the commercial castes. Instead of levying the *mohturfa* on individual merchants or craftsmen, the officers of the State demanded a consolidated sum of money from the heads of different castes, leaving them free to distribute this demand among their caste-fellows. Such a procedure left the way open for the leading members of a caste to transfer a heavy burden of tax on caste-fellows who were poor and lacked influence and prestige. But in fact this never happened and the *mohturfa* was distributed among the members of the caste accord-

[1] *BA:* H. T. Graham to G. Giberne dated 3 October 1828: R.D., Vol. 53/250 of 1833.

THE POONA DISTRICTS IN 1818

ing to their ability to contribute to the collective obligation. The principles which informed the breakdown of the *mohturfa* into the shares of individual craftsmen can be illustrated by looking into the tax paid by the weavers of Mulligaum. The caste of weavers in Mulligaum had a strength of forty-two, and it was required to pay a *mohturfa* of Rs. 312. The major share of this *mohturfa* was paid by thirty-one moderately prosperous weavers, each of whom made a contribution of Rs. 8. However, the three flourishing weavers of the town paid Rs. 48 towards the common fund, while the eight weavers whose business had yet to be established were required to pay only Rs. 2 per head.[1]

The principles underlying the levy of the *mohturfa* illustrate the organisation of urban society, and they highlight the popularity of values which prevented the accumulation of capital in any section of the community. Such values stood in the way of progress and mobility, and they were instrumental in creating a society in which the wealth and status enjoyed by an individual were determined by prescription and inheritance, rather than by his industriousness, or by the extent to which he exercised initiative and enterprise. The foundations of this society rested upon caste, which was an institution committed to stability and order, and which mitigated the tensions between individuals and classes through directing their allegiance to a common corpus of secular and spiritual values. The institution of caste was the bed-rock of society, and it shaped more than anything else the social climate of Maharashtra.

At the apex of society in Maharashtra stood a cluster of brahman castes, of which the most important were the chitpavans and the deshasths.[2] The deshasths were numerically the most significant of the brahman castes, and they regarded themselves as the first settlers in the region. They also believed that they were the highest of all brahmans. Upon the chitpavans who had come into prominence after the rise of the Peshwas they looked down with scarcely veiled contempt as *parvenus*, barely fit to associate on terms of equality with the noblest of the *dvijas*. A chitpavan who was invited to a deshasth home was

[1] *BA:* Report on the Mohturfa Taxes by T. W. Langford dated 31 January 1840: R.D., Vol. 97/1181 of 1840. Also see J. Briggs to W. Chaplin dated 5 November 1821: R.D., Vol. 26/50 of 1822.
[2] I am indebted to Professor Irawati Karve for the concept 'caste cluster'. See her *Hindu Society: An Interpretation* (Poona, 1961), pp. 9–10.

D   37

a privileged individual, and even the Peshwa was denied the right to use the ghats reserved for deshasth priests at Nasik on the Godavri. The deshasths were closely integrated into the social fabric of the villages, and as *kulkarnis* and *joshis* they featured more prominently in the eyes of the peasants than any other brahman group. Before the rise of the Peshwas, the administration was almost entirely recruited from their ranks. But even though the rise of Balaji Vishwanath undermined their monopoly over the administration, they still controlled considerable power over rural society in the role of *kulkarnis* and *deshmukhs*.[1]

Prior to the British conquest of 1818, the administration of Maharashtra was dominated by the chitpavans, who possessed greater intellectual agility and political acumen than the deshasths, and who were consequently able to exercise a more profound influence over the region. Indeed, members of the chitpavan caste virtually shaped the style of life in Maharashtra before 1818, through their close connection with the Peshwas, and through the social and political power which this connection bestowed on them. The caste produced men of distinction in politics, in the field of scholarship and in the art of war. True, there were chitpavans steeped in the unlovely intrigues of court life who struck even the sympathetic observer as 'intriguing, lying, corrupt, licentious and unprincipled'.[2] But the caste was better served by skilled diplomats like Nana Furnavis; or administrators of integrity like Ramashastri; or *advaitists* of repute like Mulhar Shrotee; or scholars of distinction like Raghu Acharya Chintamun.

The opportunities which the rise of the Peshwas opened up for the chitpavans can best be illustrated by looking into the histories of two chitpavan families of slightly more than ordinary distinction in the 18th century. The Ranades were a *khoti* family of the village of Pacherisada in the Chiplun *taluka* of Ratnagiri District. Bhagwantrao, a younger son of the family, migrated to the village of Karkamb near Pandharpur in the second quarter of the 18th century, when Maratha power was making itself felt north of the Narbada under the ambitious

---

[1] *Gazetteer of the Bombay Presidency*, Vol. XVIII, Ahmednagar District (Bombay, 1885), pp. 50–63. Also see Enthoven, *op. cit.*, pp. 242–4.
[2] Report by M. Elphinstone on the Maratha States dated 25 October 1819: *East India Papers*, Vol. IV.

leadership of Baji Rao I. His son, Bhaskarrao, attached himself as a *sillahdar* to Chintamun Rao Patwardhan, one of the brahman landed chiefs whom the Peshwas had ennobled in a bid to consolidate their authority. Bhaskarrao fought with distinction in the contingent of the Patwardhan chief, and he was rewarded for his service by a *jagir* which he passed on to his descendants. The Kurlekars were yet another chitpavan family who had profited from the rise of the Peshwas. They belonged to the village of Nerren in Ratnagiri, and contemporaneously with Bhagwantrao, Balambhat Chiplokar, a member of the family, migrated to the village of Kurla near Aundh. His two sons, Bajipant and Mankojipant, first fought under the *Pant Pratinidhi*, and then joined the regiment of Chintamun Rao Patwardhan. Both the brothers were killed in action. But their sacrifice did not go unrewarded, and earned for Ganpatrao, the posthumous son of Bajipant, an extensive *jagir* which was in turn inherited by his children.[1]

The control of political and social power by the chitpavans through their connection with the Peshwas, and the intellectual hegemony which they exercised by virtue of their caste, created a degree of brahmanical dominance in Maharashtra to which there existed no parallel in the rest of India. This dominance was expressed in institutions like the *dakshina*, which represented an informal alliance between the chitpavans and the State. The *dakshina*, literally a gift, was the means through which the Peshwas extended support to the brahmans in their role as the custodians and the propagators of the values of Hinduism. It involved the distribution of charity to scholarly but impecunious brahmans after they had been examined by a body of *Shastris* who ascertained their knowledge of the sacred texts of Hinduism. The recipients of *dakshina* looked upon it as a most important institution, and in return for the recognition which it accorded to their role, they were unstinting in the support which they extended to the State. But apart from the vulgar exigencies of politics, the brahmans of Maharashtra also looked upon the *dakshina* as an instrument of moral order in society:

A knowledge of the Hindu Shasters [they pointed out to the British Government when it threatened to discontinue the

[1] *Ranade: His Wife's Reminiscences*, trans. by K. Deshpande (Bombay, 1863), pp. 17–19 and 28–29.

dakshina] is of the utmost importance, and . . . the Shasters are indisputably necessary, so that those who study them are entitled to the dakshinnah, as a gift which has been from a remote period continued, and many being thereby incited to the study of Hindu science have ultimately become eminent by their great learning. . . .[1]

Besides distributing charity to their caste-fellows, the Peshwas supported *pathshalas* or schools which were run exclusively for high-caste pupils, and which communicated the values of Hinduism to young brahmans. The extent of this system of high-caste education is indicated by the fact that in Poona alone there were 164 *pathshalas* where the religious texts of Hinduism were taught to young men through the medium of Sanskrit. The *pathshalas* were free institutions, since the *Shastris* were not expected to exploit their learning and scholarship for the sordid business of earning a livelihood. But if tradition obliged the *Shastris* to provide free education, it also imposed upon the rulers the duty of providing for their subsistence. The Peshwas, of course, fulfilled this obligation with an enthusiasm which may not have been shared by non-brahman rulers. The distinguished scholar, Vithal Upadhaya, who presided over a Sanskrit College in Pandharpur, was merely one of hundreds of *Shastris* who were encouraged through generous grants to spread education in the brahman community.[2]

The dominance of the brahmans was an important factor in promoting social cohesion and in ensuring political order in society. Since the brahmans were the leaders of society, and the guardians of the values of Hinduism, they enforced good behaviour on members of their community through a policy of voluntary restraints. In the case of the non-brahmans, however, good behaviour had to be enforced through the institution of caste assemblies, and through the authority of caste heads and *Shastris* versed in custom and law. The caste assemblies debated all questions which affected the interests of the community involved. The brahmans of Poona, for instance, met frequently to discuss points of custom, or novel problems facing the com-

[1] *BA:* Petition by 500 Brahmans of Poona to the Bombay Government dated 4 November 1836: G.D. (General Department), Vol. 15/385 of 1837.
[2] *BA:* H. D. Robertson to W. Chaplin dated 2 January 1824: G.D., Vol. 15/73 of 1824.

munity, on the initiative of leading *Shastris* like Waman Shastri Sathe or Neelkunth Shastri Thute. Such meetings provided opportunities for lively discussion and debate, and they were characterised by active participation on the part of the ordinary members of the community:

> There were present [according to one account of a meeting of the brahmans of Poona] Mulhar Shrotee, the most highly respected Brahmin in the country; Nilcunt Shastree Thuthey and Wittal Oopaddea of Pundharpur, esteemed the most able men, and the most deeply versed in the whole of the Deccan in the learning of the shasters, who have instructed and still instruct many young Brahmins; Raghoo Acharya, an eminent scholar, the Principal of the school at Poona; Hurbhut Caseekur, a beneras brahmin of great celebrity; Chintamun Dixit, Ganesh Shastree of Rajapur; and many eminent shastrees from all quarters. The number of persons assembled was at least five hundred, and the streets leading to Boodwar Palace were filled with people curious to know the result of discussions regarding suttees, and the right of sonars to perform certain Brahmanical ceremonies, which last was also a question appointed to be determined at the meeting.[1]

Because of an inferior level of education, caste assemblies in the lower and middle ranks of society possessed neither the popularity nor the liveliness of brahmanical congregations, and the power to make decisions in such assemblies was vested in a small group of individuals rather than in the rank and file. The brahmans decided issues on the basis of consensus, while in the middle castes power was vested in an 'elective' head who consulted the leading members of the community before embarking upon a course of action. Castes located at the bottom of the social scale were subject to the dictates of an hereditary head who imposed his will on the basis of the authority which he had inherited. But even among the lower castes, the position of the head was by no means completely arbitrary. Whenever he confronted a difficult question, he consulted the *Shastris*, and accepted their advice as reflecting values to which high and low castes subscribed with equal enthusiasm. As a result, even though caste assemblies served to widen the gulf between different castes, they were nevertheless instrumental in linking

---

[1] H. D. Robertson to W. Chaplin dated 10 December 1823: printed in R. D. Choksey, *The Aftermath* (Bombay, 1950), pp. 220–5.

them to a common tradition of moral values and social behaviour.[1]

Integration and cleavage, paradoxically enough, were the twin foundations of stability and order in Maharashtra. Integration flowed from the great tradition of Hinduism, and from its popular derivative, the *bhakti* cult, which linked remote rural communities and clusters of urban castes in an intimate relationship, and which moulded the identity of the *kunbi* as well as the brahman. Integration also flowed from the *deshmukhs* and *mamlatdars*, who set up a chain of command between the Peshwa and the *kunbi*; and from the *vanis* and *sowcars*, who tied urban to rural society. Yet this integration was undermined by values and institutions which divided the region into isolated and self-sufficient communities. Such were the villages of Maharashtra, with their *jathas*, their *bullotedars* and their local Gods. Such also were the clusters of urban castes, with their autonomous assemblies and their distinct styles of life.

The institutions and values of Maharashtra had conjured into existence a society whose stability was related to its overall structure, rather than to the position of a particular individual or a specific caste within it. As a result of such a stability, the rise of a new ruling group did not bring about any radical changes in society, except possibly for the introduction of a tension between the new rulers and the wider community. The stability of Maharashtra was in fact reinforced by the clash of interest between caste and caste, and class and class, and the consequent jockeying for positions of power and influence contributed to, instead of undermining, the overall condition of equipoise.

But this stability was undermined by the influences which impinged upon the region after 1818, and which provide us with an insight into the social changes which took place in Maharashtra in the 19th century.

[1] Vide Steel's *Summary of Hindu Laws*. Steele's account is based on information obtained from the leading *Shastris* of Poona, and from the heads of various castes.

II

The Politics of Moderation

The fall of Baji Rao Peshwa invested the Government of Bombay with the responsibility of administering territories which had formed the hub of an extensive empire in western and in central India in the 18th century. We have already discussed the social and political institutions which flourished in these territories under the Peshwas, and we have focused attention in particular on the bonds which tied different castes and classes in Maharashtra to a common corpus of religious values. The consensus between the high and the low castes stemmed from the dissemination of the concept of *advaita* and the values of Hinduism through a folk literature which ranged from the compositions of Jnaneshwar to the *abhangas* of Namadeva and Tukarama. Besides narrowing the gulf between the élite and the plebeian castes, the literature of *bhakti* inspired the heroic figures of Maharashtra, and it evoked an ethos which has been equated with the spirit of nationalism by some modern historians of the region.

The brahmans of Maharashtra were not only linked to the *kunbis* and other inferior castes through common religious values but they also enjoyed a special position of predominance to which there existed no parallel in the rest of India. This was particularly true of the chitpavan brahmans, who had come to occupy many important positions in the administration, and who had also been awarded substantial grants in land after the accession to power of the Peshwas, who were their caste-fellows.

Of the significant concentrations of power in society, namely, the institutions of religion, the administration and the ownership of land, the chitpavans virtually controlled all three. Their status in the scale of caste assured their supremacy over the institutions of religion; their ties with the Peshwas secured for them a monopoly over the administration; and finally, the ties of caste once again encouraged the Peshwas to create a landed aristocracy which was recruited from brahman families, and in whose loyalty they could rely in all circumstances. This is not to altogether deny the existence in Maharashtra of landlords or administrators or soldiers who were non-brahmans. This is merely to assert that the privileges enjoyed by the chitpavans through their special ties with the Peshwas enabled them to dominate the rest of the community.

I

The administration of the territories acquired from Baji Rao Peshwa presented Mountstuart Elphinstone, who was appointed the first Commissioner of the Deccan by the Government of Bombay, with a host of novel and pressing problems. The solutions which Elphinstone proposed for these problems were shaped by his intimate knowledge of Maharashtra under the Peshwas, and by his firm belief in morality rather than expediency as the basis of politics. A contemporary portrait of Elphinstone reveals him as a man of sensibility and intelligence, personable in appearance, but with a melancholy cast of features whose underlying sadness is heightened by their sensitivity. He joined the East India Company in 1795 as a junior civilian, and after serving for a few years in Benares as a subordinate executive officer, he entered the 'foreign' service of the Company, and thereafter represented it at the courts of Indian princes like the Raja of Berar and the Scindhia of Gwalior.[1] In 1811 Elphinstone was appointed the Resident at Poona, and as the representative of a power which had reinstated Baji Rao as Peshwa in 1802, he virtually controlled the political destiny of Maharashtra even before 1818. But the events of that year, and his appointment as Commissioner, conferred new responsibilities on him. Elphinstone's tenure as Resident at Poona, and the relations he conducted with the Peshwa and his court in that

[1] T. E. Colebrooke, *Life of Honourable Mountstuart Elphinstone* (London 1884).

capacity, provided him with a deep insight into the politics of Maharashtra, and into the values and institutions of her people. But it simultaneously prevented him from gaining that practical experience of administration which was acquired by civilians who spent most of their time in executive posts. As a result of this, Elphinstone was unable to apply to the problems of administration that insight and that depth of comprehension which informed his policies in the sphere of politics.

The policies which Elphinstone initiated as Commissioner stemmed from his close acquaintance with Maharashtra, and from his cautious approach to innovation and reform. He believed that social institutions and moral values were deeply rooted in the traditions of a society, and he also believed that any attempt to change them overnight could only lead to disaster. Despite his flirtation with radical ideas at an early age, when 'he wore his hair long in imitation of the French Republicans, and was fond of singing "Ça ira"',[1] Elphinstone remained all his life a Whig of the old school, who saw statesmanship of the highest quality in the politics of moderation, rather than in hasty reform and in attempts to bring about sweeping changes. His natural ability to discern, and to appreciate, the quality of a society with deep-rooted traditions was heightened by the training he received from men like Samuel Davis, the Magistrate at Benares and his mentor in the Indian Civil Service, who was a distinguished scholar of Sanskrit, and who compiled the first scientific account of the astronomy of classical India. Elphinstone's political vision, however, was not shaped by any romantic notions about the past. Instead, it stemmed from a belief that every community was endowed with qualities which were unique, and which shaped its identity in a manner which set it apart from other communities. Elphinstone's ability to grasp those unique qualities which mould the identity of a society, and his vision of progress, are both vividly reflected in entries in his journal which speak of his concern over the controversies connected with the Reform Bill which was passed in Great Britain in 1832:

> Yesterday I found the club in a hustle [he observes] from the news of the Duke of Wellington's resignation, in consequence of being in a minority on the Civil List. . . . The first expectations that

[1] ibid., Vol. I, p. 6.

present themselves for the future are that the Whig ministry, which we may suppose will be formed, will be embarrassed by its pledge in favour of retrenchment, which to any great extent is impracticable; and of reform, which beyond due limits would be perilous in the extreme. Many well-intentioned but ill-informed persons, who may favour it at first, will be driven by this to join the Radicals, to whom the Whigs are always objects of detestation. The Ministry will sink, and with it all confidence in moderate reformers; power will either pass directly into the hands of violent reformers, or will come to them with more tumult and danger after having been for a time entrusted to ultra-Tories. Universal suffrage, preponderance of democracy, might be expected to follow, and to be accompanied by the annulment of the national debt . . . and other revolutionary measures. . . . No contingency can render it safe or wise to withhold reform, or to delay making the necessary alterations in parts of the constitution, while there is sufficient attachment to the whole to prevent it being subverted during the operation.[1]

Elphinstone's reaction to the political storm which threatened the constitution of Great Britain in 1832 demonstrates that he was not a blind opponent of change. He believed that innovation and reform were essential parts of the social process. In the evolution of a community, ran his argument, institutions and values which had once performed a creative role and satisfied a genuine need often became completely purposeless. It was foolish and even dangerous to oppose the abolition of such values and institutions. For mere antiquity was insufficient to preserve inveterate abuse, and it was no defence of an outmoded order that it was an inheritance from the past. Those who supported values and institutions merely because they had been handed down from the past were guilty of defending the prescriptive order as though it was of divine origin, and as if its growth was unconscious and even spontaneous. They refused to accept that values and institutions originated in answer to specific social requirements, and that throughout the course of history they changed in response to the changing needs of society.

Because he held a view of society which approved of progress that did not involve any break with tradition, Elphinstone was quite prepared to initiate reform in response to the law of change which, so he believed, determined the course of human

[1] ibid., Vol. II, pp. 297–8.

development. But he was convinced that arbitrary reform, arbitrary because it rode roughshod over tradition, could only undermine the foundations which gave stability, and the values which imparted cohesion, to a community. The task of the reformer was, therefore, to reinvigorate and to reaffirm the underlying moral principles of a community, maintaining all the while a fine balance between progress and stability. Reform, Elphinstone argued, ought to reconcile the conflicting principles of conservation and correction, for the reformer assumed that some of the attributes of his society were worthy of being preserved. True reform accepted the moral foundations of a society and sought to establish their supremacy in the midst of change. It also made use of existing institutions, and even in modifying them attempted to reinforce their spirit and to reinvigorate their style. True reform embodied, in other words, the traditional order of a society shorn of obsolete forms and stultifying excrescences.

Since Elphinstone was intimately acquainted with the politics of Maharashtra under the Peshwas, and because he was opposed to reform which undermined the traditions of a society, as Commissioner of the Deccan he asked himself a series of questions which would not have suggested themselves to a less discriminating, or a more impetuous, individual. What were the most fruitful policies to be pursued in the conquered territories? To what extent was the old system of administration to be incorporated in the new? How were dominant groups like the chitpavan brahmans and the landed aristocrats to be treated? To what extent were their special privileges to be recognised by the British Government? What would be the fate of the institutions of self-government within the village? Would it be necessary to encroach upon their authority? Would it also be necessary to bring about a redistribution of social power within the villages? Finally, what was to be done with values which approved of discrimination based on an individual's status in the scale of caste, and which were so intimately related to the religion of the people?

If Elphinstone had subscribed to the values of Hinduism, and if he had approved in principle of the social and political institutions which flourished under the Peshwas, it would have been possible for him to provide simple answers to the questions which he faced as the Commissioner of the Deccan. But since he disapproved of the values of Hinduism, and since he also

47

disapproved of progress which was achieved through undermining the traditions of a society, the creation of a new system of administration presented him with a serious dilemma. His views on the moral principles which sustained society in Maharashtra were clear and unambiguous. A religion which sanctioned the institution of caste and approved of a most gross form of social discrimination was highly offensive to Elphinstone. He also believed that in the peculiar conditions of Maharashtra, measures of reform which strengthened the moral foundations of the community would heighten social injustice and stimulate political iniquity. It was therefore necessary to do away altogether with the framework of society which Elphinstone had inherited from the Peshwas. It was also necessary to propagate new values in the community, and to foster the growth of appropriate social and political institutions. However, Elphinstone's conservative cast of mind and his vision of social progress prevented him from embarking upon so drastic and so comprehensive a programme of reform. He therefore tried to transform the institutions which he had inherited from the Peshwas into instruments for the reform of Maharashtra.

Elphinstone's attempt to exploit existing institutions for the infusion of new values in Maharashtra is reflected most vividly in his decision to continue the patronage which the Peshwas had extended to the brahmans through the distribution of the *dakshina*. He took this decision out of political calculation, rather than out of any sentimental concern for the welfare of the brahmans, since he had no illusions about them, and looked upon them as narrow and bigoted in their attachment to their privileges. What prompted Elphinstone to continue the *dakshina* was the importance of the role which the brahmans had played in Maharashtra before 1818, and the influence which they consequently continued to exercise after the transfer of power into the hands of the Government of Bombay. Indeed, the concentration of political power in the hands of the Peshwas had heightened brahmanical dominance to an extent to which there existed no parallel in the rest of India, for the *dakshina* had been merely one of the institutions through which the Peshwas had indicated their approval of the hegemony of the brahmans, and their attachment to the values of Hinduism. True, under Baji Rao II the sum distributed as *dakshina* had been reduced from the imposing figure of Rs. 1,000,000 to an extremely modest amount. But despite his straitened circumstances, the last Peshwa had given gifts to as many as 50,000 brahmans, over and above the prizes which he awarded to *Shastris* who distinguished themselves by their proficiency in the sacred texts of Hinduism. The Peshwas had thus supported a class of individuals who devoted their time exclusively to the study of religious literature, and who handed down from generation to generation the religious traditions of the community.[1]

Though the *dakshina* represented an alliance between the Peshwas and the brahmans of Maharashtra, and though it served to reinforce and to reinvigorate the values of Hinduism, Elphinstone desisted from abolishing it, even though the institution held no 'moral' significance for the political system which was introduced in the Poona territories under British aegis. Indeed, Elphinstone even refrained from altering the agency through which the *dakshina* had been distributed under the Peshwas. He appointed a committee of five distinguished *Shastris* of Poona, headed by Raghu Acharya Chintamun, to supervise the distribution of bounties to the brahmans. This committee scrutinised the list of brahmans who had enjoyed patronage in former days; it then examined them in those fields in which they claimed a special interest; and finally it determined the sums of money they were to receive as *dakshina* on the basis of their scholarly attainments. In 1820 Raghu Acharya Chintamun submitted a list of 2,665 brahmans whom he had examined and found proficient; and he recommended that they be paid a sum of Rs. 75,000, which was reduced to Rs. 45,000 by the Government of Bombay.[2] Elphinstone regarded the distribution of the *dakshina* as more than just a sop to the susceptibilities of the brahmans, or a concession to the religious prejudices of the Hindu community. The *dakshina*, he argued, could be exploited to weaken the attachment of the brahmans to their traditional values, and to encourage them to take an interest in the arts and the sciences of the West. After British rule over Maharashtra was firmly established, Elphinstone pointed out, 'the *dakshina* might still be kept, but most of the prizes, instead of being

[1] *BA:* Minute by Governor of Bombay dated nil: G.D., Vol. 8/63 of 1826.
[2] *BA:* W. Chaplin to Government of Bombay dated 15 April 1820: Political Department, Diary No. 482 of 1824.

conferred on proficients in Hindu divinity, might be allotted to those more skilled in more useful branches of learning—law, mathematics, etc., and a certain number of professors might be appointed to teach these sciences'.[1]

The Hindu College established by Elphinstone in Poona was equally informed with the view that the most effective means of converting the brahmans to western values lay in creating an institution that would lead them gradually from the study of Hindu religious texts to an examination of the philosophy and the sciences of the West. Since the College was established with the object, in the first instance, of imparting a catholic education to 'young men of the caste of brahmins in the several branches of science and knowledge which usually constitute the subjects of study of the learned Indians',[2] it incorporated professorial chairs for the study of *Vedanta*, of the *Shastras*, of Vyakaran, *Nyaya*, *Jyotish*, *Vydic* and *Alankar*, and junior professorships for the study of the Vedas. Elphinstone had no illusions about the values which the Hindu College would disseminate in the community:

> But we must not forget [he pointed out] that we are forming, or rather keeping up with no modifications, a seminary among a most bigoted people whose knowledge has always been in the hands of the priesthood, and whose science itself is considered a branch of religion. In such circumstances, and supporting the expenses from a fund devoted to religious purposes, I do not think we could possibly have excluded the usual theological professorships without showing a hostility to the Hindu faith which it was our object to avoid, and irritating those prejudices of the people which it was the professed desire of the institution to soothe or remove.[2]

Although Elphinstone did not underestimate the tenacity with which the brahmans clung to their traditional values, he still desired to prepare them for the changes which lay ahead, and Raghu Acharya Chintamun, the *Mukhya Shastri* or Principal of the Hindu College, was instructed to 'direct the attention of the College principally to the shastras as are not only most useful in themselves, but will prepare their minds (i.e. the minds

[1] See Minute by Mountstuart Elphinstone in G. W. Forrest (ed.), *Selections From the Minutes and Other Official Writings of the Honourable Mountstuart Elphinstone*, pp. 334–5.
[2] *BA*: Address by W. Chaplin on the opening of the Poona Hindu College dated 10 April 1821: G.D., Vol. 10 of 1821.
[3] *BA*: Minute by Governor of Bombay dated nil: G.D., Vol. 8/63 of 1824.

of the students) for the gradual reception of more useful instruction at a later time'.[1] To ensure this objective, scholars admitted to the Hindu College were required to know enough Sanskrit to commence straightaway with the study of the *Shastras* or *Vyakaran* or *Alankar*. Besides, while the study of the Vedas was not discouraged, it was held inferior to the study of the *Shastras*, and no scholar was permitted to devote his time exclusively to the former. A student who chose to study the Vedas was also required to study the *Shastras*, and his proficiency in the *Shastras* was looked upon as his main qualification. The curriculum of the Hindu College emphasised knowledge which was utilitarian as opposed to metaphysics and philosophy, and Elphinstone had every intention of heightening this emphasis with the passage of time. He believed that once the Hindu College became a popular institution among the brahmans of Maharashtra, it would be easy to modify the courses which it offered to students, and to transform it into an instrument for disseminating western values.

While Elphinstone was anxious to prevent the alienation of the brahmans, if only because of the great influence which they exercised over the rest of the community, he did not overlook the problems of popular education. The state of popular education could, of course, bear looking into. In cities like Poona and Nasik young men of the upper castes had the opportunity of attending *pathshalas* run by distinguished scholars like Waman Shastri Sathe or Neelkunth Shastri Thute, who subsisted upon bounties granted by the Peshwas. But there was no provision for the education of the children of *kunbis* even in the immediate vicinity of Poona. As Table B indicates, the 650 villages which occupied an area of 1,728 square miles around Poona had between them only twenty-seven schools.[2]

But even if the number of schools in the villages had been greater, it is doubtful whether the *kunbis* could have made any extensive use of them. For the great majority of the *kunbis* were so poor, and they lived so near the level of subsistence, that they were compelled to send their children to work on the fields from a very tender age. Literacy in the rural areas was confined to the

[1] *BA:* W. Chaplin to Government of Bombay dated 24 November 1821: G.D., Vol. 10 of 1821.
[2] *BA:* Report on the Poona District by Colonel Sykes dated nil: R.D., Vol. 154B of 1826.

TABLE B

Showing the Number of Schools in the Villages around Poona

Name of district	No. of villages	Area in miles	No. of schools
Naneh Mawal	92	159	0
Pown Mawal	32	190	1
Unaur Mawal	28	62	0
Powar Mawal	84	167	4
Turuff Goreh	16	27	1
Turuff Kheir	36	201	7
Turuff Ambegaon	40	47	1
Turuff Chakan	65	205	5
Turuff Wareh	79	206	2
Turuff Haveli	82	207	4
Turuff Mawal	36	64	1
? Turuff	49	150	1
Mosah Khoreh	3	$2\frac{1}{2}$	0
Part of Moteh Khoreh	2	$35\frac{1}{2}$	0
Total	650		27

kulkarnis, the *joshis* and the *vanis*, and the village schools were
run by ill-educated brahmans called *puntojis*, who taught their
pupils little apart from the rudiments of arithmetic and the
myths of Hinduism. The *kunbis*, of course, were in no position
to exploit even the limited opportunities for schooling that were
open to them. 'I believe not one cultivator in a hundred would
be able to write',[1] observed a British officer who travelled in the
villages around Poona in the 1820s. Despite their liveliness and
their natural intelligence, the illiteracy of the *kunbis* placed them
at a great disadvantage in their dealings with the *vanis* or the
kulkarnis. Perhaps it was these disadvantages which made them
anxious to educate their children. The Collector of Poona, for
instance, observed with considerable satisfaction how 'extremely
fond parents . . . (were) of getting their favourite and eldest son
taught'.[2] If a *puntoji* resided in a village, then all the *kunbis* who
could afford to work their fields without the assistance of their
children sent them to the *puntoji* to learn how to read and write.
Indeed, it was usual for prosperous *kunbis* to engage a brahman
teacher to reside in their village for the benefit of the children
of the community. Landed families of respectability, of course,
engaged learned brahmans as tutors for their sons.

[1] ibid.
[2] *BA:* H. D. Robertson to Government of Bombay dated 20 January 1824: E.D.
(Education Department), Vol. 1 of 1825.

The contrast between the state of schools in the cities and in the villages underscores the limited opportunities for education open to the *kunbis*. It also underscores the extent to which the brahmans exercised intellectual dominance over the rest of the community. In the city of Ahmednagar, for instance, out of a total of thirty-six schools eighteen were meant exclusively for the children of brahmans, and only offered courses in the Vedas and the *Shastras*. The total number of children who attended school in Ahmednagar was 571, out of which 275 were brahmans, while the rest were drawn from the Muslim community, or from the caste of *kunbis*. Children of low caste parents seldom went to school in the city. A caste breakdown of schoolteachers is even more revealing of the extent to which the brahmans dominated the intellectual life of the community, since twenty-six out of thirty-six teachers hailed from the brahman caste.[1]

Elphinstone sought to organise education along lines which would introduce the brahmans of Maharashtra to the arts and the sciences of the West; he also sought to destroy the monopoly which they exercised over the profession of teaching. He found an excellent instrument for his education policy in the Bombay Education Society. This Society was created in 1815, and it concerned itself, in the first instance, with the education of European children in Bombay, seeking to bring them up in in 'pious attachment to the principles of Christianity'. Because it was committed to the propagation of education on Christian principles the Bombay Education Society was not equipped to spread literacy in the Hindu community. But when Elphinstone was appointed the Governor of Bombay he encouraged the Society to acquire new responsibilities, whereupon it opened in 1820 a branch called the Native Education Society with the object of providing facilities for the education of the native community through the acquisition of already existing schools, and also through the institution of new schools. Besides, the Native Education Society aimed at providing the schools under its aegis with teachers trained in English, and in western science and philosophy.[2]

[1] *BA:* H. Pottinger, Collector of Ahmednagar, to Government of Bombay dated 18 August, 1824: E.D., Vol. 1 of 1824.
[2] Extract from the First Report (1824) of the Bombay Native Education Society in R. V. Parelkur and C. L. Bakshi (ed.), *Selections from the Records of the Education Department, Government of Bombay, Volume II (1815–1840)* (Bombay, 1955), pp. 43–5.

E

Encouraged by Elphinstone, the Native Education Society presented a memorandum to the Government of Bombay in which it emphasised the need for popular education along lines which would open the minds of the non-brahmans to the arts and the sciences of the West.[1] While the brahmans, the Society pointed out, possessed a strong tradition of scholarship, and while they were firm in their allegiance to the values of Hinduism, precisely the reverse was true of the non-brahmans. But apart from the absence of scholastic traditions among the non-brahmans, there did not exist in Marathi, the only language with which they were conversant, literary works which could form the basis of a sound education. It was consequently necessary to translate into Marathi works dealing with western science and philosophy 'which without interfering with the religious sentiments of any person, may be calculated to enlarge the understanding and inspire the character...'[2] The Native Education Society drew up for translation a list of books which embraced fields as diverse as Newtonian physics and a scientific account of evolution. Behind the Society's desire to transform, indeed, to revolutionise popular education lay the assumption that since the non-brahmans lacked an intellectual tradition of their own, they could straightaway be introduced to the arts and the sciences of the West. Such a move, the Society was confident, would be opposed only by the old-fashioned *puntojis*, whose vision was confined to the traditional world of Hinduism, and who fed their pupils on a diet of irrationality and superstition. To prevent their opposition from frustrating a sound policy in education the Society proposed to set up centres which would train a new generation of schoolteachers. Such schoolteachers could be relied to disseminate values among the non-brahmans which would tie them in firm bonds of loyalty to the British Government in India. The effective execution of its policy, the Native Education Society pointed out, depended upon the moral and the material support which it received from the Government of Bombay. But to deny this support would mean a calculated weakening of the foundations of British rule over Maharashtra:

[1] *BA:* Letter from G. Jervis, Secretary to the Bombay Native Education Society, to the Government of Bombay dated 4 October 1823: G.D., Vol. 8/63 of 1824.
[2] ibid.

With means so disproportionate [ran the memorandum of the Native Education Society] the Committee are immediately prompted to look towards the government for pecuniary assistance; the more especially as it has shown such readiness hitherto to support the views of the Society. From the dissemination of education, the cultural and moral improvement of the human mind, there are consequences as truly advantageous to the governing as to the governed; and it is not without any presumptuous feeling the Committee express their opinion, that it appears more beneficial and glorious to check at first the propensities and vice, by affording subjects the means of judging between right and wrong, than eventually to make a display of that power with which providence has entrusted the British Government, for the suppression of crime and maintenance of order.[1]

Since Elphinstone supported the Hindu College and the Native Education Society with equal enthusiasm, we can infer that he was as much concerned with élite as he was with popular education, and that he wanted to disseminate western values both among the brahmans and among the non-brahmans. Elphinstone, in fact, sought to transform Maharashtra into a society which would respond creatively to the stimulus of the West, and which would also absorb liberal and rational ideas. While the objectives which informed Elphinstone's policy in education were significant in themselves, the means he devised for their realisation were even more significant, and reflected his deep insight into the structure and values of society in Maharashtra. Elphinstone recognised, for instance, the tenacity with which the brahmans clung to institutions which held out for them a dominant role in society. He also recognised the absence of intellectual traditions among the non-brahmans, and their lack of affection for values which relegated them to a position of subordination. Elphinstone's policy in education was, therefore, based on the conflicting attitudes of the brahmans and the non-brahmans towards the values and institutions of Hinduism. A 'brahmanical' institution like the Hindu College, for instance, was to commence with the study of traditional disciplines, and to introduce its students to western science and philosophy very gradually. Schools meant for the plebeian castes, however, were to start straightaway with the rational disciplines of the West. The effect of such a policy, so Elphinstone believed, would be to

[1] ibid.

55

transform the values of the entire community without creating any tensions between different social groups, and without weakening the social fabric of Maharashtra.

II

The creation of values which would undermine the unlovely social institutions of Maharashtra was only one of the problems which confronted Elphinstone as the Commissioner of the Deccan. Questions concerning the state of the rural economy, and the policy best calculated to ensure the prosperity of the peasants, confronted Elphinstone with an urgency which was more compelling than anything else, if only for the reason that the land-tax paid by the *kunbis* formed a major share of the revenues of the State. These questions hinged upon one decisive issue: How was the produce of the land to be divided between the *kunbis* who tilled the soil, the intermediaries who assisted him in various ways, and the State, which ensured the social peace and protected him against aggression from without? The prosperity of the *kunbis*, indeed, the prosperity of the entire community depended upon a satisfactory answer to this question. An equitable tax on the land could mean plenty for the *kunbi* and for society as a whole; an inequitable tax could mean poverty for the peasants and impoverishment for the wider community.

When he took over the territories of the Peshwa, Elphinstone found the administration of the land-tax in a state of complete confusion. The institutions of self-government within the villages, and the balance of power between the *deshmukhs* and the *mamlatdars*, had ensured an element of rough and ready justice in the collection of the land-tax so long as a watchful ruler presided over the destinies of Maharashtra. But Baji Rao II had thrown discretion to the winds, and he had adopted a host of arbitrary practices which undermined the checks and balances that were meant to ensure the efficiency of the administration. The office of the *mamlatdar*, for instance, was no longer conferred on administrators of experience who could be recalled if their conduct proved unsatisfactory. Instead, it was put to annual auction among the courtiers and the favourites of the Peshwa, who were expected to bid high for the office, and fell out of favour if they failed to do so. The *mamlatdars* appointed in this fashion had neither the time nor the inclination to inquire into the resources of the districts which fell under their charge. They were also indifferent to the prosperity of the *kunbis*. They often let out a district at an enhanced rate to farmers of revenue, who repeated the operation until it reached the *patil* in the village. A *mamlatdar* who had purchased the rights of collection of revenue for a district became absolute master over it for the term of his lease, and the *kunbis* under his control could not lodge complaints against him through the *deshmukhs*. If the *patil* of a village, mindful of his role as the leader of the *kunbis* and the protector of their interests, refused to farm his village at an exorbitant rate, the *mamlatdars* of Baji Rao entrusted the collection of tax to their personal attendants, who performed their duties with a lack of consideration that imposed great suffering on the peasants.[1]

Immediately after the conquest of the Peshwa's territories, Elphinstone tried to revive the old system of the administration of land-revenue, purging it of the anomalies which had crept into it under Baji Rao. The revenue divisions of the former administration were regrouped into compact districts, each one of which yielded from Rs. 50,000 to Rs. 75,000 as tax. These districts were placed under native *mamlatdars*, who were in turn subordinated to the control of British officers designated Collectors. The *mamlatdars* were instructed to abolish the practice of farming the revenue, and they were also instructed to settle the land-tax in negotiations with the *patils* and the principal cultivators of the villages under their charge. They were to levy the tax according to the area of land actually under cultivation; to make the assessments light; to impose no new taxes; and to abolish none unless they were positively harmful. But above all they were to introduce no innovations.[2] The *mamlatdars* were required to settle the tax on villages as a whole, instead of settling it on individual peasants, though some *mamlatdars*, under instructions from their Collectors, executed this principle with greater rigour than it had ever been executed under the Peshwas. W. Chaplin and H. Pottinger, the Collectors of Dharwar and Ahmednagar respectively, settled the land-tax of a village

[1] *East India Papers*, Vol. IV: Report on the Maratha States by Mountstuart Elphinstone dated 25 October 1819. Hereinafter referred to as M.E.'s Report on Maratha States.

[2] Mountstuart Elphinstone to Lord Hastings dated 18 June 1818: Reproduced in R. D. Choksey, *The Aftermath (1818–1826)* (Bombay, 1959), pp. 153–76.

in negotiations with the *patil*, and then apportioned the tax among individual cultivators, giving each of them a deed or *puttah* which set out his obligations to the State. Grant at Satara, and Robertson at Poona, settled the tax with the *patil*, and gave him a *puttah* setting out the collective obligations of his village. But they did this only after they had ascertained the amount that would be required of individual cultivators, and had inquired of the cultivators whether they were satisfied with the arrangements.[1]

Despite Elphinstone's attempt to revive the system of administration as it had flourished before Baji Rao Peshwa, and despite his reluctance to undermine the institutions of self-government within the village, the disintegration of the traditional institutions of government was inevitable. For Elphinstone brought to bear on the problems of administration concepts of efficiency and responsibility which held revolutionary implications. The office of the *mamlatdar*, for instance, was completely transformed after 1818. The *mamlatdar* was formerly an officer who exercised considerable initiative. He now became a supine instrument of the Collector's will, and his actions were controlled by a narrow and precise set of regulations. The *deshmukh*, whose informal yet intimate connection with the peasants had played so important a role in ensuring the efficiency of the former administration, suffered a similar eclipse. The Collectors were inclined to look upon him as a parasite, and they were reluctant to utilise his services in negotiating the land-tax with the *patils* and the *kunbis*. The *patil*, too, retained very few of the prerogatives which had made him so important a member of the village community. He could no longer induce *uprees* to settle in his village on preferential leases, nor could he gift away the right of ownership in land 'from his free will and pleasure...[2] The new restrictions on the authority of the *patil*, and the attempt of Collectors like Grant and Robertson to negotiate *puttahs* directly with the cultivators, weakened the ties of association between the *kunbis* and the *patil*. The sentiments of solidarity which inspired the cultivators of a village were largely, though not entirely, a consequence of the fact that the total

[1] M.E.'s Report on Maratha States.
[2] *BA:* Translation of *Meeras Puttah* by the Patil of Multan dated July 1814: Appendix to Section II of Report on Poona District by Major Sykes: R.D., Vol. 26/50 of 1822.

burden of tax on the village was apportioned into individual shares by consultations between the *patil* and the principal *kunbis* without reference to any outside authority. The administration of the Peshwas had often attempted to undermine the autonomy of the villages in the distribution of the tax on individual peasants, but the strength of the institutions of self-government within the villages had prevented it from doing so. The *vox populi* in the villages, as represented in the *rivaj* rates, had always triumphed over measures like the *kamal* survey, which had attempted to establish a direct relationship between the *kunbis* and the central government at Poona, through the exclusion of intermediaries like the *patils* and the *deshmukhs*.

Although his inexperience in the administration of land-revenue prevented him from formulating a clear-cut policy of land-taxation, Elphinstone's belief in an efficient and rational system of administration led him to support the view that it was necessary for the peasants' obligations to the State to be defined on the basis of precise principles by the officers of revenue, instead of being left to the discretion of the *patils* and the dominant *kunbis* of the village. Elphinstone's attempt to establish a contractual relationship between the State and the *kunbi* was a stupendous undertaking, since it involved a most fundamental change in the institutions which had for so long determined the tax to be paid by the peasant. A system of land-tax which rested on a legal contract between the peasant and the State was bound to undermine the solidarity of the villages, since it affected the collective responsibility for the land-tax which held the cultivators of a village in ties of close association. Elphinstone's belief in the equity of a revenue system in which the tax to be paid by the peasant was fixed by the officers of revenue, instead of the *patil* and a few dominant cultivators, stemmed from the suspicion that the poor peasants had suffered great hardship under the *rivaj* rates. Whether this suspicion was true or not, Elphinstone's attempt to determine the equitable tax on every single peasant, instead of leaving the detailed distribution of the obligations of a village to its *patil*, added significantly to the prevailing confusion. It was relatively easy for the Collectors to determine the total tax that could be demanded of a village; but it was extremely difficult for them to divide this sum into the shares of individual peasants. A number of most intricate questions had to be answered before the Collectors could set aside the traditional machinery for calculating the tax on individual peasants. What was the proportion of the produce which the State could claim as its own? What was the criterion on which this proportion was to be based? How was this criterion to be applied? Indeed, even if a satisfactory criterion was to be devised for the land-tax, the application of such a criterion could conceivably alter the existing obligations of the peasants to an extent which would ruin them. What was to be done in such a situation?

There were, in fact, no easy solutions to the problems of land-revenue administration in Maharashtra. A hasty and impetuous attempt at reform in the system of administration by John Briggs, the Collector of Kandesh, merely demonstrated the pitfalls that could trap the unwary.[1] Briggs had a particularly difficult charge. Kandesh was a wild and desolate district, infertile and inhospitable, and it supported a thin population of which the untameable Bhil tribes formed a significant proportion. Briggs found the revenue accounts of the villages of Kandesh in a state of complete disarray. The *kulkarnis'* ledgers were incoherent and undecipherable; the classification of fields was incredibly complex and intricate; and no two fields in a village had been measured in the same unit of area. Immediately after he had assumed charge of Kandesh, Briggs resorted to the expedient of settling the revenue of villages with their *patils*. But this expedient proved useless when a failure of the crops obliged him to remit part of the revenue. Since Briggs had settled the tax on villages as a whole instead of settling it on individual cultivators, it was impossible for him to ensure that the remission of revenue was actually transmitted to the peasants, instead of being appropriated by the *patils* and the *kulkarnis*.

To ensure that the *kunbis* of Kandesh were not cheated of remissions in revenue, Briggs decided to scrap the *rivaj* rates, and to ascertain through personal inquiry the taxes which the peasants could equitably pay to the State. According to the *rivaj* in Kandesh cultivable land was divided into three categories: *patusthal*, or land irrigated by public waterworks: *motusthal*, or land irrigated by privately constructed wells; and

[1] *BA:* J. Briggs, Collector of Kandesh, to W. Chaplin dated 9 November 1821: R.D., Vol. 26/50 of 1822.

zorayet, or unirrigated land. Rates on *patusthal* land were levied on the basis of the crop which was actually grown, while in the case of fields belonging to the second and third classes the tax was levied on the productivity of the land. Briggs considered the practice of taxing *patusthal* lands on the basis of the actual crop grown by the cultivator a most objectionable practice, since it did not offer the *kunbis* any incentive to cultivate crops which yielded high profits. The profit which a peasant could have made on a superior crop was appropriated by the State in the form of an enhanced rate. The peasants of Kandesh, consequently, turned to the cultivation of inferior crops merely to escape the unwelcome attentions of the *mamlatdars* of Baji Rao:

> In addition to the chance of under- or over-assessment [Briggs pointed out] is the circumstance of the ryot not being able to cultivate what he chooses, in consequence of the difference of rates in the different kinds of produce. For the extra rates on the superior sorts of cultivation naturally drive him to rear the poorer kinds in preference to the more valuable production of sugar and rice, which are not only precarious in their returns, but are taxed at so much higher a rate than crops of an inferior value. Admitting this to be the case, it seems that the system is considerably defective.... It is, therefore, advisable to equalise the rates of *patusthal* lands....[1]

Besides abolishing a system of assessment which discouraged the peasants from growing crops which yielded a high rate of profit, Briggs reduced the sixty-eight scales of tax on *motusthal* land to eight, and he also reduced the 122 scales of tax on *zorayet* land to eleven scales. A settlement based on these principles was introduced in Kandesh in 1821.

Before Briggs' settlement could be appraised on the basis of the reaction it evoked from the *kunbis* of Kandesh, W. Chaplin, who had succeeded Elphinstone as the Commissioner of the Deccan, struck a note of serious alarm. Chaplin's objection to the survey conducted by Briggs stemmed from his desire to 'abstain for the present from making any considerable change in the former revenue system, beyond that of removing such abuses as are obviously calculated to affect the prosperity of the country'.[2] Since Chaplin was a conservative of the same hue as

[1] ibid.
[2] *BA:* W. Chaplin, Governor of the Deccan, to J. Briggs dated 3 January 1822: R.D., Vol. 26/50 of 1822.

Elphinstone, he was not opposed to the idea of a new survey as such. But his experience as a revenue officer under Sir Thomas Munro had convinced him that a survey which was not based on 'known and fixed principles that had already been approved by experience' was unlikely to prove successful. When Chaplin examined the survey conducted by Briggs he discovered that it did not rest on any fixed principles, nor did it show any consideration for the prescriptive rights of the peasants. Chaplin conceded that the practice of taxing *patusthal* land on the basis of the crop which was sown, rather than on the basis of its fertility, provided the peasants with no incentives to increase productivity. But, he pointed out, it was doubtful whether Briggs' decision to substitute a simple scale of assessment for the complex *rivaj* rates would necessarily improve the condition of the peasants. Referring to the new categories in the classification of soils which had replaced the old categories in the *motusthal* and the *zorayet* lands, Chaplin observed that if the new classes were based on reliable data, then there was every reason to assume that the simplicity of the new system would constitute an improvement:

> But how have this data [Chaplin wondered] the acquirement of which in other countries has occupied many years ... been ascertained and verified; surely not in a single year of labour of the mamlatdars and their deputies. The classification and assessment of fields, which is everywhere so nice and difficult a process, is not to be well accomplished by such easy means and such unprincipled agents; and the basis of the system being therefore imperfect, if not incorrect, the superstructure will be entirely liable to its fall. ...[1]

A sound revenue policy, Chaplin pointed out, had to satisfy other requirements besides being based on rigorous principles. It had to make an occasional bow to expediency, and also to make allowance for rights whose antiquity made them inalienable. The principle that the land-tax should be based exclusively on the productivity of land was unexceptionable. But was it expedient, indeed, was it even possible to follow this principle when it led to a sudden increase in the burden of tax on a peasant? Chaplin referred to a *kunbi* in the village of Ootran who

[1] ibid.

owned 50 *beegahs* of land, of which 10 *beegahs* were rated first class, and the remainder were divided equally between the second and third categories, on the basis of the *rivaj*. Briggs' survey had shown that all the land owned by the *kunbi* belonged to the first category. It would, consequently, have been perfectly legitimate for Briggs to double the burden of tax on the *kunbi*. 'But the ryot in question has all along been enabled only by moderation of rent to hold so much land,' Chaplin pointed out. 'The rent now being raised to the full, he must of course throw up his land.'[1]

Was it expedient to force such a peasant to throw up his land in the name of abstract principles?

Two distinct, though not necessarily conflicting, issues were thus involved in devising a satisfactory revenue policy. It was necessary to work out a rational body of principles on whose basis the claims of the State and the peasants could be equitably adjusted; but it was equally necessary to ensure that a new system of taxation did not bring about a drastic alteration in the existing obligations of the peasants. Chaplin looked upon both these principles as being of equal importance. Briggs' survey, of course, failed on both counts, and consequently threw the revenue management of the entire district into complete disorder. What Chaplin observed in the village of Bhanmod, for instance, was typical of the effects of the new settlement. The total sum for which Briggs had settled Bhanmod was equitable, and it did not differ significantly from past assessments. But when Chaplin proceeded to Bhanmod to see how it had fared under the new survey, he was met on the outskirts of the village by an outraged group of sixty to seventy peasants 'who were loud in their outcry against the new classification and assessment',[2] since their burden of tax had been raised by 50 to 60 per cent. While the peasants whose obligations had been enhanced complained bitterly against the new survey, Briggs had also reduced the tax on forty-six peasants in Bhanmod, and this group was very pleased with the new rates. Since the confusion caused in Bhanmod was characteristic only of those villages whose total assessment had not been altered, it is easy to visualise the effect of the new settlement on villages whose total tax had been

---

[1] *BA:* W. Chaplin to J. Briggs dated 22 January 1822: R.D., Vol. 26/50 of 1822.
[2] ibid.

raised. Briggs' survey, and the reaction it evoked from the *kunbis* of Kandesh, confirmed Chaplin in his belief that it would be a serious mistake to determine the pitch of the land-tax on individual peasants on the basis of 'objective' principles in complete disregard of the *rivaj* or the custom of villages:

> It must be considered a revenue axiom [Chaplin pontificated] that no settlement that is not conducted with the general assent of the village authorities and the great body of the ryots can possess any stability. The classification and assessment of the lands must therefore be made in a great measure by the corporation of each separate village. To assist in determining the evaluations, the patels and the kulkarnis, and a few of the principal ryots of the adjacent villages should be assembled and consulted. All these persons assembled together, and aided by an intelligent and experienced karkoon from the district, and another from the Huzoor Kutcherry, might inspect and class each field with respect to its quality. . . . (The) evidence of the ryots themselves, checked as I have suggested, will in general furnish the means of discovering pretty accurately what were the former rent and produce of the field, which point being determined, its classification may be safely left to the patel and the principal ryots.[1]

The problems which confronted Briggs in Kandesh were no different from the problems which confronted other Collectors in the districts under their charge. But although the *kunbis*' reaction to Briggs' survey discouraged other Collectors from embarking upon similar schemes of reform, it was clear even to conservatives like Chaplin that the *rivaj* rates could no longer be accepted as the basis of the land-tax. Yet Chaplin had no clearcut notion how the profits of agriculture could be equitably distributed between the peasants and the State. His diffidence, however, was not shared by Robert Keith Pringle, a young civilian who had studied Ricardian economics under Malthus at the East India College at Haileybury, and who was in charge of the *talukas* of Pabul and Sewnere under the Collector of Poona. Impetuous to the point of rashness, with a doctrinaire cast of mind, and with a sense of personal loyalty that was destined to prove his Nemesis, Pringle believed that political economy had discovered a rational explanation of agricultural profits in the Ricardian law of rent, and armed with this belief

[1] ibid.

he launched a frontal attack on those administrators who were reluctant to disturb the *rivaj* or customary rates of tax in the villages of Maharashtra. Pringle's belief in the Ricardian law of rent was not the only reason why he differed from the conservatives. Unlike Chaplin and Elphinstone, who approved of the institutions of self-government in the villages, Pringle felt that these institutions merely served to cloak the domination of the *patil* and the principal cultivators over the village. The *kamal* survey of Madhav Rao Peshwa, he argued in his appraisal of the 'revenue axiom' outlined by Chaplin, had been designed to absorb all the rent of the land, leaving to the *kunbis* the wages of their labour and the profits on their capital. But Madhav Rao's attempt to base the pitch of the land-tax on a rational principle had provoked the hostility of the dominant cultivators in the villages, who had exploited the *rivaj* rates to transfer a predominating share of the village rental on the shoulders of the poor cultivators. The *mamlatdars* of Madhav Rao Peshwa, however, were unable to crush the opposition of the dominant cultivators; and although they were able to exploit the findings of the *kamal* survey in levying taxes on villages as a whole, they failed in reducing the local power of the *patil* and the dominant cultivators, and they failed also in imposing the *kamal* rates on individual cultivators.[1]

Pringle showed how the *patil* and the principal cultivators dominated rural society, and exploited the poor *kunbis*, by examining how the *rivaj* rates were applied to the village of Oswaree. The unit of measure according to the *rivaj* was the *chowar*, and a field which measured a *chowar* paid a standard assessment irrespective of the quality of its soil. The *chowar* was not a fixed unit, and its dimensions were meant to vary inversely with the quality of the soil, thus bringing about an equalisation of the assessment. However, the *kamal* survey of Madhav Rao Peshwa which took account of the quality of the soil, and at the same time employed a standard *beegah*, demonstrated this to be untrue. In the village of Oswaree, for instance, the holdings of the Mallee *jatha* measured $4\frac{1}{40}$ *chowars*, while the holdings of Indoree *jatha* measured five *chowars*, and their *rivaj* or customary assessments therefore stood in the proportion 17:20. But the

[1] *BA:* R. K. Pringle to H. D. Robertson dated 20 November 1823: R.D., Vol. 10/94 of 1824.

surveyors of Madhav Rao discovered that the estate of the Mallees was superior in quality than was indicated by the *rivaj*, and they therefore fixed the assessment of the two *jathas* in the proportion 275 : 234. Since the Mallees were therefore obliged to pay a higher tax than before, they could hardly be expected to be over fond of the *kamal* survey. It was also obvious, to Pringle at any rate, that the Mallees had exploited their social position in the village to secure a light assessment for their holdings under the *rivaj* survey.

The dominance of the *patil* and the principal *kunbis* over the villages of Mahrashtra, Pringle argued, could only be undermined through a new survey based on rational principles. The *rivaj* rates reflected the control exercised by a small group of cultivators over the village, and it would therefore be a serious mistake to take any notice of their sentiments in carrying out a new survey. Rent, as defined by Ricardo, provided an objective criterion for determining the share of agricultural produce which the State could claim as its own:

> The character which land revenue has always borne throughout India [Pringle concluded] is essentially that of rent, and not a personal or property tax. It ought not to be equal to all individuals, nor vary with the circumstances of individuals. But it ought to be regulated only by such incidents as affect rent; and the circumstances which affect rent are the powers of production and the value of the produce. The rent payable to government should depend upon these, and the net profit of the ryot should be the same in all lands, and under all circumstances. . . . To regulate the respective rights of government and its subjects under this principle appears to have been the object of the different systems of administration under every Indian Government. . . .[1]

Despite the striking clarity which characterised his suggestions for a new revenue policy, Pringle's recommendations made little impression on his superiors in the Deccan, since they were anxious to preserve the traditional institutions of rural society, and since they also looked upon the former system of administration with sympathy. Both of Pringle's immediate superiors, Henry Robertson, the Collector of Poona, and William Chaplin, the Commissioner of the Deccan, refused to support the radical, indeed, the revolutionary changes he had suggested in

[1] ibid.

66

the revenue system. Robertson took the sober view that 'in the present situation of our government in the Dekhun, the ascertainment and preservation of rights, laws and customs of society subject to our control should be our first concern. . . .'[1] He repudiated Pringle's interpretation of the *kamal* survey, and refuted the thesis that the State had formerly looked upon itself as the supreme landlord in the country. The *kamal* survey, Robertson pointed out, had been instituted to find out the resources of the villages, and also to find out the tax which they could conveniently pay to the State. The *kamal* was never intended to supersede the *rivaj*, and its findings were never meant to be applied to individual cultivators or to particular estates. This was not so because the *mamlatdars* of Madhav Rao Peshwa were incapable of enforcing the *kamal* rates; this was so because the *kamal* rates rested on inadequate evidence. In assessing fields, for instance, the surveyors of Madhav Rao had taken only the quality of the soil into consideration, and they had overlooked a host of other factors like proximity to markets or the state of communications in the region:

> By the kamal [Robertson pointed out] the same quantity of land is rated at different values. By the old custom of the villages, variable quantities of land are rated at the same value. . . . By the algebraical process of alteration, these data would produce the same results. But . . . you will perhaps admit that the accuracy of the particulars of the one is not to be put in competition with that of the other. The kamal rates were things of theory. They were the same in every village and in every talook. They were an estimate in general terms of what the assessment of lands of different qualities might be. They may therefore be termed accurate on the whole, but erroneous in detail. To say that the kamal rates were not applicable to particular estates or fields is not to prove that the realisations from such particular estates according to the old village rivaj were actually fair—but if we reflect on the constitution of village society, there is every reason to believe that the burdens of the corporations were originally equally distributed, however much the improvement of their lands by some holders may have enhanced at a subsequent period their apparent value. . . .[2]

[1] *BA:* H. D. Robertson to R. K. Pringle dated 22 December 1823: R.D., Vol. 10/94 of 1824.
[2] ibid.

Since the principles underlying the *rivaj* rates had been weakened under the corrupt administration of Baji Rao II, both Chaplin and Robertson agreed with Pringle on the need for a reinvestigation into the resources of the villages of Maharashtra. A new survey, they believed, would furnish the Collectors with a complete record of the conditions on which the peasants held their land, and of the productivity of the villages. It would, therefore, provide the basis for a relationship between the State and the peasant in which the rights and obligations of both the parties would be clearly and equitably defined. However, while Chaplin and Robertson supported the idea of a new survey, they differed from Pringle on the expediency of adopting a theoretical criterion for regulating the cultivator's dues to the State. It was, they believed, a fallacy to assume that these dues could be determined solely by reference to the fertility of the land, since the 'rent which the assessment is intended to fix is that of government, not that of the ryot and his tenant; . . . the government rent should be that which can be produced by the ordinary means of cultivation in ordinary seasons . . .'.[1] In fixing the assessment a new survey would, therefore, have to take account of what the cultivator could actually produce, and the tax which he had paid in the past. Since the pitch of the land-tax under the Marathas had not been based upon fixed principles, inflexible reliance upon past realisations could jeopardise the success of a new survey. But detailed investigations conducted under British aegis would prove a useful check in cases involving gross injustice. Once such a survey had been conducted, Chaplin and Robertson stated, the *kunbis* could be made to enter engagements, severally for their own rents, and collectively for the rents of their villages. At the same time, the State could reserve to itself the right of levying extra assessments to recover losses in revenue arising out of individual failures.

Clearly, then, Chaplin and Robertson were no apologists for the *status quo*. They eschewed reform in the administration of land-revenue, as they eschewed it in other fields, only to the extent that it involved a departure from tradition. A revenue survey which was designed to remove obstacles in the progress of rural society, and which did not completely disregard the

[1] *BA:* Circular letter to the Collectors of the Deccan by W. Chaplin dated 13 September 1824.

rivaj rates, had the full support of Chaplin and Robertson. But despite their concern to strengthen the institutions of self-government in the villages of Maharashtra, and despite the caution with which they formulated their proposals, it is obvious that they were proposing the creation of a new, and in some respects revolutionary, relationship between the peasants and the State. The land-revenue policy advocated by Chaplin and Robertson was not only dependent upon the creation of a new system of administration but it was also designed to undermine the cohesion of rural society.

How radical were the changes advocated by Robertson and Chaplin became clear when their proposals were attacked by administrators who were committed to a rigorous conservative position. G. More, the Secretary to the Government of Bombay, voiced his opposition to a revenue survey because of the dislocation it would cause by suddenly raising or lowering the obligations of the peasants.[1] He also emphasised the impolicy of setting fixed standards for the payment of tax by the cultivators, since the efficiency with which they cultivated their fields varied so much from one year to another that it was impossible for them to pay a fixed land-tax. Indeed, More argued, even if the pitch of the land-tax was based on a rational criterion, the Collectors would still be obliged to negotiate the land-tax on an annual basis with the *patils* and the principal cultivators. F. Warden, a member of the Bombay Executive Council, raised an even more basic objection to a revenue survey. Warden looked upon a survey as an 'inquisitorial' probe into the rights and privileges of the peasants. The State, he believed, lacked the moral authority to carry out such an investigation. Besides, he argued, the institution of a direct relationship between the peasant and the State involved a radical departure from the former system of administration, and it was therefore in conflict with that spirit of moderation which informed the policies of the Government of Bombay under the stewardship of Elphinstone.[2]

The differences between a utilitarian like Pringle and conservatives like Chaplin and Robertson touched upon fundamental

---

[1] *BA*: Memorandum by G. More dated 13 September 1824: R.D., Vol. 18/102 of 1824.
[2] *BA*: Memorandum by F. Warden dated nil: R.D., Vol. 18/102 of 1824.

questions of policy, and they stemmed from conflicting visions of society. Similarly, the objections advanced by More and Warden to the institution of a new survey, even a survey which refrained from violating 'traditional' principles, served to illustrate how conservatives could espouse the cause of reform in the peculiar circumstances of Maharashtra. Because of the conflicting advice which he received from his Collectors, Elphinstone was unable to formulate a revenue policy with the clarity which characterised his policy towards *dakshina*, and towards education for the brahmans and the non-brahmans. His failure to do so was partly a result of the complexity of the problem, since it was impossible to devise a revenue policy without an investigation into the rights and obligations of the peasants. But it was equally a consequence of his inexperience in the problems of land-revenue administration. While Elphinstone was incapable of providing satisfactory answers to the problems concerning the collection of the land-tax, his belief in gradual change led him to support the views of Chaplin and Robertson. The strongest argument in favour of a new survey, Elphinstone observed, was the confusion which characterised the collection of land-revenue under the Peshwas. If the territories of the Deccan had been in a flourishing condition, then it would have been pointless to embark upon a new survey. But the districts acquired in 1818 were in a hopeless condition. The *rivaj* rates had fallen into a state of chaos because of the greed of the revenue farmers employed by Baji Rao II. The disorder which they had inherited from the former administrators obliged British officers to make their annual settlements in complete ignorance of the actual resources of the villages. Their settlements were therefore arbitrary, and likely to injure the interests of the peasants. But if British officers had a careful survey to guide them in fixing the assessment, then they were unlikely to act as obstacles in the way of progress and prosperity. Of course, the question whether the settlements should be made with the peasants severally, or with the villages jointly, could be answered only on the basis of the evidence which the survey would bring forth. 'The survey must be ryotwar. . . , that is, it must be based on an inspection of each field,' Elphinstone summed up. 'Which mode of settlement to adopt is a question for further decision. The one which I had the honour to propose for adop-

tion when the survey should be completed was the mauzewar.
...'[1]

In the administration of land-revenue, as in the creation of
new schools and colleges, the policies advocated by Elphinstone
were characterised by his concern for continuity in the midst of
change. He wanted to abolish the corruption which characterised the administration of revenue under the Peshwas; but he
also wanted to retain the desirable features of the former government. He wanted to resolve the contradictions between the
kamal and the *rivaj* through a new survey; yet he did not desire
to abolish the prescriptive rights of the peasants. Finally, he
wanted the pitch of the land-tax to be based on a rational principle; but he did not want such a principle to undermine the
rivaj of the village. In short, Elphinstone wanted to incorporate
in his administration features of the former government which,
so he believed, were of enduring value.

But despite the cautiousness with which Elphinstone formulated his reforms, the old order was bound to disintegrate under
the impact of British rule. It was bound to disintegrate because
of the new concepts of legality, efficiency and responsibility
which inspired the reforms of Elphinstone, and which were
conspicuously absent in the administration of the Marathas. To
take a specific example it was impossible, despite the best
efforts of Elphinstone, for the *patil* and the *deshmukh* and the
mamlatdar to retain under British aegis the position which they
had occupied under the Peshwas. They were formerly powerful
because their obligations were nowhere defined, and because
they were not subject to any rigid rules. Elphinstone's attempt
to integrate them into his administration was bound to prove
a failure, since the restrictions to which he subjected them
undermined the initiative which they had exercised under the
Peshwas, and consequently weakened their position. Elphinstone's attempt to reinforce the sentiment of solidarity in rural
society was equally futile, since this sentiment was intimately
related to the values and institutions which had flourished under
the former administration. Because of the principles which
informed the new government, even the most cautious policies
of reform could not fail to undermine the bonds which held

[1] *BA*: Minute by Governor of Bombay dated 22 December 1824: R.D., Vol.
14/204 of 1826.

together the classes and castes of Maharashtra before the British conquest of 1818.

III

Despite the instability of politics and the arbitrary principles which informed government, social life in Maharashtra on the eve of the British conquest of 1818 was characterised by stability and order rather than by chaos and disquiet. This is not to deny that even conservatives like Elphinstone found much to detest in the values and in the institutions which flourished under the Peshwas. This is merely to emphasise the undercurrent of stability, indeed, of stagnation which characterised the territories of the Peshwa. Such a state of society reinforced Elphinstone's natural reluctance to embark upon sweeping programmes of reform, for it proved to his satisfaction the enduring, and hence commendable, quality of the values and institutions of the former administration. Behind the stability and order which characterised society in Maharashtra lay the strength of caste institutions, which fulfilled the contradictory functions of differentiation and integration. Even an 'outcaste' like Elphinstone was impressed with the vitality of the institutions of caste, and could not but be impressed by the important role they played in the life of the community. 'The influence of caste and public opinion as associated with religion is very strong,' he observed, 'and the censures of the priest have perhaps in general more weight than the terrors of the magistrate.'[1]

The strength of caste institutions in Maharashtra stemmed partly from an accident of history which bestowed political power on the brahman Peshwas, and partly also from the skill with which the *Shastris* of Poona conducted the affairs of their community, and assisted the lower and middle castes in enforcing order on their members. The values of Hinduism and the sanctions of caste combined to create social cohesion, and to mitigate tension between different orders and classes. Elphinstone, for instance, was struck by the standards of public morality in Maharashtra, and by the entire absence of that violence which characterised so many provinces in India, not excluding territories under British control:

[1] *BA:* Minute by Governor of Bombay dated 22 December 1824: R.D., Vol. 14/204 of 1826.

Judging from the iniquity [he pointed out] with which crimes might be committed ... we should be led to fancy the Maratha country a complete scene of anarchy and violence. No picture, however, would be further from the truth. . . . It is most important to ascertain the causes which kept the country in a state superior to our oldest possessions (i.e., Bengal) amidst all the abuses and oppression of a native government. . . .

The Maratha country presents in many respects a complete contrast to ... (our territories in Bengal). The people are very few compared to the quantity of arable land; they are hearty, warlike, and always armed till of late years; the situation of the lower orders was very comfortable, and that of the upper prosperous. . . . All the powers of the State were concentrated in the same hands, and their vigour was not chastened by any suspicion on the part of the government or any scruples of their own. . . . (Men) knew that if they were right in substance, they would not be questioned about the form. . . . The mamlatdars were considerable persons, and there were men of property and consideration in every neighbourhood; Enamdars, Jagheerdars and old Zamindars. They were associated with the ranks above and below them, and kept up the chain of society to the prince; by this means the higher orders were kept informed of the situation of the lower, and as there was scarcely anyone without a patron, men might be exposed to oppression, but could scarcely suffer from neglect.[1]

The strength of institutions which 'kept up the chain of society' explained, so Elphinstone believed, the absence of violence and anarchy in Maharashtra. It simultaneously pointed to the means through which social peace and political order could be maintained by the Government of Bombay in the territories conquered from the Peshwa. The highest body in the territories could either be a Court, or an individual, vested with general control over the various branches of the administration. This Court had to be frequently in circuit, and it had to be responsible for the general superintendence of the administration, rather than be required to pay detailed attention to any part of it. The actual business of administration could be conducted by Collectors under the control of the Court, and these Collectors could be entrusted with supreme authority over the districts under their charge, and could also supervise the work of the native administrators like the *mamlatdars*.

[1] *Vide* M.E.'s Report on Maratha States.

Although Elphinstone believed that a system of administration created under British aegis could profitably imitate some of the features of the administration of the Marathas, he was equally convinced that to ensure efficiency in government it was necessary to define the obligations and the responsibilities of various offices in the administration. Elphinstone also believed that it was necessary to rewrite the sacerdotal and customary laws which guided the judicial institutions that had flourished under the Peshwas into a simple and comprehensible code. He wanted, in effect, to frame a body of regulations which would spell out the structure of an efficient system of administration, and which would also clarify the complex, and often contradictory, legal principles which had formerly shaped the decisions of indigenous courts of law. The Benthamite inspiration behind such an objective hardly needs any emphasis. But Elphinstone's enthusiasm for Bentham was tempered with a regard for tradition, and a concern for continuity in the midst of change. He described him as 'a man of first-rate ability, but also of first-rate eccentricity; which, both in his doctrines and in his personal habits, probably arises from his little intercourse with the world'.[1] It was all very well to advocate, as Bentham was given to advocate, a simple and rational body of laws in preference to archaic and ill-defined legal principles. But, Elphinstone argued, 'foreigners should certainly be cautious how they made a code for a nation which they imperfectly know'.[2] Hindu law contained the most glaring inconsistencies, and it was imprecise to a degree which defied comprehension. But despite its inconsistencies and its incomprehensibility, the people of the region were deeply attached to a system of justice which they had inherited from their forefathers. The creation of a new body of laws could only confuse them and would undermine their allegiance to habits of thought and action which were the best guarantee of social peace and public morality in Maharashtra.

Such were the considerations which inspired Elphinstone to initiate an investigation into *The Laws and Customs of Hindoo Castes within the Dekhun Provinces subject to the Presidency of Bombay*[3]

[1] Mountstuart Elphinstone to Edward Strachey dated 3 September 1823: quoted in Colebrooke, *op. cit.*, p. 114.
[2] ibid.
[3] A. Steele, *Summary of the Laws and Customs of Hindoo Castes Within the Dekhun Provinces Subject to the Presidency of Bombay* (Bombay, 1827).

74

which was conducted by Arthur Steele, a civil servant attached to the Government of Bombay. Similar principles determined the creation of a Regulation Committee to draft a new Code for the provinces controlled by the Presidency of Bombay. In his instructions to Steele, Elphinstone outlined the reasons which had prompted him to initiate an inquiry into the laws of Maharashtra. The law books of the Hindus, he stated, were a collection of texts which were inconsistent and vague, and which were further obscured by the interpolation of later commentaries. To make matters more complicated, in many instances the law of the *Shastras* had been substituted by the custom of different castes and communities. In such circumstances, Elphinstone pointed out, an administrator could adopt either of two conflicting courses of action. He could formulate a completely new code based on rational principles, or he could compile

> a complete and consistent code from the mass of written law and the fragments of tradition, determining on general grounds of jurisprudence those points where the Hindu books and traditions present only conflicting authorities. . . . The first of these courses, if otherwise expedient, is rendered completely impracticable here by the attachment of the natives to their own institutions, and by the degree to which their laws are interwoven with their religion and manners. The second plan is, therefore, the only one which it is in our power to pursue. . . .[1]

How the Committee set up by Elphinstone reconciled 'Maratha mamool with Jeremy Bentham' is best illustrated by a discussion in the Government of Bombay over the powers and jurisdiction of the judiciary and the executive. Contrary to the traditions of administration in India, the reforms instituted by Lord Cornwallis in the provinces of Bengal had made the judiciary completely independent of the executive, with consequences which British civil servants in the subcontinent had come to recognise, and to apprehend, by the 1820s. But despite the unhappy experience of Bengal, the Regulation Committee wanted to establish the supremacy of the judiciary by investing it with the authority to interpret the regulations in questions

[1] *BA*: Minute by Governor of Bombay dated 25 April 1823: J.D. (Judicial Department), Vol. 42/51 of 1823.

affecting the powers of the courts of law. Charles Norris, a member of the Regulation Committee, argued the case for an independent judiciary along familiar Whig lines. Since the regulations could be looked upon as a compact between the State and its subjects, he pointed out, it would be wrong to give either party the right to interpret this compact, least of all the party which had framed it. But apart from considerations of equity, it would be politically inexpedient to deny supremacy to the judiciary. It was often necessary to apply regulations in circumstances which antagonised important sections of the community. If in such circumstances the executive could point to the judiciary as the source of its sanctions, then it would escape the opprobrium which would otherwise have discredited it in the eyes of the community. Norris also examined the argument that a strong executive ensured efficiency in administration. This argument, he observed, was devoid of any force whatsoever, since the pronouncements of the courts of law on various questions would yield a body of knowledge which could guide the executive in the application of the regulations. Of course, it was always open to the executive to pass new regulations in response to novel situations, and in the fulfilment of new political objectives. But the interpretation of these regulations ought to rest with the courts of law.[1]

The arguments put forth by Norris were disputed by Elphinstone, and by other members of the Executive Council of the Government of Bombay, who had seen the disastrous consequences arising of the system of administration created by Cornwallis in Bengal. According to G. C. Pendergast, a member of the Executive Council, Norris was guilty of confusion between 'laws' and 'regulations'. Laws dealt with fundamental issues like the ownership of private property, and unless civilised principles of government were to be completely abandoned, the supremacy of the judiciary in such issues was to be unquestioned. The regulations, on the other hand, set out the duties of the courts of law and defined their powers. If the notion of judicial supremacy advanced by Norris was accepted, then in a conflict between a higher and a lower court the latter would sit in judgement over a dispute to which it was a party. The absurdity of such a situation was patent, and it would be a positive contri-

[1] *BA:* Memorandum by Charles Norris dated nil: J.D., Vol. 42/51 of 1823.

bution to efficiency in administration if the executive was invested with the authority to resolve such disputes. Elphinstone fully supported the arguments advanced by Pendergast. 'What I would recommend, therefore,' he stated, 'would be, that the *Sudder Adawlut*'s decisions in the interpretation of the Regulations be final in all cases when the question did not relate to an extent of its authority, but that in such cases, a reference should be made to the government. . . .'[1]

But if Elphinstone was reluctant to invest the judiciary with supreme authority, he was equally unwilling to transform the executive into a *Juggernaut* answerable to none. His commitment to Whig principles led him to look upon the executive and the judiciary as counterpoised institutions of government. It also led him to veto the attempt of the Regulation Committee to invest the Collectors with unlimited authority in the administration of land-revenue. The Regulation Committee was in favour of investing the Collectors with such powers because of the difficulties involved in determining the pitch of the land-tax to be paid by the peasants. The problem of defining a fair land-tax was, of course, a very real one. For, the Committee argued, although it was easy to postulate the State's share of agricultural production as a certain proportion of the gross produce, the application of this principle presented a serious problem. If the jurisdiction of the courts of law was extended to disputes between the *kunbis* and the revenue officers over the quantum of the land-tax, then the *kunbis* would always contest the Collector's evaluation, since they knew full well that it was impossible for the Collector to demonstrate the equity of his evaluation before a court of law. In order to eliminate the possibility of such litigation, which could virtually deluge the courts of law, the Regulation Committee proposed to invest the Collectors with the authority to confiscate the holdings of 'obstreperous' *kunbis* in order to lease them to more accommodating cultivators. The Committee made such a recommendation in full awareness of the arbitrary powers its proposals would bestow on the Collectors. But it saw no alternative to the exercise of such arbitrary powers by the officers of the administration. 'Probably the ultimate authority,' the Committee confessed, 'for decision between

---

[1] *BA*: Memorandum by G. C. Pendergast dated 9 March 1823: J.D., Vol. 42/51 of 1823.

the cultivator and the Collector must be arbitrary. Native arrangements have ever been so, in fact, however nominally modified; and it is not obvious that the state of proprietary landed interest admits of any other interpretation of the State's rights.'[1]

Elphinstone, however, would have nothing to do with so arbitrary a proposal. He pointed out that even if the officers of the former government had exercised such a power, a Collector armed with similar authority was capable of far more mischief than a revenue officer of the Peshwas, because of the greater concentration of power in the administration under British aegis. The proposal undoubtedly secured the interests of the administration, but 'it would not be equally efficacious in protecting those of the ryot, . . . (who was) left no resource in the event of excessive demand from the Collector, but that of . . . giving up his lands'.[2]

The insight which Elphinstone possessed into the enduring qualities of the administration of the Peshwas, and his ability to reproduce these qualities in a new system of administration, is brought out in bold relief in the judicial institutions which he created in Maharashtra. His approach to the problem of dispensing cheap and efficient justice was simple and ingenious. He believed that most of the disputes between the *kunbis* concerned trivial issues, and could best be settled through institutions with which they were well acquainted. It would, therefore, be a mistake to abolish the *panchayats* through which a majority of rural disputes had been resolved in the past. Yet *panchayats* could not be expected to dispense justice according to western notions of social equity. He therefore superimposed upon them an imposing structure of courts of law which dispensed justice according to western legal principles.

If Elphinstone upheld the *panchayats*, he did so because he regarded them as an indispensable inheritance from the past, and not because he had any illusions about them. 'I kept the panchayats because I found them,'[3] he told his confidant, Edward

---

[1] *BA:* Regulation Committee to Government of Bombay dated 17 August 1821: R.D., Vol. 16/99 of 1823.
[2] *BA:* Bombay Government to Regulation Committee dated 17 August 1821: R.D., Vol. 16/99 of 1824.
[3] Mountstuart Elphinstone to Edward Strachey dated 21 April 1821: quoted in Colebrooke, *op. cit.*, II, p. 124.

Strachey. He was aware of their dilatory methods of procedure; their inability to execute their own awards; and the lack of integrity among their members. But he also recognised that despite these failings the *panchayats* were popular with the *kunbis*, who referred to them as *Punch Prumaishwar* (i.e. the *panchayats* are like the Gods). The reason for the popularity of the *panchayats*, he argued, lay in the inability of the former administration to dispense cheap and efficient justice to its subjects. Since the officers of the Peshwa were well aware of the limitations of their power, they left it to the people to procure justice for themselves through autonomous institutions which rested upon popular initiative. As a result, these institutions had become an integral part of society, and their abolition would impose suffering and misery on the *kunbis* who looked upon the *panchayats* as their only protection against social injustice and oppression.

The role of the *panchayat* in the new administration was spelt out at considerable length in a draft regulation. This regulation stressed the need for *panchayats* in order to secure 'the easy and amicable settlement of disputes of a civil nature. . . .'[1] It also indicated that as in former times, there was to be no restriction on the complexity of the cases that could be referred to a *panchayat*, so long as the disputing parties were agreed upon the need for such arbitration. The members of a *panchayat* were to be selected by the disputants, but no individual could be compelled to serve on a *panchayat* unless he held the office of a *patil* or a *kulkarni* in the village. Behind this stipulation lay the assumption that the village officers were morally bound to devote a part of their time to public business, but that nothing was to be gained by foisting allegiance to and interest in *panchayats* on ordinary cultivators. Finally, a *panchayat* was free to give its awards orally, or in writing, but a higher court of law could take cognisance of its decisions only if they were written in a prescribed form. A written award made by a *panchayat* could not be set aside by an executive officer, but a disputant was at liberty to appeal to a higher court if he had reason to believe that he had been denied justice. Such a limitation on the authority of the *panchayats* was essential to provide safeguards against corrupt or partisan decisions. 'Although it is essential

[1] *BA:* Draft of Regulation concerning Panchayats dated 16 August 1821: J.D., Vol. 48 of 1822.

that awards should be final . . .' the Committee pointed out, 'yet it is necessary to guard against injustice arising out of wilful impartiality on the part of arbitrators, and this can best be done by a suit to set aside arbitration.'[1]

While the *panchayat* thus became an integral part of the new system of justice, it is clear that it became so because of its popularity with the *kunbis* rather than because of the efficiency with which it resolved disputes between the cultivators. It is also clear that the courts of law superior to the *panchayat* were to draw exclusively upon western principles of law and western concepts of social equity. Applying the Benthamite principle that cheap and efficient justice could best be administered by the delegation of original authority to subordinate courts, and the retention of powers of supervision and control in a supreme court, the Regulation Committee proposed the creation of a three-tiered judicial system, comprising the *Sadar Adawlat*, the *Zillah Adawlat* and the Native Commissionerships of Justice. The judicial institutions proposed by the Committee corresponded to Bentham's three grades of courts—the parish court, the district court and the provincial court. The coping stone of the judicial system was provided by a *Sadar Adawlat* which was vested with supreme civil and criminal jurisdiction over the entire territories. In its civil capacity the *Sardar Adawlat* could hear appeals against the decisions of the district courts; while in its criminal capacity it could superintend matters relating to the administration of criminal justice by the Magistrate-Collectors. The *Adawlat* was, in addition, authorised to appoint Puisne Judges to hold courts of circuit for the trial of capital and other offences. While on circuit, the Puisne Judges were required to inspect the proceedings of the Magistrates, and to guide them in the interpretation and the application of criminal law.[2]

The district or *Zillah* court was the most important institution in the judicial system. The *Zillah* Judge presided over two courts, one of which possessed civil, and the other possessed criminal, jurisdiction over the district. In his civil capacity the *Zillah* Judge was competent to try civil cases of every description in his district. His jurisdiction also extended to appeals against original suits tried by judicial officers subordinate to

[1] ibid.
[2] *BA:* Draft of Regulation concerning the Judiciary: J.D., Vol. 48 of 1822.

him. Indeed, the *Zillah* Judge's primary responsibility was to supervise the work of the lower courts, rather than to attend to original cases, since the Regulation Committee was 'disposed to relieve the Zillah Judge as much as can conveniently be done from the cognisance of original suits ... in order that he may have the leisure to superintend and regulate the proceedings of the inferior courts ... '[1] The *Zillah* Judge was equally powerful in the administration of criminal justice, since he was competent to try 'all natives and other persons not British subjects committing any offence within the Zillah'. To enable him to discharge his responsibilities efficiently he was helped by Assistant Judges, whose duties were assigned by him, and he was further required to supervise their conduct and to hear appeals against them.

The integration of a Benthamite judicial system with institutions like the *panchayats* was achieved through officers who were designated Native Commissioners of Justice. These officers were appointed by the *Zillah* Judges; they could only try cases in which natives were included; and their original jurisdiction was confined to suits of less than Rs. 500. The appointment of the Native Commissioners was expected to relieve the *Zillah* Judges of trivial cases, which added significantly to the total volume of litigation, and which prevented the *Zillah* Judges from attending to more serious business. 'The greatest inconvenience to the judicial system throughout India,' the Regulation Committee pointed out, 'has been the wide range of suits which could only be tried by European agency, providing an accumulation, and, in some instances a stagnation of business in the chief courts of the Zillah. ...'[2] But apart from relieving the *Zillah* Judges of a part of their work the Native Commissioners were also required to investigate appeals against the decisions of *panchayats*, a task which it was assumed their knowledge of local sentiment would enable them to perform much better than the *Zillah* Judges.

That the Native Commissioners of Justice were expected to follow judicial principles quite different from the judicial principles followed by the *Zillah* Judges is clear from a debate within the Government of Bombay regarding the rights of pleaders to represent disputants in courts of law. The Regulation Committee made short shrift of the argument that the very existence

[1] ibid.   [2] ibid.

of pleaders encouraged litigation, and that pleaders defeated the ends of justice by diverting the attention of the courts from the real points at issue in a dispute. Whenever courts of justice based upon western principles were instituted, the Committee pointed out, litigation which was formerly handled by a large number of *panchayats* was brought within the ambit of a single institution, thus creating the illusion of social conflict where none had existed before. Once such courts had been established, the disputants had to be permitted to have their cases represented by lawyers on grounds of convenience, and because of the complexity of legal procedures. In other words, pleaders, whether good or evil, were an inevitable consequence of the creation of courts which rested on western principles of law. The practical question was whether the ends of justice would not be better served if pleaders were required to possess legal and academic qualifications. 'We propose, therefore,' the Committee stated, 'to limit pleaders so far as to ensure their being qualified for their duty. . . .'[1] But while all this was true of the *Zillah* courts, any person could act on behalf of disputants appearing before the Native Commissioners, since these Commissioners based their awards upon popular notions of justice and social equity.

The recommendations made by the Regulation Committee, and the principles which inspired these recommendations, formed the basis of the Elphinstone Code of 1827. Since Elphinstone played a decisive part in shaping this Code, it stands as an eloquent tribute to the sophistication of his outlook and the catholicity of his vision. The Code also reveals the depth of Elphinstone's insight into Maharashtra. It sets him apart from conservatives who were opposed to change in any form whatsoever; it also sets him apart from reformers who denied the role of tradition in the life of a community. Elphinstone's cautious approach to reform; his belief in politics as a moral activity; and his commitment to innovation tempered with a sense of continuity, made him fully aware of the complexity of the task which he confronted as the head of the Government of Bombay. He saw, for instance, the futility of the notion that the brahmans who were steeped in centuries of tradition could be transformed overnight into men who were 'English in tastes, in morals, and

[1] ibid.

in intellect'.[1] His policy in the field of education was, therefore, geared to the slow but steady dissemination of western values among the brahmans of Maharashtra. Similarly, Elphinstone realised the danger of abolishing the former system of administration, and substituting in its place the system of administration created by Cornwallis. His reluctance to do so explains his attempt to retain institutions like the *panchayat*, and offices like the *patil*ship, as subordinate but none the less important elements of his administration.

The reforms initiated by Elphinstone exercised a decisive influence over Maharashtra in the 19th century, even though some of his policies were rejected by his successors. Elphinstone's most striking contribution was his policy towards education, which took account of the deep hold of traditional values on the brahmans of Maharashtra, and sought to win them over to liberal and rational ideas without alienating them from their own community. As a result of this policy, the brahmans of Maharashtra were able to acquire western values without weakening the fabric of society, and without losing their sense of identity. Indeed, as we shall later see, the most westernised of the brahmans of Maharashtra were also the most Maharashtrian of the brahmans of the region. All this was in no small degree due to Elphinstone.

But if Elphinstone's policy in the field of education was successful to a remarkable degree, quite the reverse was true of his attempt to strengthen the traditional institutions of society. This was partly due to the fact that his successors repudiated some of his policies in the field of administration. But it was equally due to the new concepts of legality and responsibility which inspired and sustained the system of administration created by Elphinstone. These new concepts undermined the 'chain of society' which had formerly held together the rulers and the ruled, and they stimulated fundamental changes in the structure of society, and in the relationship between different castes and classes in Maharashtra.

[1] Minute by Lord Macaulay dated 2 February 1835: *Selections from Educational Records, Part I, 1781–1847*, ed. by H. Sharp.

III

The Utilitarian Deluge

Eʟᴘʜɪɴsᴛᴏɴᴇ's attempt to bring about a gradual change in the values and institutions of Maharashtra exercised an irresistable appeal over men like Chaplin and Robertson, who were committed to the politics of conservatism. But despite the appeal which they exercised over conservative administrators, the policies advocated by Elphinstone were characterised by a deep-rooted contradiction. The crucial question facing Elphinstone hinged upon the necessity of reform in a context where the reformer did not subscribe to the values of the society whose problems he was called upon to resolve. In such circumstances the reformer could not avoid facing problems that could only be resolved through drastic solutions which involved a break with tradition. The alternatives before him were an abject surrender to social iniquity and political tyranny, or the creation of institutions and values which would wholly remould society. Elphinstone, however, refused to accept the existence of such a dilemma. Consequently, he could not provide satisfactory answers to a host of questions because of his refusal, either to accept the institutions which he had inherited from the former rulers, or to implement bold policies of reform. However, there is a limit to which compromise can serve as a grand principle in politics, and the violence of the tide of reform which swept across Maharashtra after Elphinstone's departure stemmed, in equal parts, from his fruitless endeavour to preserve the institutions and values of the past, and from the refractory quality of the problems which confronted the Government of Bombay in the territories conquered from Baji Rao Peshwa.

The refractory quality of the problems which confronted Elphinstone is most clearly expressed in questions concerning the administration of land-revenue, questions which constituted the subject of continuous debate during his term as the Governor of Bombay. The issues at stake in the administration of land-revenue were of outstanding significance for Maharashtra. Was the *kunbi* to be alienated from his fellow-cultivators in the village through the institution of a *ryotwari* system? Did there exist a class of rich peasants which dominated the villages of Maharashtra and exploited the poor cultivators? Were rationality and objectivity to ride roughshod over prescription and tradition as principles sustaining the new administration? In the answers given to these questions by different administrators lay conflicting commitments to ideology, and rival concepts of the objectives of British rule in India.

The two significant trends of opinion within the Government of Bombay were represented, on the one hand, by conservatives like Chaplin and Robertson, and on the other, by utilitarians like Pringle who had come under the influence of Malthus at the East India College at Haileybury. Pringle scoffed at the timidity of the conservatives who took their cue from Burke, and who were therefore deeply concerned with continuity in the processes of social change. His vision of society differed fundamentally from the conservative vision of society as an organism which embraced conflicting social groups and antagonistic interests in a state of equipoise. Instead of looking at society through social groups like class or caste, Pringle focused his attention on the individual in the community, and he drew inferences regarding the attitudes and the proclivities of men through the insights he thus gained into social processes. As a result of his atomistic approach to social problems Pringle placed a strong emphasis on the separate and distinct identity of the individuals who made up a society. He also combined with his vision of society as composed of individuals rather than of social groups a conviction in the effectiveness of rational action. Because of his commitment to rational action, Pringle believed that once a logical solution had been devised for a

G   85

particular problem, all that was required of the reformer was the rigorous application of this solution to particular problems.

Pringle's advocacy of a *ryotwari* system of land-revenue stemmed from his belief in the economics of Ricardo and in the principles of utilitarianism. He was convinced that the sentiment of solidarity which tied the *kunbis* of a village in a close relationship of interdependence, a sentiment which flowed from the collective responsibility which they bore for its land-tax, constituted a great obstacle in the progress of rural society. The revenue system of the Peshwas had, therefore, to be completely reorganised, since it sapped the cultivator's will to improve his position through the exercise of initiative in the operations of agriculture. To reorganise the former system of revenue administration, so Pringle believed, it was necessary to substitute the role played by the *jathas*, the *patils* and the *deshmukhs* in the collection of tax by a legal and rational relationship between the *kunbi*, as a tenant, and the State, as the supreme landlord in the country. The share of agricultural produce appropriated by the State would then be the rent payable to a landlord, leaving the wages of labour and the profits of capital to the cultivator who tilled the land.[1] In 1823, when Pringle first suggested that Ricardo's law of rent could provide an excellent basis for a new system of land-revenue, conservatives like Chaplin and Robertson voiced strong opposition to his proposal. Robertson, in particular, argued that the assumption that the State stood as the supreme landlord in India would undermine the prescriptive rights of the *thulwaheeks*, or the *meerasdars*, and it would unleash a disastrous revolution in rural society. The *thulwaheeks*, who were descended from the *jathas* which had established new villages, had a clear proprietary right in the soil, a right which was substantiated by the numerous sales of land which had taken place in the rural districts around Poona before 1818. To protect the proprietary rights of the *meerasdar*, Robertson would have him pay the tax for all the fields which stood in his name in the village register, even if he was unable to cultivate some of them in a particular season:

> The ground upon which government had a demand of right upon meeras land [he pointed out] arise from the nature of the tenure,

[1] *BA:* R. K. Pringle to H. D. Robertson dated 20 March 1823: R.D., Vol. 10/94 of 1824.

i.e., the usufructory right of such land being exclusively vested in certain individuals and families, and government being bound, if it acts justly, not to infringe this right, so long as those enjoying it perform the conditions concomitant on its acquisition. . . . Tell a meerasdar who endeavours to be freed from the assessment of the waste land—'You must resign your title to the usufructory possession of a portion of your good, bad and indifferent land of your whole estate, yielding a rent or tax equal to that portion left waste for which you did not pay tax', and remark his answer, 'How can I do this? How can I part with my land?'[1]

Although Elphinstone's conservatism predisposed him to the views advanced by Robertson, he was struck by Pringle's brilliant analysis of the *kamal* survey, and he was also struck by the boldness and clarity with which Pringle had outlined a new system of revenue administration. Besides, Elphinstone was aware of the influence to which the Court of Directors was exposed in the person of James Mill, who was the Chief Examiner of the East India Company. Since the revenue dispatches from the Court of Directors were filled increasingly with short disquisitions on the virtues of the new political economy of Ricardo and Smith, Elphinstone thought it expedient to appoint Pringle as the Superintendent of the 'Revenue Survey and Assessment of the Deccan'. But while he entrusted the survey to a radical like Pringle, Elphinstone did not shed his distrust of policies likely to provoke a social upheaval or to disturb long-established rights. In instructing Pringle to initiate a new survey he therefore struck a note of caution to check his protégé's exuberance.[2] The rights of the *meerasdars*, he pointed out, would be the principal concern of the survey, since these rights featured so prominently in the organisation of rural society. The proprietary rights of the *meerasdars* were based upon indisputable grounds of prescription, and they could not claim as of right any remission in tax if they did not cultivate a part of their holdings in a particular season. However, it would be a mistake to apply such a principle rigorously, more particularly because the former administration had always taken into consideration

---

[1] *BA:* H. D. Robertson to R. K. Pringle dated 22 December 1823: R.D., Vol. 10/94 of 1824.
[2] *BA:* Minute by the Governor of Bombay dated 14 August 1826: R.D., Vol. 13/145 of 1826.

the actual condition of the cultivators before fixing its demand. Elphinstone resolved this problem through a characteristic gesture of compromise. 'My present opinion is,' he stated, 'that it will be most expedient to allow meerasdars to throw up such portions of their land as they think proper; and to make a corresponding deduction in their payments until they shall be able to resume the land, which for a certain period at least, they should retain the right to do.'[1] He then proceeded to enunciate the principles on which the new survey was to be based. Instead of advocating the 'net produce' criterion favoured by Pringle, Elphinstone wanted the survey to be carried out in two stages. In the first instance, a rough assessment of each village was to be made on the basis of the rents levied in the past. Next, this rent was to be apportioned among individual cultivators, the share of each *kunbi* being determined by the productivity of his land, and by an evaluation of what he could equitably pay, 'but with such allowance in forms of privileged tenures as have been enjoined in the orders of government . . . '.[2]

I

The *taluka* of Indapur, a revenue subdivision of Poona, was the first district in which Pringle tried to determine the fiscal obligations of the cultivators to the State on the basis of the Ricardian law of rent. The choice of Indapur for the introduction of a new system of land-revenue was unfortunate, for although the *taluka* was by no means atypical of the rural districts around Poona, it nevertheless possessed characteristics of climate, fertility and population which were unlikely to contribute to the success of a new experiment in the administration of land-revenue.

Indapur lay between the rivers Neera and Bhima, which formed a junction towards the south-eastern extremity of the *taluka*. It contained eighty-six villages of which ten were alienated as *enams* to various Maratha chiefs. Most of these villages were located on the banks of the Neera or the Bhima. The location of the villages would indicate that their soil was very fertile, but since the *taluka* was fairly mountainous, only the fields lying very close to the rivers possessed fertile soil, while the highlands between the river-banks and the mountainous ridges were

[1] ibid.   [2] ibid.

barren and stony, and could produce little apart from a crop of *jowri*. The barrenness of the soil was heightened by a rainfall which was notoriously scanty, and which fluctuated considerably from one year to another. The scarcity and the uncertainty of the rainfall could partly have been remedied by the excavation of wells and tanks for irrigation. But the nature of the soil, which lay thinly on a rocky outcrop, and the lack of initiative among the cultivators, of which more later, combined to prevent any significant development of irrigation in the *taluka* of Indapur.[1]

The cultivators of Indapur had done very little to develop the resources of the *taluka*, partly because they were lacking in enterprise, but partly also because of circumstances which were not of their creation. During the 18th century, Indapur, like other districts around Poona, had provided the armies of the Peshwas with the *sillahdars* or soldiers of cavalry who formed the backbone of Maratha military strength. These *sillahdars* were assigned land for their maintenance by the Maratha Government. But since they were better soldiers than farmers they took little interest in the land, apart from renting it to *uprees* who actually cultivated the soil. Yet despite the indifference of the *sillahdars* to cultivation, and despite the tenuousness of the ties which held the *uprees* to the land, Indapur was on the whole fairly prosperous, because of the care and attention bestowed upon it by the Maratha Government, and also because of the 'wealth' which the *sillahdars* brought with them into the *taluka* from the wars they fought for the Peshwas.

After 1794, however, a number of factors combined to drain Indapur of its resources, and to inflict misery and suffering on its peasants. The *taluka* first experienced a number of bad seasons in close succession, and it was then exposed to the revenue farmers of Baji Rao, who extorted money from the *kunbis* in a bid to reap quick profits for themselves. To heighten their misery, in 1802 the *kunbis* of Indapur were pillaged by the army which marched to Poona under the Holkar in order to establish his control over the Peshwa. As a result of all this Indapur became so impoverished that even Baji Rao was roused to action, and in 1807 he entrusted the affairs of the *taluka* to Mulhar Mukund,

[1] *BA:* R. K. Pringle to John Bax, Secretary to the Government of Bombay, dated 6 September 1828: R.D., Vol. 225 of 1828.

a Maratha administrator of considerable ability and imagination. Mulhar Mukund faced a most difficult charge since war and famine and misgovernment had combined to devastate the *taluka* and drain its resources. The cultivators, who were mostly *uprees*, had fled in large numbers to the neighbouring districts while those who remained behind were incapable of any sustained effort. In order to restore the *taluka* to its former prosperity, Mulhar Mukund tried to persuade *uprees* to settle in the villages of Indapur through offering them leases on attractive terms. But his efforts were only partially successful, and when the Government of Bombay took possession of the *taluka* in 1818, it was still in a state of depression. The *cusbah* of Indapur was the only substantial township in the *taluka*. It was once a place of considerable importance, but its fortunes had declined with the fortunes of the rest of the *taluka*, so that by the 1820s its manufactures were confined to the fabrication of coarse cloths which met the requirements of the surrounding villages. The *cusbah* also provided a *petah* for the export of a small surplus of agricultural produce to Poona and to the cities on the coast.

Immediately after 1818 the administration of Indapur devolved upon the Collector of Ahmednagar, who was saddled with the responsibility of repairing the damage done by the revenue farmers of Baji Rao. The difficulties facing the Collector of Ahmednagar were heightened by the fact that the mismanagement of the former government had encouraged the *kulkarnis* to hide, if not to destroy, the account books and registers which set down the rights of cultivators, and which also recorded the rents they had paid to the Maratha Government. All that the Collector could unravel was the bare outline of the revenue history of the *taluka*. The first attempt at restoring the revenue administration of Indapur to order had been made by Malik Amber at a time when the *taluka* formed a part of the kingdom of Ahmednagar. The *tankha* settlement introduced by Malik Amber in the 1620s was a cash rental which took away from the cultivators one-third of the gross produce of agriculture. The *tankha* was evaluated on a *mauzewar* basis; that is, it estimated the obligations of entire villages instead of individual cultivators, and it left the breakdown of the total rent on a village into the shares of individual cultivators to the *patils* and the dominant cultivators of the rural communities. When Indapur was captured by the Marathas, no attempt was made to disturb the settlement of Malik Amber. But in 1784–85 the Maratha Government extended the operations of the *kamal* survey to the *taluka*. Unlike the *tankha* settlement, the *kamal* survey was based on an evaluation of individual holdings rather than of entire villages. It was undertaken to provide the Maratha administration with an accurate record of the resources of Indapur, so as to enable it to raise the rents without oppressing the *kunbis*. But whatever be the reasons which inspired Madhav Rao to embark upon such a measure, the *kamal* survey was very unfortunate in its effect on the *taluka*. For although Indapur had made considerable progress since the institution of the *tankha* settlement, the surveyors of Madhav Rao over-estimated the resources of the *taluka*, and in raising its rent from Rs. 122,000 to Rs. 222,000, they imposed a crippling burden on the *kunbis* of Indapur.[1]

The pitch of the *kamal* rates was one reason, though it was not the only reason, why Baji Rao rejected the traditional machinery for the collection of the land-tax, and entrusted the administration of Indapur to farmers of revenue, with consequences which we have already discussed. After 1818 the Collector of Ahmednagar repeated the mistakes of his predecessors, though it is only fair to point out that his mistakes stemmed out of ignorance, rather than out of greed and unscrupulousness. British revenue officers believed that the findings of the *kamal* were reasonably accurate; they also believed that when Indapur had recovered from the ravages of war, famine and misgovernment it would be possible to fix the rents to be paid by the *kunbis* on the basis of the *kamal* rates. Their assumptions led British officers to offer leases on low rates to *uprees* in an attempt to persuade them to return to the villages of Indapur in conscious imitation of the measures adopted by Mulhar Mukund before 1818. But since these low rates were based on the findings of the *kamal* survey they achieved only partial success in restoring Indapur to a state of prosperity.

All this is vividly reflected in the attempt of Henry Robertson, the Collector of Poona, to reduce the revenue administration of

[1] Report on the *taluka* of Indapur by Colonel J. Francis dated 12 February 1872: *Selections from the Records of the Bombay Government, New Series*, No. CLI.

Indapur to order when in 1825 the *taluka* was transferred to his charge.[1] Despite the best efforts of the Collector of Ahmednagar, the condition of Indapur in 1825 was no better than its condition in 1818, when the *taluka* had fallen into British hands. Robertson, consequently, decided to reconstruct the revenue system of Indapur from its very foundations. To do this, he visited every village in the *taluka* in order to persuade the *patils* to enter into *cowls* or engagements which obliged them to collect a stipulated sum of money as rent on behalf of the government. Robertson's ignorance of the resources of the *kunbis* forced him to deal with the *patils*, but since he suspected their integrity, he instructed them to give deeds or *puttahs* to the *kunbis*, setting forth the tax they were required to pay annually to the State. By these means, Robertson hoped to keep a check on corruption, and he also hoped to gain a precise idea of the resources of the villages and of the cultivators who lived in the villages. Such information, so Robertson believed, could form the basis of a lasting revenue settlement of the villages of Indapur.

Yet Robertson's experiment was destined to prove a failure. This was so because the *patils* of only forty-six out of seventy-six villages could be persuaded to take up *cowls* obliging them to collect the tax on behalf of the government. The thirty *patils* who refused to enter into any engagements with the Collector looked upon the rates demanded by him as excessive. But even the *patils* who had signed *cowls* treated them in a cavalier fashion. The *patils* of Indapur had been free of all constraint under the former government, and they were unaware of the implications of a legal contract. Consequently, not only did they fail to provide the *kunbis* of their villages with *puttahs* setting out their obligations but when 1826 turned out to be an unfavourable year they granted leases on low rates of their own discretion, and thus represented the Collector with a *fait accompli*. The 'irresponsibility' of the *patils*, who violated the *cowls* without any thought as to its possible results, made nonsense of the experiment launched by Robertson in order to ascertain the resources of Indapur.

The administration of the thirty villages whose *patils* had re-

[1] *BA:* R. K. Arbuthnot to H. D. Robertson dated 22 July 1826: R.D., Vol. 20/174 of 1827. Also see H. D. Robertson to W. Malet dated 13 December 1826 in *ibid.*

fused to enter into *cowls* was conducted on principles which were even less satisfactory than the principles which informed the administration of the forty-six villages whose *patils* had entered into *cowls* with Robertson, if only to break them immediately afterwards. R. K. Arbuthnot, the Assistant Collector of Inda-pur, wrote a circular letter to the *patils* of these villages setting out the conditions on which they could offer leases to the *uprees*.[1] In the concessions which it offered to the *kunbis*, Arbuthnot's letter almost struck a note of desperation. To induce cultivators to settle in Indapur the *patils* were free to offer leases at as. 10 ps. 4 per *beegah* for the superior soils, and as. 9 per *beegah* for the middling and inferior soils. Over the first two years of cultiva-tion the *uprees* were required to pay less than the standard rates; and if they cultivated a field continuously for seven years, then they were to 'have the same claim on the land as if it were meeras'.[2] However, to prevent the *kunbis* from taking up fresh land on low rates every year, a cultivator was permitted to throw up his fields and acquire a new holding only if he agreed to cultivate it for a period of seven years.

By offering such favourable terms to the *kunbis* of the thirty villages whose *patils* had refused to sign *cowls*, Arbuthnot pre-vented a complete breakdown in the administration of Indapur, although he did so by surrendering a substantial proportion of the State's share in agricultural produce. What the government actually lost in revenue is clear from the following account of collections in the thirty villages. The *kamal* assessment of these villages, admittedly a fictitious figure, amounted to Rs. 74,684; the *tankha* assessment, a more reliable guide to their resources, was Rs. 35,153. In 1826, the year in which Arbuthnot took over from Robertson, the villages yielded Rs. 19,779 as rent. In 1827 Arbuthnot expected to collect a sum of Rs. 21,134.[3]

The Government of Bombay, however, was not the only loser in the confusion which characterised the administration of land-revenue in Indapur. Despite the instructions of Arbuthnot and Robertson the *patils* of Indapur had consistently refused to issue

[1] *BA:* Memorandum to the Patils of Indapur by R. K. Arbuthnot dated 22 July 1826: enclosed in Arbuthnot's letter to Robertson dated 22 July 1826: R.D., Vol. 20/174 of 1827.
[2] ibid.
[3] *BA:* W. W. Malet to H. D. Robertson dated 20 February 1827: R.D., Vol. 20/174 of 1827.

puttahs to the *kunbis* setting out their annual obligations of tax. Their refusal to do so convinced Arbuthnot that the rents actually collected by the *patils* bore little relation to the official rates of assessment, and that considerable sums of money stuck in the hands of the village officers while being transferred from the *kunbis* to the public treasury. Corruption became all the more acute in bad seasons, as in 1827, when a failure of the rains obliged the government to remit a part of its demand. Since the Collectors were unable to intervene effectively in relations between the *patils* and the *kunbis*, they were obliged to entrust the detailed breakdown of the remission to the village officers, even though they fully realised that the remission in revenue, instead of alleviating the misery of the poor cultivators, would be appropriated by the dominant men in the villages. According to Arbuthnot such remissions not only reinforced the corrupt power of the village officers but they also undermined the sentiment of solidarity in the villages, and encouraged rich and poor peasants alike to enter into an unholy alliance to defraud the government of its revenues:

> The system of granting large remissions in reference to the quality of crops [he pointed out] is of so bad an effect, that I feel very averse to putting it in practice to any great extent; for as soon as it is understood that collections are to be made on this principle, it becomes the object of everyone to deceive the government. . . . When it is generally understood that all of one family assist each other in their concerns and that if the crop of one should particularly fail, he has recourse to his neighbour to lend him for this year, in expectation, that he will be called upon in his turn in the following, there appears no injustice, where the *assessment is moderate* in insisting on it being paid, nor is it likely to produce injury throughout the country. (Emphasis in original.)[1]

The confusion arising from ignorance of the true resources of Indapur was heightened by the complexity of the tenure on which the *uprees* and the *meerasdars* held their land. The villages of Indapur were divided into *sthuls* or estates, which were further apportioned into *teekas*, several of which were held by the same cultivator, though often in different *sthuls*. The cultivable land in the village was also divided into areas of *ghutcool* and

[1] *BA:* R. K. Arbuthnot to H. D. Robertson dated 1 March 1827: R.D., Vol. 20/174 of 1827.

meeras tenure. The cultivating community was made up of *meerasdars* and *uprees*, of which the former were organised into families or *jathas*, each one of which comprised a group of related families of *meerasdars*, and of such cultivators as had entered a *jatha* through the purchase of land. The *sthul* and the *jatha* were originally corresponding and co-extensive designations. But when the Government of Bombay took over Indapur, members of the same *jatha* often held fields in different *sthuls*; and the ownership of a *sthul* was often vested in more than one *jatha*. The situation was further complicated by the fact that the *meerasdars* could on occasions enjoy *ghutcool* land, and the *uprees* cultivate the plots of the *meerasdars*, with sometimes each holding portions of both.[1]

The complexity of land rights can also be illustrated by looking into the ownership of land in the village of Mettur, which contained in all five *sthuls* or estates. Of these *sthuls* the estate of four *chowers* owned by the Mawleh *jatha* was the only estate which was still owned in its entirety by a founding family of the village. Most of the estates, like Guhwan *sthul*, or Zalleh *sthul*, were either completely deserted; or they were inhabited by a lone descendent of a once-flourishing *jatha*, like Appa Scindiah Dhungar, who cultivated less than one *chowar* of the Scindiah *sthul* of four *chowers*, and permitted the *patils* to do what they wanted with the rest. The individuals who benefited most from such a state of affairs were the *patils* of Mettur. For apart from land which they held as *enam*, and besides the holdings which they administered on behalf of the village, they claimed the ownership of extensive estates whose original owners had died, and to which they possessed no clear title. Bapu Patil Geteh of Mettur, for instance, was firmly in control of the Jendeth *sthul* of three *chowars* which, so he claimed, his ancestors had purchased from the Jendeth *jatha* 500 years ago! Similarly, Yashwant Patil Power held 6½ *chowers* of land in different *sthuls* which belonged to *jathas* that were extinct. How he had come to possess all this land was a question to which the Power *patil* could provide no simple answer.[2]

[1] *BA:* R. K. Pringle to J. Bax, Secretary to the Government of Bombay, dated 28 July 1827: R.D., Vol. 28/1811 of 1827.
[2] *BA:* Major Sykes' Report on the Poona Districts dated nil: R.D., Vol. 154B of 1826.

To clear the confusion which he had inherited from the former administration, Pringle 'recruited a number of brahmans for surveying and assessing the land, the surveyors having over them brahman assessors, and the assessors' work being supervised by head-assessors, who were also brahmans. Over the whole department was a Huzoor Cutcherry, composed of twelve brahmans and an English gentleman (i.e., Pringle himself).'[1] Perhaps the most important person in this huge army of brahman officers, certainly far more powerful than Pringle himself, little though the young civilian realised this, was Sideshwar Shastri Tokekar, the *daftardar* of the 'Revenue Survey and Assessment of the Deccan'.[2] Sideshwar Shastri was a most remarkable person, although he was not atypical of the new men who climbed into positions of prominence under British aegis. He came from a family of modest means, and he was reasonably well educated, though he possessed qualities of shrewdness and unscrupulousness which had little to do with the formal education of a young brahman. The Shastri first met Pringle as his tutor in Marathi when the young civilian was serving as the Assistant Collector at Junere. Pringle was immediately struck by the outstanding ability of his tutor, and there sprang up between them a friendship which was to bear important consequences. He first appointed the Shastri a *carcoon* at Junere, and then promoted him to the rank of a *munsif*. On being appointed the Superintendent of the 'Revenue Survey and Assessment of the Deccan', Pringle persuaded his old brahman tutor to accept the office of the *daftardar*, or the ranking native officer in the survey establishment. 'He is a man of excellent character, very superior talents, and extensive information on revenue and general subjects,'[3] Pringle wrote to a fellow-civilian about Sideshwar Shastri. But while everyone agreed about the 'superior talents' of the Shastri, not all British officers reposed the same confidence in his incorruptability as Pringle. Robertson, for instance, found him 'a clever man, . . . (but) the dexterity with which he coils himself in a general principle or rule or a

[1] *BA:* R. K. Pringle to J. Bax, Secretary to the Government of Bombay, dated 6 September 1828: R.D., Vol. 225 of 1828.
[1] *BA:* Letter to T. Williamson, Revenue Commissioner of the Deccan, dated 25 May 1833: R.D., Vol. 38/505 of 1833.
[3] *BA:* R. K. Pringle to T. Williamson dated 23 May 1831: E.D. (Financial Department), Vol. 6 of 1831.

fallacy renders it difficult to follow him ... '.[1] Besides Pringle and the Shastri, the *Huzoor Cutcherry* or the Head Office of the Survey Department contained ten other brahman officers like Vishwanath Baji Joglekar, the *munshi*; Chintopunt Bhave, the expert on *Hukdars;* and Balloji Dhondu, the authority on village officers. Under the *Cutcherry* functioned more than a thousand surveyors and assessors who measured the fields and assessed the quality of their soil. By carefully appointing his protégés in the *Huzoor Cutcherry*, Sideshwar Shastri was able to establish an intricate system of control over the Survey Department which he exploited for purposes on which we shall dwell at some length later.[2]

Despite the radical principles which inspired Pringle, he could hardly be accused of setting a new precedent in recruiting the native officers of the Survey Department from the caste of brahmans. But the criterion on which he based the pitch of the *kunbis'* rent involved a complete repudiation of the traditional principles on which the assessment was evaluated. The tax or rent on land in India had always been a certain share of the gross produce of agriculture. A British authority on revenue administration like Sir Thomas Munro had accepted this principle and had applied it in his surveys in the districts of Madras. However, Pringle rejected the traditional principle of assessment since it made no distinction between rent, which was the landlord's share of agricultural produce and a consequence of the fertility of the land, and the profits of capital and the wages of labour, which rightfully belonged to the cultivator. The proportion of the gross produce which could be levied without trenching upon profits varied with the fertility of the land, and it decreased progressively from the superior to the inferior soils. Pringle conceded that the surveys of Munro had probably left a fraction of the rent to the cultivator even on the inferior soils. But such a concession did not lead him to accept the traditional principle of assessment, which was concerned solely with the gross produce of the land:

> It is obvious that the surplus which remains from the gross produce of the land [Pringle pointed out] after deducting all expenses

[1] *BA:* Letter to T. Williamson dated 25 May 1833: R.D., Vol. 38/505 of 1833.
[2] *BA:* Statement by Vishwanath Baji Joglekar, chief munshi of the Survey Department: R.D., Vol. 38/505 of 1833.

is the fair measure of its power to pay an assessment. But as that surplus varies in its relation to the whole produce in different soils, any tax proportional to the latter only must be unequal. . . . (This) inequality by creating an artificial monopoly in favour of the soils yielding the greatest proportion of net produce . . . will have a tendency to check production. . . . It has always appeared to me that, as the net produce is the only accurate standard of exaction, and as in proportion the assessment is regulated by it, it will be distributed in the manner most favourable to the general wealth and prosperity of the community, it ought therefore to be distinctly recognised as the basis of our operations. . . .[1]

After having defined the principles of a scientific survey Pringle instructed the Survey Department to apply them to the *taluka* of Indapur. The actual survey of Indapur was carried out in three distinct stages: in the first instance, the surveyors measured the holdings of the *ryots;* next, the assessors classified the fields so measured; and finally, the data collected by the surveyors and assessors was utilised by Pringle to calculate the net produce of soils of different fertility. After he had calculated the net produce Pringle fixed the rent as 55 per cent of this figure.

In presenting the results of his survey to the Government of Bombay Pringle emphasised the fact that he had left the natural advantages of the different fertilities of soils completely unimpaired. He also emphasised the fact that his rates enabled the landlords to levy rents which increased progressively from the worst to the best soils. The settlement was, he conceded, dependent upon the accuracy of the data from which he had calculated the net produce. But Pringle found no reason to doubt the honesty of the native officers of the Survey Department, or to question the accuracy of their findings. The crucial question was the effect of the new survey on the rates which the *uprees* and the *meerasdars* had formerly paid to the State. Pringle was struck by the drastic changes which the survey had produced in the fiscal obligations of the peasants individually, and of the villages collectively. But, he argued, these were consequences which ought to surprise no one. If the assessment on the cultivators and on the villages had been equitable under the former administration, then there would have been no need for a new survey. If it was

[1] *BA:* R. K. Pringle to J. Bax, Secretary to the Government of Bombay, dated 6 September 1828: R.D., Vol. 225 of 1828.

unequal, a survey based on scientific principles was bound to change the position of the cultivators regarding their obligations to the State.

Because he was a doctrinaire ultilitarian, Pringle was convinced of the infallibility of the principles which informed his survey of Indapur. But he also realised that 'this (survey) is not a mere question of political economy, and that, affecting as it does the rights and interests of a large portion of the community, it must be considered on broader and more general grounds'. He had no apprehensions about cultivators whose financial burden had been reduced by the survey. But the position of cultivators whose obligations had been enhanced required serious consideration. Pringle believed that although it was desirable to equalise the pitch of the assessment on different cultivators it would none the less be a serious mistake to violate long-established rights by trenching into the profits which the peasants had traditionally derived from their holdings. It was in this context that alterations in rent impinged upon the prerogatives of the *meerasdars*, who possessed a clear proprietary interest in the land. As the idea of a new survey had gained ground in the Government of Bombay it was argued by conservatives like Chaplin and Robertson that the assessment on *meerasdars* ought in no circumstances to be increased, since an increase in their rent would amount to an encroachment on their rights of property. Yet Pringle failed to see why the *meerasdars* could not be required to pay a rent higher than the rent they had paid under the former government.

> I am at a loss to discover [he pointed out] the grounds on which this notion of the right of meerasdars to exemption from increased payments on a general revision of the assessment was originally taken up. I have looked in vain for any confirmation of it in the numerous notices and regarding the rights and immunities of this class.... I have looked in vain for it in the deeds by which the land is transferred.... I can find no trace of it in the management of our predecessors.... I have frequently conversed on this subject with intelligent natives ... and I have never heard from them but one opinion.... Arbitrarily to raise the assessment of an individual meerasdar beyond that of his fellows would be an outrage to public feeling. But they have no conception of the existence of any contract to prevent government from causing it to be

apportioned on the fields either of meerasdars or uprees in any way which in its wisdom it may think fit.[1]

However no inconvenient questions were raised by the survey of Indapur, since it reduced instead of raising the burden of rent on the *meerasdars*. It was the *uprees* rather than the *meerasdars* who were adversely affected by the new arrangements. But Pringle held that since the *uprees* cultivated land on short leases they had no reason to expect an indefinite extension of the low rents which they had formerly enjoyed, and that they were at liberty to fend for themselves. This could well be described as a cavalier attitude, but it stemmed from a doctrinaire and not from an opportunistic cast of mind. Pringle, in fact, realised that his survey could bring about a decrease in the area of cultivation in Indapur. But such a prospect did not impair his confidence in the equity of his rates of assessment. Besides, he believed that an extension of cultivation was not necessarily desirable in all circumstances. The practice of attracting *uprees* to villages through low rents was in his opinion ill-conceived and even mischievous. It stimulated a ruinous competition against the *meerasdars*, and it encouraged inefficient and slovenly cultivation on the part of the *uprees*. 'Like the poor law in England,' Pringle pointed out, 'it is a system which sets out upon the principle of making the poor rich by making the rich poor, and ends by making paupers of us all'.[2]

The cogency with which Pringle set out the principles of his survey is reflected in the fact that a conservative like Sir John Malcolm, who had succeeded Elphinstone as the Governor of Bombay in 1828, not only accepted the validity of his findings but also recommended that the new system be extended to other districts in Maharashtra. According to Malcolm the reasons put forth by Pringle for fixing the assessment on the basis of the net instead of the gross produce were so convincing that 'I must believe it to be rather apparently than actually the case that the assessments were at any time not so fixed'. Malcolm conceded that mistakes in survey or assessment could seriously effect the success of the rates proposed by Pringle. But he saw no reason to doubt the accuracy of the findings of the Survey Department. Indeed, he looked forward to an era of increasing prosperity in rural society as the survey was extended to new areas:

[1] ibid.   [2] ibid.

Without (the survey) . . . we proceed in darkness. With it we have light [Malcolm stated]. The minuteness of our acquaintance with the receipts, the rights, and the condition of every individual instead of limiting our liberality, enables us to give it a just direction, and so to render the benefits we confer on the community real blessings for their being given with a discrimination that ensures their happy operation.[1]

II

The rates calculated by Pringle were introduced in the *taluka* of Indapur in 1830 in a remarkable mood of optimism, since they rested, on the one hand, on the laws of political economy, and on the other, on the investigations conducted under the supervision of a civilian who had a reputation for brilliance which bordered on precocity. However, the scale of rates proposed by Pringle possessed one characteristic which would have caused him grave anxiety, if only he had been less of a doctrinaire, and if only he had reposed less confidence in Sideshwar Shastri Tokekar and the native officers of the Survey Department. Pringle, we must remind ourselves at this juncture, believed that the *patils* and the dominant men in the villages of Maharashtra had formerly exploited the *rivaj* rates to secure light assessments for their holdings. Indeed, Pringle's case for a new survey, and for a *ryotwari* as opposed to a *mauzewar* settlement, rested on the supposition that the dominant cultivators had paid ridiculously low rents to the former government. But as the results of his survey poured in, Pringle observed to his utter astonishment that the burden of rent on the *meerasdars*, whom he regarded as the 'exploiters' of rural society, would be reduced instead of being enhanced under the new rates of assessment. In the *talukas* of Pabul and Sewnair, for instance, the rent on the *meerasdars* was reduced from Rs. 355,827 to Rs. 267,196, which represented a diminution of more than 20 per cent in the total demand.[2] Such a drastic alteration in the burden of tax on the *meerasdars*, who represented the dominant section of rural society, would have undermined the confidence of most men in the findings of the survey.

[1] *BA:* Minute by the Governor of Bombay dated 18 November 1828: R.D., Vol. 225 of 1828.
[2] *BA:* Collector of Poona to Government of Bombay dated 1 April 1830: R.D., Vol. 7/287 of 1830.

But Pringle refused to be haunted by any doubts. Executing a neat sleight of hand he explained the diminution in the burden of tax on the *meerasdars* on the ground that they had formerly over-taxed themselves in order to attract *uprees* to the villages on low rents!

Although the survey undermined his belief that the *meerasdars* had formerly exploited their poor fellow-cultivators, Pringle found the reduction in the burden of rent on the *meerasdars* most convenient, if only because of the important position which they occupied in rural society. Since the question of a survey had first been raised in the Government of Bombay, conservatives like Chaplin and Robertson had been apprehensive, largely because of Pringle's analysis of the distribution of power in the villages of Maharashtra, that an assessment based on scientific principles would raise the burden of rent on the *meerasdars*, and would therefore encroach upon their rights of property. But Pringle could now turn on his critics and claim that his survey had reinforced and not weakened the position of the *meerasdars*:

> There is [Pringle observed] no class of the community which will benefit so much by the survey as the meerasdars. Indeed, were it otherwise, I should entertain much greater doubts of the advantages than I do. I am fully sensible of the importance, with a view to the welfare of society, and every purpose of good government, of maintaining and promoting that independence of spirit, elevation of character, and attachment to the soil, which is the result of proprietary rights. . . . So far from advocating any system which will lead to annihilate them, I should be glad to see them extended to a much wider sphere than they at present occupy.[1]

The real test of a survey, however, was the reaction it evoked among the poor but numerically significant cultivators. So far as the poor cultivators were concerned it soon became obvious that the experiment launched with such hopes was doomed to failure. Early in 1830 Robertson received reports from the Assistant Collector of Indapur of the difficulty he experienced in persuading the *kunbis* to cultivate land under the new rates of assessment. Even more disturbing was the virtual desolation of the villages of Indapur through the migration of the *kunbis* in large numbers to the neighbouring territories of the Nizam in a

---

[1] *BA:* R. K. Pringle to J. Bax, Secretary to the Government of Bombay, dated 6 September 1828: R.D., Vol. 225 of 1828.

bid to escape the rigours of the settlement. The peasants had virtually voted against the new survey with their feet! The elements, too, joined in a conspiracy against Pringle, since there was a partial failure of the monsoon in 1830. But the collection of revenue made it clear that the vicissitudes of the weather had been reinforced by an ill-conceived scale of rates to precipitate a disastrous situation. In 1829 Indapur was assessed at Rs. 58,702, and actually yielded a revenue of Rs. 42,299. Pringle had assessed the *taluka* at Rs. 91,569. But so many peasants had fled from Indapur after the introduction of the new rates that even the wildest optimist could not have forecast a collection exceeding Rs. 16,410 in 1830. The Collector of Poona was reluctant to pass any verdict upon the rates introduced by Pringle after so brief a trial. But he advocated the reintroduction of *cowls* in order to persuade the *kunbis* of Indapur to return to their villages and cultivate their ancestral lands.[1]

Since the intransigence of the *kunbis* threatened to undermine the results of his survey, Pringle turned to the defence of the new rates of assessment with a strength born of desperation. He touched upon the extensive inquiries into the rights of the *kunbis* which had been carried out under the survey, and he also referred to the statistics on productivity and resources upon which the calculation of the net produce, and of the actual rates of assessment, were based. To claim infallibility in the conduct of so intricate an operation would be foolhardy. But, Pringle argued, it was easy to see why a measure having for its object the correction of inequalities in assessment had provoked the opposition of those whose rents had been increased. The refusal of the *kunbis* to pay the new rates, therefore, should not shake the government's confidence in the accuracy or in the equity of the survey:

> For I am persuaded [Pringle concluded] that in the opinion of the majority of the people . . . the magnitude and importance of this work are fully appreciated, and held to be worthy of the government by which it was undertaken. It is certainly looked upon with hope, and will come to be recognised and relied upon with confidence, as the character of their privileges over a point so interesting to our Indian community as the adjustment of the land-tax

[1] *BA:* Letter from the Assistant Collector of Poona to the Bombay Government dated 1 April 1830: R.D., Vol. 7/287 of 1830.

and the rights and claims connected with it become increasingly clear. . . .[1]

The magnitude of Pringle's failure, however, was too calamitous to be dispelled either by pious platitudes or by a reiteration of the principles which informed his survey. Conservative administrators like Robertson had always been sceptical of Pringle's ability to base the pitch of the assessment exclusively on the laws of political economy. They now demonstrated how the survey had disastrously altered the rents paid in the past by villages, and how it had also affected the fortunes of individual cultivators. From the inquiries which they conducted in villages surveyed by Pringle these administrators were able to locate the fallacies in his revenue policy, and in the application of this policy to the survey of Indapur.

Robertson looked upon the decrease in the burden of rent on the *meerasdars* as the most disturbing feature of the survey. Pringle, of course, was aware of this decrease, but it took a detailed investigation by Robertson to bring out how the *meerasdars* had actually fared under the new rates of assessment. The rent calculated by Pringle on the village of Mauze Kowrey, for instance, was identical with the *kamal* assessment of Rs. 3,304. However, the survey assessment on the holdings of the *meerasdars* of the village, who owned the most fertile fields, lowered their rent from Rs. 2,152 to Rs. 1,815, while the *uprees'* share of the total demand on the village was raised from Rs. 1,152 to Rs. 1,343. These alterations were effected through a simple expedient. The fertile fields held by the *meerasdars*, which were formerly assessed at the maximum rates, had been transferred to the category of *jerayet* or inferior land by the native officers of the Survey Department, who had at the same time upgraded the inferior holdings of the *uprees*. The collection of rent from Mauze Kowrey before and after the introduction of the new rates constituted a telling indictment of the survey. In 1829 the village yielded a sum of Rs. 2,690; in 1830 the collection was anticipated to be Rs. 1,819.[2]

[1] *BA*: R. K. Pringle to T. Williamson dated 18 July 1831: R.D. Vol. 20/426 of 1832. Also see Pringle's letter to Williamson dated 8 March 1831 in R.D., Vol. 48/375 of 1831.
[2] *NAI* (National Archives of India): H. D. Robertson to Government of Bombay dated 20 January 1834: Home Department, Revenue Branch, Consultation No. 4 of 30 July 1834.

The survey had not only reduced the burden of rent on the *meerasdars* but it had also disturbed the proportion in which the *meerasdars* had formerly distributed the total demand on a village among themselves. This became clear to Robertson when he investigated the effect of the new rates of assessment on a *jatha* which owned the *sthul* of Kurdela in the village of Kurra. The Kurdela *jatha* comprised six families which had divided the *sthul* in the not too remote past on the basis of their several rights of inheritance. According to the *rivaj* of Kurra, the first four

TABLE C

Showing the Effect of the Pringle Survey on the Kurdela *Jatha*

Head of the family	*Rivaj* survey		Pringle survey	
	Area (*beegahs*)	Assessment (Rs.)	Area (*beegahs*)	Assessment (Rs.)
Pandojee Kurdela	20	24	21	12
Arjunah Kurdela	20	24	20	10
Kassee Kurdela	20	24	24	16
Goondji Kurdela	20	24	29	17
Byheroo Kurdela	40	48	59	34
Andojee Kurdela	30	36	28	24

families of Kurdela *jatha* held equal shares in the ancestral estate; the fifth family held a double share; and the sixth and last family held a share and a half. However, when the native officers of the Survey Department surveyed Kurra, they discovered that the area of the fields held by different families did not correspond with the picture set out by the *rivaj*. The holdings of Byheroo Kurdela, for instance, measured thrice the holdings of Pandoojee Kurdela, although the *rivaj* put them as twice the size of the holdings of Pandoojee. The effect of the survey was, therefore, to alter radically the burden of rent on the families of Kurdela *jatha*. True, the *jatha* as a whole bore a lighter burden of tax than before, but the different families in the *jatha* were affected to different degrees by this diminution in demand. Arjunah and Pandoojee Kurdela, for instance, had their rents halved, while the demand on the rest of the *jatha* was reduced by only 33 per cent.[1]

The members of the Kurdela *jatha* were completely baffled by this inexplicable change in their fortunes. The *patils* of Kurra, Luxman Patil Gonday and Balloojee Patil Dholay, explained to Robertson that when the Kurdela *sthul* was partitioned, the various families had resolved the problem of differential fertility in different parts of the estate by apportioning shares in *beegahs* of varying superficial extent. The *rivaj beegah* in Kurra, in other words, took into consideration both the area and the fertility of a field. The measurement of holdings in such a unit considerably simplified the administration of revenue. The Marathas, for instance, had levied a rent of Rs. 1 as. 4 per *beegah* on Kurra. If their *mamlatdars* raised the demand on Kurra in a particular year, the *patils* of the village were able to meet the enhanced demand through distributing it evenly on the number of *beegahs* under cultivation. By disturbing the traditional distribution of rent among the families of Kurdela *jatha*, Pringle had undermined the principles which determined the shares of these families, just as much as he had undermined the principles which determined the breakdown of the total demand on the village. To neutralise the effect of the new rates, the *patils* of Kurra told Robertson, it was likely that the families comprising the *jatha* would redistribute the *sthul* so as to 'bring their shares back to an equality'.[2] The *patils*' verdict on the long term consequences of the survey, however, was more disturbing and more ominous: 'All the people do not yet know the effect of it (i.e. the new survey),' they told the Collector of Poona, 'but as soon as they comprehend it, we think that the *meerasdars* will generally quarrel among themselves.'[3]

The confusion which the survey had introduced in the affairs of Kurra highlights the arbitrary treatment of the *meerasdars* by

[1] *BA*: H. D. Robertson to Government of Bombay dated 1 November 1831: R.D., Vol. 434 of 1832.
[2] *BA*: Report of an interview between H. D. Robertson and the *patils* of Kurra enclosed in Robertson's letter dated 1 November 1831: R.D., Vol. 434 of 1832.
[3] ibid.

Pringle. His attitude towards the *meerasdars* was shaped by his original suspicion that they had paid very light rents to the former government, and that their contribution to the public treasury was both unequal and inequitable. These suspicions blinded Pringle to fallacies in the principles which informed his survey, or to errors in the application of these principles. They also led him to repose complete confidence in the findings of the native officers of the Survey Department, even when these findings flatly contradicted the *rivaj* of the villages. Finally, Pringle's belief in the discretionary right of the government to raise the rent on the *meerasdars* virtually ensured the failure of his survey:

> That meerasdars [Robertson pointed out] had their assessments raised or lowered by government is true; but government has no right to raise or lower the assessment of only one meerasdar of a village. It must raise or lower the assessment of all in equal proportions, for their assessments were originally equalised by their tenures and joint responsibility, and any alterations of the proportions, except in singular circumstances of fraudulent concealment, is precisely rendering their assessments unequal. . . .[1]

Since Robertson's inquiries revealed how the *meerasdars* of Indapur had emerged with substantial reductions in rent through the new rates of assessment, they provided a convincing explanation for the failure of Pringle's survey. But it required the detailed investigations of yet another revenue officer, namely, Robert Shortrede, to establish Robertson's findings on a firm foundation. The prosecution of the survey by the native officers of the Survey Department had involved two distinct stages: the measurement of the area of holdings, and their classification into soils of different fertility. Pringle's surveyors had carried out the measurement of fields with reasonable accuracy. But their classification was so notoriously undependable that 'in two instances only did . . . (Shortrede) find three successive fields correctly assessed'.

> I have called the misclassification general and systematic [Shortrede observed] because had it been otherwise, had the class of each field been determined by lot, it might have been expected where there were nine classes, that one field in nine should have

[1] *BA:* H. D. Robertson to Bombay Government dated 1 November 1831: R.D., Vol. 434 of 1832.

been correct, and of the remaining eight, four should have been above and four below the proper class. In order to try the classification in this way, I made a spinning top on which I made nine-marks corresponding to the nine classes, and in several villages I found that the class determined by the spinning top was nearer the truth than that determined by the survey.[1]

The conclusion was irrefutable, so Shortrede believed, that the errors committed by the native officers of the Survey Department in the classification of fields were deliberate and not accidental. The conclusion was also irrefutable that these errors were inspired by the dominant men in the villages of Indapur in order to cheat the government of its revenues. The holdings of Masaye Patil Galande in the *cusbah* of Indapur, for instance, had been classed as inferior red by the Survey Department despite the obvious superiority of their soil. Similarly, the 750 acres of superior black soil owned by the *kulkarnis* of Indapur were grossly under-assessed by the surveyors of Pringle. So far as the *kulkarnis* were concerned, the surveyors had committed errors both in the assessment and in the measurement of their estate. Only 23 acres of the estate had been entered as superior black in the official accounts; of the rest, 299 acres were registered as middling black; 166 acres as inferior black; and 140 acres as red, making in all only 628 acres. The *kulkarnis* of Indapur, therefore, paid an assessment which bore little relation to the productivity of their holdings.[2]

The concessions extended to the *patil* and the *kulkarnis* of Indapur clearly speak of collusion between the native officers of the Survey Department and the dominant men in the villages. Behind this collusion lay the web of intrigue which was woven by Sideshwar Shastri Tokekar in the Survey Department. The surveyors and assessors who went out to the villages were instructed by the Shastri to accommodate those who were willing to pay for the unfair advantages which they demanded. Gopal Punt, who was a *Sir Turrim* or chief surveyor in the Survey Department, collected Rs. 500 from Suntaji Patil Tope and the principal cultivators of Hadapsar, and in return he reduced the rent they were required to pay to the government, and con-

[1] *NAI*: Report on the *taluka* of Indapur by Robert Shortrede dated 24 October 1835: R.D., Proceedings No. 4 dated 23 January 1837.
[2] ibid.

firmed their ownership over fields to which they possessed no clear title. Similarly, Govind Rao Gunpule, an officer of the *Huzoor Cutcherry*, received Rs. 155 from the villagers of Umra as a bribe for a reduction in the demand on the village.[1] From the key position which he occupied in the *Huzoor Cutcherry*, Sideshwar Shastri Tokekar thus controlled a machinery of corruption which reached out to the remote villages of Indapur. Vishwanath Rowji Joglekar, a creature of the Shastri, described the working of this machinery to Robertson in the following terms:

> I may give as an example that when I was *Sir Turrim* of Junere, and had under me as *Turrims* Pandurung Gungadhar Udas and Naro Ganesh, the latter person classed the lands of Dholivir village. But afterwards, being converted into the Huzoor munshi, my successor Rowji Mule altered the classes of from 50 to 75 numbers (i.e., holdings) having previously settled matters without my knowledge with Govind Row. When I found it out I said to Govind Row: 'This village was assessed when I was *Sir Turrim* and I investigated the work and now alterations have been made where there are no grounds for making them and nothing good will come out of this. If Mr. Pringle or Shastri Bawa (i.e. Sideshwar Shastri Tokekar) should ask me about it, what shall I answer?' Then he (i.e. Govind Rao) replied: 'Nobody will ever ask you about it, only just hold your tongue, and nobody will challenge the affair. We have got Rs. 300 by it.[2]

The unholy alliance between the native officers of the Survey Department and the *meerasdars* was, therefore, the principal reason behind the diminution in the burden of tax on the dominant men in the villages of Indapur. 'I am credibly informed,' Robertson pointed out, 'that in most instances where the aggregate assessment of a village is now less than it formerly was, a contribution was raised from the village officers and ryots.'[3] But in focusing exclusively on the dishonesty of the native officers of the Survey Department, and in refusing to take account of the social anarchy and the ruthless individualism which Pringle had unleashed by introducing a new system of assessment, both Robertson and Shortrede failed to grasp the

[1] *BA:* Letter to T. Williamson dated 25 May 1833: R.D., Vol. 38/505 of 1833.
[2] *BA:* Statement of Vishwanath Rowji Joglekar, chief *munshi* of the Survey Department: R.D., Vol. 38/505 of 1833.
[3] *BA:* H. D. Robertson to Government of Bombay dated 1 November 1831: R.D., Vol. 434 of 1832.

full implications of the *ryotwari* system of land-revenue, just as they failed to grasp the significance of the social climate which encouraged corruption on so massive a scale. The most important feature of the administration of revenue under the Marathas was the collective responsibility which the *meerasdars* of a village bore for its rent. Again, it was the *meerasdars* who distributed the total demand on the village into the shares of individual cultivators, once this demand had been fixed through negotiations between the *patil*, the *mamlatdar* and the *deshmukh*. Pringle's belief in the dominance of the *meerasdars* over the villages was based on sound logic, since it was natural for the *patil* and a few principal *kunbis* to control the levers of social power in the rural community. But his inference that the dominant men in the villages were able to transfer a portion of their fiscal burden on the shoulders of the poor cultivators, an inference which he drew from a comparison between the *kamal* and the *rivaj* surveys, was wholly incorrect. The *meerasdars* could, in fact, extract very little from the *uprees*, because of their poverty, and also because the *uprees* could always migrate to a new village if they were oppressed beyond a point. Indeed, for the *meerasdars* to bully the *uprees* amounted to killing the goose which laid the golden eggs, for if the *uprees* fled from a village the *meerasdars* were still obliged to make good the collective demand on the village to the *mamlatdars*.

All this was no longer true once the obligations of the *meerasdars* to the village community were abolished through the introduction of a *ryotwari* system of land-revenue, which established a direct relationship between the *meerasdar* and the State. Under the *ryotwari* system, a *meerasdar* stood to gain if he could secure a diminution in his share of the village rent, since it was the responsibility of the government to ensure payment of the rent from the cultivators severally, instead of the community collectively. In thus introducing a new mode of assessment, therefore, Pringle threw open to the *meerasdars* and to the village officers of Indapur a means for bettering their position which had not existed before. This explains the alliance between the native officers of the Survey Department and the dominant men in the villages which was responsible for the more dramatic features of the Pringle survey. Pringle was right in postulating the existence of dominant men in the villages of Maharashtra; but their dominance was social rather than economic; and ironically enough, the means he adopted to undermine their power only strengthened their hold over rural society.

It would, however, be a grave mistake to attribute the failure of Pringle's survey solely to the corruption of Sideshwar Shastri Tokekar and his minions, or to the selfishness of the *meerasdars* of Indapur. The calculation of the 'net produce' was so difficult that in many cases mistakes in assessment arose out of genuine error rather than out of dishonesty. But no matter how they originated, mistakes in assessment had the most serious repercussions on the prosperity of rural society. The fate of the village of Oolhi, for instance, provides a revealing glimpse of the damage which Pringle's impetuousness could inflict upon a prosperous rural community:

> One of the most heavily assessed villages is Oolhi, distance from Sholapur 8 miles [pointed out a revenue officer who was instructed to revise Pringle's rates of assessment in 1840]. The rate here is Rs. 2 as. 10 per acre. This place I well recall a flourishing village 7 years ago, it had a couple of shops, and was to all appearances populous. It is now mostly deserted. The shops are ruined, all the trees disappeared, walls down, and the place in ruins; and of 4,000 acres 2,475 are waste; revenue fallen from Rs. 1,066 to Rs. 618. Patel and kulkarni both ruined, being involved in defalcations they could not prevent. An acting patel and kulkarni doing duty, and an outstanding balance of Rs. 3,466. Several of the villagers now cultivate in the neighbouring villages. The year prior to the Pringle survey the village produced net revenue Rs. 2,000. The rest of the over-assessed and mis-classified villages have all partaken more or less similar ruin and misery. . . .[1]

Oolhi, of course, was only one of the many villages which had been reduced to a state of utter desolation by the new rates of assessment. The survey thus dealt a death blow to the prosperity of Indapur; and in doing so, it completely discredited the principles which informed Pringle's *ryotwari* system of land-revenue.

Although Pringle's critics did not completely grasp the implications of the *ryotwari* system which he had introduced in Indapur, the failure of his settlement finally scotched any attempt to base the rates of assessment exclusively on the laws of political

[1] *BA:* J. D. Bellasis to G. Wingate dated 26 January 1839: R.D., Vol. 114/1198 of 1840.

economy. Robert Grant, who had succeeded Malcolm as the Governor of Bombay in 1831, voiced a widely shared opinion when he stated that the only general rule that could be laid down for the conduct of a new survey was that 'there ought to be a patient, searching, and accurate enquiry into the individual nature and capabilities of every beegah of soil. . . . No abstract principles can be applied in such a case.'[1]

The scepticism of British administrators in the laws of political economy was reinforced by a growing understanding of social organisation within the villages of Maharashtra, and of the institutions through which the former government had collected the rent on land. The confusion which characterised the revenue policy of the Government of Bombay in the districts acquired from Baji Rao Peshwa for a decade and a half after 1818 was in some measure due to the fact that most of the Collectors in the Deccan had gained their initial experience in the administration of revenue under Sir Thomas Munro in the districts of Madras. They were, therefore, inclined to apply their experience of Madras to the Deccan without allowing sufficiently for local variations in the social organisation of the villages, and in the traditions of administration. After Pringle had failed at Indapur, however, conservative administrators who had opposed him from the very outset tried to re-examine the methods of the former government in the hope of devising an efficient system of revenue administration. Prominent among these administrators was Thomas Williamson, who had succeeded Chaplin as the Revenue Commissioner of the Deccan. Being an enlightened conservative in the tradition of Elphinstone, Williamson was a great exponent of continuity in the processes of change, and he believed in the futility and in the folly of drastic attempts at reform:

> The results of all my researches and experience [Williamson pontificated] have strongly impressed me with the idea that there is no system as good as the established custom of the country, and that when it has apparently failed, we have been misled by signs which did not properly belong to that system, but were the consequence of confusion, or decay, arising from it being neglected, or misunderstood. . . . (Of) our own well meant plans for the ameliora-

[1] *BA*: Minute by Governor of Bombay dated 12 October 1836: R.D., Vol. 11/698 of 1836.

tion of this country, none have proved so successful as those directed at the support and restoration of local institutions, and none
so unfortunate as those which have a contrary direction.[1]

In searching for the reasons which led to the failure of
Pringle's survey of Indapur, Williamson gained a new insight
into the revenue administration of the Marathas, although he
was unable to transform this insight into a practical policy. Unlike Pringle, Williamson defined a *ryotwari* system as one in
which the rights and obligations of the *kunbis* were first ascertained severally, and then made the basis of the total rent of the
village. The superiority of such a system, so Williamson believed,
lay in the precision with which it defined the dues of the cultivator, and in doing so prevented excessive taxation by the
government, and arbitrary exactions by the village officers.
Williamson saw a perfect expression of the *ryotwari* system in the
bhayachara settlements of the North-Western Provinces, where
the survey officers first instituted a detailed inquiry into the
productivity of a village, and the rent evaluated by them was
then apportioned into the shares of individual *kunbis* by the
members of the village community. He recognised that the
shares so determined did not necessarily have equal productivi-
ties, since some estates and holdings were better looked after
than others. But it would be wrong to levy an additional rent
on that account. Such a limitation was in fact the most striking
feature of the system. For it offered economic incentives to the
kunbi without alienating him from his fellow-cultivators in the
village. The *kunbi* was no longer induced to drift from one
village to another in search of leases on low rents. Instead, he
was encouraged to tie himself firmly to a piece of land, and to
direct his energies exclusively to its improvement. It would be
a serious mistake, Williamson concluded, to weaken the *kunbi's*
attachment to his land through a new assessment which would
tax improvements effected under the impression that they would
not lead to an increase in rent.

The principles enunciated by Thomas Williamson were
applied by Richard Mills, the Collector of Dharwar, to the
settlement of some of the villages in his district. Mills seized
upon the basic weakness of the *ryotwari* system when he pointed

[1] *NAI:* T. Williamson to Government of Bombay dated 30 July 1834: Home Department, Revenue Branch, Consultation No. 3 dated 30 July 1834.

out how Pringle's survey had weakened the cohesion of the villages through alienating the *kunbis* from their fellow-cultivators, and how it had thereby encouraged large scale corruption in Maharashtra. However, the alternative adopted by Mills was open to equally serious objections. Mills gave leases for a decade on moderate rents to the *patils* of eleven villages of Dharwar. By giving such leases he hoped to preserve the sentiment of solidarity among the cultivators, and to provide them with incentives for improvement. Because of Robertson's experience with the *patils* of Indapur in 1825, Mills had been doubtful whether the *patils* of Dharwar would be willing to undertake the responsibility of collecting the rent on behalf of the government. But what encouraged him to bring his experiment to the notice of the Government of Bombay was the enthusiasm with which the *patils* and the cultivators of Dharwar responded to his initiative. However, Mills' experiment was so reminiscent of the system of farming which had prevailed under Baji Rao, and it could so easily have been exploited by the *patils* and the substantial *kunbis* to enrich themselves, that it was not considered seriously by the Government of Bombay.[1]

Indeed, it was in fact impossible to revive the principles which had determined the collection of revenue under the Peshwas, not the least because the *rivaj* rates had been 'obliterated' by the farmers of revenue who had collected the rent on behalf of Baji Rao II. A fair and practical system of revenue, therefore, had to be based on a compromise between the traditional principles of assessment, on the one hand, and the laws of political economy, on the other. Such a compromise was advocated by Shortrede in the form of a scale of rates based on a proportion of the gross produce which diminished progressively from the superior to the inferior soils. Shortrede's proposal highlighted the extent to which he was willing to abandon rational principles when confronted with practical problems, and as we shall presently see, precisely because he was willing to do so, his suggestion met with considerable success. Williamson, for one,

---

[1] *NAI*: R. Mills to Government of Bombay dated 30 May and 1 June 1839: Home Department, Revenue Branch, Consultation No. 10 dated 14 December 1840. Also see Memorandum by L. P. Reid, Secretary to the Government of Bombay, dated 10 August 1839, and Reid's Memorandum dated 11 January 1840 in ibid.

threw himself squarely behind Shortrede's suggestion, since 'from the simplicity of the system, and the moderation of the rent, it would at once be intelligible and acceptable to the people'.[1] The Revenue Commissioner's support of Shortrede's proposal was completely vindicated by subsequent events. For as soon as Pringle's rates were abolished, and the rates recommended by Shortrede substituted in their place, the situation in Indapur took a turn for the better. When Williamson journeyed through the *taluka* shortly afterwards, he observed that the *kunbis*' confidence in the good intentions of the government had been restored, and they were consequently returning in large numbers to their villages. 'An interesting group of men, women and children who passed my camp the other day,' he noted in his journal, 'said they had left the Nizam's country and were going to their native village in Indapur in consequence of the security now enjoyed there.'[2]

Despite the *kunbis*' favourable reaction to the revival of the *rivaj* rates, Shortrede's proposal was too arbitrary, and too discriminatory in the burden of rent it imposed on different cultivators, to form the basis of a permanent revenue settlement. It was left to H. E. Goldsmid and G. Wingate to devise a system of land-revenue which reconciled the laws of political economy to the *rivaj* of the villages of Maharashtra. In devising such a system they laid down the foundations of land settlement policy in the Deccan. Goldsmid opposed Shortrede's suggestion that the survey carried out under Pringle's supervision be rejected in its entirety, and that the measurement of land in the traditional unit of the *chowar* be revived. Equally ill-conceived, so Goldsmid believed, was the notion of attracting *uprees* to the villages of Indapur through the low rates proposed by Shortrede. Such a measure would not only cause a serious loss of revenue to the government but it would also create a grave imbalance in the economy of the districts which surrounded Indapur by inducing the *kunbis* who lived there to throw up their fields and migrate to villages where they could rent land on very attractive terms.

[1] *BA:* T. Williamson to Government of Bombay dated 26 March 1835: R.D., Vol. 73/933 of 1838.
[2] *BA:* T. Williamson to Government of Bombay dated 30 January 1836: R.D., Vol. 73/933 of 1838.

However the most important characteristic of the revenue policy proposed by Goldsmid and Wingate consisted in the rejection of Pringle's attempt to fix the rates of assessment on the basis of the net produce of the land. Pringle had aimed at rewarding the *kunbis* on the basis of the fertility of the land which they cultivated, rather than on the basis of the capital which they invested in their holdings, or the effort they put into the operations of agriculture. Such a policy, he had argued, would be justified both on grounds of morality and of expediency. Ricardo had demonstrated that the benefits reaped by cultivators ought to be determined by the fertility of the land which they tilled, and that these benefits should decrease progressively from the best to the worst soils. Politically, the introduction of such an inequality in the rates of assessment was most desirable, since it would enable the more substantial *kunbis* to build up reserves of capital which they could reinvest in the land to secure high profits for themselves. The accumulation of capital by a section of the *kunbis* would stimulate the growth of a class of rich peasants whose prosperity would be based on the laws of political economy, rather than on the exploitation of their fellow-cultivators. Such a class of rich peasants, so Pringle believed, would not only contribute to the moral and material progress of rural society but it would also provide a stable social base for British rule over Maharashtra.

According to Goldsmid and Wingate, Pringle's attempt to foster a class of rich peasants was the most serious fallacy in his revenue policy, and the most important reason behind the failure of the survey of Indapur. In an inquiry which they conducted in eighty-six villages of Indapur, they observed, like Robertson and Shortrede before them, that while the measurement of fields had been conducted with reasonable accuracy, their classification was completely undependable. However, Goldsmid and Wingate did not attribute the failure of the survey solely to errors in classification. They recognised that the new rates of assessment were resisted by the *kunbis* because they had raised the rent on inferior and lowered the rent on superior soils. But this feature of the survey, they pointed out 'cannot be accounted for ... (exclusively) by the numerous cases of error and defect exposed by Lt. Shortrede; it is so general and unusual, that we must look for its cause in the system, and not in the execution of the survey'.[1] Goldsmid and Wingate pinpointed in Pringle's application of Ricardo's law of rent the reason why his survey had dealt so harshly with *kunbis* who cultivated land of low fertility. Pringle had defined the net surplus as the rent which a tenant could pay to his landlord after deducting costs of capital and wages of labour. But he had overlooked the fact that the soil of the poorest quality taken into cultivation at a particular moment did not yield a rent to its owner. In imposing a tax on soils of the lowest quality, Pringle had therefore trenched into the profits of the poor cultivators, and he had levied rates of assessment which favoured the dominant as against the poor cultivators.

Pringle's application of Ricardo's law of rent made nonsense of his claim that his rates had left undisturbed the benefits which would have accrued to the cultivators from the natural fertility of the soil. But although they recognised where Pringle had erred in the application of the laws of political economy, Goldsmid and Wingate did not attempt to base their rates of assessment on the net produce of the land. In subsequent discussions they cited the net surplus of the land as the theoretical basis of their rates, but in practice they employed pragmatic criteria for fixing the assessment on different soils. While Pringle's settlement favoured those who cultivated the fertile fields, and while it aimed at fostering the growth of a class of rich peasants, Goldsmid and Wingate regarded his rates as ill-conceived and injudicious. For instead of rewarding *kunbis* with identical reserves of capital and identical skills in agriculture to the same extent, they showered benefits on them according to the fertility of the land which they cultivated. Wingate, for instance, showed how a *kunbi* having at his disposal a capital outlay of Rs. 100 would, according to the rates levied by Pringle, make a profit of Rs. 32 as. 8 on the best soil, and a profit of Rs. 12 as. 8 on the worst soil.[2] Such a scale of assessment, so Wingate believed, violated all notions of social equity. A fair assessment ought to leave the *kunbis* with the same margin of profit, irrespective of the quality of the land they cultivated. That a settlement based on the principle recommended by Wingate would have violated the 'net surplus' criterion is obvious; and a

[1] *BA:* A. Nash to G. Wingate dated 23 March 1838: R.D., Vol. 73/933 of 1838.
[2] *BA:* G. Wingate to R. Mills dated 17 April 1838: R.D., Vol. 73/933 of 1838.

TABLE D

Comparison between Pringle's Scale and Wingate's Egalitarian Scale

Type of soil	Area of land cultivated with Rs. 100	Net produce per acre
	1	2
	Acres	Rs. as. p.
1st black	28–36–0	2 8 0
2nd black	29–15–0	1 15 3
3rd black	34–33–0	1 7 9
1st red	29–13–0	2 0 6
2nd red	35–1–0	1 5 3
3rd red	40–29–0	0 14 4
1st *burud*	40–14–4	1 2 1
2nd *burud*	40–34–6	0 13 2
3rd *burud*	43–33–0	0 10 0

Pringle's rates			Wingate's rates		
Rate per acre	Total rent	Profit	Rate per acre	Total rent	Profit
3	4	5	6	7	8
Rs. as. p.	Rs. as. p.	Rs. as. p.	Rs. as. p.	Rs. as. p.	Rs. as. p.
1 6 0	39 11 9	32 8 3	1 12 1	50 11 6	
1 1 3	31 10 9	31 10 9	1 3 6	35 13 0	
0 13 0	28 4 9	28 4 9	0 13 10	30 2 2	
1 1 9	32 8 6	27 0 7	1 4 9	38 0 2	
0 11 9	25 11 6	20 16 9	0 11 6	25 15 4	23 8 9
0 7 9	19 11 3	16 12 5	0 5 10	14 14 9	
0 10 0	25 3 6	20 6 1	0 9 7	24 0 8	
0 7 3	18 8 2	15 1 7	0 4 9	12 0 10	
0 5 6	15 1 0	12 5 3	0 2 2	5 13 4	

comparison of columns 3 and 6 in Table D illustrates how drastic a change it would have necessitated in the rates proposed by
Pringle. Rent on the best soils like 1st black and 1st red would
have to be raised by 25 per cent, while rent on the worst soils
like 3rd red and 3rd *burud* would have to be reduced to 33 per
cent of the rates levied by Pringle in Indapur.

Although Goldsmid and Wingate repudiated Pringle's attempt
to foster the growth of a class of rich peasants, it would be a
grave mistake to think that their revenue policy was influenced
in any degree by considerations of egalitarianism. The fate
of Pringle's survey was clear enough warning of the dangers of
a doctrinaire approach to the problems of revenue administration. But Goldsmid and Wingate were as a matter of principle disinclined to attach any exaggerated significance to theoretical considerations in the solution of practical problems.
While Pringle had relied exclusively on the laws of political
economy in devising his scale of rates, and while he had entrusted the measurement and the assessment of fields to the
native officers of the Survey Department, Goldsmid showed
a shrewd awareness of the pitfalls it was necessary to avoid in
devising rates which were reasonable and practical:

> It is absolutely necessary [he pointed out] that in assessing the
> land every field should be visited, and its soil and situation care-
> fully assessed (by the European Superintendent of the survey). To
> conduct such an assessment wholly by myself . . . would be work
> requiring years for its completion. Nor is it requisite that I should
> attempt to do so. For although I can place no confidence in native
> officials of the class we can afford to employ, still I should enter-
> tain four natives, unconnected with the districts, whose duty it
> would be to prepare statements of the quality, quantity and situ-
> ation of the land, and although not probably wholly present in the
> very fields in which the carcoons are present, I should take care to
> be so near at hand . . . as to prevent the possibility of fraud on the
> part of the native subordinates. . . .[1]

Goldsmid and Wingate accepted with minor alterations the
measurement of fields carried out under Pringle's supervision.
The classification of holdings by the native officers of the Survey
Department, however, they found to be completely worthless,
and decided to conduct anew. They graded the fields of the

[1] *BA:* H. G. Goldsmid to R. Mills dated 27 June 1835: R.D., Vol. 44/660 of 1835.

kunbis into nine different categories according to the fertility of the land. But instead of calculating the net surplus of each grade of soil, and then fixing its rent as 55 per cent of this figure (as Pringle had done), Goldsmid and Wingate derived their rates of assessment 'from local enquiry and the experience of qualified persons, without any very minute investigations into actual produce. . . '.[1] The rates at which they assessed fields of different fertility are set out in column 4 of Table E.

Two features of the rates proposed by Goldsmid and Wingate deserve special mention. Taken as a whole, their assessment indicates a considerable diminution in the demand on the land, a

TABLE E

Comparison between the Rates of Pringle, Goldsmid and Wingate

Type of Soil	Pringle's rates	Wingate's rates	Difference %	Goldsmid's rates	Difference %
	1	2	3	4	5
	Rs. as. p.	Rs. as. p.		Rs. as. p.	
1st black	1 6 0	1 12 1	27	0 12 0	−45
2nd black	1 1 9	1 4 9	17	0 8 0	−53
3rd black	1 1 3	1 3 6	12	0 9 7	−47
1st red	0 13 0	0 13 10	9	0 6 10	−46
2nd red	0 11 9	0 11 5	−5	0 5 2	−57
3rd red	0 10 0	0 9 7	−7	0 4 2	−66
1st *burud*	0 7 9	0 5 10	−25	0 3 0	−63
2nd *burud*	0 7 3	0 4 9	−30	0 2 5	−71
3rd *burud*	0 5 6	0 2 2	−62	0 1 0	−67

diminution which they justified on the plea that Pringle had used inflated figures for the prices of food-grains in calculating the net produce. More significantly, while they reduced the rent on all grades of soil, the reduction in rent on the inferior soils like the *buruds* was significantly greater than the reduction in rent on the superior soils like the blacks. As a result of this, while both the *meerasdars* and the *uprees* had their rents lowered under the new rates of assessment, the rents paid by the *meerasdars* were lowered to a lesser extent than the rents paid by

[1] ibid.

the *uprees*. Goldsmid and Wingate thus redressed that imbalance in the burden of rent on the poor cultivators which was the most objectionable feature of Pringle's survey of Indapur. Nevertheless, their rates of assessment were far removed from the egalitarian scale devised by Wingate, which sought to put all cultivators on the same footing, irrespective of the fertility of the soil which they cultivated. All this becomes clear through a comparison of columns 3 and 5 in Table E. To apply the egalitarian scale recommended by Wingate, Goldsmid had not only to reduce the rates levied by Pringle on the inferior soils by 25 per cent but he had also to raise the rates levied by Pringle on the superior soils by 25 per cent. However, Goldsmid was guided by practical considerations rather than by abstract notions of social equity in his survey of Indapur. Instead of basing his rates on the laws of political economy or on egalitarianism, he therefore relied upon 'local enquiry and the experience of qualified persons' in calculating the rent on soils of different fertility.

Although Goldsmid's rates of assessment were less favourable to the *meerasdars* than the rates of Pringle, they were still instrumental in widening the gulf in incomes between the dominant and the poor cultivators in the villages of Maharashtra. This was so because the rates levied by the former government had pressed heavily on the villages, and had trenched deeply into the profits of the dominant *kunbis*, who were responsible for the total demand on the villages, and were therefore required to make up by large personal contributions the sums which the *patils* had contracted to pay to the *mamlatdars*. By virtue of the Goldsmid settlement, however, the *meerasdars'* obligations were fixed for the period of the settlement, and they could not be called upon by the government, or by the village community, to make any additional contributions of rent. The resulting improvement in the condition of the dominant cultivators struck the attention of British officers most forcibly when they resurveyed the Deccan in the 1870s. Throughout the districts of Maharashtra the dominant cultivators had exploited the security and the status which they enjoyed under the *ryotwari* system of Goldsmid and Wingate by erecting *chowries* and *dharamsalas*, which enhanced the respectability of their villages, and by investing their surplus capital in the excavation of wells and tanks for irrigation. So conspicuous was the improvement in the condition of the dominant cultivators that the British officers who resurveyed the districts of Maharashtra mistook their prosperity for the prosperity of rural society as a whole, although this impression was rudely shattered by the Deccan Riots of 1875.[1]

Since the principles of ultilitarianism exercised so powerful a hold over British administrators in India, Goldsmid's reliance upon 'local enquiry and the experience of qualified persons' in determining his rates of assessment was a matter of serious concern to the Government of India. Commenting on his revised rates for Indapur, for instance, Lord Auckland, the Governor-General of India, conceded the harm done by Pringle's survey and the consequent need for a new survey of the *taluka*. But he insisted that it was important to know 'upon what principles the new survey and assessment were to be made'.[2] However, conservative officers like Thomas Williamson refused to pay any attention to such objections, since they believed that 'to introduce an entirely new assessment on a uniform system . . . (could) be liable to be vitiated by the very same errors as the (Pringle) survey itself'. In illustration of the principles which informed the rates of assessment fixed by Goldsmid and Wingate, Williamson recounted the instructions on whose basis they had revised the survey of Indapur. He had asked them to

> restore and revive the *mamool* (or rivaj) assessment where that system was tolerably complete, carefully correcting the survey rates when it was found not difficult to discover and remedy their defects—and when the *mamool* system was obliterated, and the survey was found not to admit of corrections, introducing an entirely new assessment, combining as far as possible moderation and simplicity with correctness, and permanency, suiting, in short, the measure to be adopted to the peculiar circumstances of each village, reverting where practical to the ancient customs with regard to the assessment of the land, and where that could not be done, attempting to fix a sufficiently fair assessment, with as little violent change as possible.[3]

[1] See Report on the *taluka* of Indapur by Colonel J. Francis dated 12 February 1872: *Selections from the Records of the Bombay Government, New Series*, No. CLI.
[2] *NAI:* Minute by the Governor-General of India dated 26 November 1836: Home Department, Revenue Branch, Consultation No. 4 dated 12 June 1837.
[3] *NAI:* T. Williamson to Government of Bombay dated 13 April 1837: Home Department, Revenue Branch, Consultation No. 4 dated 12 June 1837.

Despite the conservative principles which inspired the *ryot-wari* system of Goldsmid and Wingate, and despite the cautious-ness with which they were required to look upon 'the ancient customs with regard to the assessment of the land', the extent to which their revenue policy undermined the traditional insti-tutions of rural society was brought out by J. Thornton, the Secretary to the Government of the North-Western Provinces, in a memorandum in which he reviewed the 'Bombay Plan of Survey and Assessment'.[1] The revenue policies of the Govern-ment of Bombay, Thornton pointed out, were based on a mis-conception of the communal ownership of land in India. It would, for instance, be a mistake to imagine that the cultivators of the North-Western Provinces could not hold land as private property, or that they did not enjoy the fruits of their labour. The communal ownership of land only meant that the holdings of the cultivators were subject to certain common obligations, and that a part of the profit which they derived from their land could be requisitioned to meet the collective obligations of the village community:

> The village communities of upper India [Thornton observed] might easily be reduced to the same state as those in the Deccan. The process would be first, to fix the payments to be levied from such shares, field by field, for the term of settlement, instead of allowing them to vary, as now, with the extent of cultivation in the villages, and other circumstances; secondly, to destroy the joint responsibility; thirdly, to collect the revenue from each man separately, instead of through the representatives of the body; fourthly, to assume possession on the part of the govern-ment 'ghutcool' of all land the owners of which might die without immediate heirs. We should then find, in one or two generations, the precise state of things which exists in the Bombay Presidency.[2]

The most serious consequence of the *ryotwari* system of Goldsmid and Wingate, so Thornton believed, was the aliena-tion of the *kunbi* from his fellow-cultivators in the village. Be-cause of this alienation the *kunbi* was deprived of the moral and

---

[1] Memorandum by J. Thornton, Secretary to the Government of the North-Western Provinces, dated 11 July 1850: *Parliamentary Papers*, Vol. LXXV for 1852–53, pp. 439–45.
[2] ibid.

material support which he had formerly received from the village (organised as a community). The *ryotwari* system, in fact, created a climate of individualism, indeed, of social anarchy in which every cultivator looked after his own interests, or turned to the Government for help, since he could no longer depend upon his fellow-cultivators for assistance. The weakening of the sentiment of solidarity in the villages of Maharashtra was the most harmful consequence of the *ryotwari* system, since it impoverished the *kunbis* morally and materially, and undermined those values of co-operation which had enabled them to triumph over adverse circumstances despite their poverty and their helplessness.

While the *ryotwari* system, Thornton further argued, had weakened the ties of community in the villages of Maharashtra, it was none the less incapable of encouraging the *kunbis* to take fresh land under cultivation, just as it was also incapable of transforming a rural economy based on subsistence into a rural economy based on accumulation. Because of the peace and stability created by British rule there would arise in the cities professional and commercial classes with substantial reserves of capital. In the North-Western Provinces such classes could invest their capital to purchase whole villages, or large and contiguous estates. But because the villages of Maharashtra had been split up into small fields it was impossible for the prosperous urban classes with idle capital in their hands to invest it in agriculture. Even the most fanatical advocate of the *ryotwari* system, Thornton pointed out, could not deny the benefits which the owners of large landed estates bestowed on rural society, since only they were in a position to embark upon new experiments in agriculture, which on proving successful, were emulated by small peasant proprietors who possessed limited reserves of capital.

The *mauzewar* system of the North-Western Provinces, according to Thornton, not only reinforced the sentiment of solidarity in the villages, and promoted innovation and progress in agriculture but it also afforded economic incentives to the cultivator which were not offered to him by the *ryotwari* system. This was so because the former system left the waste land of the villages at the disposal of the village community on the payment of a nominal rent. The cultivators could, therefore, bring this land under cultivation without taking upon themselves any additional financial burden. The situation was quite different under the *ryotwari* system. Goldsmid and Wingate had surveyed and assessed each field in the village, whether it was cultivated or not, and a *kunbi* who wanted to bring waste land under cultivation had to pay its full rent from the outset.

The criticism which Thornton directed against the *ryotwari* system of Bombay was conceived, so Goldsmid and Wingate believed, in equal parts of ignorance about conditions in the villages of Maharashtra, and of misapprehensions about the objectives of the revenue policies of the Government of Bombay. Long before Thornton had attacked their settlement policy, Goldsmid and Wingate had put forth the principles which informed their survey of Indapur in two documents which embody the most succinct exposition of their system. These documents are the 'Joint Report' written by them in 1840, and the additional 'Report' which they wrote together with D. Davidson in 1847. While these documents set out practical solutions to the problems of survey and assessment, they do not in any respect depart from the principles which Goldsmid and Wingate had applied to the survey of Indapur; more particularly, they make it clear that their rates of assessment were based on 'local enquiry and the experience of qualified persons' rather than on the calculation of the net produce of different soils. In answering the criticism levelled against their system by Thornton, Goldsmid and Wingate drew heavily upon the Reports of 1840 and 1847.

While Thornton looked upon a direct relation between the *kunbi* and the State as the great weakness of the *ryotwari* system, Goldsmid and Wingate regarded such a relationship as the means through which the *kunbis* would be aroused from inertia and apathy, and as the great instrument of progress in rural society:

> The limitation of a landholder's liabilities to his own estate [they pointed out] under the Bombay plan of survey, must tend to foster free and independent habits of thought and action, which are greatly wanting in the agricultural population of India, ground down into slavish subserviency and apathy by long ages of despotic rule. . . . (Yet the) municipal institutions have in no wise been destroyed in the surveyed districts. It does not appear that the villages of the surveyed districts are less favourably placed for

acting in concert than those of parts of India where joint responsibility for the discharge of assessment obtains.[1]

Not only was Thornton mistaken, argued Goldsmid and Wingate, in believing that the *ryotwari* system undermined the cohesion of the villages but he was also mistaken in believing that
the *mauzewar* system offered the cultivators great incentives for
extending the operations of agriculture. The extension of agriculture depended upon the amount of surplus capital controlled
by the *kunbis*, and the system which permitted the most rapid
accumulation of capital was the one which provided the maximum encouragement for the extension of agriculture. On such
grounds the *ryotwari* system enjoyed a clear superiority over
other systems of revenue administration. The limitation of the
rent to the land actually under cultivation left a larger surplus
of capital in the hands of the cultivators in the *ryotwari* than in
the *mauzewar* system, which obliged the cultivators to pay an
assessment, admittedly a light assessment, even on the cultivable
waste of the village. Once they had surplus capital in their
hands the *kunbis* were not only encouraged to take waste land
under cultivation but they could afford to pay the full rent on
this land. The superiority of the *ryotwari* system, Goldsmid and
Wingate argued in conclusion, was incontestable, 'since in all
the surveyed districts of Bombay, it is probable that cultivation
was extended beyond what the amount of agricultural capital
warrants, and the revenue returns subsequent to the survey
settlements show that . . . (they) have greatly augmented cultivation. . . .[2]'

In contrast to the *ryotwari* system of Pringle, the settlement
policy advocated by Goldsmid and Wingate was neither based
exclusively on the laws of political economy, nor did it calculatedly foster the interests of the dominant cultivators of Maharashtra. Nevertheless, the settlements of Goldsmid and Wingate
were as much concerned with the problems of economic growth
and social progress as the settlements of Pringle. Nevertheless,
also, in the conditions which prevailed in the 19th century, the
only cultivators who could reap any advantages from their settlements were the substantial *kunbis*. In their report of 1847, for

[1] Memorandum by H. G. Goldsmid and G. Wingate dated 21 December 1850:
Parliamentary Papers, Vol. LXXV for 1852–53, pp. 445–52.
[2] ibid.

instance, Goldsmid and Wingate pointed out that 'the chief reason for a revenue survey may be defined as . . . the progressive development of the agricultural resources of the country. . .'. In saying this they were not implying that they were concerned only with the accumulation of agricultural capital or with the fate of the dominant men in the villages. Indeed, Goldsmid and Wingate actually stated that their system was more favourable to the small farmer than the *mauzewar* system of the North-Western Provinces. In saying this they were merely asserting that their revenue policies favoured the substantial as against the poor cultivators, and in doing so ensured progress in rural society.

While Goldsmid and Wingate abolished Pringle's emphasis on the laws of political economy, they still subscribed to the utilitarian, though not only the utilitarian, belief that the springs of creativity could be tapped only by individuals like the *kunbis*, and not by organised social groups like the *jathas*. This belief was the great driving force behind the *ryotwari* system of land-revenue, which sought to establish a direct relationship between the *kunbi* and the State on the assumption that the *jathas* or the village community merely undermined the initiative of the cultivators. The effect of such a policy, as we shall later see, was to stimulate the growth of a class of rich peasants whose aspirations exercised a decisive influence over the politics of Maharashtra.

IV

The Twilight of the Watandars

DESPITE its far-reaching implications the *ryotwari* system of land-revenue was only one facet of the utilitarian programme of reform for Maharashtra. Pringle and other administrators who were influenced by Bentham were equally anxious to reform other parts of the administration which they had inherited from the Marathas. Since they subscribed to the principles of legality and rationality, and since they also subscribed to the belief that the centralisation of authority ensured efficiency in government, the utilitarians looked upon the administration of the Marathas with marked disapproval. The absence of clear channels of authority in the former government; the ambiguity in the obligations and responsibilities of the *mamlatdars* and other officers; and finally, the arbitrary powers exercised by hereditary officers like the *deshmukhs* and the *patils* were anathema to the utilitarians. An efficient administration, so they believed, was one which possessed a simple and centralised structure, and in which the powers and responsibilities of the various officers were clearly defined. An efficient administration, they further believed, was one which exercised strict control over hereditary officers like the *patils* and the *deshmukhs*, who possessed strong ties of tradition with the villages under their control, and who had consequently been a source of constant trouble to the Peshwas. While the rigorous rationality which characterised Pringle's system of land-revenue had aroused the hostility of administrators like Chaplin and

128

Robertson, the utilitarians and the conservatives were both agreed upon the need for substantial reforms in the rest of the administration. As a result of such a consensus, the institutions of government which grew up under British aegis represented far more drastic a break with tradition than the *ryotwari* system of land-revenue after it had been modified by Goldsmid and Wingate.

Of the institutions which they had inherited from the former government the office of the *deshmukh* was one institution which British officers without exception regarded as completely useless. Under the Marathas, as we have already seen, the *deshmukhs* played a key role in the collection of land-revenue. Indeed, because of their intimate ties with the villages under their charge, and also because of the weakness of the central government at Poona, 'the whole revenue administration was in their hands, though nominally supervised by the *mamlatdars*'.[1] The existence of such powerful subjects was a matter of serious concern to the Government of Bombay, and in 1831 it issued instructions to the Collectors that 'the deshmukhs, etc., should be restricted from all direct interference in the revenue management of the country', and that they were not to be employed as 'agents between the government and the ryots in revenue transactions . . . '.[2] However, while they were no longer permitted to play an important role in the administration of land-revenue the *deshmukhs* were still required to assist the Collector in the collection of rent from the villages. In the language of an official circular the *deshmukhs* were obliged to attend 'to the orders of the camvisdars (native revenue officers) in all matters connected with the ensuring of the prosperity, cultivation, and regular collection of the revenue of the different villages . . . '.[3]

The *deshmukhs* of Maharashtra, however, were men of independent spirit who found the restrictions imposed upon them by the Government of Bombay most irksome, and who preferred to withdraw from their public responsibilities rather than to acquiesce in the inferior status imposed upon them under British rule. Nothing was more indicative of their inferior status

---

[1] *BA:* J. Vibart, Revenue Commissioner, to L. R. Reid, Secretary to the Government of Bombay, dated 21 January 1839: R.D., Vol. 40/1003 of 1839.
[2] ibid.
[3] *BA:* J. Vibart to L. R. Reid dated 26 June 1839: R.D., Vol. 40/1003 of 1839.

than the provisions of Regulation XVI of 1827, which conferred on the Collectors unquestioned authority over all *watandars*. According to Section XVII of this Regulation, the *deshmukhs* and other hereditary officers were required to 'render the usual services of his office, as far as the same may be required by the Collector, under the penalty of suspension from office, pay and emolument'.[1] The reaction of the two *deshmukhs* of Barsi, Wygaji Rao and Daji Dharmaji, to the diminution in their status and authority was by no means atypical of the reaction of the *deshmukhs* as a class, though relations between the administration and the *deshmukhs* did not always result in a crisis. The forefathers of Wygaji Rao and Daji Dharmaji had received the *deshmukhi* of Barsi from Madhav Rao Peshwa in the second half of the 18th century. Prior to 1818 their *watans* had been confiscated by Baji Rao Peshwa on trumped-up charges of treason. When the Government of Bombay assumed control of Barsi, the two *deshmukhs* were restored to favour, although the value of their emoluments was reduced from Rs. 2,454 to Rs. 1,000. Before the sequestration of their *watans*, Wygaji Rao and Daji Dharmaji had provided the *mamlatdars* of the Maratha Government with half a dozen *carcoons* who assisted them in settling the villages of Barsi. But in view of their reduced emoluments under the new dispensation, while the two *deshmukhs* continued to offer their personal services to the Collector of Poona, they flatly refused to provide *carcoons* for the assistance of the revenue officers:

> The government has got our watan [Wygaji Rao and Daji Dharmaji pointed out] yielding a large revenue, and we have only our nemnooks (pensions) for our support; we will render the customary service as we have hitherto done *in person*, but we cannot maintain carcoons. If government wants them, they ought to pay them from the profits they derive from our watans—or give us back our watans, when we will supply carcoons.[2]

The intransigence of Wygaji Rao and Daji Dharmaji reduced the work of settlement in Barsi to a standstill, since the detailed local knowledge of the *deshmukhs* or their *carcoons* alone enabled the officers of the Government of Bombay to fix equitable rents

[1] See Text of Regulation XVI of 1827.
[2] *BA:* T. Williamson to L. R. Reid dated 8 April 1837: R.D., Vol. 41/799 of 1837.

on the *kunbis* and on the villages of Barsi. Yet the *deshmukhs* had played their cards so shrewdly that it was impossible for the Collector of Poona to take disciplinary action against them. As Thomas Williamson, the Revenue Commissioner of the Deccan, pointed out, 'all the fault which the mamlatdar finds with them is that "his lad" (i.e., the deshmukh's son) cannot get through his thirty villages fast enough for the government *carcoons*; but he says at the same time, *that he is at work*'.[1] Moreover, since the Government of Bombay had already decided to reduce the *deshmukhs* to a position of insignificance, the only course open to its revenue officers was to acquire information on their own initiative which would enable them to dispense with the services of such hereditary officers. Indeed, one of the objectives of the surveys conducted by Goldsmid and Wingate was to acquire information which would make British officers of revenue independent of the *deshmukhs* of Maharashtra.

The inferior status of the *deshmukhs* under British aegis, on the one hand, and the concentration of power in the hands of the administration, on the other, were both embodied in the Settlement of 1868 between the Government of Bombay and and the *deshmukhs* of Maharashtra. Such a settlement, which formally reduced the *deshmukhs* to a position of complete impotence, could hardly have been attempted before their duties had become 'obsolete and useless by the introduction of the revenue survey settlements . . . '.[2] The settlement of the *deshmukhs'* claims was entrusted to a Commission comprising Mr. Stewart St. John Gordon, a civil servant attached to the Government of Bombay; the Honourable Madhavrao Vithal Vinchurkar, a member of the Maratha landed aristocracy; and last but not the least, Rao Bahadur Keshav Ramchandra Jog, a retired *daftardar* of the Survey Department. In the inquiries which it conducted among the *deshmukhs* and other hereditary officers the Commission confined itself to two basic questions: first, whether the *deshmukhs* still desired to perform for the government the services which they were required to perform under the terms of their *watans*; and secondly, what proportion of their emoluments

[1] ibid.
[2] Resolution by the Government of Bombay dated 7 March 1863: *Selections from the Records of the Bombay Government*, No. CLXXIV, New Series.

were they willing to surrender in order to be set free of such obligations.

Since the regulations of the Government of Bombay had imposed such irksome restraints upon the *deshmukhs*, few of them exhibited any enthusiasm to perform for the British the services which they had performed for the Marathas. 'We are fairly convinced that the universal feeling is against the acceptance of service,'[1] the Commission pointed out to the Government of Bombay. What compelled the *deshmukhs* to adopt such a stance was more than just the legislation enacted by the Government of Bombay to control hereditary officers. The spirit of the new administration; the principles which sustained it; and the objectives for which it was created were quite different from, if not actually opposed to, the spirit of the former administration under which the *deshmukhs* had thrived. They were men of proud bearing, men who had formerly enjoyed a high status in society, who despised the petty ways of bureaucracy, and who found it humiliating to assist the *camvisdars* and the *daftardars* who were socially their inferiors in the business of settling villages for British officers of revenue.

The discussions between the Commission and the *deshmukhs*, therefore, devolved upon the terms on which the latter could be relieved of their obligations to the administration. The Government of Bombay was of the opinion that all hereditary officers who claimed exemption from service ought to surrender one-fourth of the emoluments of their *watans*. It was also of the opinion that *watans* ought to be convertible into 'saleable property' on the payment of a *nazarana* of one anna in the rupee. These terms formed the basis of the negotiations between the Commission and the *watandars* of Maharashtra. The Commission's proposals, needless to say, did not appeal to all the *watandars*. Indeed, there were 'families of influence, and possessing huge watans' which held out for exemption from service on a deduction of two annas in the rupee. But most *deshmukhs* agreed that the proposals of the Commission represented 'a fair compromise between the rights of the government and the vested interest of the watandars'.[2] The financial implications of the

---

[1] Report of the Commission for the Settlement of the Claims of the District Hereditary Officers dated 21 April 1865: *ibid.*
[2] *ibid.*

Settlement of 1868 can be illustrated by examining the affairs of the *deshmukhs* of Satara. The Commission was called upon to settle the affairs of six substantial *deshmukhs* in the taluka. Waman Shridhar Angapurkar, the most significant of them all, had his emoluments reduced from Rs. 1,342 to Rs. 1,007 per annum; Bapuji Appaji Guzar was obliged to sacrifice Rs. 146 out of an annual income of Rs. 584; and the remaining four *deshmukhs* were similarly obliged to surrender one-fourth of their *watans* as the price of exemption from service. Yet the financial losses suffered by the *deshmukhs* by no means reflected the full consequences of the settlement, since its political implications outweighed its financial implications. More than anything else, the settlement revealed the extent to which men who were formerly the leaders of rural society had abandoned all pretensions to such a role, and had in fact become the instruments of British rule over Maharashtra.

I

Despite the importance of the role which the *deshmukhs* had played under the Marathas, and despite the patronage which they had extended to the *kunbis*, the Government of Bombay did not find it difficult to displace them from power, partly because their links with the *kunbis* were indirect, and partly also because the settlements conducted by the Survey Department made them expendable if not actually superfluous. But the position of the hereditary officers within the villages, namely, the *patils* and the *kulkarnis* was quite different from the position of the hereditary officers outside the villages, namely, the *deshmukhs* and the *deshpandeys*. The *patil* and the *kulkarni* were an intimate part of the village community, and they played a most important role in making it self-sufficient. The abolition of the offices of the *patil* and the *kulkarni* would have necessitated an extension of the administration which the imagination boggles to contemplate. Indeed, whether they were utilitarians like Pringle, or conservatives like Elphinstone, all British administrators were agreed on the indispensability of the *patil* and the *kulkarni*; they were also agreed upon the necessity of reinforcing their authority in order to ensure progress in rural society. That the steps taken by the Government of Bombay to reinforce the position of the village hereditary officers did not necessarily

K

have the desired effect was, of course, an entirely different question.

In our portrayal of the distribution of social and economic power in a typical village like Ambola, and in our portrayal also of relations between Babu Rao Patil Scindiah and the dominant cultivators of this village, we have already indicated some of the sources of the *patil*'s authority. However, to fully understand the position occupied by the *patil* in rural society before 1818, it is necessary to show the extent to which his actions were controlled by the Maratha Government, just as it is also necessary to emphasise the importance attached to social status in a society in which sharp distinctions in wealth were unknown. Both these issues are highlighted in a *muhujur namah* (statement of proceedings) which records an agreement between the *patils* of the village of Kuweeteh in the District of Poona in 1725.[1]

The differences between the *patils* of Kuweeteh stemmed from a long and complicated dispute. At the turn of the 18th century, the *patelki* rights in the village were enjoyed jointly by two families named Khanolkar and Goreh. However, the incompetence of the *patils* combined with a series of natural calamities to reduce the affairs of Kuweeteh to a state of complete confusion, and the village was consequently unable to pay the revenues due to the government. In desperation the *patils* of Kuweeteh 'fell upon the neck' of one Suryaji Waghuree, a scion of a family of *patils* from a neighbouring village, and borrowed a sum of Rs. 1,112 from him to pay arrears of revenue. But this assistance was purchased at a heavy price, since the *patils* Goreh and Khanolkar were in return obliged to share the rights of their office with Suryaji Waghuree:

> At the present moment [stated Vithoji Patil Khanolkar and Hiraji Patil Goreh in a statement setting out their agreement with Suryaji Waghuree] there are large arrears due by the village on account of the jummahbundy and the village has not the means of paying them. In consequence we have importuned you (Suryaji Waghuree) and in conjunction with all the families and lineages in the village, you and we are now as brothers in the affairs of mukudam (or patil). You shall be a third brother, and we will equally enjoy all the rights, privileges, enams etc. of the office, and

[1] *BA:* Appendix to Major Sykes' Report on Poona dated nil: R.D., Vol. 154B of 1826.

perform the pandre (services) together, preserving to us only the precedence. . . . We have now made you our brother and so let it be.[1]

Despite its effusive language, however, the agreement between the *patils* Goreh and Khanolkar, on the one hand, and Suryaji Waghuree, on the other, remained a dead letter. The agreement remained a dead letter because Vithoji Patil Khanolkar and Hiraji Patil Goreh shrewdly exploited the unwillingness of the *kunbis* of Kuweeteh to accept an outsider as their leader, unless he could muster overwhelming force to buttress his pretensions. However, since Suryaji was cheated of the rights which he had acquired through fair and open purchase, it was now his turn to cast around for support. He chose to 'fall upon the neck' of one Anand Rao Powar, a member of a powerful landed family which exercised considerable influence at Satara, then the seat of the Maratha Government. Suryaji Waghuree sold his rights of office to Anand Rao for Rs. 200, and Anand Rao then made a representation at the court of Satara, whereupon the Raja of Satara instructed the *Pant Pratinidhi* to investigate the dispute. The *Pant Pratinidhi* requested the disputants to present their cases before him for arbitration at Pabul on 13 December 1725. However, since the rights of an hereditary office could not be decided solely on the basis of an administrative fiat the *Pant Pratinidhi* simultaneously issued invitations to the *deshmukhs* of the neighbouring districts and the *patils* of the surrounding villages, whose presence could be expected to impart legitimacy to the proceedings of the assembly.

Because Anand Rao Powar belonged to an influential family he secured for himself the rights of a 'third brother' in the *patil-ship* of Kuweeteh at the meeting of 13 December. The *patils* Goreh and Khanolkar, for instance, severally enjoyed an *enam* of 35 *tuckas* of rent-free land in the village. Each one of them was obliged to surrender one-third or $11\frac{1}{2}$ *tuckas* of his *enam* to Anand Rao, providing for the Powar *patil* an *enam* of 23 tuckas. The *meeras* holdings of the *patils* were divided on a similar basis. Khanolkar gave up $11\frac{3}{4}$ *tuckas* of his holding of $35\frac{1}{4}$ *tuckas*; similarly, Goreh surrendered 9 *tuckas* out of his holding of 28 *tuckas*, leaving him with 19 *tuckas*. Anand Rao Powar, of course, thereby accumulated $20\frac{3}{4}$ *tuckas*, while the Goreh and Khanolkar

[1] ibid.

patils were left with 19 and 23¾ *tuckas* of land respectively. The social privileges attached to the *patil*ship were also divided equally between the three *patils*. If Khanolkar had the right to throw the first cake of bread at the burning of the *holi*, then Goreh could claim precedence in receiving *pan supari* on social functions, while Powar enjoyed the right of collecting *sir pao* or presents from the Government on the occasion of the annual revenue settlement. In this manner dignities of the first (*adhemaun*), second (*mudeelmaun*) and third (*magelmaun*) orders were equally divided between the three brothers who shared the rights of *patil*ship over Kuweeteh. The agreement negotiated under the aegis of the *Pant Pratinidhi* and the *deshmukhs* and *patils* of the surrounding districts was embodied in a 'legal' document which bound the disputing parties to strictly honour its clauses. 'As the children of one mother,' the *muhujur namah* stated, 'Khanolkar and Goreh, and Powar and Waghuree are to be united in the service of the (community). . . . In case of disputes in the same mode as formerly he (the perpetrator) will be out of his caste and will be amenable to the Dewan. . . . '[1]

In view of the fate which overtook the *patils* of Maharashtra after 1818 two features of the dispute over the *patelki* rights of Kuweeteh between the Khanolkars and Gorehs, on the one hand, and the Waghurees and Powars, on the other, deserve special mention. These features touch upon the sources of the *patils*' power, and the principles which sustained the administration of the Marathas. The purchase of a share in the *patil*ship of Kuweeteh by Suryaji Waghuree was a transaction of irreproachable legality. But the ties of tradition counted for so much in the villages of Maharashtra that the old *patils* of Kuweeteh successfully prevented Suryaji Waghuree from exercising the rights which he had acquired through fair and open purchase. In the absence of traditional ties only a person like Anand Rao Powar, whose family possessed substantial landed interests and exercised considerable influence over the court at Satara, could establish himself successfully as a 'new' *patil* in a village. The importance of traditional ties is also reflected in the composition of the assembly which met under the aegis of the *Pant Pratinidhi* to resolve the dispute over the *patil*ship of Kuweeteh. In inviting the *deshmukhs* of the surrounding districts, and the *patils* of the

[1] ibid.

surrounding villages, the *Pant Pratinidhi* was clearly acting on the assumption that the court of Satara was no more powerful than the established leaders of rural society in questions affecting the rights of the hereditary officers.

For the hereditary officers in general, and the *patils* in particular, enjoyed under the Marathas a position which it was impossible for them to enjoy under the British Government. Indeed, since the Maratha Government did not attach any exaggerated significance to legality the *patils* had acquired under the former administration habits of independence which led them to exercise their discretion in a way which often embarrassed British officers of revenue after 1818. It is highly unlikely, for instance, that the *patils* of Indapur who entered into *cowls* with Robertson in 1826, and immediately afterwards leased holdings to *uprees* below the stipulated rates, were acting out of malice towards the Collector of Poona. It is much more likely that they were following a practice on which the Maratha Government would not have looked askance, for under the former administration the *patils* 'knew that if they were right in substance, they would not be questioned about the form. . . '.[1]

The principles which distinguished the British administration from the Maratha administration are reflected most clearly in the attempts of the Government of Bombay to exercise a retraining influence over the *patils* and the *kulkarnis* of Maharashtra without undermining their capacity for exercising initiative. These differences stemmed from British concern for efficiency in administration; for the precise definition of the rights and responsibilities of the officers of the government; and for the establishment of unambiguous rules of procedure. However, since the position of the hereditary officers was tied up with the principles which had sustained the former government, the attempts of the Government of Bombay to introduce efficiency in administration, and rationality in bureaucratic procedures, often served to frustrate the objectives which had inspired them in the first instance.

Why the attempts of the Government of Bombay to promote efficiency in administration proved abortive can be appreciated only when we examine how the village hereditary officers like the *patils* fared after 1818. We have already focused on the

[1] Mountstuart Elphinstone's Note on the Maratha States.

sources of the *patil's* power, which rested, on the one hand, on his ties with the *kunbis* of the village, and on the other, on his position as an officer of the State. However, we have still to see how the privileges and the prerogatives of such hereditary offices were disbursed to their incumbents.

The dispute over the *patelki* rights of Kuweeteh indicates that the perquisites of office in that village were shared equally between three families, namely, the Khanolkars, the Gorehs and the Powars. In a majority of the villages, however, the position was far more complicated, and the rights of *patil*ship were

TABLE F

The Principal Sharers and Sub-sharers in the *Patil*ship of Dapoare, *taluka* Ambroli, Ahmednagar District

(There are three principal sharers and thirty-eight sub-sharers in the village)

The *Patil*ship of Dapoare

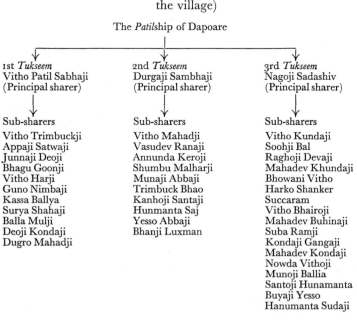

1st *Tukseem*	2nd *Tukseem*	3rd *Tukseem*
Vitho Patil Sabhaji	Durgaji Sambhaji	Nagoji Sadashiv
(Principal sharer)	(Principal sharer)	(Principal sharer)

Sub-sharers	Sub-sharers	Sub-sharers
Vitho Trimbuckji	Vitho Mahadji	Vitho Kundaji
Appaji Satwaji	Vasudev Ranaji	Soohji Bal
Junnaji Deoji	Annunda Keroji	Raghoji Devaji
Bhagu Goonji	Shumbu Malharji	Mahadev Khundaji
Vitho Harji	Munaji Abbaji	Bhowani Vitho
Guno Nimbaji	Trimbuck Bhao	Harko Shanker
Kassa Ballya	Kanhoji Santaji	Succaram
Surya Shahaji	Hunmanta Saj	Vitho Bhairoji
Balla Mulji	Yesso Abbaji	Mahadev Buhinaji
Deoji Kondaji	Bhanji Luxman	Suba Ramji
Dugro Mahadji		Kondaji Gangaji
		Mahadev Kondaji
		Nowda Vithoji
		Munoji Ballia
		Santoji Hunamanta
		Buyaji Yesso
		Hanumanta Sudaji

jointly shared by an enormous brood of *bhowbund* (brothers) whose members squabbled and intrigued incessantly for the perquisites of office. The *patelki* rights of the village of Dapoare in Ahmednagar District, for instance, were jointly shared be-

tween three families or *tukseems* which were headed by Vitho
Sabhaji, Durgaji Sambhaji and Nagoji Sadashiv respectively
(see Table F).[1] However, instead of controlling the one-third
share of the *patil*ship by himself, the head of each *tukseem* merely
represented the interests of his kinsmen, each one of whom
looked upon himself as a candidate for the position of the officiating *patil*. Vitho Sabhaji, for instance, was nothing more than
the spokesman of a large family of eleven kinsmen, who in no
way looked upon themselves as his inferiors, and who were just
as anxious as he was to share the perquisites of office. Similarly,
Durgaji Sambhaji headed a family of ten co-sharers, and Nagoji
Sadashiv represented the interests of no less than seventeen
kinsmen! All told there were forty-one co-sharers in the *patelki
watan* of Dapoare. The *kulkarni*ships, too, were divided among

TABLE G

The Sharers in the *Kulkarni*ship of Malwadi in Sholapur District

The *Kulkarni*ship of Malwadi

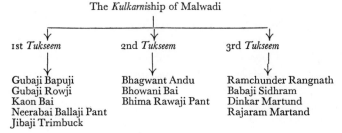

1st *Tukseem*	2nd *Tukseem*	3rd *Tukseem*
Gubaji Bapuji	Bhagwant Andu	Ramchunder Rangnath
Gubaji Rowji	Bhowani Bai	Babaji Sidhram
Kaon Bai	Bhima Rawaji Pant	Dinkar Martund
Neerabai Ballaji Pant		Rajaram Martand
Jibaji Trimbuck		

large numbers of co-sharers. Thus in the village of Mulwadi in
Sholapur District the office of *kulkarni* was divided between
twelve claimants whose shares in the perquisites of office are set
out in Table G.

The *bhowbunds* of *patils* or *kulkarnis* in a village 'elected' one
from among their midst to perform the duties of office. Under
the Maratha Government, however, there was little competition for election to office, since the officiating *patil* or *kulkarni* did
not receive any special privileges to compensate him for the
responsibilities which he was required to shoulder. This does not

[1] *BA:* Statement concerning the nomination of a *patil* in the village of Dapoare,
Ahmednagar District, dated 15 April 1848, by the Collector of Ahmednagar: R.D.,
Vol. 78 of 1848.

mean that the officiator did not do any better than the rest of the *bhowbund*. Indeed, if he possessed even a modicum of shrewdness, which he usually did, then the officiator could make substantial if illicit sums of money while discharging the responsibilities of his office. His illicit gains were often more substantial than his official remuneration if only for the reason that very rarely did the tax collected in a village find its way into the public treasury without enriching the hereditary officers.

The existence of a swarm of squabbling and intriguing co-sharers behind every officiating *patil* or *kulkarni* provided insuperable difficulties in the way of ensuring efficiency and removing corruption in the administration. According to Regulation XVI of 1827 the Collector was entitled to dismiss a hereditary officer if he was guilty of gross misconduct in the discharge of his duties. However, since the dismissal of an officiator merely provided the *bhowbund* with yet another opportunity to elect one from among their midst to office, the powers vested in the Collector held no terrors for the *patils* and *kulkarnis* of Maharashtra, and proved singularly ineffective in restraining the hereditary officers from indulging in acts of corruption and dishonesty.

When the Government of Bombay tried to make the whole *bhowbund* responsible for the officiating *patil* or *kulkarni*, and issued a directive stating that if a *watandar* was guilty of gross misconduct, then the 'watan of that entire family shall be resumed', the hereditary officers of Maharashtra were quick to see the threat to their position, and protested vigorously against the decision of the government. Quite frequently, they pointed out, the co-sharers in a *watan* entrusted their rights to the officiator, and then left their native villages in search of new opportunities. To hold such *watandars* responsible for the actions of the officiator would be most arbitrary. Besides, the decision of the Government of Bombay was contrary to former practice, and would impose great *zoolum* (cruelty) on the *watandars*:

> We beg to submit, that during the several powers which have hitherto swayed over us, no such rule as above described has ever been enforced [the hereditary officers said in a petition to the Government of Bombay]. . . . (It) is repugnant to the law, that a watan which exists from time immemorial should be resumed, because of one of the members of a family to which it belongs, com-

mitted an offence. It is, however, the right of government to punish him who may commit any fault. . . . We, the watandars, have not been guilty of any offence, so as to incur such a displeasure of government. It is, therefore, a matter of surprise that government should issue such orders as above.[1]

The Government of Bombay, however, was not convinced by the arguments advanced by the *watandars* in their petition against its directive. Its stand was set out in a minute by Mr. J. Farish, a member of the Bombay Executive Council. The only security which the government possessed for the proper performance of a *watandar's* duties, Farish pointed out, was the *watan* itself. It was, therefore, quite legitimate for the government to insist that the *bhowbund* as a whole be held responsible for the integrity of the officiating *watandar*. 'I can see no injustice in making the whole watan responsible for the conduct of the officiating officer,' Farish stated. 'He is for the time in possession of the whole office. The duties, and therefore the responsibilities, of the whole (watan) are centred in him.'[2]

The decision of the Government of Bombay to confiscate entire *watans* as punishment for grave misconduct on the part of officiating *watandars* was formally enshrined in Act XI of 1843, which was enacted to remedy the defects of Regulation XVI of 1827. However, the most important provision of Act XI did not concern the punitive powers over the hereditary officers to be vested in the administration. The most important provision of the Act concerned the conditions determining the election of officiating *watandars*. As we have already pointed out, the officiators were in theory 'elected' by members of the *bhowbund* even before the British conquest of 1818. But because the officiating *watandar* had received the same remuneration as the non-officiating *watandars*, such elections had rarely been the source of serious friction between the members of the *bhowbund*. In most cases the *tukseemdars* delegated their powers to the most enterprising and the most energetic member of the *bhowbund*, who compensated himself for the extra burden which fell upon him by illegal exactions from the *kunbis*.

[1] *BA:* Substance of a Petition from the *Watandars* of Ratnagiri *Taluka* to the Government of Bombay dated 15 August 1838: R.D., Vol. 40/1003 of 1839.
[2] *BA:* Minute by Mr. James Farish, Member of the Bombay Council, dated 1 November 1838: R.D., Vol. 40/1003 of 1839.

The relationship between the *watandars* and the administration was dramatically transformed by Act XI of 1843. In the interests of greater efficiency in administration, and in the interests also of strict control over the hereditary officers, the Act vested the Collector with a decisive voice in the selection of the officiating *watandar*. As a concession to popular sentiment in the villages, the Act still required that 'the sharers in a watan shall nominate a fit and proper person from among their number, who shall hold office as the representative of the family. . .'. But in the event of the *bhowbund* being unable to elect a 'fit and proper person' as their representative, the Act required the Collector 'himself to exercise the power of selection, subject to the approval of the Governor in Council'.[1]

The Collectors were obliged to exercise this power all too frequently. This was so because the Government of Bombay had made the position of the officiator far more attractive financially than it had been under the Marathas. Formerly the officiator had received the same remuneration as other members of the *bhowbund,* and he compensated himself for the extra work which fell upon him through illicit exactions. The Government of Bombay looked upon such an arrangement with strong disapproval, and while it enforced honesty upon the *patil* or *kulkarni* by making him subservient to the Collector, it simultaneously raised the emoluments of his office in order to make his job financially attractive. The result of all this was a sudden intensification of social conflict within the villages of Maharashtra, with rival factions of *tukseemdars* squabbling and intriguing among themselves in order to push their nominees into office.

The dispute over the *patelki* rights of the village of Baburwadi in Ahmednagar District illustrates how Act XI of 1843 intensified social conflict in the villages of Maharashtra.[2] It simultaneously illustrates how the concepts of legality and efficiency which sustained the British administration transformed the climate of rural politics. The *patil*ship of Baburwadi was vested in two families, namely, the Khares and the Pomnes. In 1867, when the office of the *patil* fell vacant, the members of the

---

[1] See Text of Act XI of 1843.
[2] *BA:* Petition of Babuji Patil Pomne to the Governor of Bombay dated nil: R.D., Vol. 57 of 1870. Also see Memorandum by the Revenue Commissioner dated 9 July 1870 in ibid.

bhowbund were unable to select an officiator from the two candidates, namely, Manaji Pomne and Babuji Pomne, who pressed their claim to office. As a result of this, the Assistant Collector of Poona appointed Manaji Pomne as officiator, on the ground that the only evidence which Babuji Pomne could produce in support of his claim was that his father, Vithoji Pomne, had served as *patil* from 1828 to 1830. Babuji Pomne appealed against the decision of the Assistant Collector to the Collector of Poona, and he persuaded his collaterals of the Khare *tukseem* to support his candidature before the Collector. The Collector, thereupon, revised the decision of the Assistant Collector, and appointed Babuji Pomne as *patil* of Baburwadi from 1868 to 1873. It was now Manaji's turn to refuse to acquiesce in the victory of his rival. He, therefore, made a representation to the Revenue Commissioner, emphasising that a judicial inquiry conducted in 1862 had revealed that Babuji's claim to the *patil*-ship was null and void. The Revenue Commissioner then reversed the decision of the Collector of Poona, and installed Maruti Pomne, the elder brother of Manaji, as *patil* of Baburwadi.

The conflict between the cousins Pomne had by now attained such a level of intensity that instead of accepting the award of the Revenue Commissioner as final, Babuji Pomne decided to initiate proceedings at the highest level. In a petition to the Governor of Bombay, Babuji pointed out how his cousins Manaji and Maruti had usurped his rights, and how the Assistant Collector and the Revenue Commissioner had refused to accept the legitimacy of his claim. Babuji's representation to the Governor of Bombay had a startling sequel. When the history of Baburwadi was closely investigated it was discovered that neither the Pomnes nor the Khares had any rights in the *patil*-ship of the village. The Government of Bombay, therefore, decided that 'the present incumbent (Maruti Patil Pomne) may be continued in office until his term expires'.

The intrigues and counter-intrigues which prevented the Pomnes Manaji and Babuji from serving effectively as *patils* represented a state of affairs that was repeated in tens upon hundreds of villages in Maharashtra. The litigation inspired by Act XI of 1843 created a climate of tension and strife in rural society which was all the more destructive because it devolved upon issues which were personal and trivial rather than public and momentous. Compared to the Khanolkers and Gorehs of Kuweeteh in the 18th century, the Pomnes and Khares of Baburwadi were men of straw, men who were completely subservient to the will of the administration, and who lacked an independent position in rural society. They fought for the spoils of office rather than for power or prestige. Altogether, they were lesser men than their forefathers, and whether in office or out of it, they were incapable of furthering the interests of the villages.

Contrary to the expectations of the Government of Bombay, therefore, Act XI of 1843 made it virtually impossible for the officiating *patils* and *kulkarnis* of Maharashtra to perform their duties effectively. The Collectors who were required to implement the new legislation were consequently unanimous in their opposition to the Act, just as they were also unanimous in their determination to get it repealed. 'The Act gives to the watandars or the bhowbund, power to elect the officiating member of the watan, and this election affords a perennial subject of dispute, intrigue and litigation in every village throughout the country,'[1] stated Mr. Ashburner, the Collector of Kandeish. His views were identical with the views of Mr. O'Daly, the Collector of Ahmednagar, who had watched the Act undermine the peace of of the villages of Maharashtra:

> Nothing can exaggerate the evil of the present system [O'Daly pointed out]. The amount of labour which it involves is enormous. In this Collectorate about 700 appointments are annually made under the Act.... The present system altogether fails to give satisfaction to the watandars. Endless heart-burnings arise from the appointments, and one half of the petitions which are presented to me are in connection with some appointment which has been made or is about to be made under the Act. . . .[2]

Clearly, then, the necessity of amending Act XI of 1843 soon became obvious to the Collectors, just as it also became obvious to them that the machinery of administration in the villages could grind itself to a halt if the *bhowbunds* were given free rein to squabble and to intrigue among themselves for the rights of

[1] *BA:* Letter by the Collector of Kandeish dated 30 June 1863: R.D., Vol. II of 1867.
[2] *BA:* Letter by the Collector of Ahmednagar dated 1 July 1863: R.D., Vol. II of 1867.

office. A proposal setting out the lines along which Act XI could be amended so as to reduce tension in the villages of Maharashtra was first made by O'Daly, the Collector of Ahmednagar.[1] As a preliminary step, O'Daly suggested, the Government of Bombay ought to embark upon the compilation in each village of a register of rights which would record the names of the various *tukseemdars*, and their shares in the perquisites of office. After such a register had been compiled, so O'Daly believed, the process of selecting an officiator would become relatively simple. When the responsibility of providing an officiator fell upon a particular *tukseem* or family, the *tukseemdars* of other families could quite properly be debarred from using their right of franchise. 'The amendments which I have proposed will, by narrowing the field of selection and reducing the number of claimants, tend less to foster animosities than the present system,'[2] O'Daly stated in conclusion.

The draft Bill prepared by the Government of Bombay to amend Act XI of 1843 went considerably beyond O'Daly's recommendation in restricting 'popular' participation in the selection of officiating *watandars*. In moving the Bill in the Legislative Council, Mr. Chapman, the Member for Land Revenue in the Executive Council, emphasised that its primary objective was to put an end to the squabbling which characterised the selection of *patils* and *kulkarnis* in the villages of Maharashtra:

When Act XI of 1843 was enacted [Chapman told the Legislative Council] rotation (of officiators) was recognised, but unfortunately no provision for providing the proper regulation of shareholders was made. The result has been deplorable. The omission has given rise to a most corrupt scramble among all parties to obtain office. There was no authoritative list from which the nominating officer could make his selection. The consequence was that intrigue, bribery, and corruption were rife amongst all the offices, from the Mamlatdar's up to the Revenue Commissioner's. I believe that I am correct in saying that the great object of the Bill now before us is to amend and simplify the manner in which these appointments are made.[3]

[1] ibid.   [2] ibid.
[3] See Proceedings of the Council of the Governor of Bombay assembled for the passing of Laws and Regulations, 1874, Vol. XIII (Bombay, 1875), pp. 27–33.

According to the provisions of the Bill, popular participation in the selection of officiating hereditary officers was restricted in two specific directions. In the first instance, the Bill provided for a register of rights in each village in order to prevent *tukseemdars* with dubious credentials from swelling the ranks of those entitled to exercise the right of franchise. Secondly, and this was a most revolutionary proposal, the Bill provided that the officiating *watandars* be selected exclusively from the 'representative watandars' or the heads of the *tukseems*.

The notion of a 'representative watandar' was central to the draft Bill, and it went considerably beyond O'Daly's recommendations in narrowing the field of selection for an officiating *watandar*. The implications of this notion can be illustrated through its application to the *patil*ship of Dapoare, which contained three *tukseems* or families comprising forty-one co-sharers. Under Act XI of 1843, all the forty-one co-sharers could aspire to the position of the officiating *patil*. By virtue of the draft Bill, however, only the heads of the three *tukseems*, namely, Vitho Sabhaji, Durgaji Sambhaji and Nagoji Sadashiv could serve as officiating *watandars*. The Bill was, therefore, a most radical step towards controlling 'politics' in the villages of Maharashtra.

The *watandars* protested vigorously against the novel principle which the draft Bill introduced in the selection of officiators. This, at any rate, was what was discovered by A. C. Trevor, the Assistant Collector of Nasik, who was the only officer who bothered to consult the *watandars* about the Bill.[1] Men like Ramji Nave, the *patil* of Dabhui; Parshuram Govinda, the *patil* of Nampur; Gopalrao Parmanand, the *deshmukh* of Andersol; and Shridhar Bapuji, the *kulkarni* of Khambgaon told Trevor that the principle of primogeniture was 'entirely foreign to the constitution of the village watans', and that to introduce it would alienate a large and important section of rural society. Yet officers like H. Erskine, the Collector of Nasik, were disinclined to attach any significance to the views of the *watandars*. If the object of the Bill had been to appease the squabbling *bhowbunds*, Erskine pointed out, then it would completely fail to achieve its purpose. But if its object was to ensure efficiency in the performance of the duties of the hereditary officers, then

[1] *BA:* Memorandum by A. C. Trevor, Assistant Collector of Nasik, dated 19 January 1874: R.D., Vol. 36 of 1874.

'the wishes of the majority (of the *bhowbund*) are not of so much importance as the wishes of the government. . .'[1].

Within the Legislative Council the restriction of the rights of office to the representative *watandars* was opposed by Rao Sahib Vishwanath Narayan, who pointed out that the Bill was contrary to the principles of Hindu law, which did not recognise the right of primogeniture. Besides, the Rao Sahib argued, in extinguishing the rights of the co-sharers the Bill would lower and not raise the quality of men who served as officiating *patils* and *kulkarnis*. In the absence of a tradition of primogeniture, the ablest and most energetic member of a *tukseem* was usually elected to represent the interests of the entire family. Under the new dispensation, however, only the heads of the *tukseems* would enjoy such a privilege, and there was no reason to believe that they were necessarily the fittest persons to lead the village.[2]

Although the Government of Bombay refused to pay any attention to the objections raised by the *watandars* of Maharashtra, and Act III of 1874 disenfranchised all but the 'representative watandars' of the *tukseems*, the new legislation did not undermine the established mores of rural society to the extent apprehended by men like Rao Sahib Vishwanath Narayan. This was so because of the conservatism which influenced the application of the Act. In piloting the Bill through the Legislative Council, for instance, Chapman had made it clear that the government was not seeking to bring about any revolutionary changes in rural society. 'I do hope,' he stated, 'that the officers to whom the working of this Act will be entrusted will be very chary in interfering with the past, and restrain that craving for uniformity, which is to my mind the most unpleasant, and I believe the most unpopular feature of our administration.'[3] The conservative spirit behind the Act was brought out with even greater emphasis in a resolution passed by the Government of Bombay with the object of explaining its provisions to British officers of revenue. The resolution commenced with the declaration that 'it is the greatest desire of government to make as little change as possible'. In the appointment of representative

---

[1] *BA:* Memorandum by H. Erskine, Collector of Nasik, dated 11 February 1874: R.D., Vol. 36 of 1874.
[2] Same as footnote 3, on p. 145.
[3] ibid.

watandars with exclusive rights of service the resolution required the Collectors to proceed with the utmost of caution. After the establishment of British rule, it pointed out, the officiating *patils* and *kulkarnis* had often been selected from a single *tukseem*, and co-sharers belonging to other *tukseems* had acquiesced in such arrangements 'on the understanding that their rights subsisted unaffected'. It was impossible to prove the legal existence of such arrangements, but the Government required the Collectors to 'bring as much work and expenses as possible to their judgement on the evidence, taking care that mere accident shall not prejudice just rights . . . '.[1]

The conservatism which inspired Act III of 1874 is vividly reflected in its application to disputes between rival *tukseemdars* for the right of performing service in hereditary offices. In the village of Sukhane in Nasik District, for instance, the rights of *patil*ship were initially bestowed after a careful inquiry on three *tukseemdars*, namely, Dada Sukhdev, Bhikaji Ganguji and Abha Ganpati.[2] However, Dada Sukhdev claimed to be the sole representative *watandar* in the village, and he consequently petitioned to the Collector of Nasik that the names of Bhikaji Ganguji and Abha Ganpati be struck off the register of rights. Dada Sukhdev advanced three arguments in support of his claim: first, that he was a representative of the eldest branch of the *tukseem*; secondly, that his ancestors had acted as officiators both before and after 1843, whereas the ancestors of the other two claimants had never acted as *patils*; and thirdly, although the families of the other claimants had been consulted in the selection of officiators, such consultation was an empty formality and did not involve the recognition of any specific rights. The reasons advanced by Dada Sukhdev in support of his pretensions carried conviction with the Collector of Nasik, who made a recommendation to the Revenue Commissioner that according to Act III of 1874 the rights of office ought to be vested exclusively in the person of the petitioner. But the Revenue Commissioner took the position that the Collector's decision violated the conservative spirit in which the Government of

---

[1] *BA:* Resolution by the Government of Bombay dated 8 September 1875: R.D. Vol. 37 of 1875, Pt. II.
[2] *BA:* Petition by Dada Sukhdev to the Government of Bombay dated 26 April 1883: R.D., Vol. 267 of 1883.

Bombay wanted the Act to be implemented. The new legislation had not established the right of primogeniture, and it was
also doubtful whether the officiating *patils* of Sukhane had always been drawn from members of Dada Sukhdev's family. In
the light of such considerations, the Revenue Commissioner rejected the petition of Dada Sukhdev and confirmed all the three
co-sharers, namely, the petitioner, Bhikaji Ganguji and Abha
Ganpati in the rights of office.

A similar spirit of conservatism characterised the resolution of
disputes between the *tukseemdars* of the villages of Pimpri and
Ralegaon in Poona District.[1] In the former village, before 1874
the rights of office had been shared equally between two families called Jadhav and Kute respectively, of which the latter was

TABLE H

A Genealogical Table of the Kute Family of Pimpri Showing the
Officiating *Patils* between the Years 1825–65

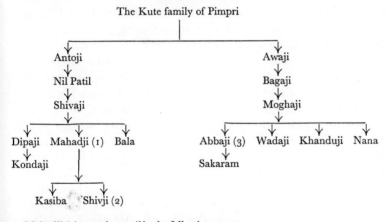

The Kute family of Pimpri

Mahadji (1) served as *patil* in the following years:
1825–26, 1827–28, 1833–34, 1840–41 and 1842–43.
Shivji (2) served as *patil* in the following years:
1853–54 and 1864–65.
Abbaji (3) served as *patil* in the following years:
1841–42, 1842–43, 1855–56 and 1861–62.

divided into two collaterals, namely, Shivji Mahadji and
Abhaji Mogaji (see Table H). When the register of rights for
Pimpri was prepared in 1878 Shivji Mahadji was appointed the

[1] *BA:* Memoranda by the Patils of Pimpri and Ralegaon dated nil and 10 February
1881, respectively: R.D., Vol. 206 of 1881.

representative *watandar* of the Kute *tukseem*, whereupon Abhaji Mogaji petitioned to the Governor of Bombay, presenting in substantiation of his claim a genealogical table which showed that he had officiated as *patil* on various occasions. On the basis of the evidence produced by Abhaji Mogaji, the Governor of Bombay reversed the decision of the Collector of Poona, and appointed both Shivji Mahadji and Abhaji Mogaji as representative *watandars* of the Kute *tukseem*.

Despite appearances to the contrary, therefore, Act III of 1874 did not bring about any dramatic changes in rural society, nor did it significantly lower the intensity of social conflict in the villages of Maharashtra. In the first flush of enthusiasm the Collectors often appointed single representative *watandars* for families in which the rights of office had formerly been shared between two or more *tukseemdars*. But such decisions were invariably reversed by the Government of Bombay, which in the course of time established precedents that ensured the application of Act III of 1874 along truly conservative lines. The net result of the legislation passed under British aegis to control the hereditary officers was, therefore, to set *tukseem* against *tukseem*, and co-sharer against co-sharer, in a sordid scramble for the emoluments of office. This is not to imply that disputes between rival claimants for office were unknown before 1818. Under the Marathas, as the example of Kuweeteh illustrates, the *tukseemdars* of the *watans* were often divided into hostile factions which squabbled over the rights of office. But the stakes in such conflicts in the 18th century were quite different from the stakes in similar conflicts in the 19th century. The *patils* of Kuweeteh fought for the rights of leadership over the village; in contrast, their compeers in the villages of Sukhane and Pimpri fought for the emoluments of office. The Gorehs and the Khanolkars were men of substance and power, over whom the central government exercised a precarious control. The Kutes and the Jadhavs of the 19th century were mere creatures of the administration, incapable of exercising any initiative, and alienated from the *kunbis* whose affairs they supervised. Their intrigues and their politics were designed to secure for them nothing more substantial than the emoluments of office.

V

The Deccan Riots of 1875

THE redistribution of social power in the villages of Maharashtra which stemmed from measures of reform inspired by utilitarianism led to a growth of social tension that erupted in the disturbances of 1875. While all the social groups in rural society were affected by the reforms introduced by the new rulers of Maharashtra, the tensions which resulted from these reforms found their clearest expression in the relationship between the *kunbis* and the *vanis*. Even before the British conquest of Maharashtra, rural indebtedness was widespread in the region, and an inquiry into the condition of a village like Lony in 1820 illustrates something of its extent.[1] But under the Marathas the *kunbis* dominated the villages despite their indebtedness to the *vanis*, because they enjoyed a numerical preponderance, and also because the *vanis* were isolated from their caste-fellows in other villages. The *mamlatdars* who represented the government were unconcerned about the *vani*'s fate so long as he kept the rural economy on the move. The only judicial institution to which the *vani* could appeal for the recovery of his debts was the *panchayat*. But since the *panchayat* was dominated by the *patil* and other influential *kunbis* in the village, it was hardly an institution that gave fair consideration to the *vani*'s claims. Because the *kunbis* controlled the institutions which dispensed justice within rural society, the *vanis* were prevented from exercising

[1] T. Coats, 'Account of the Present State of the Township of Lony', *Transactions of the Literary Society of Bombay*, III (London, 1823), pp. 183–250.

a social dominance over the villages comparable to the economic dominance they exercised over the rural communities.

I

The most crucial of the changes in Maharashtra after the British conquest was the introduction of the *ryotwari* system of land-revenue. The *ryotwari* system weakened the sentiment of solidarity in rural society through abolishing the collective responsibility which the *kunbis* had formerly borne for the fiscal obligations of the villages. It was also responsible for reorganising rural credit along novel lines. Under the Marathas, the role of the *vani* who resided in the village was sharply differentiated from the role of the *sowcar* who resided in the city. The *vani* was a member of the village community, and he was obliged to acquiesce in its judicial and its executive authority. He was a shopkeeper as well as a moneylender, and his meagre resources of capital were tied up either in small advances in money to the *kunbis*, or in loans of grain to cultivators who had exhausted their reserves before the harvest. Due to his physical isolation, and because he was dependent upon the *kunbis* for the security of his person and property, the *vani* never presented any threat to the village. The *sowcar*, on the other hand, was a somewhat different person, not only because of the scale on which he conducted his business but also because of his position *vis-à-vis* the rural community. Instead of dealing with the cultivators directly, he advanced loans to villages through their *patils* in order to enable them to fulfil their fiscal obligations to the government. By advancing such loans the *sowcar* was able to control all the surplus produce of the village for disposal in the *pethas* of the cities. However, he did not desire to establish a more intimate control over the economy of the villages, even though it was possible for him to do so, since it was contrary to the style of his caste to participate directly in agriculture. Thus when in 1827 the Government of Bombay tried to relieve the villages of their indebtedness by giving grants in land to the *sowcars*, the *sowcars* revealed their unwillingness to take upon themselves direct responsibility for agriculture by refusing to accept land in compensation for the loans they had advanced to the villages.[1]

[1] *BA:* R. K. Arbuthnot to Bombay Government dated 23 September 1826: R.D., Vol. 43/196 of 1827.

The introduction of the *ryotwari* system, however, changed the role of the *sowcar* in the supply of credit to the village. Since the new system emphasised the responsibility of the individual for the payment of the land-tax, credit was now required by the peasant, and not by the village community. The *sowcar*, therefore, no longer had any dealings with the *patil* as the head of the village community. Instead, he dealt with each peasant individually. But since it was difficult for the *sowcar* to conduct business directly with the peasant, he preferred to work through his caste-fellows, the *vanis* in the villages. As a result of such a reorganisation of rural credit the *vani* developed business relations with his caste-fellows outside the village to a far greater extent than ever before. Also as a result of the reorganisation of rural credit, the *sowcar* supported the *vani* in every possible way to fulfil the new role which had become open to him. All this not only strengthened the position of the *vanis* vis-à-vis the *kunbis* but it also increased the intensity of friction and the occasions for conflict between the two castes. Indeed, in the decades following the British conquest, the antagonism between the *kunbis* and the *vanis* became the most disturbing source of tension in the villages of Maharashtra.

Nothing did more to heighten this tension than the awards of the new courts of law which were instituted by the Government of Bombay. These courts not only wrested judicial authority from the *kunbis* but their awards were based upon concepts of equity and legality which favoured the *vanis* rather than the *kunbis*. The consequences of such awards were brought to the notice of the Government of Bombay in a petition presented by the *ryots* of Thana in 1840. The petition opened with an enumeration of the blessings which British rule had conferred on Maharashtra. Life and property, the *ryots* pointed out, were secure as they had never been secure before; arbitrary taxes had been abolished; and the *deshmukhs* and other hereditary officers who had formerly oppressed the cultivators were firmly under the control of the government. But, the *ryots* continued, 'though we live under such protection and prosecute out labour free of any apprehension of oppression, yet our families are reduced to a miserable condition, so much so that their ordinary wants even cannot be supplied'. The reason behind the 'miserable condition' of the *kunbis* was simple. To cultivate their fields properly, the *ryots* were forced to borrow money from the *vanis*. Under the former rulers, the *vanis* had levied interest on loans of money at rates varying from 25 to 50 per cent; and on loans of grain at rates varying from 30 to 60 per cent. In the case, however, of *usmani sultani* (natural or artificial calamities) the *vanis* had recovered their advances with moderation, since the Maratha Government

> never allowed its ryots to be oppressed by usurious demands, and consequently the Sahookar did not carry any complaint to the Government. Considering the Sahookar as our parent and that he would save our lives at a critical moment, we settled our claims according to our circumstances. Thus both the ryot and the Sahookar were able to sustain their situations.[1]

But the relationship of trust and confidence between the *ryots* and the *vanis* had been transformed through the institution of the courts of law, and the promulgation of the regulations, into a relationship of acute antagonism. The *vanis* now inveigled the *ryots* into legal contracts of dubious equity, and if a *ryot* failed to fulfil such a contract, the *vani* instituted a civil suit against him. As a result, the 'whole of his (i.e. the ryot's) property is disposed of; and he is reduced to such a condition as never to regain his footing in society'. This was possible because the *ryots* were unaware of the implications of legal contracts, and could be persuaded to sign agreements whose significance they failed to comprehend. In contrasting their miserable plight under the Government of Bombay to their condition under the Peshwas, the *ryots* pointed to the obvious solution of the problem:

> Under the late Government we suffered great oppression, but no one could sell our immovable property or lands, etc., and therefore we were able to endure the oppression both of Government and of the Sahookars. . . . Under the present Government, by the sale of our immovable property we are reduced to a starving condition in the same manner, as a tree when its roots are pulled out, dies. We are neither Shroffs, nor traders, and we are not acquainted with the regulations of the Courts. The Vakheels whom we employ, extort money from us in the first instance, under various pretences, and when the cause is lost, advise us to make an appeal.

[1] *BA:* Petition signed by 7,215 *Ryots* of Thana District dated 27 July 1840: R.D. Vol. 110/1194 of 1827.

Let Government therefore consider whether the cultivator is able to litigate with the Sahookar. . . . (We) beg . . . that our cases may be referred to the Panchayats, who should decide on the claims and liabilities of the parties with reference to the circumstances of each, agreeably to the ancient custom.[1]

The appeal of the *kunbis* of Thana pointed to a social malaise of an intensity which was both alarming and explosive. It is true that in representations to the government the peasants as a matter of habit painted their misery in lurid and heightened colours; but the accuracy of the *kunbis'* description of their condition was confirmed by an official inquiry into the state of the rural districts of Maharashtra. Because rural indebtedness had been widespread even before 1818, the seriousness of the problem caused little surprise to the Government of Bombay, even though a Collector pointed out that in the *talukas* of Khair and Mamul under his charge there was scarcely a village in which it was possible to find 'three persons, ryots or zamindars, *not* in debt for sums above rupees one hundred'.[2] But what perturbed the Government of Bombay was the stranglehold which the moneylender was gradually acquiring over the *ryot*. Within two decades of British rule the predominance of the *vanis* had become so characteristic a feature of the villages of Maharashtra that not a single administrator questioned its existence, even though District Officers differed in their assessment of its implications for the future of rural society, and for the administrative policies of the government. The majority of British officers attributed the problem to the rapacity with which the *vani* conducted his financial dealings with the *kunbi*.[3] But administrators like Pringle believed that the *vani* was a much maligned creature. They also believed that his rates of interest were in keeping with his risks and did not exceed the normal profits of capital. Indeed, when Pringle looked at the condition of rural society in Maharashtra, he characterised the *vanis* as a class which formed the only connecting link between 'civilisation and barbarism'. He also argued that although the *kunbis* were 'loud in their complaints against their creditors, yet I imagine they would be the

[1] ibid.
[2] *BA:* B. Frere, Assistant Collector of Poona, to P. Stewart, Collector of Poona, dated 2 July 1840: R.D., Vol. 1664 of 1844.
[3] *BA:* M. Rose, Assistant Collector of Poona, to P. Stewart dated 15 July 1840: R.D., Vol. 1664 of 1844.

first to suffer by, and not less ready to complain against, any restrictions which would deprive them of the aid of so useful a class'.[1]

When Pringle focused attention on the part played by the *vanis* in the rural economy, he could hardly lay claim to any great originality. For British officers who looked upon the *vanis* as rapacious recognised only too well the significance of their role. The *ryots* rarely possessed any reserves of capital, and they seldom had access to liquid money. It was the *vanis* who helped them to pay their land revenue, and it was the *vanis* once again who enabled them to fulfil such obligations of caste and religion as were essential to their self-esteem and status in society. The *vanis* were consequently valuable members of the villages, without whose assistance the cultivators could be reduced to great distress. What the 'anti-*vani*' British officers deplored, however, was the unscrupulousness with which the *vanis* conducted their dealings with the *kunbis*. In the districts which surrounded Poona, for instance, an officer like Bartle Frere regarded a return of 10 per cent as reasonable in a region where there was so little employment for capital. Yet interest on loans in the villages around Poona ranged from 25 to 60 per cent. When Frere looked at the cost at which the *vani* met the needs of the cultivators, he described him as 'one of the greatest obstacles upon the prosperity of society'.[2]

In the decades which followed upon 1818, therefore, relations between the *kunbis* and *vanis* progressed along lines which boded ill for the future. With his greater sophistication, and his greater ability to grasp the implications of the laws and regulations, the *vani* became more and more of a power in rural society. His progress towards social dominance was facilitated by the new courts of law. The increase in civil suits instituted against the *kunbis* proves that the *vani* recognised in these courts a most convenient instrument for furthering his interests. In the District of Ahmednagar, for instance, cases involving *ryots* increased by practically 100 per cent (from 2,900 to 5,900) between the years 1835 and 1839. This increase clearly demonstrates the 'knowledge

[1] *BA:* R. K. Pringle, Collector of Kandesh, to Bombay Government dated 17 July 1840: R.D., Vol. 1664 of 1844.
[2] *BA:* B. Frere, Assistant Collector of Poona, to P. Stewart, Collector of Poona, dated 2 July 1840: R.D., Vol. 1664 of 1844.

that the Marwarree has acquired of the Regulations, and of the powerful regime they afford him for exacting the fulfilment of the most usurious contracts which ever disgraced any country. . . '.[1] A substantial proportion of these suits resulted in the transfer of holdings from the *kunbis* to the *vanis*. But since the social values of the *vanis* prevented them from cultivating the land, they permitted the former proprietors to cultivate their fields, and appropriated all the profits of their labour after providing them with the bare means of subsistence. The style of life of the *vanis* was, indeed, the most formidable obstacle in the progress of rural society. For it prevented a transformation through which the small peasants of Maharashtra would have given way to a class of capitalist farmers who possessed large landed estates, and who also possessed the resources to cultivate them efficiently. The *vani*, a District Officer pointed out, did not

> by a liberal expenditure of his part of his gains make up for the poverty of the ryots. . . . Seldom do you see them (the vanis) improving any property that may have come in hand, or in embarking on any speculation such as sugar plantations, cotton or the cultivation of silk. Their thoughts and speculations are confined to their ledger and money transactions, and in no instance have I ever found a banian step forward . . . to aid in any work of public activity.[2]

The transfer of dominance over the villages from the *kunbis* to the *vanis* proceeded at a rapid pace after the rural districts of Maharashtra had been settled on the basis of the *ryotwari* system of Goldsmid and Wingate. Barely three decades after the completion of the first revenue surveys, the Commissioners who investigated the Riots of 1875 discovered that in one village after another the *kunbis* had been gradually dispossessed of their holdings by the *vanis* who thrived under the new dispensation. In village after village the Commissioners observed identical changes. The *patil* and the principal cultivators, who had formerly presided over the affairs of the village, were reduced to the position of tenants who tilled the fields owned by the *vanis*. Their position as the most privileged social group in rural

[1] *BA:* Letter from the Collector of Ahmednagar to Bombay Government dated 30 October 1840: R.D., Vol. 1664 of 1884.
[1] *BA:* B. Frere, Assistant Collector of Poona, to P. Stewart, Collector of Poona, dated 2 July 1840: R.D., Vol. 1664 of 1844.

society was a thing of the past. It was the *vanis* who now dominated the villages of Maharashtra. But caste prejudices and a
deep-rooted sentiment of conservatism prevented the *vanis* from
exercising that active leadership over rural communities which
had formerly been exercised by the cultivators whom they had
dispossessed.

The rise of a *nouveau-riche* caste of *vanis* to positions of dominance in rural society can be illustrated by examining the affairs
of a village like Parner in the Ahmednagar District.[1] Parner
was a substantial village, the headquarters of a *taluka*, and a
mamlatdar's station. In it resided fifty *vanis*, mostly marwaris by
caste, whose financial dealings were not confined to Parner but
also extended to the neighbouring villages. The *patil*ship of
Parner was held by a family called the Kowreys. At the time
of the British conquest it was a coveted office, with the *patil* owning 160 acres of fertile land. In 1840 the Kowrey estate was partitioned into two shares of 80 acres each. A further subdivision
took place soon afterwards, with Rowji Kowrey and Babaji
Kowrey, two grandsons of the *patil* at the time of the British conquest, receiving shares of 40 acres each. In 1863 Rowji Kowrey
borrowed a sum of Rs. 200 from Rajmull Marwari to buy a
standing crop. He paid a sum of Rs. 150 on the original bond
by the sale of his own standing crop, and signed a second bond
of Rs. 100 for the balance. He then paid Rs. 24 yearly for three
years, and in 1866 the bond was renewed for Rs. 175. Rajmull
subsequently sued him for a sum of Rs. 388, and obtained a
decree on the strength of which he acquired Rowji's share of the
Kowrey estate. Since he was dispossessed of his holdings, Rowji
Kowrey migrated to his wife's village, where he eked out a
miserable existence as a labourer on daily wages. Babaji
Kowrey's fate was no better than the fate of his brother, since
his share of the family estate was in possession of Vittoo Marwari of Parner. Between them the marwaris Rajmull and Vittoo
had thus humbled the once proud Kowreys to the dust. 'There
is not now one yoke of bullock or acre of land in Parner village
held by the Kowreys,' the Report of the Deccan Riots Commission stated, 'though some of the family are still cultivating land
in the hamlets.'[2]

[1] *Report of the Deccan Riots Commission* (Bombay, 1876), II, Appendix C, pp. 66–9.
[2] ibid.

The decline of the *kunbis* and the rise of the *vanis* can also be illustrated through contrasting the eclipse of the Kowreys with the emergence of a marwari family like the Karamchands of Parner:

> The first immigrant of this family was Karamchand, who came to Babulwari in Parner, about 60 years ago. Karamchand had four sons. Tukaram, the eldest, came to Parner about 39 years ago as his father's agent; served him in that capacity for two years. Then the father lent him Rs. 150 at annas 12 per cent, per mensem, and he set up on his own account. Now his khata in Parner and Nagar talukas is Rs. 664 for government assessed land . . . (which) represents an annual produce of Rs. 3,600. How much land is mortgaged to him, and what may be the amount of his annual dealings, it is impossible to say with any accuracy. . . . (The) kulkarni states that Tukaram was assessed in 1871–72 at Rs. 2,000 per annum.[1]

The fate of the Kowreys and the Karamchands is not an isolated instance of the decay of the *kunbis*, or of the rise of the *vanis*. The *deshmukhs* of Parner, for instance, held 500 acres in 1818, but between 1818 and 1875 all their land had passed into the hands of the local marwaris. At a more prosaic level came *kunbis* like Andu Dhondiba, once the proud owner of 30 acres of land, all of which were now mortgaged to a *vani*; or Tantia bin Bapu Gaikwad, whose holding of 150 acres had passed over to Kapurchand Marwari for the paltry sum of Rs. 75; or Navji bin Trimbakji, whose 48 acres were held by Oodaram Marwari against a loan of Rs. 35 contracted in 1860. Typical *vanis* whose rise in affluence and status coincided with the decline of the *kunbis* were individuals like Chandrabhan Bhuban, who started from humble beginnings in 1840, and had acquired land assessed at Rs. 2,000 by 1875; or Hariram Bhuban, who hailed from a family which had settled in a village near Parner in 1818, and who had since amassed a small fortune for himself within half a century.

The dominance of the *vanis* over rural society in 1875 is also reflected in the affairs of a village like Oorli which was located in Poona District.[2] Oorli had a population of 1,264 souls, an annual assessment of Rs. 3,735, and 2,158 acres of land under cultivation. It was also the happy hunting ground of five *vanis*,

[1] ibid. [2] ibid.

whose total claims amounted to Rs. 16,000. Tukaram was the most substantial of the *vanis* of Oorli. His biggest debtor was Buggaji Panduji, who owed him a sum of Rs. 1,300, and paid him in return Rs. 75 worth of produce and cash every year. In addition, Tukaram had acquired control over the holdings of two *kunbis* called Marooti and Genoo Subaji, and he proposed to institute civil proceedings against another *kunbi* called Jotee. Only two of the other moneylenders of Oorli, namely, Muniram Marwari and Govinda Vani, were men of any substance. Muniram had claims amounting to Rs. 2,500, while Govinda had loaned Rs. 1,000 to different *kunbis* in the village. Between them the *vanis* of Oorli controlled all the *kunbis* of the village, and they appropriated the agricultural surplus of Oorli for disposal in the *petah* of Poona.

While the extent to which the *kunbis* were losing out to the *vanis* is revealing in itself, the full implications of the growing dominance of the *vanis* can be appreciated only if account is taken of the style of life of the *kunbis*, and of the wider economic context in which they were being dispossessed of their holdings. The changes which we have described in rural society were not accompanied by the growth of cities or by any marked increase in industrial activity. Because there was no outlet to the cities, the dispossessed peasant was forced to eke out a wretched existence as a landless labourer, often on those very fields which he had formerly cultivated as an independent proprietor. However, even if the growth of economic activity in the cities had provided an alternative avenue of employment for the *kunbis*, it is doubtful whether their social values would have permitted them to adapt themselves readily to a new style of life. All this meant intense suffering and frustration for the *kunbis*, who were being dispossessed of their holdings by the *vanis* through legal processes which they were unable to comprehend, and which were opposed to their notions of social equity.

II

The increasing bitterness between the *kunbis* and the *vanis* of Maharashtra contained the seeds of a bitter conflict. But while the dispossession of humble *kunbis* like Andu Dhondiba or Navji bin Trimbakji was serious enough in itself, the simultaneous decline of influential men like the Kowreys or the *deshmukhs* of

Parner generated social tension of an intensity that was bound
to cause an upheaval. What was implicit in the social climate
became explicit through two factors which heightened antagonism between the *kunbis* and the *vanis*, and added to the atmos-
phere of disquiet in rural society. The revision of the Goldsmid
Settlement in the 1860s combined with the dislocation in the
economy of Maharashtra caused by the Civil War in America
to transform the dormant antagonism between the *kunbis* and
the *vanis* into open conflict in rural society.

The revision of the tax on land was an important undertaking
in the rural districts of Maharashtra, where virtually all sections
of the community subsisted on the produce of agriculture. The
importance of the revision was enhanced by the principles of
political economy which sustained the revenue system. According to these principles the State was the supreme landlord in
India, and could alter at will, and according to the dictates of
political expediency, the share in the profits of agriculture
which it awarded to the cultivators. A resurvey involved an
assessment of the changes in the profits of cultivation, and it
simultaneously involved an assessment of the proportion of these
profits which the State could claim as its own. A revision of the
tax on land was therefore bound to stimulate excitement, and
could easily arouse discontent, among the cultivators.

The changes which characterised Maharashtra over the
thirty years of the Goldsmid Settlement can be seen clearly
through focusing attention on Poona, the former capital of the
Peshwas, and on the *taluka* of Haveli, which surrounded it.
Poona itself had fallen into reduced circumstances in the 1860s,
though it was still a considerable city, with a population of
75,000. The deserted palaces of the Peshwas, and the empty
houses of those landed chiefs whose fate we have already
sketched at some length, bore silent testimony to its political
decline. But the institution of a municipality in 1864, which was
managed by a class of educated Maharashtrians of whom more
later, and which had cleaned and widened the principal streets of
the city within three years, spoke in clear accents of the shape of
things to come. Similarly, the flourishing *petah* which assembled
each day in front of the deserted Shanwar Palace, the former
residence of the Peshwas, epitomised the change that had come
over Maharashtra after the British conquest of 1818.

For the establishment of the *Pax Britannica* had transformed Maharashtra in a way it had never been transformed before. Peace, stability in politics and the rule of law were three of the more obvious influences at work under the new dispensation. But there were, besides, a host of other influences which moulded society in Maharashtra in a new shape. The state of communications, for instance, had altered beyond recognition. Since Haveli surrounded a city of the size and importance of Poona, it was particularly fortunate in this respect, but what happened in Haveli was by no means atypical of the rest of Maharashtra. In contrast to the primitive state of communications under the Marathas, a railway line now ran through the *taluka*, and it stopped at four stations within the territorial limits of Haveli. Besides, there were roads of good quality which linked Poona with places like Bombay, Nasik, Satara and Sholapur. Since all the roads converged on the former capital, they afforded easy access to the supplies of food and consumer goods which were required for so large a city. The increase in facilities for the transport of agricultural produce, and the growth of markets for their disposal, stimulated the growth of population and the extension of cultivation in the rural districts of Maharashtra. The population of eighty-one villages in Haveli for which figures are available rose from 37,695 in 1840 to 58,829 in 1870. While statistics are not available for the preceding decades, it is highly likely that the population did not register any significant increases before 1818. The increase in population led to an increase in the area of land under cultivation, and equally inevitably, inferior soils were taken up for agriculture. In the eighty-one villages of Haveli under consideration the area under cultivation rose from 176,974 acres to 204,135 acres during the thirty years of the Goldsmid Settlement. Already Maharashtra appeared to be poised on the edge of a Malthusian abyss![1]

Such were the altered conditions which confronted J. Francis and W. Waddington, the Superintendents of the 'Revenue Survey and Assessment of the Deccan', when they applied themselves to the revision of the Goldsmid Settlement in 1867. Like Robert Keith Pringle in the 1820s, Francis and Waddington

[1] Report on the Taluka of Indapur by Col. J. Francis dated 12 February 1867: *Selections from the Records of the Bombay Government*, New Series, No. CLI. Henceforth referred to as Francis' Report on Indapur.

first turned to the *taluka* of Indapur in the hope of devising a scale of assessment which could then be applied to other districts after appropriate changes on the basis of local variations in productivity. The principles which guided their operations were quite different from the doctrinaire presuppositions which had inspired Pringle's survey of 1830, and which had also ensured the failure of that survey. But while Francis and Waddington were not pedantic utilitarians, they none the less subscribed to the Ricardian view that the extension of cultivation which had taken place under the Goldsmid Settlement indicated a rise in the profits of agriculture which could justify an increase in the rents levied by the State. With this assumption George Wingate, one of the founders of the 'Bombay System of Survey and Assessment', was in complete agreement:

> The land assessment . . . is not a tax at all [stated G. Wingate in a memorandum approving of Francis' Report on Indapur], but a share of the rent which the land yields to its possessors. This share of the land rent has from the dawn of history formed the great fund from which expenses of government in India have been defrayed, and in an agricultural country like India the land must ever remain a great source of taxation from which the expenses of Government will have to be supplied. The government right to increase the land assessment is the property of the public, and forms a sacred trust, which, in my humble opinion, the government is bound to transmit to its successors unimpaired. . . .[1]

The theoretical reason for a revision of the rates levied by Goldsmid was reinforced by the errors discovered by Francis in the measurement of fields by the former surveyors. All these errors were not fortuitous, for Goldsmid had concerned himself exclusively with the measurement of the better quality of land, and he did not take into account inferior soils. However, apart from land which was left deliberately unmeasured by Goldsmid, holdings had increased in area because the Survey Department had not erected the boundaries of fields till a decade after the first settlement, during which interval the *kunbis* had surreptitiously taken under cultivation the unclaimed land which surrounded their fields. In the villages of Baura, Kalas, Shetphal

---

[1] Memorandum by Sir G. Wingate (on Francis' Report on Indapur) dated 12 February 1869: *Selections from the Records of the Bombay Government*, New Series, No. CLI.

and Nagunda in Haveli, for instance, the *ryots* had appropriated between 1,500 and 2,000 acres of land of which the records of the Survey Department made no mention. The surreptitious extension of their holdings by the *ryots* obliged Francis to devise a new classification of fields. The need for reclassification became obvious to Francis when, on remeasurement, a field which had been recorded as 30 acres under the old survey turned out to be 40 acres in area. If the 30 acres formerly taken into account were of medium fertility, and the 10 acres 'added' by the *ryot* of a poor quality, then the entire field had to be reclassified if its owner was to escape over-assessment.

However because the revenue system was based on the principles of political economy enunciated by Ricardo, the need for a revised scale of assessment existed independently of the surreptitious extension of their holdings by the *kunbis*. Since there were no intermediate proprietors whose increased rentals could provide an index of the rise in profits of agriculture over the

TABLE I

Table Showing Fluctuation in the Price of Jowri between 1836 and 1866

Price	Year		Year	Price		Year	Price
	1836–37	43	1846–47	65		1856–57	32
	1837–38	36	1847–48	48		1857–58	39
	1838–39	67	1848–49	72		1858–59	32
	1839–40	44	1849–50	72		1859–60	39
	1840–41	64	1850–51	38		1860–61	33
	1841–42	56	1851–52	40		1861–62	27
	1842–43	68	1852–53	56		1862–63	16
	1843–44	72	1853–54	56		1863–64	13
	1844–45	60	1854–55	29		1864–65	16
	1845–46	36	1855–56	32		1865–66	18
Average	$56\frac{1}{2}$			$45\frac{3}{4}$			$26\frac{1}{2}$

thirty years of the Goldsmid Settlement, Francis was obliged to rely on a more fallible criterion in calculating the increase in the net surplus of different soils. The rise in the price of *jowri*, the staple crop of the region, during the currency of the Goldsmid Settlement constituted in the circumstances, the most reliable criterion for a new scale of taxation on the *kunbis* of Indapur.

During the first decade of the Goldsmid Settlement (see Table I) the price of *jowri* fluctuated from 72 seers per rupee in 1843–44 to 36 seers in 1845–46, and the average over the ten years was 56½ seers. The following decade opened with a poor season, when conditions of acute scarcity raised the price of the food-grain to 48 seers per rupee. However, in 1848–49 *jowri* plummeted to 72 seers per rupee. A steady increase in price set in after 1847–48, and in 1856–57 the grain was selling at 32 seers, the average for the entire decade being 45¾ seers per rupee. Commencing with a price of 32 seers per rupee in the last decade of the lease, *jowri* did not experience any dramatic fluctuation in the first few years, and till 1861–62 its price remained stable at the figure of 30 seers. But thereafter, the outbreak of the Civil War in America caused a sudden dislocation in the economy of Maharashtra. The export of raw cotton from the United States ceased abruptly during the Civil War, whereupon India was called upon to meet the requirements in raw material of the textile industry in England. Indapur had not produced much cotton before the 1860s. But as soon as reports of the profits reaped from the cultivation of cotton reached the *kunbis*, they applied themselves to its growth, and by 1867–68, 30,000 acres of land was devoted to the cultivation of cotton. The diversion of so large an area to the cultivation of cotton gave a boost to the price of food-grains, and *jowri* registered an immediate rise to twice its normal price, raising the average to 26 seers per rupee in the last decade of the settlement.[1]

The exceptional conditions created by the outbreak of a Civil War in America, Francis argued, could hardly provide the basis of a new scale of rates because of the inflationary conditions caused by the sudden, and temporary, demand for raw cotton. During the thirty years of the Goldsmid Settlement, therefore, the price of *jowri* in Indapur in effect rose from 66 to 55 seers per rupee. But before this rise could be transformed into an increase in the profits of agriculture, Francis had to answer two important questions: at what stage during the currency of the settlement had the *kunbis* accumulated enough capital to cultivate their fields efficiently? and what was the price of grain at this stage?

To answer these questions Francis relied upon an appraisal

[1] Vide Francis' Report on Indapur.

of the economy of Indapur during the thirty years of the Gold-smid Settlement. The introduction in 1836 of the rates proposed by Goldsmid had lowered the rent on the taluka from Rs. 203,000 to Rs. 89,000. This reduction gave considerable encouragement to cultivation, and in the five years which followed upon 1836, the area under cultivation in Indapur increased by 60,000 acres, and there was a corresponding increase in the yield of land revenue. But it soon became obvious that the low rates proposed by Goldsmid had tempted the *kunbis* to spread their resources far too thinly in order to establish their proprietary rights over as much land as was possible. When the inevitable reaction set in, the *kunbis* were not only forced to throw up a substantial proportion of the land they had initially taken up for cultivation but they were also compelled to seek remissions in rent. Late in the 1840s the *kunbis* stabilised their position, and from then onwards they neither threw up any land nor did they seek any remissions in revenue from the Government of Bombay. This favourable trend continued throughout the 1850s, which indicated that the condition of the *kunbis* had improved to such an extent that they could pay their rents without much trouble in bad as well as in good seasons. It could also be inferred that by the end of the 1840s the *kunbis* had built up substantial reserves of capital, and that they could cultivate their land with reasonable efficiency. Francis, therefore, looked upon the 1850s as a turning-point in the economy of the rural districts of Maharashtra:

> I think, therefore, [he stated] we may fairly assume that towards the latter end of the second decennial period (1846–47 to 1855–56) the cultivators had acquired *that amount of capital and that well to do position* which we could assign to them in the name of profit to be left to them after payment of the government assessment. I am consequently of opinion that we may take the average price of grains during the latter half of the second decennial as the index by which we may estimate from prices what our present assessment ought to be. In other words, the percentage increase which has taken place during the last ten years will represent generally the high percentage addition to the present assessment which may now be made.[1] (Italics in original.)

Since the increase in assessment was to be computed on the

[1] ibid.

basis of the increase in the price of *jowri* during the decennial preceding the outbreak of the Civil War in America, Francis' task was relatively simple. The average price of *jowri* during the last five years of the second decennial of the Goldsmid Settlement was 42 seers per rupee; the corresponding figure for the decennial ending in 1865–66 was 26 seers per rupee, a difference of 16 seers in all. 'We may assume, therefore,' Francis stated, 'that between 50 and 60 per cent is the addition (calculated solely with reference to the price of grain) which may be made to the present assessment.'[1] The rate at which Goldsmid had assessed the best soil in Indapur was 12 annas per acre. Francis raised this rate to one rupee per acre, which constituted a rise of 33 per cent. The total assessment, however, was raised by practically 50 per cent, because of the surreptitious cultivation unearthed by Francis, and his survey, therefore, increased the rent of Indapur from Rs. 89,000 to Rs. 124,700.

III

When confronted with the high rates imposed by Pringle in 1830 the *kunbis* of Indapur had forced the Government of Bombay to resurvey the *taluka* through the simple expedient of migrating in very large numbers to the neighbouring districts. The events of the 1830s reveal that even though the officers of the Survey Department did not consult the peasants before making a revenue settlement, the peasants could still exercise a decisive influence on the pitch of the tax on the land. The success of the new rates recommended by Francis in 1867, therefore, hinged very largely on their acceptance by the *kunbis*. However, the timing of a new scale of rates was just as crucial an issue as their pitch, and so far as the question of timing was concerned the Government of Bombay could not have chosen a worst moment for introducing a new settlement in Indapur. By 1870 the stimulus given to the rural economy of Maharashtra by the Civil War in America had yielded to an acute depression which left the peasants impoverished, and in a discontented frame of mind.

The imposition of a new burden of tax at a time when the termination of the Civil War in America had seriously dislocated

[1] ibid.

the rural economy of Maharashtra could hardly be expected to evoke a favourable reaction from the *kunbis*, particularly when we consider the effect of the new scale of rates on individual *ryots* and on specific villages. Francis, on his part, was not unaware of the fact that while he had raised the rent on Indapur as a whole only by 50 per cent, the increase in rent was as high as 200 per cent in the case of some villages.[1] What he had never bothered to investigate, however, was how individual *kunbis* were affected by the changes he had recommended. The state of affairs in the village of Kullum was in this respect typical of the consequences of the new survey. From the changes proposed by Francis in the fiscal obligations of the cultivators of Kullum it is clear that a *kunbi* like Madoo Mitoo, whose assessment had been increased from Rs. 6 to Rs. 24 because of the 10 acres which he had surreptitiously added to his holding of 20 acres, was bound to become hopelessly indebted under the new settlement. A similar fate awaited *ryots* like Madhoo Bawanee and Naroo Rowji, whose assessment had been raised from Rs. 7 to Rs. 19, and from Rs. 12 to Rs. 21, respectively.[2]

But it was impossible for the *kunbis* of Indapur to adopt in the 1870s the tactics which they had so successfully adopted in the 1830s because of the great increase in the population of the *taluka* in the intervening period. Apart from an increase in population, the creation of rights in property, and the generation of acquisitiveness through the light rates of the Goldsmid Settlement, had tied the *ryots* to their holdings in a way which made it impossible for them to throw up their fields and migrate to new villages in search of more attractive leases. However, the abandonment of their villages was not the only way in which the *kunbis* could protest against arbitrary and excessive taxes. When confronted with such problems under the Marathas, the *kunbis* had utilised the services of their hereditary officers to make representations to the central government at Poona. While the increase in the power of the administration after 1818 had robbed the hereditary officers of their position as the patrons of rural society, the *deshmukhs* still exercised considerable influence over the *kunbis* of Indapur. They consequently turned to a traditional

[1] ibid.
[2] *BA:* Petition from the *Ryots* of Kullum dated 5 October 1874: R.D., Vol. 96 of 1874.

leader like Gopal Narsingh Deshmukh, who had assumed the sobriquet of 'Agent of the Ryots of Indapur', to communicate their resentment against the rates proposed by Francis to the Government of Bombay.

The petition presented by Gopal Narsingh Deshmukh on behalf of the *kunbis* of Indapur to the Government of Bombay was a most remarkable document, both for the sentiments which it expressed, and for the use it made of a traditional and supposedly defunct channel for communication between the peasants and the government. The petition originated at a meeting held in July 1873 in the *cusbah* of Indapur. This meeting was attended by a number of substantial cultivators who had assembled to formulate their grievances for transmission to the Government of Bombay. The appeal drafted at the meeting in Indapur was circulated in the villages of the *taluka* until 2,694 *ryots* had attached their signatures to it. The authorship of the petition is all too obvious from the values which inform its rhetoric, namely, a romantic yearning for the glories of the past; a refusal to take account of realities; a naïve faith in a benevolent ruler who would redress the injustice perpetrated by the agents of his administration; and finally, a belief that the mere expression of dissastisfaction would persuade such a ruler to concede popular demands.[1]

The principal theme set out in the petition of the *kunbis* of Indapur was the striking contrast between the prosperity of the *ryots* under the liberal rates of the Goldsmid Settlement, and the poverty to which the new scales of assessment introduced by Francis and Waddington had reduced them. Pringle's attempt in 1830 at devising a new scale of rates for Indapur had left the *taluka* desolate, and when the 'popularly beloved Mr. Goldsmid' was appointed to resurvey the district he realised that the peasants were impoverished to such an extent that only a very light assessment would persuade them to recultivate their fields:

A moddel (sic) survey of the taluka was aimed at, [the ryots pointed out] and such were the settled rates, that after defraying all expenses of cultivation etc., including the assessment, they (i.e. the peasants) received no less than ⅓th of the produce as a reward

[1] *BA:* Petition from the *Ryots* of Indapur to Bombay Government dated 29 July 1873: R.D., Vol. 96 of 1874.

to the cultivators. Moreover, an ample provision had been made by these truly circumspect officers for our cattle, etc., in excluding all and every sort of waste land, amounting to about 43,000 acres which had been used by us as grazing lands, but are since the late survey about all assessed along with the cultivable lands proper.[1]

To the *kunbis* of Indapur it appeared as though Francis and Waddington were guided by principles completely opposed to the liberal principles which had influenced their predecessors. The new rates of taxation, they observed, were not only excessive but also the transference of what had formerly been regarded as waste land into assessable land made them positively ruinous. Yet such alterations in the burden of tax had been recommended by Francis 'without reflecting for a moment what calamities he was about to bring on the helpless poor. . . '. The effect of what was an oppressive scale of rates to start with was heightened by the harshness with which British officers of revenue enforced the payment of the land-tax. Because of insufficient rain in 1871 and 1872, the yield of agricultural produce had been only 50 to 75 per cent of the normal yield, but when this had been brought to the notice of the Collectors, 'not the slightest notice had been taken of all our cries for exemption from this heavy tax'. Did the Collectors [the *ryots* posed the rhetorical question] pause to consider the damage they were inflicting by selling land worth thousands of rupees in order to realise a few beggarly instalments of revenue? Did they realise the misery and suffering they were imposing on peasants already impoverished through natural calamities over which they had no control? When the *kunbis* were confronted with the cruel demands of the revenue officers, they were forced to turn to the *vanis* for assistance in meeting their obligations. But such assistance ensured for the peasants a fate worse than death, for they were thereby reduced to being the bonded slaves of the *vanis*. 'The monstrosity of our subordinate rulers has been so great that words cannot express them,' the *ryots* stated in conclusion:

> The usurpation of our rights by both the moneylenders and the government together, really brings to our recollection the jolly old times in which our fathers swayed the sceptre in prosperity. It really cuts one to the core to reflect on the past and present con-

[1] ibid.

ditions; i.e. the freedom and affluence in which our fathers lived
and died, and the serfdom in which we are doomed to live and
die! From past history it is evident that during the 2,000 years
back a great many rulers have been in possession of India; but
notwithstanding their great abilities and power, no sooner they
manifested a desire for worthless gain ... the Almighty God sup-
planted them by others more human; for God will hear the cries
of the afflicted and punish the wicked.[1]

The significance of the petition of the *kunbis* of Indapur lies in
the light it throws, first, on the romanticism of the peasants,
secondly, on the extent to which they still looked upon the
deshmukhs as their leaders, and thirdly, on their reaction to the
new settlement of Indapur. Whether the petition was able
to prove that the rates proposed by Francis were excessive, which it did not, is irrelevant to these considerations.
For basically the problems of the *kunbis* stemmed from the dislocation caused by the Civil War in America and by a succession of bad harvests, which had combined to trench into their
slender accumulations of capital, and to render their condition
most precarious.[2]

But despite the depression which followed the Civil War, and
notwithstanding the run of bad harvests which trenched heavily
into the slender resources of the cultivators, the grievances expressed in the petition of the *kunbis* of Indapur were by no
means unrelated to the new scale of rates proposed by Francis.
However, it took civil servants like Sir Auckland Colvin, a revenue officer who was a member of the Deccan Riots Commission,
and W. H. Havelock, the Commissioner of the Northern Division, to translate the emotive accusations of the petition into a
rational analysis of the repercussions of Francis' Settlement.
Colvin questioned the assumption that the *kunbis* had accumulated new wealth over the thirty years of the Goldsmid Settlement, and that this increase in wealth justified the enhanced
rates they were required to pay to the government. In support
of his view that a high assessment had contributed to 'disturb
(for the worse) the relation of creditor and debtor in the Poona
District', Colvin drew attention to the Malthusian nightmare
which had already cast its grim shadow over the rural districts

[1] ibid.
[2] *BA:* Petition from the *Ryots* of Indapur to the Bombay Government dated 15
February 1875: R.D., Vol. 106 of 1875.

of Maharashtra. Pointing to the increase in population in the three *talukas* of Indapur, Haveli and Pabul during the thirty years of the Goldsmid Settlement, Colvin observed that although the growth in population had been accompanied by an increase in resources, it was 'very significant that the growth in population is out of all proportion to the growth of plough cattle or homes. . . . (It seems) that individual property in stock has declined. . . .'[1] The problem acquired a new gravity if account was taken of the manner in which the increase in population had forced the *kunbis* to cultivate soils of marginal fertility. Indeed, the extent to which what had formerly been looked upon as waste land was being pressed into cultivation expressed the problems confronting the *kunbis* with unmistakable clarity (see Table J). It simultaneously demonstrated, so Colvin believed,

TABLE J

Table Showing the extension of Cultivation in the three *Talukas* of Indapur, Haveli and Pabul during the course of the Goldsmid Settlement

	Indapur	Haveli	Pabul
i. Waste land at the end of the first decennial (in acres)	24,510	10,000	18,885
ii. Waste land at the end of the second decennial	1,300	1,922	18,349
iii. Waste land at the end of the third decennial	930	639	3,264

that the increase in the area of cultivation had kept pace with the rise of population 'until, generally speaking, the whole available area has been occupied. For further rise of population there is no further margin of waste.'[2]

Colvin's critique of Francis' Settlement was damaging enough by itself. But the most devastating indictment of the new scale of rates came from Havelock, who was requested by the Government of Bombay to investigate the charge made by some *kunbis* from Sholapur that the new rates weighed more heavily on inferior soils than they weighed on superior soils. To

[1] Memorandum by A. Colvin dated 8 November 1875: *Report of the Deccan Riots Commission, Vol. I.*
[2] ibid.

ascertain the authenticity of this charge, Havelock analysed the effect of the revised rates on villages like Alipur in Barsi *taluka* in the District of Sholapur. On doing so he discovered that the rates on inferior soils had been increased by 67 per cent, whereas the rates on medium and superior soils had been enhanced by only 18 per cent. The results of his inquiry convinced Havelock that

> there had been a judicious increase (of rates) in the highest class of lands; but that, notwithstanding a most salutary and well designed reduction in the two lowest classes of the ... (Goldsmid) scale, and a slight reduction in the 7th class, the new scale has not suited the special circumstances of the region; that the application of the revised classification at too high a rate on much of the former unculturable land, and on the lower and medium lands, has raised the assessment to be too high on such lands.[1]

What was the reason behind such an imbalance in the new scale of assessment? The rates proposed by Pringle in 1830 had proved to be so disastrous because they were a result of collusion between the dominant cultivators in the villages and the native officers of the Survey Department. However, collusion on so extensive a scale was impossible in the 1870s. Havelock, therefore, attributed the imbalance in the new rates to Francis' assumption that Goldsmid and Wingate had left a standard proportion of the net surplus to the poor as well as to the dominant peasants. This belief, he pointed out, was based upon a misapprehension because Goldsmid and Wingate did not base their scale of rates on abstract principles of political economy. Instead, their rates were based upon the principle that the poor cultivators deserved a larger share of the net surplus than the prosperous cultivators. In revising Pringle's rates, which were rigorously based upon Ricardo's law of rent, Goldsmid and Wingate had reduced the rent on superior soils only by 40 per cent, but the rent on soils of medium and inferior quality had been reduced by 60 per cent and 70 per cent respectively, 'with the entire success which had been recognised at all hands'. Francis had repeated Pringle's error in trying to ensure a margin of profit to the cultivator which bore a fixed relationship to the net produce of the soil, irrespective of the quality of the land

[1] *BA:* Memorandum by W. H. Havelock dated 20 April 1874: R.D., Vol. 97 of 1874.

he cultivated. But a practical scale of rates, so Havelock believed, had to be based upon a progressive decrease in the pitch of the assessment as it proceeded from the best to the worst soils.

IV

The reasons why the *kunbis* of Indapur opposed the introduction of Francis' rates were highlighted by Colvin and Havelock with a clarity that was conspicuous by its absence in the petition presented by Gopal Narsingh Deshmukh. In his failure to seize upon the true weaknesses of the rates proposed by Francis, the *deshmukh* revealed the inability of the traditional leaders of rural society to channelise discontent creatively under British rule. The influence of the *deshmukhs* and the old landed families was something to be reckoned with in the 1870s. But their values, political and social, were so different from the values of the new rulers of Maharashtra that their effectiveness in the role of leaders was somewhat limited. Contrast, in this context, the emotive, and consequently ineffectual, rhetoric of the petition by the *kunbis* of Indapur with the cogent case for a revision of the rates proposed by Francis made by Colvin and Havelock. How much more effective would have been the arguments of a Colvin or a Havelock if they had been put forth by the 'Agent of the Ryots of Indapur'? Could the Government of Bombay have overlooked so telling an indictment of its revenue policy by a 'natural' leader of the people? And finally, would a rational belief in the righteousness of their cause not have imparted additional strength to the *kunbis* of Indapur?

To raise these questions is to focus on the need for new and effective leaders in the community. In response to this need a group of brahmans in Poona founded in 1867 an organisation called the Poona Association. The Poona Association was created with the dual object of creating opinion among the educated classes on the crucial issues of the day, and communicating the views of these classes to the Government of Bombay. In 1870 the Association was reorganised as the *Poona Sarvajanik Sabha*. The *Sabha* not only claimed the patronage of landed aristocrats like the *Pant Pratinidhi* of Aundh and the Maharaja of Kohlapur but it also counted among its active members young brahman intellectuals like Mahadev Govind Ranade, the most sophisticated thinker of his day in Maharashtra, and

Ganesh Vasudev Joshi, a liberal, and a leading figure in the politics of Poona. While the support of the landed aristocrats gave legitimacy to the *Sabha*, its political activities were controlled by men like Ranade and Joshi who represented the western educated classes. The popular base of the *Sabha* was provided by ninety-five representatives from different cities of Maharashtra who attended the inaugural meeting of 2 April 1870. These representatives had been 'elected' by 'over 6,000 persons, representing all castes, creeds, and interests . . . '.[1] Soon after the establishment of the *Sabha* in Poona, a number of affiliated branches were established in the principal towns of Maharashtra such as Satara, Wai, Sholapur, Nasik, etc. The object behind the establishment of these *Sabhas* was set out with unmistakable clarity in the preamble to their constitution:

> Whereas it has been deemed expedient that there should exist between the government and people some institution in the shape of a mediating body which may afford to the latter facilities for knowing the real intentions and objectives of Government, as also adequate means of securing their rights by making timely representations to government of the real circumstances in which they are placed, an association has been formed and organised with the appellation of Poona Sarvajanik Sabha.[2]

The *Sarvajanik Sabha* has often been dismissed as an organisation which concerned itself exclusively with presenting cautiously phrased petitions to the British Government in India. But leading members of the *Sabha* like Ranade and Joshi did not envisage for it a purely passive role, since they were anxious to establish rapport with rural society, and since they were also anxious to build for themselves a place in the affections of the peasants. The *Sabha* resembled a caste organisation to the extent that it provided a forum for the political activities of sophisticated urban castes like the chitpavan brahmans. But it also tried to assume the role of the landed aristocracy as a bridge, and as a channel of communication, between rural society and the

---

[1] Memorandum on the founding of the Poona Sarvajanik Sabha taken from the unpublished recollections of *Bombay State Committee for a History of the Freedom Movement in India*. Henceforth cited as *BSCHFMI*.

[2] From an article by V. M. Potdar on the history of the Poona Sarvajanik Sabha in *BSCHFMI*.

administration. The members of the *Sabha* were not only brahman intellectuals whose politics was inspired by Burke and Mill but they also looked upon themselves as '*deshmukhs*' defending the interests of the *kunbis* through invoking the laws of political economy and the principles of utilitarianism.

The resurvey of the rural districts of Maharashtra by Francis, and the opposition of the *kunbis* to the enhanced scale of rates proposed by him, offered the *Sabha* a unique opportunity to broaden its social base by championing the cause of the *kunbis*. Immediately after the introduction of the new survey, therefore, Ranade and Joshi tried to channelise the *kunbis*' opposition to the enhanced rates, and to secure a diminution in the land-tax, in conscious imitation of the role formerly played by the *deshmukhs*. Their attempt to channelise the discontent of the *kunbis* was expressed in political activity at two levels, namely, the drawing up of petitions which communicated the *kunbis*' grievances to the government, and the dispatch to the villages of cadres who were expected to acquaint the peasants with the reasons responsible for their impoverishment. A class of persons who combined traditional and modern techniques of agitation with a commitment to western political ideals presented a serious threat to British authority over the country, and the significance of this development was not lost on the British Government in India.

The 'Report of the Sub-Committee of the Poona Sarvajanik Sabha' on the Francis Settlement, which was presented to the British Government in 1873, concerned itself with themes identical to the themes expressed in the petition of the *kunbis* of Indapur. But in contrast to the romantic idiom of the petition, the report was couched in the rational language of political economy, and the arguments which it advanced to demonstrate the progressive impoverishment of the *kunbis* were quite different in style and in content from the arguments on which Gopal Narsingh Deshmukh based his indictment of Francis. Though written contemporaneously, the petition and the report stood worlds apart in the outlooks they represented. They highlighted the cleavage between the old landed classes which subscribed to traditional political values, and the western educated brahmans who were trying to establish their leadership within the community. The agitation of the *Sabha* undoubtedly created a greater impact on the government as well as on rural society, since its leaders combined a comprehension of the political values of the new rulers with a readiness to exploit the techniques of agitation with which the *kunbis* were thoroughly familiar.[1]

The arguments advanced in the report of the Sub-Committee of the *Poona Sarvajanik Sabha* in support of the charge that the *kunbis* were being progressively impoverished put the Government of Bombay on the defensive, and it immediately conducted an inquiry into the condition of the rural districts of Maharashtra. Those officers of the Government of Bombay who were involved in the administration of the rural districts did not reject the report as a polemical tract devoid of all objectivity. But they emphasised that the changes in the social values of the *kunbis* were just as important as statistics concerning productivity and average incomes in any balanced appreciation of conditions in rural society. Men like A. Wingate, the Collector of Satara, argued that adverse assessments of the state of rural prosperity quite frequently stemmed from the increase in the level of expectations engendered as a consequence of British rule. Under the Marathas the material requirements of the ordinary *kunbis* were extremely modest. '(The) . . . wants of a man scarcely exceeded those of an animal. . . . (A) few bits of rags, a hut, and a cooking pot or two constituted the family accumulations. . . .' All this was related to the fact that in a society where the means of communication were primitive, and markets undeveloped, the surplus produce of agriculture could easily be appropriated by the State and by a few dominant men in rural society. Such conditions in turn produced cultivators who were apathetic and lacking in initiative, and who were easily reconciled to their wretched conditions of existence. The situation had changed dramatically under British rule. A generation of peace and stability, and a rational revenue policy, had encouraged acquisitiveness and the accumulation of capital and it had simultaneously opened the eyes of the *kunbis* to a new range of material wants. These influences had also revealed to the

[1] I have been unable to trace the Report presented by the Sub-Committee of the Poona Sarvajanik Sabha to the Bombay Government. This inadequate precis of the Report is taken from extensive quotations of the same given in a dispatch to the Secretary of State by the Bombay Government dated 27 December 1875: R.D., Vol. 44A of 1875.

kunbis how they could satisfy these wants, and in doing so had planted the seeds of dissatisfaction in their minds. A competitive spirit, acquisitiveness and a desire for the good life had generated a revolution in the social outlook of the *kunbis*:

> Western energy [Wingate pointed out] is introducing the element of labour to eastern apathy and with the desire to accumulate comes the necessity to work. People are no longer content with what satisfied them 50 years ago; their own and their neighbours' estimate of the fitness of things has changed. . . . For example, one mamlatdar states that during the decade 1820–30 the ryots' condition was all that could be desired. The crops ripened well, grain was plentiful, and the instalments in kind were easily given. Great men in the State supported numerous retainers, and these in turn supported their families, so that labour was cheap, the necessity for buying little and so long as the rains fell seasonally, everybody got enough to eat. . . . It is true that there were no shops, no roads, no trade, and little encouragement for labour; no one could afford either to leave his village or to purchase his clothes or ornaments or fair stock. But then . . . (these things) were not wanted. . . .[2]

The *Pax* had thus created an undercurrent of discontent among the peasants by generating a desire for a life that was rich and materially satisfying. It had also stimulated the rise of a class of *kunbis* whose habits of consumption, and whose accumulations of capital, were 'in every way so superior to what the same people were 40 years ago as it is possible to conceive'.[2] But the 'affluence' of these peasants stood in striking contrast to the poverty of the great majority of the *kunbis*. This was vividly reflected in the widening gap between the wages of agricultural labourers and the prices of the major food-crops, on the one hand, and the decreasing margins of profit on the inferior soils which were being taken under cultivation through a rise in population, on the other. In the District of Ahmednagar, for instance, the wage of an agricultural labourer had risen from Rs. 28 per annum to Rs. 60 per annum during the course of the Goldsmid Settlement. But this rise did not represent any real gain, since the price of food-grains like *jowri* and *bajra* had risen

[1] *BA:* A. Wingate, Collector of Satara, to Bombay Government dated 3 October 1874: R.D., Vol. 44B of 1875, Pt. II.
[2] ibid.

by 250 and 185 per cent respectively over a corresponding period.[1]

The inquiries conducted by the Government of Bombay in response to the report of the *Poona Sarvajanik Sabha* demolished the picture of increasing rural prosperity which formed the background to Francis' revision of the Goldsmid Settlement. But while the report attributed the deterioration in the condition of the *kunbis* to the revenue policy in general, and to the rates proposed by Francis in particular, the Government of Bombay ascribed their impoverishment to the increase in population which followed the British conquest of Maharashtra, and also to the want of habits of thrift and prudence among the peasants. In the opinion of the government, an uncontrolled rise in population in a country which did not possess an expanding economy could lead to only one result. The pressure on the land would force the peasants to take soils of inferior quality under cultivation, and such a trend would slowly but surely lower the profits of agriculture. 'Some experienced officers under us are already of opinion that the land is less productive now than formerly,' the Government of Bombay pointed out in a dispatch to the Secretary of State for India. But there were obvious limitations to what the government could do in the circumstances. All civilised societies exercised voluntary restraints on the growth of population, but in India the balance was struck by famines and by epidemics. According to Hinduism marriage was obligatory, and the possession of heirs was the precondition of salvation. Small wonder then that the *kunbis* of Maharashtra lived and multiplied 'with the only check to the rise of population being starvation and disease'. The persistence of such social values was responsible for the creation of a dangerous state of affairs, since whereas

a government can do much to foster the development of the country, it can do little or nothing to enrich such of its subjects as are wanting in thrift or enterprise. . . . (Progress) depends more on the desire of the people to learn than on the capacity of the government to teach, and after all the principal object of government is to afford protection to life and property, and the accumulation of wealth must be left to individual action. It cannot be

[1] *BA:* H. B. Boswell, Collector of Ahmednagar, to Bombay Government dated 28 August 1874: R.D., Vol. 44B of 1875.

denied that as regards security of life and property, opportunity of education, etc., there is no comparison between present and former ideas. . . . But still the people are worse off than they were ten or fifteen years ago. . . .[1]

The ability of the *Sarvajanik Sabha* to put the Government of Bombay on the defensive illustrates the effectiveness of the educated young brahmans in contrast to the impotence of traditional leaders like Gopal Narsingh Deshmukh. But to play the role of *deshmukhs* effectively, it was necessary for the young brahman leaders of the *Sabha* to persuade the *kunbis* to participate actively in their campaign against the Francis Settlement, not the least because their roots were wholly urban, and they therefore lacked that intimate connection with the *kunbis* which lay behind the influence of the traditional leaders of rural society. To activate the peasants the *Poona Sarvajanik Sabha* sent some of its members to the villages, to whip up the *kunbis'* opposition to the new rates, and to acquaint them with the reasons behind their impoverishment. The *Sabha's* success in arousing the peasants against the survey was dramatic, and became immediately apparent to British officers of revenue. An officer of the Survey Department, for instance, encountered organised opposition when he tried to introduce the rates recommended by Francis to the *ryots* of Barsi *taluka*:

> I had scarcely concluded my explanatory remarks [Waddington wrote to Francis] when most of the assembled ryots stood up, refusing to have their 'khatas' examined, and declaring their intention to pay no more assessment than they had hitherto been in the habit of paying. I endeavoured to reason with them and to point out the grounds on which it was but equitable that their payments should be raised; but without success, and so excited and disrespectful was their demeanour that I felt myself bound to report the matter to you for further instructions. . . . I have little doubt that the opposition has been fostered by the Sarvajanik Sabha of Sholapur.[2]

Waddington's experience was not an isolated instance of the *Sabha's* ability to arouse opposition to the new scale of rates. The revised assessment had been introduced without any trouble in

[1] *BA:* Dispatch to Secretary of State for India dated 27 December 1875: R.D., Vol. 44A of 1875, Pt. I.
[2] *BA:* Letter from W. Waddington dated 18 April 1874: R.D., Vol. 104 of 1874.

the *talukas* of Madhe and Sholapur in 1872. But while the *kunbis* quietly accepted the new rates in the first instance, they refused to pay the enhanced assessment the moment agitators connected with the *Sabha* appeared in their midst, and told them that in raising the rent the Survey Department had encroached upon their rights and was depriving them of the fruits of their labour. The Collector of Satara believed that these agitators had urged the *kunbis* 'to refuse to pay the new assessment, trusting to them, the Sarwajanik Sabha (sic), to make it all right for them to do so'.[1]

V

The disaffection aroused by the agitation of the *Poona Sarvajanik Sabha* thoroughly alarmed the Government of Bombay, particularly when the depth of this disaffection was reflected in the reports which poured in from one *taluka* after another of the resistance which the *kunbis* were offering to the payment of the new rates. True, a majority of the revenue officers believed that the intransigence of the *kunbis* stemmed from their impoverishment due to a succession of bad harvests. But the *kunbis'* inability to pay the rent was not the only reason behind their truculence, as Waddington discovered to his utter astonishment while introducing the new taxes in the *taluka* of Barsi. The high pitch of the rates proposed by Francis had created an alliance between the traditional leaders of rural society and the emerging leaders of the *Poona Sarvajanik Sabha*, and this alliance was an important influence in shaping the *kunbis'* attitude to the new settlement. The Collector of Poona, for instance, pointed to the active role which a few leading landed families of the *taluka* of Bhimthari had played in the 'no-tax' campaign launched by the *Sabha* and observed: 'It may seem strange to connect a general failure in the collection of a whole taluka long under our rule, with the discontent of a few families. . . . But it must be remembered that these families had considerable influence under the former Government, which still exists to some degree. . . .'[2]

The situation in Indapur, Bhimthari and the neighbouring

---

[1] *BA:* Letter from Collector of Sholapur dated 3 December 1873: R.D., Vol. 97 of 1874.
[2] *BA:* Letter from Collector of Poona to Bombay Government dated 14 December 1873: R.D., Vol. 97 of 1874.

districts took so serious a turn that in the month of April 1874 W. H. Havelock, the Revenue Commissioner, called a meeting of the officers of the affected districts in order to devise measures which would relieve the tension and disquiet that prevailed in the rural areas around Poona. In a letter to the Collector of Poona on the eve of the meeting, Havelock outlined his views on rural discontent, and the means he considered expedient to resolve this discontent. He would consider sympathetically appeals for reductions in tax from *kunbis* who were genuinely unable to pay their rents, but he would not yield an inch to the spirit of opposition created by the *Poona Sarvajanik Sabha* and the disgruntled landed families.[1] However, the discussions which took place at the meeting called by Havelock revealed how difficult it was to come to any definite conclusions regarding the *kunbis'* ability (or inability) to pay the new taxes. Rao Saheb Balwant Sitaram, the *mamlatdar* of Bhimthari, felt that the *kunbis* were genuinely unable to pay the new rates, because the opposition to these taxes 'was as great in the revised villages that had good crops, as in those that had bad crops'. But the *mamlatdar's* opinion was challenged by the Collector of Poona, who held that the opposition fostered by the *Sabha* in alliance with the disaffected landed families had influenced the *kunbis* to such an extent that they were thirsting for a collision with the Government of Bombay. The solution suggested by the Collector was of a piece with his analysis of the true causes of rural discontent. Once the spirit of the landed families had been broken by the confiscation of their estates, he pointed out, the *kunbis* would no longer dare to oppose the new settlement.[2]

But the Government of Bombay refused to embark upon the course of repression outlined by the Collector of Poona. It refused to do so because its inquiries into the economic conditions of the *kunbis* had brought to light some extremely disturbing facts, and more particularly, because the new rates had hit the poor cultivators harder than they had hit the prosperous *kunbis*.[3]

[1] *BA:* Letter from H. D. Havelock to the Collector of Poona dated 26 December 1873: R.D., Vol. 97 of 1874.
[2] *BA:* Letter from Collector of Poona dated 13 May 1874: R.D., Vol. 97 of 1874. Also see Minutes of a Departmental Conference held in Poona on 14 April 1874: R.D., Vol. 97 of 1874.
[3] Resolution by Bombay Government dated 29 October 1874: R.D., Vol. 97 of 1874.

Instead of accepting the suggestions of the Collector of Poona, therefore, the Government of Bombay extended a series of concessions to the *kunbis* in order to make the new rates acceptable to them. It resolved that in no case should the assessment of a *taluka* or of a group of villages be raised by more than 50 per cent; or the rent of a single village raised by more than 75 per cent. It also resolved that if a cultivator was unable to pay his tax, then the Revenue Department would in the first instance attach his movable property, and that his holdings would be auctioned only when his movable property proved insufficient to cover the full amount of the tax.[1]

The imposition of a ceiling on the extent to which the assessment could be raised dampened the hostility of the *kunbis* to the new settlement in particular, and to the Government of Bombay in general. But the decision to attach the *kunbis'* movable property if they failed to pay the land-tax held implications which heightened social conflict in the villages of Maharashtra. We must remember that despite the opposition provoked by the new settlement, the disquiet which prevailed in rural society stemmed basically from the loss of their holdings by the *kunbis* to the *vanis*, and the dominance which the latter had consequently acquired over the villages. It is true that the dislocation caused by the Civil War in America and by a series of bad harvests had combined to create an unusual degree of unrest in the villages. But the most important source of conflict in rural society remained none the less the antagonism between the *kunbis* and the *vanis*. Because the *kunbis* depended upon the *vanis* for the payment of the land-revenue, the decision to first auction a *kunbi*'s movable property if he was unable to meet his obligations of tax was a concession which was immediately exploited by the *vanis*. The *vanis* had formerly advanced the assessment to the *kunbis* in the knowledge that if the *kunbis* defaulted, then the only security which they had to offer, namely, their land, would be attached by the Revenue Department. Since the Government of Bombay had now resolved to attach the *kunbi*'s movable property in the first instance, the *vani* did not see any threat to his holdings and consequently refused to advance him the land revenue in 1874.

The antagonism between the *kunbis* and the *vanis* was

[1] ibid.

thereupon transformed into an open conflict in rural society. It would be misleading to look upon this conflict as stemming from a single cause. The dislocation of the rural economy by the Civil War in America; an ill-conceived revision of the land-tax by Francis; the agitation initiated by the *Poona Sarvajanik Sabha* and supported by some influential landed families; and finally, the long standing hostility between the *kunbis* and the *vanis*, all combined to contribute to the tension and frustration which resulted in the Riots of 1875. The complexion of the social groups involved in the disturbances was determined by that decision of the Government of Bombay which encouraged the *vanis* not to advance money to the *kunbis*; it was also determined by the fact that the nexus between the *kunbis* and the *vanis* was the weakest link in the chain which held together different social groups in rural society.

In contrast to the opposition to the rates proposed by Francis, the Riots of 1875 were spontaneous and did not bear any evidence of the careful preparation that was responsible for the 'no-tax' campaign launched by the *Sarvajanik Sabha*. Moreover, while the 'no-tax' agitation had revealed the extent to which the old landed families still exercised influence over rural society, the upsurge against the *vanis* brought into focus the conflict among social groups whose close interdependence was formerly a distinguishing feature of the villages of Maharashtra. The *patil*, for instance, had become so closely identified with the administration that he was now incapable of leading the *kunbis*, and was in fact looked upon by them with suspicion as somebody who did not belong to the village. Similarly, the partial introduction of a money economy, and the spread of acquisitiveness, introduced a note of acrimony in relations between the *kunbis* and the *bullotedars* which had formerly been conspicuous by its absence.

In the initial stages of the disturbances of 1875 the *kunbis* took recourse to social sanctions against the *vanis* in an attempt to browbeat them into acquiescence without resorting to violence. Their moderation is brought out in a *sama patra* (bond of agreement) executed by the *kunbis* of Kallas in the *taluka* of Indapur, which document simultaneously illustrates the absence of cohesion between different social groups in the villages of Maharashtra in 1875. The main fire of the *sama patra* was directed against the *vanis*, since it pointed out that any *kunbi* who cultivated the fields of a *vani*

> will neither be allowed to come to caste dinners nor intermarry amongst his own society. Such person will be considered outcaste. He will not be allowed to join the community without their unanimous consent, and will have to pay the fine which the community may inflict on him, and further to give one meal to the community.[1]

But it spoke with equal clarity of the absence of any sentiment of solidarity between the *kunbis*, on the one hand, and the hereditary officers of the village and the *bullotedars*, on the other. The *bullotedars* were threatened with the termination of their customary dues if they did not fall in line with the rest of the village in the boycott of the *vanis;* and the *patil* of Kallas, in-instead of leading the *kunbis* to whom he was related by bonds of class and caste, had to be warned that 'if he joins the money-lending people, his hereditary rights will be discontinued. . . '.

The coercion of the *vanis* along the lines set out in the *sama patra* executed by the *kunbis* of Kallas spread like wildfire in the villages of Poona, Ahmednagar, Sholapur and Satara. Since the movement was so genuinely spontaneous, it is difficult to recapitulate how it spread from village to village in the rural districts of Maharashtra. But a letter written by the *kunbis* of Kallas to the nearby village of Akola indicates the probable means through which the movement against the *vanis* gained momentum. In this letter the *kunbis* of Kallas rebuked the *kunbis* of Akola for their refusal to co-operate with their caste-fellow in other villages and asserted:

> It is very wrong of your people to keep communication with the marwaris whom we excluded from the community of this village. Unanimity is very important at this time. You will perhaps know this if you give the subject mature consideration, and we therefore refrain from making further remarks about the matter.[2]

They then appealed to Akola in the name of the traditional ties binding the two villages ('We have always regarded Kallas and

---

[1] Substance of a *Sama Patra* by the Villagers of Kallas in the taluka of Indapur dated 7 May 1875: *Report of the Deccan Riots Commission*, Vol. II.

[2] Letter from the Villagers of Kallas to the Villagers of Akola dated 15 May 1875: *Report of the Deccan Riots Commission*, Vol. II.

Akola one') and asked it to send two responsible elders to a meeting which was being held to concert common measures against the *vanis*. The letter written by the *kunbis* of Kallas concluded with an impassioned plea for unity at so critical a period: 'We shall be helpless,' they said, 'should you take no measure to (prevent co-operation with the moneylenders). . . . For the good of all of us it is necessary that we should co-operate with each other.'

The adoption of social sanctions against the *vanis* on such an extensive scale created so tense a situation in the rural districts that a violent clash between the *kunbis* and the *vanis* became inevitable. The first outbreak occurred at Supa, a substantial village in the *taluka* of Bhimthari, on 12 May 1875. The victim of the *ryots* were the *vanis*, of whom there were a goodly number in Supa. Their houses and shops were stripped of everything which the *kunbis* could find, and then burnt, but no violence to any person was committed. Within twenty-four hours of the outbreak at Supa the leading marwari of Khairgaon, a village fourteen miles away, had his residence burnt. In the days which followed riots occurred in four other villages of Bhimthari, and threatened in seventeen more. The disturbances then spread to the *talukas* of Indapur and Purandhur. Outside the District of Poona, the disturbances were concentrated in the *talukas* of Parner, Shrigonda, Nagar and Kargat in the Collectorate of Ahmadnagar. The riot at Supa was singular in the wholesale destruction of property; and the outbreak at Damareh in the murderous assault on a *vani*. In a few other villages the *kunbis* threatened the *vanis* with violence. But on the whole the disturbances were characterised by great restraint. The object of the *kunbis* everywhere was to seize and to destroy those legal documents which proclaimed their bondage to the *vanis*. In villages where these documents were given up without any fuss, no physical injury was inflicted on anyone, but if the *vanis* refused to surrender the bonds and decrees in their possession, violence was used to intimidate them. Fortunately, the *kunbis* had to resort to extreme measures in very few instances, and the 'nonviolent' character of the movement as a whole impressed itself forcibly on the Commission which investigated the disturbances:

In reviewing the character of the disturbances generally [ran the report of the Commission] the most remarkable feature presented

186

is the small amount of serious crime. A movement which was a direct appeal to physical force over a large area usually restrained within the limits of a mere demonstration; the moderation is in some measure to be attributed to the nature of the movement itself. It was not so much a rebellion against the oppressor, as an attempt to accomplish a very definite and practical object, namely, the disarming of the enemy by taking his weapons (bonds and accounts), and for that purpose mere demonstration of force was usually enough.[1]

The distinguishing characteristics of the Deccan Riots of 1875 reflected the tensions which were generated within rural society through the policy of reform initiated by the Government of Bombay. Prior to 1818, the villages of Maharashtra were characterised by the absence of any serious friction between the social groups which resided within them, and contributed to their self-sufficiency. The dominance of the *kunbis*, which was expressed most clearly in the power and the influence of the *patils*, created the consensus which held these social groups together. It also generated a social climate in which collective responsibility rather than individual endeavour formed the basis of society. All this was transformed under the influence of policies of reform which were inspired by utilitarianism, and which tried to mould life in rural society according to the principles of individualism and acquisitiveness. The clue to the resulting changes in rural society was provided by the growing dominance of the *vanis* over the villages, and by the consequential antagonism between the former and the *kunbis*.

The growth of tension between the *kunbis* and the *vanis* of Maharashtra was merely one facet of an all embracing social process. The climate of individualism and acquisitiveness created by the policies of reform progressively undermined the corporate structure of the villages and split them into discrete social groups. It did so by alienating the *patil* from the *kunbis* through converting him into a supine instrument of the administration; by creating friction between the *kunbis* and the *bullotedars* through the partial introduction of a cash nexus; and most important of all, by transforming the harmonious relationship between the *kunbis* and the *vanis* into a relationship of acute social conflict. To an

---

[1] *Report of the Deccan Riots Commission*, Vol. I, para 15.

extent these changes were calculatedly fostered by the advocates of reform in the hope that the weakening of the sentiment of solidarity in the villages would create a social revolution along lines much to be desired. But such expectations proved abortive because of the values of the *vanis* of Maharashtra. Even after they had acquired substantial holdings in land, for instance, the *vanis* refused to have anything to do with agriculture, and they preferred to lease their holdings at rack rents to their erstwhile proprietors. In doing so the *vanis* created a climate of intense conflict and strife in the villages of Maharashtra.

The antagonism between the *kunbis* and the *vanis* was, indeed, the most important reason behind the disturbances which broke out in 1875. Factors like the growth of the rural population; the dislocation of the economy by the Civil War in America; the ill-conceived revision of the land-tax by Francis; and finally, the agitation whipped up by the young brahman leaders of the *Poona Sarvajanik Sabha* and the dominant landed families contributed to a similar end. All these influences combined to create a situation of explosive intensity in the villages of Maharashtra, a situation in which relations between different social groups were placed under great stress, though the breakdown of consensus occurred at the weakest link in the chain which held together rural society, namely, the link between the *kunbis* and the *vanis*.

VI

Reconsiderations and Reappraisals

THE Deccan Riots of 1875 revealed the limitations of the policy of reform which the utilitarians had devised for Maharashtra. The lynch-pin of this policy was the *ryotwari* system of land revenue, which was designed to undermine the collective institutions of rural society, and which was also designed to create a climate of individualism and competition in the villages. The utilitarians wanted to liberate the *kunbis* from their obligations to the *jatha* and the village community, since they believed that in doing so they would stimulate the rise of a class of affluent peasants whose acquisitiveness would form the basis for economic progress and create the conditions for stability in rural society. But the indifference of the utilitarians towards the values of the *kunbis* and the *vanis*, particularly the latter, and their lack of concern for the established institutions of rural society, led to consequences which defeated the very objectives they had in view. The breakdown of the traditional institutions in the villages, and the introduction of a revenue system based on the laws of political economy did, as we shall later see, to a limited extent promote the rise of an affluent class of cultivators. But these cultivators were eclipsed by the growing dominance of the *vanis*, who enriched themselves at the expense of the landed families whose power and prestige had formerly been the mainstay of rural society.

The consequences of the rise of the *vanis* were recognised long before the growth of tensions within the villages of Maharashtra erupted in the disturbances of 1875. But the influence of utilitarian and *laissez-faire* principles was so decisive on those who controlled power in the Government of Bombay, that they did not take any steps to ward off the dangers which loomed ahead. The inability of the British administrators to remedy the social evils arising from the growing dominance of the *vanis* is reflected in the debate provoked by the representation of the *kunbis* of Thana to which we have referred before, and which set out the dangerous proportions assumed by the influence of the *vanis* over rural society. When the disturbing picture set out in the representation of the *kunbis* was confirmed by the District Officers, the Government of Bombay raised the question whether the concepts of legality which guided British courts of law did not require modification in view of their adverse effect on the prosperity of the peasants in the villages. But so strong was the prevailing belief in the laws of political economy, and in the virtues of free competition, that while he acknowledged the magnitude of the evil, an officer like J. Vibart, the Revenue Commissioner of the Southern Division, felt that 'however injurious, in some respects, the perfectly free traffic in money may be to the advancing prosperity of the country, any interference on the part of the government, in the way of limiting the legal rate of interest . . . would be of doubtful tendency; and possibly lead to greater extortion on the part of the moneylenders. . . . '[1] While Vibart at least recognised the *vani* as a parasite, some administrators looked upon any attempt to impose restrictions upon him as impolitic and regarded his role as worthy of support and encouragement:

> The moneylenders [the Collector of Surat pointed out] have already sustained a severe injury to their trade by the introduction of one universal currency and, in our zeal to protect the poorer classes, we should not forget the policy of conciliating an industrious and very influential tribe, one of the few who are still attached by interest and inclination to our supremacy in India. These people might be seriously injured, and entirely alienated from us, by precipitate legislation on the subject under review, while our revenue might be imperilled by a stoppage of customary

[1] *BA:* J. Vibart, Revenue Commissioner of the Southern Division to the Bombay Government dated 28 February 1840: R.D., Vol. 1664 of 1844.

advances, and the ryots themselves disturbed by the very means taken to benefit them.[1]

However District Officers who were confronted with the practical tasks of administration became progressively sceptical of the relevance of the laws of political economy to the problems of rural society in Maharashtra. The dissatisfaction of such administrators with the doctrinaire approach of their superiors was reflected in the stance adopted by Bartle Frere, when as a junior officer in the District of Poona he pressed for bold action to remedy the serious turn which the situation had taken in the rural districts of Maharashtra. Frere traced the difficulties of the *kunbis* to the principles enshrined in Regulation V of 1827, according to which financial transactions between the *vanis* and the *kunbis* were governed by rates of interest regulated by the principles of free enterprise. He conceded that in a country like Great Britain which had achieved a high level of commercial and industrial development there was a lot to be said for the removal of restraints on the movement of money. But in Maharashtra 'where the population are mostly needy, thoughtless and ignorant, and the Banians enjoy a monopoly of the money market, unrestricted license . . . (is highly undesirable) . . . '.[2] Even a casual acquaintance with the conditions of rural society, Frere pointed out, revealed the irrelevance of the principles of *laissez-faire* to the economy of the village. The *kunbis* were supposedly free to deal with a *vani* of their choice, but actually they were completely dependent upon the *vani* of the village, and looked upon him as a 'wuttundar, and it would require an entire change in the constitution of the ryots to get them to seek pecuniary aid elsewhere'.[3]

The conditions which prevailed in the villages of Maharashtra led Frere to suggest that the Government of Bombay should fix a ceiling on the rates of interest which the *vanis* could charge from the *kunbis*. But while District Officers as a rule agreed with Frere that the *vanis* charged exorbitant rates of interest, they were none the less divided on the possible effects

[1] *BA:* Letter from the Collector of Surat to J. Vibart dated 29 July 1840: R.D., Vol. 1664 of 1844.
[2] *BA:* Letter from Bartle Frere to P. Stewart, Collector of Poona, dated 2 July 1840: R.D., Vol. 1664 of 1844.
[3] ibid. For a similar viewpoint, see letter from the Collector of Sholapur to the Revenue Commissioner dated 9 October 1840: R.D., Vol. 1664 of 1844.

of an artificial restraint on the rate of interest. The Collector of Poona, for instance, sympathised with the sentiments which had encouraged Frere to recommend the adoption of a ceiling on rates of interest. But he was apprehensive that an attempt to lower the rates of interest would have precisely the reverse effect. It would encourage the *vanis* to raise their rates of interest in order to compensate themselves for the risks involved in the evasion of the law, and it would also encourage them to charge high premiums for the loans they advanced to the cultivators.[1] The practical difficulties in enforcing a ceiling on the rates of interest made some British administrators chary of legislative interference in the operations of the money market, and turned their attention to indirect means for supporting the *kunbis*. Vibart, for instance, believed that the cultivators would benefit enormously if they were required to register all documents setting out their obligations to the *vanis*.[2] The registration of bonds, he pointed out, would impress upon the cultivators the conditions on which they had borrowed money. It would also prevent the evasion by the *vanis* of the principle of *dam dupat*, according to which interest on a loan could not exceed the principal. The *vanis* circumvented this principle by forcing the *ryots* to sign fresh bonds every two or three years for sums made up of the principal of the loan plus the interest. A system which required bonds to be registered would make such evasion impossible by exposing the succession of bonds through which the *vanis* dragged the *kunbis* who fell into their clutches.

The remedies proposed by Frere and Vibart for the problem of rural indebtedness were not without their merits. But these remedies hardly touched the heart of the problem. The primary cause of rural indebtedness lay in the *kunbi*'s need for credit to carry out his agricultural operations, and to fulfil his obligations to the State. Formerly, when the payment of the rent was the responsibility of the village as a community, the *patil* of the village had borrowed money from the *sowcars* to pay the tax on land. By establishing individual responsibility for the land-tax, the *ryotwari* system directed the flow of capital to the cultivator

[1] *BA:* Letter from the Collector of Poona to J. Vibart dated 20 July 1840: R.D., Vol. 1664 of 1844.
[2] *BA:* J. Vibart to the Bombay Government dated 28 February 1840: R.D., Vol. 1664 of 1844.

through the *vani*, instead of the village community. It thus created a relationship between the *kunbis* and the *vanis* in which all the advantages rested solely with the latter. The position of the *kunbis* could only be improved by providing them with an alternative source of credit that would reduce their dependence upon the *vanis*. To provide them with an alternative source of credit P. Stewart, the Collector of Poona, suggested the establishment of financial institutions similar to the *Monts-de-Piété* of Europe. Such institutions, Stewart held, would 'protect the helpless and needy (peasants) from being plundered by irresponsible persons . . . like the village banians. . . '. They would, he also believed, go a long way towards undermining the *vani*'s grip over the cultivators. But Stewart's proposal was rejected out of hand by Vibart, who argued that the Government of Bombay was under no obligation to assume the responsibilities of a banker *vis-à-vis* the *kunbis*.

A proposal which resembled Stewart's proposal, but reflected a more sensitive understanding of the problems of rural society, was the suggestion made by H. E. Jacomb, a junior officer in the Collectorate of Ahmednagar. Proceeding straight to the crux of the problem, Jacomb argued that in order to restore the *kunbis* to their former position of dominance in rural society it was essential to 'counterpoise the baneful influence of the village sowkars, and . . . (to inculcate) habits of thrift and carefulness among the rural population. . . '.[1] But before such steps could be taken, it was necessary to grasp the basis of the *vani*'s dominance over the villages. The Government of Bombay had conferred a great boon on the peasant through awarding him property rights in the soil. But the expectations with which this step had been taken had not been fulfilled. Instead of exploiting his newly acquired rights of property to enrich himself, the *kunbi* had sunk more and more into a state of impoverishment. This had come about because he lacked the resources in capital to develop the land. The poverty of the *kunbi* could be attributed to debts contracted for the payment of revenue, and also to debts arising out of social obligations. Because of his meagre resources

---

[1] Letter from H. E. Jacomb, Assistant Collector of Ahmednagar to C. E. Fraser-Tytler, Collector of Ahmednagar dated 6 December 1858: *Report of the Deccan Riots Commission*, Vol. II, Appendix A (Bombay, 1876). This report is henceforth referred to as *DRC*.

in capital and also because of an accumulated burden of debt, the *kunbi* found himself caught in a vicious circle from which escape was difficult, if not impossible. But one method, Jacomb pointed out

> by which the incubus of debt may be gradually but surely over-come (is) by endeavouring to raise small capitalists to act as a check on the listless sole possessor of money (the vani) in a village, and by which the great moral lessons of thrift and carefulness may be instilled, fostered, and nurtured, by the force of example in the minds of the native agricultural population. Could these debts be swept away or even modified, the ryots saved from their deterior-ating influence, would be free and most probably willing to ex-pend his energies, both in capital and labour, on the land so firmly guaranteed to him.[1]

The absence of a prosperous class of peasants was a serious obstacle in the success of Jacomb's scheme. But surely, he argued, most villages in Maharashtra harboured a group of cultivators who could be persuaded to save small sums of money with the object of establishing credit institutions like the English Savings Bank. The capital available with such institutions could be used to meet the needs of the poor peasants. The Savings Banks would undermine the dominance of the *vanis* and they would, therefore, reduce tension and strife in the villages of Maharashtra.

> In endeavours to improve the social system of the millions of our subjects [Jacomb stated] it is only by small commencements and by striking directly at the root of an evil that we can hope to succeed. It is in the aggregate of useful institutions that a good social system exists. But the aggregate can only be attained by careful and well considered atoms. The mechanist must bestow equal care and attention on the details as on the undertaking itself. The strategist must attend to individual training ere he can consider his organisation complete. So with Indian society the details of the system must be remodelled, if we look for collective improvement.[2]

I

The proposal put forward by Jacomb for the creation of credit institutions which were to be controlled by the *kunbis* reflects his

[1] ibid.   [2] ibid.

awareness of the imbalance in the distribution of power which the *ryotwari* system of land-revenue had created in the villages of Maharashtra. But although Jacomb attacked some aspects of the policy advocated by the utilitarians, he shared to the full the atomistic approach to social phenomena which characterised men like Pringle. Because the critics of the policies inspired by utilitarianism subscribed to some of its basic presuppositions, they failed to carry any conviction with the British Government, despite the fact that the remedies which they proposed were highly relevant to the problems which confronted the Government of Bombay.

What the critics of utilitarian policies required was a new vision of society, and a new conception of the laws and institutions necessary for the realisation of this vision. The philosophy of social action which inspired the utilitarians was a creed that owed its origin to Adam Smith and Jeremy Bentham. It was conceived when policies resting upon the principles of mercantilism stood in the way of free commercial intercourse between the nations of Europe, and when outdated laws inhibited the growth of societies which stood on the brink of an industrial revolution. The principles of utilitarianism 'had been a corrosive solvent of everything that clogged the free play of individual activity'.[1] The philosophy of utilitarianism condemned interference in the affairs of the community by the State in the name of social and economic liberty, but unfortunately, it continued to do so even when condemnation could only lead to exploitation and inhibit progress. When applied to rural society in Maharashtra, the principle of liberty merely insured the exploitation of the *kunbis* by the *vanis*. There was consequently a pressing need for a change in the principles which inspired social action and sustained administrative policies in Maharashtra.

The second generation of radical philosophers were aware of the adverse consequences which flowed from the application of utilitarian principles of law and government to the problems of social organisation.[2] It was this awareness which prompted John Stuart Mill to modify the ideas which he and his generation of radicals had inherited from Adam Smith, Jeremy Bentham and James Mill. In his essay *On Liberty*, for instance,

[1] Sir Ernest Baker, *Political Thought in England 1845 to 1914* (Oxford, 1947), p. 3.
[2] ibid., p. 3.

J. S. Mill gave a sophisticated interpretation to the utilitarian notion of liberty. Instead of defining liberty as freedom from external restraint, Mill defined liberty as that freedom of the human mind which alone could form the basis of a creative and progressive society. Similarly, in his essay *On Representative Government*, Mills bestowed a new significance on Bentham's concept of popular democracy. Instead of looking upon popular participation in government as freedom for the individual to pursue his interests at the expense of classes and social groups, he regarded representative institutions as necessary for that flowering of the individual mind and character which required to be stimulated in all directions, and which could be stimulated only if the scope of the human mind and the human will was extended to include the affairs of the whole community.[1]

While the modifications introduced by J. S. Mill in the principles of utilitarianism provided some answers, inadequate though they may have been, to the problems of an industrial society like Great Britain, the position was quite different so far as India was concerned. The problems of government in India touched upon utilitarianism at its weakest points. Administrators and reformers who were influenced by utilitarianism lacked a sense of historical perspective, and they were ignorant of social evolution as a phenomenon with a rationale peculiarly its own. These two weaknesses invested utilitarian reformers with an insensitivity towards the role which traditional values played in the life of a community, and it simultaneously invested them with a facile optimism concerning the pace at which measures of legislative reform could change the established values of a society. The weaknesses of utilitarian reformers are clearly reflected in their failure to transform the *kunbis* into acquisitive peasants anxious to exploit the *ryotwari* system to enrich themselves and to create the conditions for progress and prosperity in society.

Because of the disastrous consequences which flowed from the application of utilitarian ideas to the problems of government in India, it is not surprising that one of the most significant trends in anti-utilitarian thought is associated with an individual whose career in India exercised a decisive influence on the

[1] R. P. Anschutz, *The Philosophy of J. S. Mill* (Oxford, 1953), Chaps. II and III, *passim*.

196

development of his mind. Sir Henry Maine's ideas on social values and political institutions were conceived as a conservative reaction to Bentham's calculus of utility, and to the doctrine of natural rights enunciated by the political thinkers who influenced the course of the French Revolution; but they also drew heavily on his experience in India in defining the role of tradition in progress and change. Maine possessed an eclectic mind; yet he integrated the ideas which he had borrowed from different sources into a system which bore the unique stamp of his genius. *The Origin of the Species* by Charles Darwin preceded *Ancient Law* by two years, and it introduced Maine to social evolution, and to the scientific method which distinguished his conservatism from Burke's vision of the social order. Maine's approach to social problems was inductive and it rested on generalisations which were based upon observable facts. In an address given to the students of the University of Calcutta he outlined his approach in terms which characterised him as a thinker typical of his age:

> There can [Maine pointed out] be no essential difference between the truths of the Astronomer, of the Physiologist, and of the Historian. The great principle which underlies all knowledge of the Physical World, that Nature is ever consistent with herself, must also be true of Human Nature and Human Society which is made up of Human Nature. . . . If indeed History be true, it must teach what every other science teaches, continuous sequence, inflexible order, and eternal law.[1]

The single most important influence on Maine was the Historical School of Eichorn and Savigny in Germany, which was unequivocally opposed to social theories that rested upon natural laws like Rousseau's notion of the general will, or Bentham's principle of utility. The Historical School abandoned all *a priori* assumptions of the first causes of human society, and it embarked upon a scientific examination of social phenomena based upon the historical data of law. It analysed society on the basis of its changing legal principles and legal institutions, using a method which was historical, in so far as it was based on data arranged in chronological sequence, and comparative, in that it

---

[1] H. Maine, *Village Communities in the East and the West* (New York, 1876), p. 230. For an excellent exposition of Maine's ideas see P. Vinogradoff, *The Teachings of Sir Henry Maine* (London, 1904).

rested upon a comparison of different societies in different stages of evolution.

The uniqueness of Maine's approach to social problems lay in his firm grasp of the notion of evolution, and of the relativity of social values and political institutions. The insight provided by his approach to the social process is reflected vividly in the writings of Maine's most distinguished disciple in India, namely, Sir Raymond West, who was a judge of the Bombay High Court. In an essay entitled *Land and the Law in India* which appeared in 1873, West seized upon the crucial weakness of the utilitarians when he accused them of disregarding the values which influenced social groups like the *kunbis* and *vanis*, and of assuming that the application of sophisticated concepts of law and government would automatically transform the habits of thought which influenced the behaviour of such social groups. Progress, West believed, was a process which could not be quickened by the adoption of ideas more evolved than the stage of development which characterised a society. Progress possessed a logic peculiarly its own:

History teaches us [West pontificated] that in all nations growing up in a process of spontaneous development, a change of institutions follows regularly on a change in the dominant ideas of the people. In this way the new blends itself imperceptibly with the old, and the law is the mirror of the various aims and needs that it has to satisfy. Thus healthily evalued, it rests healthily on the tendencies from which it has sprung, and affords at each stage a fresh starting point for some new advance of the ethical or political standard. Without saying that such a course as this is possible in India under British rule, one may yet say that the circumstances which make it difficult or impossible ought to be profoundly studied; that the results should greatly control our application to this country of abstract theories or empirical laws gathered in a wholly different field; and that as our institutions are the out-growth of special character, we should before introducing any one of them ... draw the popular mind in some measure within our own sphere of thought in that particular subject. No policy can be enduring which does not find room under it for the national virtues and defects; and while we are striving to improve the moral and intellectual tone of the Hindus by the influence of new and wholesome ideas, we ought in some things to wait patiently for their fruition. If our superciliousness prevents our doing this, we may often place ourselves on some mechanical success while we may in truth have been sowing the seeds of political disaster and of a dissolution of society.[1]

Here then was the crux of the dilemma which confronted the British Government in India as seen through the eyes of a conservative thinker who was deeply influenced by the scientific spirit of the age. To every stage of social development, ran West's argument, there corresponded a set of social values and political institutions, and between the two there existed a definite and indissoluble relationship. Imperialism meant the exercise of political control by a sophisticated society over an underdeveloped society. Administrators responsible for the government of colonies, therefore, were often guided by advanced notions of law and politics, and in applying these advanced notions to the government of the colony, they equally often created difficult problems for themselves. The concepts of progress, stability and order which made West critical of the policies adopted by the utilitarians, also pointed out to him the policies which could be adopted in India without any risk of social disintegration or political chaos. The reason behind the conflicts generated in rural society under British aegis was the application of sophisticated concepts of private property and legal responsibility to the problems of social organisation in the villages of India. The solution lay in a redefinition of these notions according to the values which influenced the social behaviour of the *kunbis* and other classes in rural society.

When West tried to define the extent to which the British Government in India could regulate private property, or enforce legal responsibility, he was obliged to embark upon an historical inquiry into the development of property rights in the country. For the purposes of such an inquiry West drew upon Maine's investigations into the relationship between religious ideas and social structure in Europe, investigations which had revealed that the growth of the State's interest in the life and property of its subjects was closely connected with the development of religious ideas. In primitive societies the family first grew into the clan; then the clan became a tribe; and finally the

---

[1] Sir Raymond West, *Land and the Law in India* (Bombay, 1872): *Selections from Papers on Indebtedness and Land Transfers*, Vol. I.

tribe was transformed into a nation. The primitive State flourished under the protection of a Deity who looked after its spiritual and secular interests; this Deity had to be vanquished before a new conqueror could establish himself over the State. By the same logic, the presiding Deity was worshipped by the political community which owned collectively the agricultural land which lay within the frontiers of the State. The members of this political community were required to support the State by contributions from what they produced, and these contributions were obligatory instead of being volitional. 'A Roman proprietor could be fined for negligence in the cultivation of his own fields, as under the Hindu system he might have to make good ten-fold the loss occasioned by similar carelessness. The numerous agrarian laws were repeated assertions of the State's permanent title to the soil. . . .'[1]

Till a certain stage, so West believed, the notion that the State was entitled to a share in the produce of the land developed along parallel lines in the entire 'Aryan' world, whether it was Hindu India, or the Europe of classical antiquity. But with the emergence of the institution of caste, and the spread of brahmanical values, Hindu society entered into a course of social development to which there existed no parallel in the West. The growth of an hereditary class of priests stripped the ruling caste of their jurisdiction over the sacred world, and the brahman priests, on their part, never attempted to undermine the political authority of the rulers. While on the one hand the brahman priests erased memories in the popular mind of the priestly character of the rulers, on the other they exalted their political power in the most extravagant terms. As a result, unlike their European compeers, the common folk of India had never thought of challenging the pretensions of their rulers to the ownership of land. The absence of such a challenge explained why in India land was owned by a powerful ruler or conqueror, and not by the tiller of the soil. Of course, Hindu lawgivers saw no inconsistency between such a notion of property and the popular belief that the cultivator had an inalienable although subordinate usufructory right in the land. According to one classical authority (Yajnavalkya) 'the cultivator is not destitute of ownership, but his ownership is a

[1] ibid.

qualified one, and, being subordinate to that of the king, cannot be transferred without his consent . . . .'[1]

Since the State's rights over the land rested on such firm grounds of prescription, West argued, the extent to which it was desirable to permit the free sale of land had to be determined exclusively on grounds of expediency. Besides, the ordinary *kunbis* who carried a heavy burden of debt had to be considered separately from the landed families which were losing their position in increasing numbers to a *nouveau riche* caste of *vanis*. Just as the State possessed a prescriptive and inalienable right in the land, similarly, sentiment in the villages had always been opposed to 'the severance of the family from the family estate. . . '. The British Government in India had introduced the people of the country to the idea of free contract, which was a notion that was both progressive and sophisticated. But it was also completely out of step with the state of society in India, and had resulted in the transfer of agricultural land on an unprecedented scale to the *vanis*. The concept of free contract had enabled the *vanis* to dominate the villages, and to undermine their dominance it was necessary to exercise a check on their power by restricting the alienability of land.

The considerations which West brought to bear on the problem of the landed families which were rapidly losing out to the *vanis* were quite different from the considerations which encouraged him to support the ordinary *kunbis*. He conceded that an aristocracy which was incapable of looking after its interests deserved to be replaced by men who were resourceful and enterprising, since it was a law of nature that the weak and the incompetent should suffer a decline in fortune. However, the weakening of social classes which conferred stability on Hindu society through policies based upon notions of private property and legal responsibility which rested on alien principles would result in *anomie* and chaos rather than in progress and prosperity. Such erosion, if unchecked, would seriously weaken the foundations of British rule over India:

> This continued disappearance [West observed] of families, either of old repute, or just as their hours are mellowing by time, must be of the most serious import. India, which we are striving to make a political community, has no political nationality, no historical

[1] ibid.

consciousness greatly diffused, out of which a true nationality can be developed to give force and impulse to its future. Families of distinguished social position, impelled to a certain loftiness of feeling by the pride of ancestry, and acting on hereditary principles of political conduct, are virtually indispensable in such a community. In this, and in this alone, the sense of public honour maintains its existence. They use without effort an habitual power of command; and form a nucleus of organisations in the midst of what is else a mere chaotic mass of human atoms tending to no common centre as they are drawn by no common force.[1]

The conservative principles which West applied to problems that had defied resolution at the hands of the utilitarians created a climate of opinion which was most favourable to policies of reform that sought to protect the *kunbis* from the *vanis*. Such principles simultaneously enabled British administrators to disown allegiance to ideologies which restricted their freedom of action, and which prevented them from examining problems in politics and administration on their merits. The stultifying influence of utilitarianism is best illustrated by the doctrine of rent as defined by Ricardo, which related rights in property to the 'net surplus' yielded by the land. This doctrine enabled administrators like Pringle and Francis to represent high assessments as generous on the specious plea that the government had created for the *kunbis* rights in property which they had never enjoyed before by leaving them a proportion of the rent over and above the normal returns of capital.

When a utilitarian like J. S. Mill was confronted with the disastrous consequences which resulted from the application of Ricardo's law of rent to the administration of revenue, he became most sceptical of the relevance of abstract principles of political economy to social conditions in India. The peasant in India, he argued in his *Principles of Political Economy*, was neither a wage labourer nor a capitalist farmer. Instead, he was someone who earned his subsistence from the land through his labour and his capital. For this reason the rent he was required to pay could not be evaluated on the basis of Ricardo's law of rent, for it was determined by the pressure of population on the land, and not by the proportion between population and capital. A farmer who managed his holding on capitalist principles paid

[1] ibid.

in rent only what he produced over and above the prevailing rates of profit. But in India the peasant was forced to cultivate land as the only means of livelihood available to him, and he therefore often paid a rent which absorbed all his profits except what was necessary for his subsistence.[1] But while J. S. Mill was aware of the shortcomings of the laws of political economy, he none the less looked upon the problems of rural society from an exclusively economic standpoint, and he still supported a revenue policy based on Ricardo's law of rent.[2] For this reason, West's analysis in *Land and the Law in India* of concepts like rights in property, freedom of contract and legal responsibility introduced a breath of fresh air in an environment which had been dominated far too long by the doctrines of utilitarianism and the principles of *laissez-faire*. The principles advocated by Maine and West did not gain adherents in the dramatic fashion of philosophical radicalism a generation earlier. But these principles focused on the extent to which policies of reform had to take account of traditional values and institutions, and they encouraged British administrators to adopt a catholic approach to the problems, political, social and economic, which they confronted in India. Without disowning their commitment to utilitarianism, and without substituting belief in the principles of *laissez-faire* for belief in active intervention by the State, British administrators henceforth exhibited a new awareness of the complexity of social problems, and they exhibited to an equal degree a reluctance to believe that there existed simple solutions to these problems.

II

The conservative principles advocated by Maine not only inspired the reconsiderations and the reappraisals which were initiated by West but they also influenced the legislative measures which were enacted to restore that fine balance between the social power of the *kunbis* and the *vanis* in the villages which had been undermined by the advocates of reform. When in the 1870s W. G. Pedder, the Secretary to the Government of Bombay, assessed the changes which five decades of British rule had introduced in Maharashtra, he came to the conclusion that

---

[1] J. S. Mill, *Principles of Political Economy* (London, 1909), pp. 318–28.
[2] E. Stokes, *The English Utilitarians and India* (Oxford, 1959), pp. 156–237.

the decline of the landed aristocrats was the most significant of these changes. In a society in which all classes and social groups accepted the notion of social mobility, so Pedder believed, such a transformation would have been most beneficial. It would have stimulated the flow of new capital to rural society, and it would also have stimulated the development and the exploitation of new techniques in agriculture by the successors of the old aristocrats. But social conditions in India were quite different:

> The landowner [Pedder pointed out] who had lost his estate sinks into abject poverty, embittered by the memory of the position he has lost, and, if a man of energy or influence, becomes politically dangerous. . . . The moneylender, on the other hand, who acquires the estate, though he likes the possession of land well enough, has no idea beyond that of getting all he can out of it, and would shrink with horror from the notion of leaving the town life, the security of his caste-fellows, the business, habits, and the petty gains to which he is accustomed in order to reside in solitary dignity in a remote village.[1]

Despite the important role played by the landed families, the dispossession of the ordinary *kunbis* caused far more concern to the Government of Bombay than the decline of the territorial aristocracy. This was so because few British officers associated with the Government of Bombay subscribed to a vision of society in which the landed aristocrats played any important role. Besides, as the Collector of Ahmednagar pointed out, no government could overlook the political consequences of the dispossession of the *kunbis* on the scale on which it was being carried on in the villages of Maharashtra, more particularly because this transformation, instead of being a 'natural' change, had been stimulated by giving to the country 'laws, and I may say, advantages, for which it is not prepared'. The Government of Bombay was, indeed, faced with a number of important questions: How would the production of crops be affected when the land was almost wholly owned by the *vanis* who were ignorant of agriculture, and when it was therefore cultivated on their behalf by a class of discontented *kunbis*? What would be the effect of the dispossession of the *kunbis* on the stability of British rule? Would the existence of substantial numbers of dispossessed

[1] *DRC*, Vol. II. W. G. Pedder's Report quoted in Precis of Correspondence Regarding Indebtedness of Agricultural Classes in Bombay and Upper India, Pt. II.

and therefore disgruntled *kunbis* present any special problems of political control? But for the Government of Bombay to confine its attention to such questions was to give a very limited construction to the objectives of British rule in India. The British Government in India was not only interested in maintaining its authority but it was also interested in stimulating progress and prosperity in the country:

> The glory of the government [the Collector of Ahmednagar concluded] has been that it has hitherto secured to a great extent the prosperity of the masses, and the highest credit of our Revenue Survey has been that it appeared to have settled these on a firmer basis than ever. How then can it but be a matter of great anxiety and uneasiness to Government to discover that the prosperity of the masses is declining and their happiness passing away before the encroachments of an alien community.[1]

The refusal of the *vanis* to advance credit to the *kunbis* after the disturbances of 1875 placed the latter in so desperate a position that J. B. Richey, a member of the Executive Council, directed the attention of the Government of Bombay to the need for extension of assistance to the *kunbis* in the cultivation of their land. Richey pointed out that although the reluctance of the *vanis* to advance loans to the *kunbis* had seriously hindered the operations of agriculture, the situation was not without its redeeming features. The disturbances had left the two classes 'on more equal terms than they have ever been'. The outbreak had chastened the *vanis*, and it had driven home to them the extent to which they were still dependent upon the *kunbis* for the safety of their person and property. The *kunbis*, on their part, had seen that violence did not pay any permanent dividends. The lessons which they had learnt from the disturbances had actually drawn the *kunbis* and the *vanis* together. In several villages around Poona and Ahmednagar, for instance, *panchayats* had been called on popular initiative to settle differences between the *kunbis* and the *vanis*. In Supa such a *panchayat* had persuaded the *vanis* to accept payment on a graded scale according to the antiquity of their claims. The crux of the problem, of course, was the pressing need for credit. The *kunbis* had no money whatsoever of their own. But, Richey suggested, it would

[1] *DRC*, Vol. II. Letter to the Deccan Riots Commission by H. B. Boswell, Collector of Ahmednagar, dated 5 October 1875.

'be advisable to turn the present attitude of the sowcars and the ryots towards each other to account by assisting them to a compensation of claims'.[1] If the Government of Bombay assisted the cultivators in repaying outstanding debts to the *vanis*, then the *kunbis* could start with a clean slate, and they would be in a position to benefit from any laws which the authorities might pass for their protection.

The proposal advanced by Richey received strong support from W. G. Pedder, the Secretary to the Government of Bombay. In a memorandum which outlined the implications of the proposal, Pedder pointed out that the government would have to assist all *kunbis* who were not hopelessly involved in debt. The *kunbis*, on their part, would be required to mortgage their crops to the government till their debts were repaid. In implementing such a scheme, British officers of revenue would let the cultivators have enough grain to last through the year, and they would credit the remainder to instalments of the debt. The proposal, Pedder pointed out, was inspired by an entirely new conception of the responsibilities of the government *vis-à-vis* the *kunbis*; it involved a considerable financial risk; and it also involved an additional burden on the District Officers. But the benefits flowing from the proposal would be most substantial. 'We shall,' Pedder concluded, 'have to spend a great deal more than this if we have a famine in the Deccan and shall then only save life, instead of providing the rise of the people as well.'[2] However, even though the doctrine of *laissez-faire* no longer monopolised the minds of British administrators in India, the extent of involvement advocated by Richey appeared far too hazardous to Sir Philip Wodehouse, the Governor of Bombay. The proposal, he pointed out, would virtually oblige the State to take upon itself the role of the *vani*, who provided the *kunbi* with advances for the cultivation of his land, and for the payment of the land-tax. It would be impolitic for the Government of Bombay to assume so heavy a responsibility:

> The more I enter the subject [Wodehouse stated] the more convinced I am that any measure tending to curtail the relations of

[1] *BA:* Letter from J. B. Richey, Member of the Bombay Executive Council, to W. G. Pedder dated 30 August 1875: R.D., Vol. 118 of 1875.
[2] *BA:* Memorandum by W. G. Pedder dated 31 August 1875: R.D., Vol. 118 of 1875.

the sowcar with the ryot must work prejudicially. We cannot possibly free the latter from their dependence upon the sowcars. . . . Our aim must be to maintain friendly relations with the sowcar, to satisfy him that while we will do our best to prevent extortion we will throw no obstacle in the way of the reasonable involvement of his money. I am far from assuming that attempts in this direction will be successful; but if one attempts more, one will do great mischief.[1]

The rejection of Richey's proposal set the terms of reference for the Deccan Riots Commission, which was appointed to inquire into the disturbances of 1875, when it met to devise measures which would restore the balance of power in the villages in favour of the *kunbis*, and which would also protect their interests from encroachment by the *vanis*. The *kunbis* could be strengthened in two ways: the government could either assume the responsibility of providing them with cheap credit, or it could modify the legal system in their favour. Since a commitment to *laissez-faire* principles on the part of Wodehouse ruled out the former possibility, the remedy had to be found in reform in the principles of law and in the system of justice. The most consistent step would be the imposition of an interdict on the sale of land in satisfaction of debts. Both Pedder and West were of the opinion that such an interdict would be consistent with the level of social development which prevailed in India, and with the social values of her people. But Wodehouse was opposed to so drastic a change in the legal principles which sustained the British administration. He believed that if the State upheld the right to private property, then it was also incumbent upon it to enforce the repayment of debts which had been contracted justly, even if such enforcement resulted in the large-scale transfer of landed property into the hands of the *vanis*. Any attempt to interfere in such transfers, so Wodehouse believed, would seriously undermine the rural economy of Maharashtra.[2]

The ideological commitments of Sir Philip Wodehouse obliged the Deccan Riots Commission to seek a solution of the

---

[1] *BA:* Minute by Sir Philip Wodehouse, Governor of Bombay, dated 17 September 1875: R.D., Vol. 118 of 1875. Also see Wodehouse's minute dated 19 October 1875 in R. D., Vol. 118 of 1875.

[2] Vide letter from the Bombay Government dated 6 April 1877: *Papers Relating to Deccan Agriculturists' Relief Act.* Vol. I; *Selections from the Records of the Government of India*, No. 342. (Henceforth referred to as *DARA*.)

problem through relatively minor alterations in the system of law. The ignorance of the *kunbis*, the Commissioners pointed out, placed them under a grave handicap in their financial dealings with the *vanis* who were both shrewd and grasping. The removal of the *kunbis'* ignorance would of necessity be a slow and laborious process, and it concerned issues which fell outside the Commission's terms of reference. But until the *kunbis'* ignorance was removed, the government bore a moral responsibility to see that their lack of sophistication did not put them at a disadvantage in the courts of law. The compulsory registration of bonds by public notaries, followed by a minute record of subsequent proceedings, would greatly help the *kunbis* in keeping the *vanis* at bay. Courts in the rural districts of Maharashtra, the Commissioners further observed, were situated at great distances from most villages because of which the *kunbis* found it very difficult to attend to legal business. To enable them to defend themselves against the *vanis*, it was necessary to increase the strength of Judicial Officers, and it was also necessary to institute Courts of Circuit which would tour the country districts to try civil cases.[1]

The cautious recommendations of the Deccan Riots Commission were framed to secure the approval of Sir Philip Wodehouse, whose commitment to *laissez-faire* principles was an open secret. J. B. Richey, a leading member of the Commission, had special reason to be on guard against the limited view which Sir Philip took of the responsibilities of the government, since his proposal for the extension of credit by the State to the cultivators had already been rejected by the Governor of Bombay. But despite the moderation exercised by the Commission, it was only after Sir Philip's departure that active measures were taken to reinforce the position of the *kunbis* through reform in the system of law and judicial administration. Sir Richard Temple, who succeeded Wodehouse as Governor of Bombay, subscribed to principles of government quite opposed to the principles of his predecessor. Temple was trained in the business of administration in the Punjab under Sir John Lawrence, and he therefore combined a commitment to conservatism with a Benthamite concern for rationality and simplicity in law and administration. Temple also looked to a vision of India consisting of a community of strong and independent 'yeomen

[1] *DRC*, I, paras. 13–14.

farmers', who had to be protected from the corrosive influences of a commercial society.[1]

Temple's concern for the prosperity of the *kunbis*, and his belief that the government was obliged to defend them from the *vanis*, were reinforced by the presuppositions which West and Pedder applied to their analysis of the problems which beset rural society. When Temple assumed office in 1877, he sponsored a draft Bill which modified the system of law in favour of the *kunbis* far more drastically than had been recommended by the Deccan Riots Commission. In a minute which defined the objectives of the Bill, Temple pointed out that the natural poverty of the land, and the growth in population as a result of the conditions of stability which were provided by British rule, were factors over which the government could not exercise any control. Equally, Temple argued, the creation of rights of property in land, and the institution of a modern system of administration, were irreversible changes, even though it was legitimate to assume that they heightened social conflict in rural society. Since so many of the causes which led to the disturbances of 1875 were beyond the control of the government, there was very little that changes in the system of judicial administration could do to alleviate the situation. 'But we ought, I think,' Temple stated, 'to see that our laws do not tend to bring about this state of things. At present they actually do so. Indeed, it is probably the case that unless this were so people would not be treading such dangerous paths.'[2]

The solution, so Temple believed, lay in imposing an obligation on the courts of law to examine the detailed history of all cases of indebtedness which were brought before them for adjudication. Hitherto, courts of law had investigated such cases without reference to wider problems of social equity. When a court was presented with a bond which was properly executed, it immediately decided against the *kunbi* who had executed the bond. The *kunbis*, consequently, preferred to keep away from the courts altogether. Yet the fatal bond which handed them over to a life of slavery could be 'utterly unjust—indeed . . .

---

[1] Stokes, *op. cit.*, p. 244.
[2] Minute by Sir Richard Temple dated 12 November 1877 on 'Special Legislation For Indebtedness of Ryots of the Bombay Deccan': *Bombay Government Selection*, No. 157, New Series.

(was) generally more or less unjust'. The money originally borrowed by a *kunbi* was in most cases a small fraction of the sum for which he was sued. The rest of his debt was made up of interest which was added to the principal at successive renewals of the bond. The debt could also be an inherited debt, in which case the *kunbi* often had a very vague idea of the obligations which he had taken upon himself:

> With an innocent peasantry dealing with an astute and practised class of moneylenders [Temple stated] these circumstances constitute real grievances. *Therefore the Courts should not only be empowered, but obliged to go into all the points to separate the real debt from the fictitious debt.* There should be a limit imposed on the accumulation of debt. . . . There should (also) be a distinction between a ryot's liability for his own debts and his liability for the debts of his ancestors. . . .[1] (Emphasis added.)

Temple's draft Bill sought to redress the imbalance which had resulted in rural society through measures of reform which rested on utilitarian and *laissez-faire* principles. The Bill did not question the principles which sustained the British administration in Maharashtra; the Bill merely recommended changes in the system of law which would support the interests of the *kunbis*, and release them from the bondage of the *vanis*. Yet the measures outlined in Temple's draft Bill were opposed by the Government of India, which saw no reason to amend the existing law in favour of the *kunbis*.[2] Courts of law, the Government of India pointed out, already required proof that consideration had been received by the indebted *kunbi* according to the terms of the bond produced by his creditor. For the territories of Maharashtra, the principle was even more explicitly enshrined in Regulation V of 1827, according to which 'written acknowledgement of debt in any shape shall not be held conclusive in any Court of Law . . . if the defendant shows that a full consideration had not been received'. The existing law thus offered reasonable protection to the *kunbis*, and to provide him with any further protection was unnecessary. The draft Bill sponsored by the Government of Bombay required courts of law to

---

[1] ibid.
[2] Letter to Bombay Government dated 1 July 1878: *Bombay Government Selections*, No. 157, New Series.

investigate debts even if the *kunbi* did not put up any defence for himself. But the Government of India

doubted the expediency of legislation in this direction at present. It would cast upon the Courts an amount of work which it seems very questionable whether they could, as at present constituted, get through; it would afford many opportunities for fraud and evasion to dishonest debtors, and ought thus to be an incentive to reckless borrowing.[1]

The opposition of the Government of India did not undermine Temple's belief in the need for the imposition of an obligation on courts of law to investigate the history of cases involving indebtedness. He did not deny that there were provisions in the existing law which vigilant *kunbis* could turn to their advantage in their struggle against the *vanis*. But it was obvious, Temple pointed out, that the ignorance of the *kunbis* prevented them from doing so. It was consequently necessary to amend the law in such a way that courts of law were required to investigate the history of all cases of indebtedness.[2]

The intervention at this juncture in the argument between the Governments of India and Bombay by Lord Cranbrook, the Secretary of State for India, turned the scales in favour of the latter, and resulted in legislation which was even more specific in the protection it afforded to the *kunbis* than the draft Bill sponsored by the Government of Bombay. When Cranbrook examined the social and economic conditions which prevailed in the rural districts of Maharashtra, he was convinced of the validity of Temple's view that the poverty of the *kunbis* stemmed largely from factors over which the government could not exercise any control. The Government of India, he pointed out, had tried to stimulate prosperity by investing the *kunbis* with rights of property in land, and by developing a rational policy of land-revenue, and a modern system of administration. Its efforts had been rewarded with partial success in the rise of a small class of *kunbis* whose circumstances were reasonably comfortable. But they had simultaneously created acute tension between different classes in rural society. The creation of private property, for instance, had enhanced the *kunbis'* credit, and had encouraged

[1] ibid.
[2] Minute by Sir Richard Temple dated 30 August 1878: *Bombay Government Selections*, No. 157, New Series.

them to incur indebtedness on a scale which was impossible earlier. Similarly, the *vanis* had exploited the new courts of law to establish a position of unrivalled supremacy in the villages of Maharashtra.

This last observation [Cranbrook told the Government of Bombay] brings me to the consideration of the Bill now before me. Your government has distinctly perceived that the Courts of Justice we have constituted, and law they administer, operate most harshly, and frequently with injustice, on debtors, who form the bulk of the population. Here, therefore, is an opportunity for the beneficial interference of Government. . . . (The legislation proposed should therefore be) framed with the view of mitigating the law, and of *extending the power of judges to modify the contracts entered into* between man and man.[1]

There were, according to Cranbrook, two areas in which the Government of Bombay could profitably concentrate its efforts to assist the *kunbis*. The physical remoteness of the courts from most villages prevented the *kunbis* from defending themselves effectively. Besides, a system of justice which rested on the principle of free contract, admittedly with qualifications, induced a condition of helplessness in the peasants. Both these difficulties could be resolved through the creation of new courts which were suitably located in the rural districts, and which dispensed justice according to notions of social equity which were understood by the *kunbis*.

The principle of efficiency advocated by Bentham, and the historical approach to laws and institutions recommended by Maine, which combined to inspire the Deccan Agriculturists' Relief Act of 1879 were eloquently expressed in the speech made by T. C. Hope while piloting the Bill through the Supreme Legislative Council. Hope touched briefly upon the reasons behind the increase in indebtedness in the rural districts of Maharashtra, and the consequent growth of an antagonism between the *kunbis* and the *vanis*, and he pointed to the increasing dispossession of the former by the latter as the crux of the rural problem. It was, he confessed, legitimate to look upon the dispossession of the *kunbis* as a symptom of progress. The creation of rights of property in land was necessary to ensure progress and

[1] Dispatch to Bombay Government dated 26 December 1878: *Bombay Government Selections*, No. 157, New Series.

prosperity in society. It was also necessary that these rights should be held by those who possessed the resources and the enterprise to exploit them properly. If land was held by a class which was unable to put it to any use, and which was in addition burdened with a crippling load of debt, then it was in the interests of the community for this class to be dispossessed. But while such principles could safely constitute the bases for policy in western societies, considerable caution was necessary in applying them to India. So many of the problems which confronted the British Government in India could be traced to policies which took no account of the traditional values and the social institutions of the country. 'When one overturns by an act of legislation institutions which popular consent has maintained for centuries,' Hope stated, 'we sometimes forget that we are not the bearers of a political revelation from Heaven':

> In the present instance there seems genuine reason for doubting whether the premises on which a policy of laissez-faire is based are sound. If the present condition of the Deccan ryots is caused by inherent moral and physical defects, . . . if they encumber the land to the exclusion of a class of intelligent, enterprising and energetic capitalists, . . . then indeed we must sit down and sit out the process of gradual transfer of the rights of property from one class to another. . . . But consideration will show that no such circumstances exist in the Deccan. The Maratha kunbi is not the useless and defective creature postulated. . . . His embarrassed condition seems to be rather his misfortune than his fault, induced by the calamities of the last century, the obligation of ancestral debt, the burden of the land revenue—firstly in amount and latterly in imposition—and the facilities for extortion conferred by our laws upon his creditor. On the other hand, those into whose hands the land is now observed to be passing are not yearning for it to improve it by their capital or intelligence. With solitary exceptions, the transferees are the professional moneylenders, who have no wish even to hold the status of landed proprietors. . . . Such conditions deprive the transfer of land from distressed to moneyed classes of all the glosses with which political economy would surround it. They show that the noble gift of property in land, made by the British Government to the peasants for their sole benefit, is passing, contrary to their intentions, and in frustration of their objects to a class unfitted to receive it.[1]

[1] Speech by T. C. Hope before the Imperial Legislative Council dated 17 July 1879: *Bombay Government Selections*, No. 157, New Series.

In the districts of Maharashtra, so Hope argued, it was clearly necessary to prevent the *vanis* from taking up the position formerly occupied by the *kunbis* in rural society. But while it was necessary to restrain the *vanis*, it was equally necessary to ensure that they would continue supplying credit to the *kunbis*. Any measure which sought to help the *kunbis*, therefore, also required the approval of the *vanis*, since the prosperity of the villages depended upon a relationship of mutual trust and confidence between these two classes.

The Agriculturists' Relief Act of 1879 attempted, in the first instance, to establish safeguards against fraud by debtors or by creditors in the original transaction of the loan. For this purpose to be legally valid a bond between a *kunbi* and a *vani* had to be drawn up under the supervision of a village registrar. Next, the Act provided for Conciliators who were required to resolve disputes between *kunbis* and *vanis* through informal arbitration. If such arbitration proved abortive, and the disputing parties decided to resort to litigation, then they could proceed to newly created courts of law which were situated within easy reach of villages, and which were required to dispense justice promptly and efficiently. Over these courts presided officers called Munsiffs, who were selected from landed families of trust and respectability. The courts of the Subordinate Judges, which attended to appeals made against the awards of the Munsiffs, were reinforced in two directions. Their strength was increased from 24 to 31, and they were empowered to try a wider range of cases than before. However, in keeping with the principles of Bentham, the powers of the Subordinate Judges were counterbalanced by newly created machinery for supervision and control. This machinery was embodied in the person of a Special Judge who was expected to inspect, supervise and revise the proceedings of the Subordinate Judges. Besides reorganising the judicial machinery, the Relief Act introduced changes in the substantive law administered by the courts of law. These changes hinged upon the definition of the liability of a debtor, and they were inspired by the belief that 'the passing of a bond by a native of India is often of no more value as proof of a debt . . . than the confession of a man under torture of the crime he is charged with'. Finally, the Relief Act institutionalised the new concept of social equity advanced by Temple, and it required all courts of law to investigate the history of cases involving indebtedness in order to firmly establish the extent of a *kunbi*'s obligations before passing any judgement.[1]

III

The effect of the Relief Act on the disturbing accumulation of power in the hands of the *vanis* was immediate and decisive. Since the Act obliged the courts of law to investigate the bonds which made the *kunbis* the supine prisoners of the *vanis*, it eliminated at one stroke that bias in favour of the *vanis* which the Government of Bombay had inadvertently introduced in the administration of justice. However, the way in which rural society had changed since 1818 could not fail to influence the working of the Act. So far as the *kunbis* were concerned, the advantages they drew from the Act varied with their means and with their intellectual sophistication. Similarly, the *vanis*, being shrewd and resourceful, were able to exploit some of its provisions to defeat those very objectives for whose realisation the Act had been framed. While Temple and Hope had made no secret of their desire to restore the *kunbis* to their former position in rural society, the extent to which the *kunbis* were able to regain their lost dominance was determined by their prosperity, and by their ability to exploit the new law in their conflicts with the *vanis*. Of course, the popularity of the Relief Act among the *kunbis* was most widespread. 'In the various places through which I have passed during my late tour,' a District Officer noted in 1883, 'I have found that by *all true* agriculturists the Act is regarded as their charter of safety, and that no measure of government for many years past can be compared with it in point of popularity.'[2] Nevertheless, the *kunbis*' enthusiasm for the Act provided no index to their ability to comprehend its provisions, or to their capacity to exploit the protection it afforded them. Indeed, as we shall presently see, only *kunbis* whose circumstances were comfortable were at all able to draw any substantial benefits from the Relief Act.

To understand the effect of the Relief Act we shall find it necessary to divide the *kunbis* of Maharashtra into three classes

---

[1] ibid.
[2] Report on the Deccan Agriculturists' Relief Act by H. Woodward dated 25 June 1883: *DARA*, Vol. I, pp. 335–59.

on the basis of their indebtedness and their wealth. First we shall consider a small group of *kunbis* who represented 10 per cent of the rural population. These *kunbis* cultivated large fields of superior quality, and they possessed adequate stock and capital. Their prosperity was due to the peaceful conditions which prevailed under British rule, and to the system of land-revenue which was introduced by the Government of Bombay. Such *kunbis* possessed substantial reserves of capital, and even when they borrowed money from the *vanis*, they could always repay their debts, and must therefore be regarded as solvent and independent. A number of bad harvests, or a serious famine, could trench heavily into their resources, but such calamities could not ruin them.

The rich peasants were followed by a second group of *kunbis* who constituted 40 per cent of the rural population. Cultivators belonging to this group were most intimately affected by the Relief Act since their position was serious, but it was not beyond all hope of recovery. They owned from 20 to 70 acres of land of medium quality, and their best fields were usually mortgaged to the *vanis*. Although they cultivated their fields with considerable skill and industry, they barely produced enough to keep body and soul together, and a succession of bad seasons could reduce them to a condition of abject poverty.

For the remaining 50 per cent of the *kunbis*, who were poor even by the none too exacting standards of Maharashtra, life was a perpetual struggle against the threat of starvation. Such *kunbis* owned between 10 to 20 acres of land of such poor quality that the *vanis* were reluctant to give them loans on the security of their holdings. Since they owned insufficient cattle to plough their fields, they were obliged to depend upon their fellow-cultivators for loans of their oxen, and they repaid them either by working on their fields, or by giving them a share of the produce. Even in normal seasons *kunbis* belonging to the third group barely raised enough on their fields to feed their families all the year round. But if the rains failed, their position became desperate, and they were forced to sell their cattle, and to work as labourers on daily wages on the fields of other *kunbis*.[1]

Although the Relief Act was meant to strengthen the position of the *kunbis*, it also presented them with serious problems. Since

[1] ibid.

the Act obliged courts of law to investigate the history of loan transactions, it protected the *kunbis* from outright exploitation. But at the same time it made the *vanis* reluctant to advance money to the cultivators because of the arbitrary and inquisitorial powers, so the *vanis* believed, with which it had armed the officers of justice. The reluctance of the *vanis* to advance credit to the cultivators could, as critics of the Act were quick to point out, have grave repercussions since the *kunbis* were completely dependent upon the *vanis* for carrying out the operations of agriculture. But the Act did not precipitate any immediate crisis in the villages because *kunbis* belonging to different groups varied in their dependence upon the *vanis*, and because the extent to which their credit was affected under the new dispensation varied with their prosperity. *Kunbis* belonging to the first group were least dependent of all on the *vanis*. Their indebtedness could quite often be traced to social ostentation, and the contraction of credit which followed the Relief Act did not affect them in any significant way. The reverse was true of peasants belonging to the second and third groups, since they were forced to borrow money from the *vanis* to carry out their agricultural operations, and to pay their taxes to the State. However, since the generosity of the *vanis* was often purchased by the *kunbis* at a fearful price, the restrictions placed by the Relief Act were a blessing rather than a calamity.

The fate of the *kunbis* in the *taluka* of Kopargaon substantiates our assertion. Kopargaon was visited with a series of poor seasons after 1879, but when their crops failed the *kunbis* of the *taluka* were unable to secure any credit because of the fear in which the *vanis* held the new legislation. Since the *kunbis* were unable to obtain credit from the *vanis*, they migrated in large numbers to the neighbouring districts where they eked out an existence as labourers on daily wages. But for the Relief Act, the *kunbis* of Kopargaon would not have been obliged to migrate from their villages and to work as labourers. Yet their fields and cattle would have been pledged to the moneylenders, and they would gradually have been reduced to the status of tenants. The *kunbis* were actually better off as agricultural labourers than they would have been as the tenants of the *vanis* under the old order of things. Their wages sufficed to keep body and soul together, but they still retained their land, and so long as they retained their land they retained hope for the future. A return to normal conditions would see them back in their villages. A good rainfall would improve their situation considerably, while a succession of good harvests would restore them to their former condition of prosperity. If this was true of districts where conditions were unfavourable after 1879, the improvement in the condition of the *kunbis* was even more marked in areas where the crops were bountiful. The contraction of credit caused by the Relief Act obliged cultivators to reduce all wasteful expenditure, and since they could no longer borrow money as easily as they had done before, they were thrown back on their own resources, and did not look to the *vani* for assistance. As a result, the share of agricultural produce which had formerly been appropriated by the *vanis* as interest was now distributed among the actual tillers of the soil.[1]

While the *kunbis*, therefore, welcomed the Relief Act as a measure which protected their interests, the *vanis* looked upon it as something designed to undermine their position, and they raised a loud outcry against its 'iniquitous' provisions. But while the *vanis* protested against the provisions of the Act, they were at the same time confident that the attempt to relieve the *kunbis* of indebtedness would prove abortive, since the credit which they extended to the cultivators was essential for agricultural operations:

> The intention of the Government [the *vanis* pointed out in a representation to the Government of Bombay] is to relieve the agriculturists from indebtedness, but it is impossible to carry out the profession of agriculture without involving oneself in debt, because agriculture is a speculation. One is supposed to lay out money on land, and labour on for twelve months, maintaining himself by borrowing. If, unfortunately, the crops are damaged, the cultivator is required to ask from his creditor twelve months time to pay off the debt. . . . And the creditor, on his part, is obliged to lend money for the next year, in order to recover his past dues. Thus a creditor and a debtor stand in need of each other; but it appears that the legislators have not sufficiently considered this point.[2]

[1] ibid.
[2] Petition by the *Vanis* of Poona dated nil and forwarded in A. D. Pollen's Report dated 7 June 1880: *DARA*, Vol. I. pp. 223–6.

The crux of the problem, the *vanis* stated, did not lie in the indebtedness of the *kunbis*; the crux of the problem lay in the climate of suspicion and distrust which had been generated through the reforms instituted in the system of judicial administration. Before the British conquest of 1818, the relationship between the *kunbis* and the *vanis* had been a relationship of cooperation and mutual trust. The *vani* was then regarded as a useful member of the village community, and the role he played in the rural economy had benefited the community as a whole. 'The agricultural work . . . (was) not hindered owing to the agriculturists' dealings with a sowcar, just as the management of a family is not hindered owing to the wife having a husband,' the *vanis* pointed out. But the moment courts of law based upon western principles were introduced, the partnership between the *kunbis* and the *vanis* had broken down, since the *vanis* were then forced to secure their loans by legal documents, instead of reposing confidence in the pledged word of the *kunbis*, as they had done formerly. Because the laws became increasingly formal and inflexible, the *vanis* were forced more and more to turn the screw on the *kunbis*. As a result friction between the two classes increased by leaps and bounds and ultimately led to the disturbances of 1875. The courts of law and the legal principles introduced by the Government of Bombay had driven a deep wedge between the two most important social groups in the villages of Maharashtra. Similarly, the Relief Act had undermined the *vanis*' faith in the integrity of the government:

> The Regulations of 1827 [the *vanis* held] protected all people, and gave no trouble and expense to Government in any way. New laws were not framed every year. The traders never hesitated to carry out their dealings. Now new laws are frequently framed, and so the traders have lost their trust in laws. The traders and agriculturists do not know what laws may be framed by Government. . . . Therefore they are very cautious, and cannot attend to agricultural work. But the Government should point out a way by which the agriculturists would be enabled to get timely pecuniary aid. This would do good to all.[1]

Although the *vanis* looked upon the Relief Act as a whole with disapproval, they disapproved in particular of the provision which obliged courts of law to investigate the history of all

[1] ibid.

219

cases which involved indebtedness. Such a provision, the *vanis* believed, encouraged the *kunbis* to disown debts which they knew to be perfectly legitimate. Since the Government of Bombay had taken upon itself to support the cultivators, the *vanis* decided to discontinue their credit operations in order to impress upon everyone concerned the importance of their role in the rural economy. Their decision to restrict the flow of credit to the cultivators was reflected in a reduction of 75 per cent in loan transactions in the years after 1879. However, while the restriction of credit was a calculated attempt on the part of the affluent *vanis* to force the government to surrender, so far as the poor *vanis* were concerned it reflected a genuine inability to conduct business under the provisions of the new legislation. We have already mentioned how the *ryotwari* system of land-revenue had affected the *vani*'s role in the rural economy, since it channelised the flow of credit from the *sowcar* to the *kunbi* through the village moneylender, instead of the village community. While *vanis* like the Karamchands of Parner had blossomed into substantial men under the new dispensation, a considerable number of moneylenders possessed very little capital of their own, and they borrowed money from *sowcars* in the cities in order to advance loans to *kunbis* in the villages. The Relief Act affected such *vanis* most adversely.[1] While it did not shield them from their creditors, the *sowcars*, the *kunbis* to whom they loaned money were fully protected by the Act. The plight of the *petits vanis* is vividly reflected in their representation to the Government of Bombay:

> Before Act XVII of 1879 came into force [they pointed out] we used to borrow money from larger sowcars at a low rate of interest and advance the same with or without security to the agriculturists. As we received our dues from these agriculturists without any very serious difficulties, we were better able to support ourselves and pay off our sowcars. Since the Act came into force we are called upon to produce our accounts from the beginning in support of our claims against agriculturists. We generally do not keep accounts. Our difficulties do not end with obtaining decrees against agriculturists. The Civil Courts (now) have no powers to attach

[1] W. H. Crowe, District Judge, Poona, to Bombay Government dated 3 September 1883: *DARA*, Vol. I, pp. 399–400. Also see Memorandum by E. Hoskins, Assistant of Sholapur dated 21 August 1883: *DARA*, Vol. I, pp. 401–2.

agriculturists' movable property . . . (and) after obtaining decrees against agriculturists we are left to all intents and purposes in the same position in which one would find himself when his claim is time barred. . . . The large sowcars have now ceased lending us money, and consequently we have ceased lending money to the agriculturists. All money dealings have come to a standstill, and we are left without any means to support ourselves. Our prayer, therefore, is that the Act be cancelled and the old order of things restored.[1]

Despite the 'anti-*vani*' bias of the Relief Act, and notwithstanding the fate of the *petits vanis*, it would be a mistake to assume that the measure led to a complete suspension of credit in the villages of Maharashtra, or that it placed the moneylenders entirely at the mercy of the *kunbis*. Among other things we should bear in mind the ignorance of the *kunbis* who lived in the more inaccessible villages. A District Officer who travelled through the 'relieved' districts in 1883 found that in many villages the *kunbis* were totally ignorant of the new legislation. Such *kunbis* realised that they could no longer secure loans as easily as they had secured them formerly. But this realisation did not encourage them to find out why it was so. There were, besides, *kunbis* whom the *vanis* had always treated with indulgence and who did not, therefore, seek any protection from the government. Such *kunbis* regarded their relationship with the *vanis* as a relationship of trust and confidence, and their 'feelings . . . (were) strongly opposed to litigation, and they preferred almost any sacrifice rather than resort to the Courts'.[2]

The most important reason for the survival of the *vanis*, however, was their ability to turn certain provisions of the Relief Act to their advantage. Besides introducing changes in substantive law, the Relief Act had provided for Conciliators who were expected to resolve conflicts between the *kunbis* and the *vanis* through informal arbitration based upon traditional principles of social equity. The Conciliators were appointed from respectable landed families, and the office was expected to partially restore to such families that control over the administration of

[1] Petition by the 'Small Sowcars' of Otur, Talukar Junnar, dated 28 July 1883: *DARA*, Vol. I, p. 401.
[2] Report on the Deccan Agriculturists' Relief Act by H. Woodward dated 25 June 1883: *DARA*, Vol. I, pp. 335–59.

justice which they had formerly exercised through the *panchayats*. However, the appointment of the Conciliators rested on the assumption that the former leaders of rural society were still capable of playing an active role in the affairs of the community. This assumption was completely unwarranted. Like the Kowreys of Parner, for instance, the old landed families had mostly been eclipsed by the rise of the *vanis*. Indeed, the circumstances of the landed families had changed to such an extent that their heads hesitated to accept office because of the odium they feared to incur in discharging their duties. 'Individuals are more apt to stand apart and interest themselves less in communal matters,' a British officer pointed out. 'The Deshmukh, or mouthpiece of the community, whom every member of it looked to and heeded, is, in all but name, a thing of the past.'[1] The individuals who were persuaded to act as Conciliators bore little resemblance to the men who had formerly controlled the affairs of the villages. A majority of such men were heavily involved in debt, and they were consequently looked upon by the *kunbis* with suspicion as the supine instruments of the *vanis*.

The *vanis* immediately seized hold of conciliation as something which enabled them to defeat (what they looked upon as) the offensive provisions of the Relief Act. This is obvious from a comparison (see Tables K and L) between the relatively small number of suits filed in the higher courts of law and the flood of applications which inundated the courts of conciliation instituted under the Act. As Table K indicates, suits filed against the *kunbis* in 1880 and 1881 amounted to only 50 per cent of the suits filed against them before 1879, but this decrease was counterbalanced by the impressive volume of business handled by the Conciliators. The 'popularity' of conciliation led some British officers to view it with great suspicion. Ideally, the system required Conciliators of great integrity, and it also required disputants who were evenly matched in their knowledge of the law and in their intellectual sophistication. The conditions which prevailed in Maharashtra were quite different, since the Conciliators were often heavily indebted to the *vanis*, who were at the same time shrewder than the *kunbis* who were pitted against them. Conciliation, therefore, often led to collusive agreements, and the institution was looked upon by the *vanis* as

[1] ibid.

something which provided an escape from that 'inquisitorial' investigation into the history of debts which they regarded as the most repugnant provision of the Relief Act.[1]

Yet conciliation was not without its advantages. It saved the *kunbis* a lot of time by bringing the courts to their doorsteps. It eliminated that friction between the *vanis* and the *kunbis* which

TABLE K

Showing Decrease in Civil Suits Against *Kunbis* in 1879

District	Cases in 1881	Cases in 1880	Average over ten years
Poona	4,732	3,161	8,072
Satara	4,501	2,712	10,151
Ahmednagar	4,337	3,469	11,142
Sholapur	2,981	2,453	5,735

TABLE L

Cases before Conciliators

District	Applications for conciliation	Cases withdrawn by applicants	No. of cases decided	Cases decided by arbitration	No of failures
Poona	20,514	2,309	2,351	8	9,307
Ahmednagar	18,056	1,231	2,219	13	8,521
Sholapur	10,068	714	1,547	6	4,505
Satara	27,776	1,535	2,685	148	14,436

inevitably followed the reference of disputes to formal courts of law. Finally, it intercepted and resolved a number of cases which would otherwise have swamped the higher courts, and prevented them from carrying out the investigations into the histories of loans which they were required to conduct under the new legislation. Well-informed officers like M. G. Ranade, who

[1] Report on the Working of the Relief Act by A. D. Pollen dated 4 February 1882: *DARA*, Vol. I, pp. 290–314.

carried no special brief for the *vanis*, were of the opinion that the awards given by the Conciliators showed little evidence of collusion with the *vanis*. In the villages around Poona and Satara, for instance, Conciliators had reduced the claims of the *vanis* by 50 per cent before awarding decrees against the cultivators. Their awards, Ranade argued, 'satisfactorily disprove of the allegation that the conciliation system gives a legal sanction to the claims of the creditors. . . '.[1] A glance at Table L suggests that even though the *vanis* preferred the courts of conciliation to the regular courts, the Conciliators were by no means the supine instruments of their will. If conciliation amounted to acquiescence in the *vani*'s *diktat* by the *kunbis*, then it is difficult to explain the high rate of failure (50 per cent of the suits filed) in the Concilator's attempts to resolve cases which came up to him for arbitration. Indeed, despite the loopholes it afforded to the *vanis*, the Relief Act substantially transformed the terms of the relationship between the *kunbis* and the *vanis*. It did so by impressing upon the *kunbis* that in disputes with the *vanis* the weight of the administration would be thrown in their favour rather than against them. Such an assurance restored the *kunbis'* confidence in their ability to hold their own against the *vanis*:

> (The ryots) . . . are no longer debarred from the hope of one day being free and independent [a British civilian pointed out in 1883]. They are far from being oppressed and harassed by the creditors. They have ceased to regard him with stark dread and to accord to his dictates a submission which no one else could command. The local power and influence of the sowcar, more often abused than not, was paramount. All, or nearly all, with whom he came in contact were his debtors, and so his servants and fawning sycophants. The effect of the Act has been to change all this.[2]

The Relief Act of 1879 redressed the imbalance in rural society which was created by policies of reform that were inspired by the principles of utilitarianism. This imbalance was expressed in the dominance of the *vanis*, a dominance which they acquired by dispossessing the *kunbis* of their land, but which none the less failed to transform them into capitalist farmers.

[1] ibid.
[2] Report on the Deccan Agriculturists' Relief Act by H. Woodward dated 25 June 1883: *DARA*, Vol. I, pp. 335–59.

The Relief Act constituted an acknowledgement of this failure, indeed, of the failure of utilitarianism in general, since the transformation of the subsistence economy of Maharashtra into a capitalist economy was the single most important objective of the utilitarians. The Act was equally a triumph of the conservative principles which were enunciated by Sir Henry Maine. The concept of evolution provided the key to these principles, and when they were applied to India by disciples of Maine like Sir Raymond West, they demolished the assumption made by the protagonists of reform that a primitive society could be transformed overnight into a modern society through changes in the systems of law and administration. By focusing on the relation between the institutions and the values of a society, Maine explained why the *kunbis* had lost out to the *vanis*, just as he also explained why the *vanis* had refused to behave like capitalist farmers even after they had come in possession of substantial holdings in land!

But Maine's approach took him far beyond his analysis of the reasons behind the failure of utilitarianism in Maharashtra. It also provided him with clues as to how the problems of rural society could be resolved. Progress, he stated, could best be achieved through policies that took account of the values and institutions which obtained in a community. Failure to do so, he believed, could only lead to chaos. Maine's concern for continuity in the processes of change was reminiscent of the principles which informed the policies of men like Mountstuart Elphinstone. But Maine was the product of a milieu which had been deeply influenced by science and rationality. Consequently, his conservative principles of law and government rested on scientific assumptions which completely undermined the utilitarian vision of society. Maine substituted the facile optimism of the utilitarians by a sophisticated insight into the values and institutions of society in India.

The Act of 1879 was the first measure which attempted to reform the law in conformity with the principles of social equity which had prevailed in Maharashtra before 1818. Since the Act laid the basis for a healthy relationship between the *kunbis* and the *vanis* by throwing the weight of the administration in favour of the former, it successfully achieved its immediate objectives. But it failed to fulfil all the expectations with which it had been

launched. While presenting the Bill before the Imperial Legislative Council, for instance, Hope had stated that it would not
only undermine the power of the *vanis* but that it would also
stimulate progress in rural society.

This turned out to be wholly untrue. The Act prevented the
vanis from exploiting the *kunbis*; but it extended protection to
the *kunbis* by depriving them of that credit which was necessary
for the progress of rural society. If, however, the Relief Act
failed to achieve its wider objectives then the blame for this
failure rests on Hope who had raised unwarranted expectations
rather than on those who had framed the legislation. An Act
which merely introduced changes in law and in the administration could at best hope to create the conditions for progress; it
could do little to actually bring about such progress. Ranade
showed a clearer perception of the potentialities of the Act than
Hope when he observed that

> the proper standpoint from which the working of the Act must be
> judged appears to me to be that it is admittedly an experiment
> dictated by an emergency, and that it is further a compromise
> between the *let-alone* policy and extreme communistic suggestions.
> . . . Whenever its effects on the credit of the ryots and the economi-
> cal prosperity of the country are considered, then three charac-
> teristics of the Act, namely, that it is an experiment, a compromise
> and one of several administrative reliefs which were to have simul-
> taneous operation, should not be lost sight of. A too sanguine or
> exaggerated view of its beneficial effects is necessarily doomed to
> disappointment.[1]

The reform of the system of judicial administration could do
little to provide the *kunbis* with the capital which was necessary
for the proper cultivation of their holdings. Indeed, the Relief
Act, if it did anything at all, focused on the great scarcity of
capital in the villages of Maharashtra. By doing so it encouraged
the Government of Bombay to devote its attention to the problem of providing the *kunbis* with the capital necessary for the
operations of agriculture.

[1] Report on the Working of the Relief Act by M. G. Ranade dated 12 February,
1882: *DARA*, Vol. II, pp. 323–4.

VII

The Non-Acquisitive Society

T H E consequences stemming from the Deccan Agricultur-
alists' Relief Act of 1879 revealed that the administration of
justice was merely one of the factors responsible for the crisis
which overtook rural society in 1875. They also proved that
reforms in the administration of justice alone could not put the
kunbis on the path to progress and prosperity. What enabled the
vanis to establish their dominance over the villages of Maharashtra was the *kunbis'* need for credit to finance their agricultural operations, and to meet the social obligations imposed
upon them by their status in rural society. The Relief Act protected the *kunbis* from legal exploitation at the hands of the
vanis. But it did little to assure them of a cheap and plentiful
supply of credit, partly out of a mistaken analysis of the rural
problem by the Government of Bombay, but partly also because
of its restricted view of the responsibilities of the State towards
the community. Conservatives like Sir Richard Temple and
T. C. Hope who sponsored the Relief Act not only refused to pay
sufficient attention to the problem of rural credit but also by
amending the law in favour of the *kunbis* made the *vanis*
reluctant to conduct business with them, and created a situation
which threatened to weaken the foundations of the rural economy
of Maharashtra.

Since the *kunbis* were ignorant and helpless, and because the
Government of Bombay was committed to principles which

frowned upon minute interference by the State in the affairs of the community, it was up to the *sowcars* to propose steps which would resolve the impasse created by the Relief Act and restore the flow of capital to the villages. That the *sowcars* had a shrewd idea of the important role they played in the rural economy is obvious from the tone of their protests against the Relief Act, and from their attempt to browbeat the Government of Bombay into acquiescence through withholding credit from the *kunbis* after 1879. But the *sowcars'* bid to force the government to its knees through starving the peasants of credit turned out to be a double-edged weapon. For if the peasants were dependent upon them for carrying out the operations of agriculture, then the *vanis* on their part could not afford to let their capital lie unutilised, since they depended upon moneylending for their livelihood. Indeed, the decrease in financial transactions after 1879 was not entirely due to the intransigence of the *vanis*, since it partly reflected the inability of the *petits vanis* to conduct their business under the provisions of the new legislation. The accumulation of idle capital in the hands of the *sowcars* highlighted the need for a solution that would remove the obstacles in the flow of capital to the villages. The need for such a solution was reinforced through the rise of new social groups, like native civil servants and members of the liberal professions, which had substantial capital to invest, and whose confidence in commercial channels of investment had been destroyed during the crisis which overtook so many business houses in Bombay in the depression which followed the Civil War in America.[1]

I

The enactment of the Relief Act of 1879 by the Government of India exhausted the resources of British officers, and the initiative for further action rested entirely on the *vanis* and the *sowcars*. Being traditionally shrewd and resourceful, the latter were quick to rise to the challenge.[2] In 1882 a group of *sowcars* from Poona headed by Rao Bahadur Viziarangam Mudliar proposed the institution of Agricultural Banks which would

[1] *NAI* (National Archives of India): Memorandum by Jhaveri Lal Yajnik, a Gujerati banker, dated 9 May 1882: Department of Revenue and Agriculture (Revenue Branch), A Proceedings No. 13/20, June 1884.
[2] *Parliamentary Papers*, Vol. LXII of 1887: Communication from the Bankers of Poona to Bombay Government dated 18 August 1882.

find profitable employment for the capital that lay idle in the hands of the urban classes, and which would simultaneously provide the *kunbis* with the credit they so desperately required for the cultivation of their fields.[1] The proposal was inspired by the belief that the flow of credit from the *sowcars* to the *kunbis* through an institution which enjoyed the patronage of the Government of Bombay would ensure fair play both to the *kunbis* and the *vanis*, and would simultaneously create the conditions for prosperity in rural society. The system of rural credit which flourished before 1879 had brought about the dominance of the *vanis* over the *kunbis*; equally, the Relief Act, by amending the law in favour of the *kunbis*, had undermined the *vanis'* faith in the integrity of the Government of Bombay and had persuaded them to refuse credit to the *kunbis*. The institution of Agricultural Banks, so the *sowcars* of Poona believed, would avoid both these evils. For if the *vanis* were organised in banks which enjoyed the blessings of the government, then they would not aspire to dominate the *kunbis*, since the banks would be able to protect their interests without involving them in litigation of dubious morality.

Although their proposal for Agricultural Banks appeared unexceptionable to the *sowcars* of Poona, they were by no means inclined to underestimate the difficulties involved in launching a new experiment in rural credit. Before they took up the proposal with the Government of Bombay, they discussed the idea of a rural bank with the leading *sowcars* of various *mofussil* towns in order to win them over to the scheme. Mudliar believed that the co-operation of such *sowcars* was vital to the success of the proposal, since the Agricultural Banks would have to depend upon them for some of their capital, and because the influence which they exercised over the villages could, if directed against the banks, jeopardise the success of the scheme.

The *sowcars* of Poona bestowed equal care on the choice of a suitable site for an Agricultural Bank. They decided to locate the bank in Purandhar, which was one of the most prosperous *talukas* in Poona District, and which had a population of 75,678 distributed in 92 villages over an area of 457 square miles. Of the 15,000 peasant households in Purandhar, 13,400

[1] *Parliamentary Papers*, Vol. LXII of 1887: 'A Proposal from the Poona Bankers Regarding Agricultural Banks' dated 20 November 1882.

possessed land of their own. The distribution of holdings in Purandhar indicates the existence of a substantial number of *kunbis* who were reasonably affluent, and who owned fields which varied between 10 and 30 acres in area. The annual income of the *taluka* was Rs. 750,000, of which costs of cultivation accounted for Rs. 300,000. The government assessment for Purandhar amounted to Rs. 100,000. The *kunbis* of the *taluka* were, therefore, left with a surplus of Rs. 250,000, over and above the wages of labour and the profits of capital.[1]

Since the total indebtedness of the *kunbis* of Purandhar amounted to Rs. 1,000,000, and since they controlled an annual surplus of Rs. 250,000, it could be legitimately inferred that they were in a sound financial condition. The relative prosperity of the *kunbis* of Purandhar persuaded the *sowcars* of Poona to choose it as the site for an experimental Agricultural Bank, because there was reasonable prospect of the *kunbis* being relieved of their burden of debt with a minimum of assistance. The scheme which the *sowcars* of Poona outlined before the Government of Bombay involved, in the first stage, the liquidation of the debts of the *kunbis* of Purandhar.[2] For this purpose the *sowcars* proposed the appointment of a Commission comprising an officer of the Department of Revenue, and two private members who were expected to represent the interests of the *vanis* and the *kunbis*. This Commission was to settle the amount of debt owed by the *kunbis* to the *vanis*. After the debt had been settled the Government of Bombay was to undertake the payment of the amount due to the *sowcars*. The Commission would then arrange for the repayment of this sum to the government through annual instalments to be paid by the *kunbis*. The payments made by the Government of Bombay to the *vanis*, the *sowcars* of Poona pointed out, would be a fictitious transaction. For as soon as the Commission had concluded its inquiries the proposed Agricultural Bank would assume responsibility for all advances; and since the *sowcars* would purchase shares in the bank equivalent to the sums of money due to them the Government of Bombay

[1] *Parliamentary Papers*, Vol. LXII of 1887: Poona *sowcars* to Sir William Wedderburn dated 21 October 1885.
[2] *Parliamentary Papers*, Vol. LXII of 1887: Poona Committee to Sir William Wedderburn dated 9 January 1883.

would not actually be required to advance any money to the *kunbis*.

The crux of the *sowcars'* proposal concerned the assistance which the Government of Bombay was required to give to the Agricultural Bank for the recovery of loans from the *kunbis*. The Relief Act, the *sowcars* asserted, had made the recovery of loans impossible, and no bank could conduct business with any prospect of success so long as the Act was not amended. The loans made by the Agricultural Bank would, therefore, have to 'be a first charge on the land after the assessment, and should be recoverable through the revenue agency free of costs like the arrears of land revenue'.[1] The *sowcars* assured the Government of Bombay that whenever conditions of scarcity compelled the Department of Revenue to suspend the land-tax, the bank would follow its example. But to protect the bank's interests when the *kunbis'* defaulted in the payment of the revenue it would have to be empowered with the right to buy the *kunbis'* land, or the new owner of the land would have to be compelled to assume the obligations of the former owner. If an Agricultural Bank was assured of the support outlined in their proposal, the *sowcars* of Poona stated in conclusion, then it would provide the *kunbis* with the capital they required to build a prosperous future for themselves in Purandhar.

The fate of the proposed Agricultural Bank rested upon the attitude adopted by the Government of Bombay towards the assurances required by the *sowcars* of Poona. When Sir James Fergusson, the Governor of Bombay, met a delegation of *sowcars* from Poona on 23 November 1882 he informed them that 'he was favourably disposed towards the scheme ... (and that) he and his Honourable Colleagues would give their best consideration to the proposal'.[2] But a memorandum written by W. Lee-Warner, a senior member of the Government of Bombay, expressed the reservations with which officers who were by no means lacking in sympathy looked upon a scheme that was based on a novel conception of the responsibilities of the State *vis-à-vis* the community. Lee-Warner opened his critique with

[1] ibid.
[2] *Parliamentary Papers*, Vol. LXII of 1887: Reply by Sir James Fergusson, Governor of Bombay, to an Address by a delegation of the Poona *sowcars* dated 23 November 1882.

an emphatic repudiation of the 'exaggerated views of the duties of Government which had lately been put forward by some distinguished advocates of State assistance in this Presidency. . . '. He conceded that in a country where the State stood as the supreme landlord, the *kunbis* had a special claim on the resources of the government, and a strong case could be made for the extension of assistance by the State to facilitate the flow of capital to the villages, more particularly because in the absence of such assistance the *kunbis* were reduced to being the bonded slaves of the *vanis*. To mitigate these evils, Lee-Warner observed, it was proposed that the Government of Bombay should on the one hand extend support to the *sowcars*, and on the other protect the *kunbis* by controlling the conditions under which the *sowcars* extended them credit:

> All these statements [Lee-Warner continued] are more or less truisms, and on them I found my first proposition, that it is desirable for Government to render some assistance to capitalists or bankers who undertake to advance money to the landholders, and to exercise some control over their business. But in deciding to what lengths the Government should go, I hold that the former must be left to private enterprise, and that if this private enterprise is to be floated with cork-jackets by a Government guarantee, it will not be private enterprise, but a spurious form of State interventionism . . ., involving a check to real private enterprise. The assistance which Government must give should, therefore, . . . fall short of being any part of the weight of the liabilities of the capitalists. . . . But the State might place the business of land banks under special advantages, supplying none of its capital, taking none of its shares, and accepting none of its liabilities, but offering it special facilities for investigating titles, collecting interest, recovering arrears, and generally for carrying on its business by allowing the bank to employ the State machinery.[1]

While Lee-Warner was reluctant to commit the financial resources of the Government of Bombay to an Agricultural Bank because of his qualified belief in *laissez-faire* principles, the Revenue Officers of the Government of Bombay were apprehensive of the political repercussions of the assurances which the *sowcars* con-

---

[1] *NAI:* Memorandum on the question of State assistance to Agricultural Banks in India by W. Lee-Warner of the Bombay Civil Service dated 20 April 1882: Department of Revenue and Agricultural (Revenue Branch), A Proceedings No. 13/20, June 1884.

sidered essential for the success of their proposal. The *ryotwari* system of land revenue, they pointed out, rested upon a direct settlement of the land-tax between the *kunbis* and the government; the exigencies of the system often required the Collectors to compel the *kunbis* to pay their taxes. The application of coercion inevitably led to bitterness between the *kunbis* and the administration. But if the Department of Revenue undertook the collection of money due to the Agricultural Bank over and above its existing responsibilities, then it would be increasing friction between the *kunbis* and the administration, since the distinction between the land-revenue, and the sums collected on behalf of the bank, would be lost on the *kunbis*:

> I cannot bring myself to believe [stated one Settlement Officer] that the economic advantages which will be derived from agricultural banks in the Dekkan talukas will outweigh the political objections to Government undertaking the duties of a bill collector towards a poor community of cultivators. Since the days of the early settlements it has been the great boast of Bombay revenue officers that each cultivator has his one fixed Government demand explained to him once for all. . . . If this principle of fixity of payment is liable to be altered by the inclusion in the Government demand of fluctuating sums on account of agricultural banks, one great guarantee for the success and popularity of the Settlements will be removed. Let Government give every assistance in its power to the establishment of an Agricultural Bank, . . . but this one portion of the programme should . . . be completely abandoned.[1]

Despite the reservations voiced by Lee-Warner, and notwithstanding the possibility of increased friction between the administration and the *kunbis*, the proposal made by the *sowcars* of Poona for an Agricultural Bank was supported by the Government of Bombay as well as the Government of India. This was largely due to the interest taken in the scheme by Sir Evelyn Baring, the Finance Member of the Viceroy's Executive Council, who applied his experience of Agricultural Banks in Egypt to the problems of rural finance in India.[2] Baring agreed with

[1] *Parliamentary Papers*, Vol. LXII of 1887: Report by Survey and Settlement Commissioner dated 13 December 1882.
[2] *NAI*: Memorandum by Sir Evelyn Baring dated 17 August 1882: Department of Revenue and Agriculture (Revenue Branch), A Proceedings No. 13/20, June 1884.

the objections advanced by Lee-Warner to the indiscriminate extension of assistance to the *sowcars* of Poona, particularly if this assistance took the form of direct financial support. But he saw no harm in the recovery of the bank's advances to the *kunbis* through the machinery of the Department of Revenue. Baring admitted that in assisting the Agricultural Bank to recover its loans, the Department would be acting on behalf of the *sowcar*, and it would share with the *sowcar* the odium attached to his profession. But the consequences of inaction, Baring pointed out, could prove to be even more disastrous. Peasants who were being progressively impoverished presented a serious political danger, and unless the deterioration in their condition was checked in time, their discontent could undermine the stability of British rule in India. Baring's arguments carried conviction with the Government of India, and it recommended the proposal of the *sowcars* of Poona to the Secretary of State for India as an experiment which would not only reveal the indebtedness and the overall prosperity of the *kunbis* of Maharashtra but would also indicate the extent to which the government could contribute to the progress of rural society.[1]

At the India Office, however, caution and conservatism triumphed over the arguments in favour of a bold policy. The Secretary of State for India refused to accept the scheme proposed by the *sowcars* of Poona as a genuine example of that private enterprise on which, so he believed, rested the responsibility for financing the operations of agriculture. The *sowcars* of Poona, he pointed out, not only wanted financial support from the Government of Bombay but they also insisted that the Department of Revenue be placed at their disposal for the recovery of their loans. It would be politic to extend such support 'only on the assumption that it (i.e. the bank) is to work on behalf of the Government for political or social objects rather than be conducted on ordinary business principles'.[2] But such an assumption was entirely unwarranted. Besides, even if the political credentials of the proposed bank were accepted as genuine, there was little evidence to suggest that it would prove a suc-

[1] *Parliamentary Papers*, Vol. LXII of 1887: Revenue Dispatch No. 7 dated 31 May 1884 to the Secretary of State for India.
[2] Parliamentary Papers, Vol. LXII of 1887: Dispatch to the Government of India dated 23 October 1884.

cessful venture. The *vanis* not only advanced credit to the *kunbis* but they also provided them with a market for their surplus crops. Would the bank too try to deal in agricultural produce? If it attempted to do so, then it would be embarking upon a business which it was not equipped to handle. If not, then the *kunbis* would be compelled to maintain their relations with the *vanis*. The problems faced by Agricultural Banks were aggravated by the fact that the *kunbis* kept an open account with the *vanis* on which they drew from time to time to meet their requirements as and when they arose. A bank was incapable of conducting business on such lines and it could not, therefore, displace the *vanis* as a source of credit for the *kunbis*:

> It appears to me doubtful [the Secretary of State for India said in conclusion] whether any ingenuity can provide an effectual substitute for the operation of the ordinary laws between the ryots and those, whether sowcars or banks, from which they obtain advances; and . . . whether any bank could carry on its business with success. There is a strong presumption that Government cannot directly do much for the relief of the agricultural debtor than take care that in disputes between him and his creditors the law shall provide, and the courts shall administer, speedy, cheap and equal justice, and that the ryot shall be as little liable as possible, from his ignorance, his poverty, or his position, to be defrauded or oppressed.[1]

The dispatch of the Secretary of State for India put an end to the attempt of the *sowcars* of Poona to launch an Agricultural Bank which would restore the flow of credit to the *kunbis* of Maharashtra. The *sowcars'* scheme aimed at creating a new source of credit which would protect the interests of the *kunbis*, and at the same time prevent them from dominating rural society. The *sowcars* were justified in assuming that an Agricultural Bank would not dominate the *kunbis* in the way the *vanis* had dominated them before 1879. But to accept their arguments in no way weakens the objections put forth by those who opposed their proposal, namely, that the Government of Bombay would become unpopular if it acted on behalf of the *sowcar* in collecting his dues; and that it was impossible for a bank to take upon itself the complex role played by the *vanis* in the economy of the villages. The consequences of a policy of *laissez-faire*,

[1] ibid.

however, could prove equally disastrous. For the unpopu-
larity which the Government of Bombay would earn through
associating itself with the *sowcars* paled into insignificance when
compared with the tensions that could flow from a progressive
impoverishment of the *kunbis*.

The irony of the situation, however, lay in that the *sowcars* of
Poona as well as their supporters were mistaken in their understanding of the role of rural banking institutions. The Mudliar
Scheme rested on the assumption that the Agricultural Banks
would provide the ordinary *kunbis* with a supply of cheap credit.
This assumption was wrong, since Agricultural Banks were
equipped to deal with large landholders, rather than with
kunbis owning small plots of land. In Egypt, for instance, the
Credit Foncier conducted its transactions with farmers who possessed large holdings, and who required annual loans ranging
from £5,000 to £10,000, rather than with the *fellahin* for whom
the institution had been created in the first instance. If the
experience of Egypt had any relevance for Maharashtra, and we
must remember that the *fellahin* bore a remarkable resemblance
to the *kunbis*, then it is obvious that the *kunbis'* need for credit
could not be met by an Agricultural Bank.[1]

How then could the *kunbis* of Maharashtra be provided with
the credit which they required for the cultivation of their fields,
and for the improvement of their standard of living?

II

For an answer to this question the British Government turned
to Germany, where a remarkable experiment in co-operation
showed the improvement which could be effected in rural
society by the peasants through the organisation of their resources. The movement for rural co-operation owed its origin
to Raiffeissen, the mayor of an obscure town in Germany, who
was distressed by the way in which the scarcity of capital prevented the peasants from cultivating their fields.[2] Since Raiffeissen was a religious man who was committed to conservative political principles, he was equally distressed by the commercialisation

[1] *Parliamentary Papers*, Vol. LXII of 1887: Dispatch to Government of India dated
9 February 1885 and enclosures.
[2] C. R. Fay, *Co-operation at Home and Abroad* (London, 1948), Vol. I, pp. 19 and
42–50.

of rural society through the influx of the values of individualism and acquisitiveness. He consequently looked for means to
improve the moral and the material life of the peasants. Raiffeissen
discovered a solution for the problems of rural society in credit
societies which were organised by the peasants for mutual assistance in times of distress, and for the support of schemes of improvement in normal seasons. The striking features of the credit
societies launched by Raiffeissen were the principle of non-
acquisitiveness which inspired their conception, and the spirit
of co-operation which guided their day-to-day business. The
village banks of Raiffeissen invariably started from very humble
beginnings. The peasants of a village, who possessed neither
worldly sophistication nor an abundance of capital, would pool
their resources to launch a credit society with unlimited liability. This society would then borrow money from all available
sources, and it would advance loans to hardworking and enterprising peasants to enable them to improve their holdings. The
success of such credit societies did not rest exclusively upon the skill
of the peasants who managed them; it also depended upon their
intimate knowledge of their fellow-villagers who were also their
clients, and upon the restraint which the principle of unlimited
liability imposed on their transactions. Raiffeissen societies
flourished in Germany despite initial hostility by the State, and
they were responsible for bringing about a most remarkable
transformation in rural society:

> You should go into the valley of the Rhine [observed a British
> disciple of Raiffeissen] where the Raiffeissen Banks have been
> longest at work and observe to what extent homes have been made
> habitable and comfortable; how culture has been improved. . . .;
> how the small peasant can now buy his implements and seeds of
> the best quality at the cheaper wholesale prices, and yet . . . at six
> months credit; you should see how small industry and trade have
> developed, how the usurer, once all powerful, has been driven out
> of the fold, and these once poor men have become small capitalists.
> One is afraid of falling into strains of rhapsody in describing all
> these results.[1]

Into the valley of the Rhine went Sir Frederick Nicholson, an

[1] H. W. Wolff as quoted in F. A. Nicholson, *Report Regarding the Possibility of Introducing Land and Agricultural Banks into the Madras Presidency* (Madras, 1898), I, p. 146.
This Report is henceforth referred to as Nicholson's Report on Co-operation.

officer of the Government of Madras, to observe Raiffeissen societies in action, and to explore their relevance to the problems of rural society in India. The result of Nicholson's inquiries was a massive *Report Regarding the Possibility of Introducing Land And Agricultural Banks Into the Presidency of Madras* which provided the inspiration behind the co-operative movement in India. In his *Report* Nicholson emphasised two points: the similarity between the peasant societies of Germany and India; and the inability of Agricultural Banks (organised on the principles proposed by the *sowcars* of Poona in 1882) to provide credit for small cultivators as opposed to farmers who cultivated large holdings on capitalist principles. When Raiffeissen launched his credit societies in the middle of the 19th century, the condition of the peasants in Germany was in no way different from the condition of the peasants in India. The German peasant, like the *kunbi*, was ignorant, poor and opposed to change; he held land in small and scattered holdings; he was exploited by the moneylenders, incapable of a sustained effort to improve his condition, and unable and unwilling to exploit new techniques of agriculture. As many as 87 per cent of the peasants in Germany possessed fields which were under 25 acres in area. The Agricultural Banks instituted by the government were unable to provide any assistance to such peasants, partly because of the suspicion with which the peasants looked at these institutions, but primarily because the banks were reluctant to extend credit to hundreds upon thousands of small peasants.

When Nicholson conducted his inquiries two rival systems of co-operation had developed in Germany, both of which sought to inculcate self-confidence and thrift among the peasants and the workers, and to help them improve their conditions of existence.[1] The credit societies initiated by Raiffeissen were conducted on non-acquisitive principles, and they were concerned with the spiritual and the material well-being of the peasants. The inspiration behind such societies was conservative and clerical, and they sought to protect rural society from the crass materialism of commercial values. Raiffeissen secured his objectives by limiting the operations of a credit society to a single village, where all the cultivators knew each other inti-

---

[1] See Editorial in *The Pioneer* dated 12 November 1903.

mately; by enforcing the principle of unlimited liability, which prevented the development of acquisitiveness; by keeping the share capital to a low figure, and by enforcing a low rate of dividends, which kept in check the motive for profit; and finally, by granting loans on long terms which enabled the peasants to invest in the development of their holdings.

The credit societies launched by Schulze-Delitsch possessed completely different objectives, since he subscribed to liberal and anti-clerical principles, and because he tried to promote rather than to inhibit the growth of acquisitiveness among those who participated in co-operation. Like Raiffeissen, Schulze-Delitsch possessed an enduring faith in co-operation, and he believed that progress could be achieved only when the weakness of the individual had been transformed into strength through organisation. But the belief in co-operation formed a point of departure for these two pioneers. A Schulze-Delitsch society had little in common with a Raiffeissen Bank. It did not confine its activities to a closed community; it did not impose any limit on the share capital, or on the dividend paid to members; and finally, being committed to quick returns, it advanced loans only on a short-term basis. Because of their differing objectives, Schulze-Delitsch societies were popular with artisans and workers who lived in the cities, while Raiffeissen societies thrived in the villages.

Since Nicholson was concerned with the problems of a rural society, and because he was engaged in restoring a social fabric which had been weakened through individualism and acquisitiveness, he had little hesitation in recommending credit societies on the model of Raiffeissen Banks as the form of the co-operative movement appropriate to India.[1] The problem of rural credit, he pointed out, could not be solved by Agricultural Banks which were managed by the *sowcars* with the assistance of the State; its solution lay in credit societies run by the peasants on co-operative and non-acquisitive principles. A Raiffeissen Bank confined its operations to one village whose affairs were intimately known to its members. It also accepted unlimited liability in its financial transactions. For these reasons, so Nicholson believed, a Raiffeissen Bank would inspire confidence among the *sowcars*, and it would encourage them to subscribe to

[1] *Vide* Nicholson's *Report on Co-operation*, I, pp. 370–80.

its working capital in the form of deposits. Raiffeissen societies, in fact, possessed a number of advantages over Agricultural Banks and Schulze-Delitsch societies. Their intimate knowledge of their clients ruled out the possibility of spurious loans; their simple methods of procedure suited the unsophisticated peasants; and last but not the least, they were in a position to ensure that the sums of money they advanced were used for productive purposes.

Nicholson's enthusiasm for Raiffeissen Banks did not blind him to the difficulties which such banks would face in India. The atomisation of rural society by reforms based upon the principles of utilitarianism had made the peasants incapable of organised action; it had also made them suspicious of attempts to channelise their activities towards collective action leading to the achievement of planned objectives. The situation was further complicated by the poverty of the peasants, and by the hostility which the *vanis* were bound to extend to Raiffeissen societies. In the initial stages, Nicholson pointed out, it would therefore be necessary for the State to support co-operative societies with assistance in the form of capital and leadership. But although credit societies based on Raiffeissen's principles would be faced with tremendous problems in India, there was no reason for pessimism. The pioneers of the movement in Germany had confronted, and had triumphed over, problems which were no less formidable. Co-operation would be a resounding success in India if men of goodwill, idealism and energy threw themselves wholeheartedly into the movement:

> What is really wanted [Nicholson noted in conclusion] is the advent of men of zeal, enthusiasm, devotion and perseverance who will take up the western ideas and methods, and, by personal labour, solve the difficulties of the problems, not on paper, but in actual practice; the philanthropic reformer of the East must sit down in the villages as did their prototypes of the West, and must then establish the petty societies which, as in Europe, shall contain the germs and promise of infinite potentialities. There can be no higher honour for any man than to ... (become) the Raiffeissen of India. ...[1]

The *Report* written by Nicholson was inspired by conservative

[1] ibid., I, p. 25.

principles which were completely opposed to the principles that had inspired the utilitarian reformers in India. The utilitarians had based their policies on the aspirations of individuals rather than on the proclivities of organised social groups; and they had attempted to disseminate rationalism and acquisitiveness in rural society in order to persuade the peasants to improve their lot through industriousness and through the adoption of new techniques in agriculture. Co-operation, on the other hand, was based on collective rather than on individualistic principles of social action; and on notions of Christian brotherhood and mutual assistance rather than on values like acquisitiveness and rationality. Indeed, as conceived by men like Raiffeissen and Nicholson co-operation sought to cushion protect societies from the corrosive influence of a commercial ethic and a rational social order:

> The ideal which the founders of the co-operative movement had before them [pointed out Marshall] was that of regenerating the world by restraining the force of competition and substituting for it brotherly trust and association. They saw that under the sway of competition much of men's energy is wasted on the endeavour to overreach one another. They saw . . . the seller striving to give as little and that of as poor a quality as he could. And they saw the buyer always trying to take advantage of the seller's necessity. . . . The 'Co-operative Faith' . . . (is) that these evils can be in a great measure removed by that spirit of brotherly love and openness, which though undeveloped, is yet latent in man's nature. It looks forward to a time when man . . . shall think of promoting the general welfare as much as promoting his own interests. . . .[1]

The conservative principles which sustained the credit societies of Raiffeissen were seen with great clarity by H. Dupernex, an officer of the Government of the North-Western Provinces, who shared with Nicholson the distinction of being one of the founders of the co-operative movement in India. While Nicholson focused on the problems of rural credit, and stressed the ability of Raiffeissen societies to supply the peasants with capital without reducing them to a condition of slavery, Dupernex concerned himself with the effect of co-operation on the values and institutions of rural society.[2]

[1] Quoted in H. Dupernex, *People's Banks for Northern India*, pp. 52–3.
[2] ibid., pp. 69–70.

Dupernex was struck by the resemblance between the credit societies launched by Raiffeissen, and the village communities which had flourished in India before the British conquest. The basis of social organisation in the village communities lay in the intimate association between the cultivators of the village; in Raiffeissen societies the members of a society were held together by ties which were equally intimate. The village community acquired its unique character through the responsibility which the cultivators collectively bore for the land-tax, since this responsiblity inspired the prosperous cultivators to stimulate their less fortunate fellows to greater effort; similarly, the principle of unlimited liability obliged the prosperous members of a credit society to interest themselves in the affairs of the poor members. However, the most important similarity between Raiffeissen Banks and the village communities of India, so Dupernex believed, lay in a common approach towards acquisitiveness and the profit motive. By pooling their resources the members of a village community gained security which they could not gain otherwise. Yet this security was gained through the subordination of their personal interests to the interests of the village as a whole. Thus a cultivator would never rack-rent a fellow-villager, since life in the village rested on the subordination of profit to the principle of community. Credit societies demanded similar sacrifices from their members, since they were based upon the subordination of individual gain to collective welfare:

The two things [Dupernex pointed out] are incompatible. Once the idea of gain is allowed to obtain a footing, its ultimate predominance is inevitable, and its predominance entails the triumph of individualism over mutuality. . . . Experience teaches that the only way to safeguard the interests of the community . . . is by limiting the amount of dividend, or better still by abolishing it altogether. Profit and individualism are interchangeable terms. The desirability of eliminating profits as far as possible is apparent when it is borne in mind that where the individual is strong enough to stand alone, he should have no difficulty in obtaining a suitable reward for his efforts; but as the combination of persons into an association is for the express object of obtaining benefits which they could not obtain singly, it ought to be regarded as an inconsistency for members to seek to appropriate to themselves profits which rightly belong to the community as they are gained by the community and not by individual members.[1]

As conceived by Nicholson and Dupernex, therefore, co-operation sought the regeneration of rural society even more than it sought the restoration of the flow of credit to the villages. They believed that credit societies based on Raiffeissen's principles would check the atomisation of rural society; inhibit the spread of acquisitiveness; and retard the development of individualism. The values which Nicholson and Dupernex wanted to undermine had been generated in rural society through policies based upon utilitarianism, and they were responsible for creating conflict and tension within the villages of Maharashtra. To mitigate this conflict and tension the protagonists of co-operation proposed to create an institution which would stimulate interdependence and mutual assistance in rural society.

III

Since Nicholson and Dupernex sought to reorganise rural society on principles which were so different from the principles which had hitherto sustained the British administration in India, the initial reaction in official circles to their recommendations was one of scepticism and disbelief.[2] What made their proposals so vulnerable, however, was their confession that to be successful in India credit societies would in the first instance have to be supported with money and leadership by the State. The Government of Madras, which had deputed Nicholson to study Raiffeissen societies in Europe, pointed out that to launch credit societies with the support of the State was to destroy the very basis of co-operation. Raiffeissen had initiated the movement to create thrift, self-confidence and industriousness among peasants who had despaired of improving their conditions. The spontaneous growth of credit societies in the villages would revive the peasant's self-confidence, and would demonstrate to the world his ability to improve his lot. But if these

[1] ibid.
[2] *NAI:* Resolution of the Madras Board of Revenue on Nicholson's Report dated 6 November 1896: Department of Revenue and Agriculture (Revenue Branch), A Proceedings No. 7/10, November 1900.

credit societies were launched with the assistance of the State, the cultivators would gain little apart from access to a new source of credit. Such a facility was valuable in itself, but it had nothing to do with the objectives which had inspired Raiffeissen to organise rural credit. What he had emphasised was 'educative credit . . . based not on subventions from the State, but on the thrift and prudence of the cultivators . . . '. Credit societies which were launched on the initiative of the peasants would, so Raiffeissen believed, revolutionise their outlook and bring about a radical transformation in rural society. Since assistance by the State was designed to undermine the objectives of co-operation as conceived by Raiffeissen, the Government of Madras had 'no hesitation' in rejecting Nicholson's proposal for the creation of officially sponsored credit societies in India.[1]

However, the magnitude of indebtedness in rural society and the political implications of this indebtedness prevented the Government of India from sharing the complacency of the Government of Madras, particularly because of the pressure that was being brought to bear on the Imperial Government by the 'Indian lobby' in parliament for the adoption of steps to remedy the poverty of the peasants.[2] In commenting upon the reaction of the Government of Madras to Nicholson's *Report*, therefore, T. W. Holderness, the Secretary of the Department of Revenue and Agriculture, expressed regret at the 'cynical and unsocial' way in which it had dismissed the proposals put forward by Nicholson. The Government of Madras, Holderness pointed out, saw no difference between the assistance demanded by the *sowcars* of Poona in the 1880s, and the help which credit societies based on the principles of Raiffeissen would require for an initial period before they became self-sufficient. In France and Germany, where credit was efficiently organised, the principle of unlimited liability had established the *bona fides* of Raiffeissen societies from the very outset, and had enabled them to borrow sufficient money for their needs. But the situation in India was quite different, since urban credit was not

[1] *NAI:* Order in Council by the Madras Government dated 13 October 1899: Department of Revenue and Agriculture (Revenue Branch), A Proceedings No. 7/10, November 1900.
[2] *NAI:* Minute by E. Maconochie, Under-Secretary in the Department of Revenue and Agriculture dated 22 January 1900: Department of Revenue and Agriculture (Revenue Branch), A Proceedings No. 7/10, November 1900.

very well organised in the country. Dupernex, Holderness stated, had proposed the establishment of banks in district and provincial centres to facilitate the flow of credit to the villages. His suggestions deserved serious consideration, since they pointed to one solution of the problem. Alternatively, it was possible for the State to come forward with its resources, and to extend financial assistance to credit societies in the villages.[1]

The desultory exchanges between the Governments of India and Madras were transformed into a creative dialogue through the intervention of Sir Edward Law, the Finance Member of the Viceroy's Executive Council, who believed that co-operation on the principles advocated by Raiffeissen could improve significantly the conditions of life in the villages.[2] In December 1900 a Committee comprising Nicholson, Dupernex and Holderness met under the chairmanship of Law to examine the possibilities of establishing co-operative societies in India. After investigating the state of rural finance in the country, the Law Committee came to the conclusion that

> village associations constituted as Mutual Credit Associations, somewhat on the lines and with the objects of Raiffeissen Mutual Credit Associations, would generally be the most useful instruments of rural credit, since these or similar societies satisfy the several postulates of small, continuous, village credit, while developing conditions, habits and qualities essential to rural stability and progress.[3]

To provide the proposed village societies with credit the Law Committee recommended action on two fronts. On the one hand, the State ought to encourage the 'well-to-do, influential and educated' classes in the cities to form banks which would provide the village societies with money; on the other, the State should extend financial assistance on its own to the credit societies, particularly when they were first created. Because of the differences between the *ryotwari* communities of Maharashtra,

[1] *NAI*: Note by T. W. Holderness, Secretary to the Department of Revenue and Agriculture, dated 28 August 1900: Department of Revenue and Agriculture (Revenue Branch), A Proceedings No. 7/10, November 1900.
[2] *NAI*: Note by E. F. G. Law, Finance Member of the Viceroy's Executive Council, dated 26 September 1900: Department of Revenue and Agriculture (Revenue Branch), A Proceedings No. 7/10, November 1900.
[3] *NAI*: Resolution of the Law Committee dated 19 December 1900: Department of Revenue and Agriculture (Revenue Branch), A Proceedings No. 11/24, November 1901.

the *bhayachara* villages of the North-Western Provinces, and the permanently settled territories of Bengal, the Law Committee thought it inadvisable, and indeed impossible, to recommend precisely how the State ought to encourage co-operation in different parts of India. But the Committee believed that once the principle of assistance by the State was accepted it would be for the various provincial governments to decide how they could best encourage the movement in their respective territories.[1]

Despite the hopes which Nicholson's *Report* had aroused in Law, the Government of Bombay was doubtful whether it was possible to launch credit societies in the villages of Maharashtra.[2] Its scepticism stemmed from an appraisal of the conditions which prevailed in its territories. The atomisation of rural society by the *ryotwari* system had weakened the sentiment of solidarity in the villages to such an extent that the *kunbis* found it difficult to co-operate with each other for a common objective. The *ryotwari* system had simultaneously reduced the power and the prestige of the traditional leaders of the villages. The difficulties arising out of the breakdown of social cohesion were reinforced by the poverty of the *kunbis*. The question which the advocates of co-operation would have to answer, a senior officer of the Government of Bombay pointed out, was how the *kunbi* could be relieved of his burden of debt, and how he could rise from a state of virtual slavery to the ownership of his land.[3] The protagonists of credit societies had assumed that the *kunbi* possessed a small reserve of capital, and that his dealings with the *vani* were the dealings of a free person. Neither of these assumptions was correct. The majority of the *kunbis* had no reserves of capital, and their poverty made them so reckless in their

[1] *NAI:* Circular letter to the various Provincial Governments by J. Fuller, Secretary to the Department of Revenue and Agriculture, dated 5 November 1901: Department of Revenue and Agriculture (Revenue Branch), A Proceedings No. 1/10, November 1901.

[2] *NAI:* J. W. P. Muir-Mackenzie, Secretary to the Bombay Government, to Government of India dated 24 May 1901: Department of Revenue and Agriculture (Revenue Branch), A Proceedings No. 1/10, November 1901. Also see Letter from the Collector of Ahmednagar to the Commissioner of the Central Division dated 25 March 1901 in ibid.

[3] *NAI:* Survey Commissioner, Bombay to Bombay Government dated 2 April 1901: Department of Revenue and Agriculture (Revenue Branch), A Proceedings No. 1/10, November 1901.

dealings with the *vanis*, that without exception they were encumbered with a very heavy burden of debt. It was, therefore, difficult to see how credit societies could be launched in the villages of Maharashtra. If, however, they were launched with the support of the government, then they would be unable to undermine the dominance of the *vanis* over the *kunbis*.

The only cultivators who would benefit from the credit societies, this officer pointed out, were the 'rich' *kunbis* who owed their prosperity to the policies pursued by the British Government. Such *kunbis*, the *'crème de la crème'* of the cultivating community, alone possessed the capital to launch credit societies, and they alone possessed the qualities of leadership necessary to sustain these societies after they had been launched. Since the idea of joint responsibility had been expressly repudiated by the *ryotwari* system, it was difficult to see how the rich *kunbis* could be expected to run credit societies on the principles advocated by Raiffeissen, and how they could be persuaded to accept responsibility for loans which had been contracted to assist the poor cultivators in their villages. It was far more likely that the credit societies would refuse to accept any obligations *vis-à-vis* the poor peasants, and it was equally probable that they would give loans only to the prosperous cultivators. The support which the State would extend to these credit societies could, therefore, assist only those *kunbis* who were least in need of assistance:

> If distressed agriculturists [he concluded] could be given a method of escaping from the usurer's hands, and village associations were started to prevent them from falling back, then Government would not only be justified but morally bound, to go to any length consistent with prudence in forming the associations, but it does not appear to be quite a proper use of public money to lend it to ... (rich peasants) merely to enable them to obtain loans at a lower rate of interest than at present in the off chance that thrift and self-help may thereby be stimulated. It is even conceivable that the use of Government money may have the effect of discouraging these virtues.[1]

However the scepticism of such officers of the Government of Bombay was not shared by those who administered the more

[1] ibid.

prosperous districts of Maharashtra, where the *kunbis'* burden of debt was not beyond redemption, and where a substantial number of the peasants could be drawn into co-operative societies. The villages around Poona, for instance, enjoyed the advantages of proximity to a flourishing market, a system of communications which permitted access to these markets, and facilities of irrigation which protected crops from the vagaries of the weather. J. McNeill, the Collector of Poona, was impressed by the possibilities held out in Nicholson's *Report*, and he believed that 'the Poona District could be a hopeful field for an experiment in the formation of agricultural banks on co-operative lines'.[1] The *kunbis* of Poona District, McNeill observed, were burdened with debt like *kunbis* all over Maharashtra. But there were some villages with a sufficient number of prosperous *kunbis* who could be persuaded to start credit societies. Of course, the management and financing of such societies would present serious difficulties. But if credit societies were permitted to have as members 'landowners of some standing, (and) rich ryots, vakils and the higher government servants', then they would be greatly strengthened.

McNeill realised the possibilities of co-operation when he discussed the movement with the principal *kunbis* of Chakan, 'a large and prosperous village in the Khed taluka'. When he outlined the objectives of co-operation before the *kunbis* of Chakan, and apprised them of the extent to which the State would assist them, they exhibited considerable enthusiasm for the movement. They also assured McNeill that they could be trusted to be honest in their dealings with a credit society which belonged to the village and not to any individual. But McNeill felt that the initiative for schemes of improvement had rested for so long on individuals outside the village that the selection of a *panch* (managing committee) from Chakan would present difficulties; and the *kunbis*, too, 'doubted if a capable *panch* to manage the working of the Association would be found in the village alone'.[2] However, the government could provide in the initial stages the leadership which was lacking in the village, and which could

---

[1] *NAI:* J. McNeill, Collector of Poona, to Commissioner, Central Division, dated 26 March 1901: Department of Revenue and Agriculture (Revenue Branch), A Proceedings No. 1/10, November 1901.
[2] ibid.

develop only after the credit societies were firmly established:

> Official guidance [McNeill pointed out] is necessary if village
> banks are to be widely instituted. Perhaps official guidance might
> be adequately supplied by requiring that the Assistant Collector
> or the Mamlatdar should be members of the managing body of any
> village banking association assisted by Government capital. . . .
> Their position as members of the managing body would enable
> them to examine the workings of the bank and to put a timely
> check on any irregularities. . . . A further advantage . . . would
> be that they could initiate unpleasant measures against defaulters
> and relieve honest but weak members of the panch of the odium
> of such measures. In the early stages of village banks neither the
> associates nor the managers might have the courage of their con-
> victions, but it would not be unreasonable to hope that a sense of
> responsibility and of mutual support will grow. . . .[1]

Despite the optimism of McNeill, who looked upon co-operation as a challenge to the British Government in India, the
poverty of the *kunbis*, and the disastrous effect of utilitarian
policies upon the values and institutions of rural society, combined to make most District Officers sceptical of the success of
credit societies based upon the principles advocated by Raiffeissen. A. R. Bonus, the Collector of Nasik, spoke for such officers
when he observed that the prospect of the *kunbis* attaining prosperity through association and self-help reminded him 'of those
islanders who are said to have made a living by taking in one
another's washings. . . '.[2] The reply of the Government of
Bombay to the Government of India on the prospects of co-
operation in Maharashtra was, therefore, couched in the language of despair rather than in the language of hope. The entire
question hinged upon the individualism and the acquisitiveness
which had been deliberately fostered in rural society by policies
of reform based upon the principles of utilitarianism. While
these reforms had been carried out on the basis of experience
gained in the West, it was seldom borne in mind that the *kunbis*
lacked the sophistication which had enabled the peasant in the
West to strive for individual gain without depriving himself of the
advantages of organisation and community. Individualism had

---

[1] ibid.
[2] *BA:* Letter from Collector of Nasik to the Commissioner of the Central Division
dated 24 December 1901: R.D., Vol. 22 of 1902.

taken so deep a root in the villages, so the government believed, that it was impossible to rely on cultivators to repair embankments and irrigation channels which they had repaired without any fuss under former governments. The climate of the villages had changed to such an extent that the cultivators of a community regarded themselves as antagonists rather than as partners in a joint enterprise. 'The burden of the reports from all parts of the Presidency is that there is seldom or never found such a spirit among the rural communities as will make co-operative credit societies possible,' stated the Government of Bombay.[1] It would take a long time before the benefits of co-operation could be appreciated by such peasants, and it would also take a long time before the prosperous cultivators would interest themselves in the fate of the poor peasants.

Although British officers were far more optimistic about the prospects of co-operation in the North-Western Provinces, where the *bhayachara* system had reinforced the sentiment of solidarity in the villages, the problems posed by the movement appeared to be most formidable even in regions where the village communities had survived the ravages of time. Sir Denzil Ibbetson, who piloted the bill which launched co-operation in India, confessed that he was 'not too sanguine' about the success of village credit societies. 'The idea of co-operation for the purpose of mutual help . . . (was) familiar to the people of India . . . '. Ibbetson pointed out. '(But) the whole tendency of our rule has been to discourage such action. . . . However, we are bound to give the experiment every encouragement and a fair trial.'[2] Belief in co-operation, Sir Denzil said in effect, was an expression of confidence in the *kunbis*' capacity to rise above selfish considerations and to improve through industriousness the moral and material state of rural society.

The Act which launched co-operation in India was, therefore, an act of faith in the peasant and in his style of life. The principal objective of the Act, the Government of India pointed out

[1] *NAI:* Letter to the Government of India dated 12 August 1902: Department of Revenue and Agriculture (Revenue Branch), A Proceedings No. 1/14, September 1903.
[2] *NAI:* Minute by Sir Denzil Ibbetson dated 29 January 1902: Department of Revenue and Agriculture (Revenue Branch), A Proceedings No. 1/14, September 1903.

in a dispatch to the Secretary of State for India, was to encourage thrift and co-operation among *kunbis* of 'limited means'
through the establishment of credit societies.[1] The government
further hoped that credit societies would be organised along
similar lines in the cities, either to help the poor artisans, or to
facilitate the flow of capital to the villages. None the less, its
principal concern lay in the villages, and its sympathies were for
the poor peasant. The government was also anxious to ensure
that the assistance which it extended to the poor peasants was
not exploited by the prosperous cultivators. For this reason the
Act required that credit societies in the villages had to be organised on the principle of unlimited liability, on the assumption
that such a principle would keep the rich peasants away from
the credit societies.

Since it laid emphasis on the prosperity of the village as a
community rather than the prosperity of individual cultivators,
and because it concerned itself with the poor and not with the
rich peasants, the Act sponsored by the Government of India
sought to develop co-operation along the principles advocated
by Raiffeissen. Besides advocating unlimited liability, the Act
recommended that no dividends be paid out of the profits of a
credit society; it also recommended that the number of shares
held by an individual in a society be limited, in order to prevent
a rich *vani* or *kunbi* from acquiring control over its activities.
Since the traditional leaders of the villages had been deprived of
their power under British rule, the Act refused to leave the promotion of credit societies entirely to the initiative of the *kunbis*.
Instead, it provided for the appointment in each province of a
Registrar of Co-operative Societies, who was required to guide
and control co-operative societies, particularly when they were
first launched. Again, because of the difficulty in creating confidence in village societies in the first instance, the Act recognised pecuniary assistance to these societies as an essential part
of the government's responsibility in launching the movement.
In committing itself to such assistance the Government of
India realised the danger of subverting the principles of thrift
and self-help which formed the very basis of co-operation. But

[1] *NAI:* Dispatch to Secretary of State for India dated 3 September 1903: Department of Revenue and Agriculture (Revenue Branch), A Proceedings No. 1/14 September 1903.

it preferred a calculated risk to the consequences of inaction, because it believed that its

> advances will have a value beyond their mere use as capital, since they will be an earnest of the intensity of the government's interest in the movement, and will stimulate the interest and self-help which should be a condition precedent to this grant. . . .[1]

The Government of India's concern for the prosperity of the peasants was directly related to the stability of British rule over India and the maintenance of British authority over the country. Indeed, these considerations formed the background to the debate on co-operation, and they influenced to no small degree the attitude of the British Government towards the movement. The attempt of the first generation of British administrators to create prosperity in rural society had proved abortive because of the imbalance which the *ryotwari* system had created in the villages, and the support it had extended to the ambitions of the *vanis* at the cost of the *kunbis*. The disturbances of 1875 high-lighted the dangers of encouraging individualism and acquisitiveness among social groups which lacked a sense of responsibility to the community. The most ominous feature of the disturbances of 1875, from the standpoint of the British Government, was the 'no-tax' campaign launched by the *Poona Sarvajanik Sabha* in association with some old landed families. An alliance between the educated classes which led the *Sabha* and the landed families for the purpose of exploiting discontent among the *kunbis* could threaten the very foundations of British rule over India. The prevention of such combinations between the *kunbis*, on the one hand, and the dominant classes in urban and rural society, on the other, was an important reason behind the Co-operative Credit Societies Act of 1904. The Act was not only looked upon as the thin edge of a wedge between the *kunbis* and the educated classes which sought to lead them, but it was also regarded as something that would oblige these classes either to prove their capacity for creative leadership, or to renounce their political ambitions. In the Legislative Council of Bombay, for instance, F. S. P. Lely, the Commissioner of the Northern Division, turned to the educated classes of Maharashtra to ask why a Raiffeissen had not risen from their ranks. These classes, so Lely argued,

[1] ibid.

failed in their duty to their country in this its particular need. [For] to stir up the dreary deadness of a single village where most of the population hung upon the Government in bad times and in good times upon the sowcar . . . would be to do more service to their country, which I know they love, than to make twenty speeches however eloquent and however convincing. . . .[1]

Curzon voiced the same sentiment in the Imperial Legislative Council, when he referred to the embarrassed praise which Gokhale had showered on the Government of India for establishing credit societies in the villages, and expressed his 'pleasure to find today that we (i.e. the Government and its critics) are all so unanimous, and that in the contemplation of this measure the lion had lain down with the lamb'.[2]

IV

However J. McNeill, the first Registrar of Co-operative Societies in Bombay, was more concerned with educating the *kunbis* in the principles of co-operation than he was concerned with reproaching the educated classes for their failure to anticipate Raiffeissen in India. McNeill could scarcely have embarked upon his task with any great optimism, because the poverty of the *kunbis*, and the atomisation of rural society through the *ryotwari* system, led most British officers to look upon the prospects of co-operation with deep pessimism. But several factors combined to make a qualified success of co-operation in Maharashtra. One reason was the availability of capital in the cities which could be invested in agriculture once suitable institutions had been devised for its flow into the villages. Besides, urban castes which possessed a strong sentiment of solidarity were quick to see the benefits of co-operation, and they required little encouragement to organise themselves in credit societies. Because of poverty and the absence of social cohesion, conditions in the villages were quite different. But even in the villages McNeill discovered that with patience and skill it was possible to organise the *kunbis* into credit societies which, with the support of the government and also with the support of capital from the cities, were able to contribute significantly to the improvement of rural

[1] *Proceedings of the Bombay Council* (Bombay 1904, Vol. XL: Speech by F. S. P. Lely, Commissioner of the Northern Division, dated 21 April 1902.
[2] *NAI:* Papers Relating to Act X of 1904, Vol. I: Proceedings of the Governor-General's Council dated 23 October 1903.

society. Of course, as co-operation gained momentum social conditions in the cities and in the villages obliged the Government
of Bombay to substitute the somewhat abstract principles which
sustained the Act of 1904 for principles which were directly related to the needs of the *kunbis* or the artisans and workers.

McNeill's first year in the villages of Maharashtra did not
produce any spectacular results, but he was able to prepare useful ground for the future. He realised that although there were
no men in the villages who could be invested with the responsibility of managing credit societies, habits of association and
collective effort had not totally died out among the cultivators.[1]
Indeed, McNeill discovered that the *kunbis* were quick to grasp
the advantages of co-operation, even though it rested on principles which were totally new to them. Again, since they lacked
the qualities of leadership the *kunbis* were willing to be guided
by the Registrar, so long as they were allowed to control the
membership of the credit societies, and to grant or to refuse
loans to applicants. What struck McNeill as particularly promising was the readiness with which the *kunbis* accepted the principle of unlimited liability. McNeill had been apprehensive that
the requirement of unlimited liability would prevent prosperous
peasants from joining credit societies, and that it would therefore deny the societies of the capital and leadership which were
available in the villages. But in

> the villages which I have visited [McNeill pointed out] the ordin-
> ary agriculturist accepts unlimited liability as natural. I propose
> to register no rural society in which the liability is to be limited
> unless careful inquiry shows that it is impossible to organise a
> society on the basis of unlimited liability. Apart from the fact that
> societies with unlimited liability are more genuinely co-operative,
> the committee are more likely to exercise care in granting loans
> and the whole body of members are more interested in preventing
> default. . . .[2]

The credit societies established by McNeill faced from the
very outset the problem of finding sufficient capital to satisfy the

[1] *Annual Report Relating to the Establishment of Co-operative Credit Societies in the Bombay
Presidency for 1905* by J. McNeill, Registrar of Co-operative Societies, dated 29 September 1905. Henceforth referred to as Annual Report of Co-operative Societies.
[2] *Annual Report Relating to the Establishment of Co-operative Credit Societies in the Bombay
Presidency for 1905* by J. McNeill, Registrar of Co-operative Socities, dated 29 September 1905.

needs of the *kunbis*. Since these societies were meant to assist the poor peasants, their membership fee was kept very low, and they raised the bulk of their capital by taking fixed deposits from prosperous cultivators at an interest of $6\frac{1}{4}$ per cent. Deposits by individual cultivators ranged from Rs. 5 to Rs. 300; and most societies were able to raise between Rs. 500 to Rs. 2,000 through this source. This capital was disbursed in loans to needy and deserving *kunbis* at an interest of $9\frac{3}{4}$ per cent, and the profits made by the societies in these transactions were transferred to a reserve fund.[1]

The growth of credit societies in the villages was very slow until the organisation of Central Unions in the cities opened a new source of capital for them. But the educative value of co-operation was significant even at a stage when the movement was confined to a few prosperous villages. According to G. V. Joglekar, the officiating Registrar in 1908, the receipt of a transcript of 'Proceedings in Committee' from a credit society in some remote village couched in terms like 'first resolution', or 'voted to the chair', or 'carried unanimously', gave some indication of the changes which a successful co-operative movement could bring about in rural society:

> Let us visit Hulkoti [stated Joglekar], just by Gadag, and see what its society can tell us. We are met by the Patel, Mr. Shiddangowda, and told he is the chairman. With him are several others, more or less leaders too; and with them is the schoolmaster, who, we are told, is the Society's Secretary. We find that their capital stands at Rs. 10,500, of which Rs. 4,000 ... is entirely devoted to redemption of old debts. ... We find they are charging $9\frac{3}{8}$ per cent on loans to members, and giving $6\frac{1}{4}$ per cent on fixed deposits. We think at once of investing in the paying 'deposits', but are told that such a privilege is reserved as a rule for 'members only!' What will they give then for a loan? They look at their books and find only five demands outstanding; just at present, for loans from members, they have Rs. 175 odd at hand in the Post Office, instalments to the amount of Rs. 872 are due next month, so that altogether they have no immediate need of our money. ... Again we are disappointed. But then, remember that we are dealing with one of the best ... Rural Societies in the Presidency. ... We ask about their membership, and find there are 123 members. The liability is unlimited ... and they are together more like a little family, a village

[1] *Annual Report of Co-operative Societies for 1908.*

within a village, ruled by a panch, than a Company established by Law. . . .[1]

However the best credit society in Maharashtra cannot be expected to convey a correct impression of the difficulties faced by credit societies in less fortunate villages. Within the short space of three years the Registrar had succeeded in launching societies in forty-eight villages. But the precariousness of the majority of these societies, and the desperate methods devised by the *kunbis* to secure loans for themselves, reflected the extent to which the *vanis* still dominated the economy of the villages. Because of the scarcity of capital, and the high rates of interest, it was more difficult to launch credit societies in the central districts of Maharashtra than it was to launch them in the northern or in the southern districts. But even in the central districts the obstacles in the spread of the co-operative movement were formidable. Quite frequently the *kunbis* borrowed money from the *vanis* at high rates of interest and deposited it in the credit societies merely to create the goodwill which enabled them to raise a large loan. Besides, since it was impossible for the credit societies to accommodate the *kunbis* whenever they required a loan, their dependence upon the *vanis* was diminished, but it was by no means eliminated by the new credit institutions. Finally, the number of occasions on which a *kunbi* repaid a loan, and was advanced an identical sum shortly afterwards, indicates that the 'leaders' who managed credit societies took a cavalier view of the ethics of co-operation, and of values like thrift and prudence which the movement was meant to inculcate in the *kunbis*.[2]

The organisation of credit societies in the cities provided a great stimulus to co-operation in Maharashtra. The organisation of such societies was assisted by two factors. First, the existence of urban castes which possessed a strong sense of identity, and which took to co-operation on the principles advocated by Schulze-Delitsch with a minimum of persuasion. And secondly, the presence of *sowcars* in Bombay who wanted to invest their capital in agriculture for reasons of self-interest, and also for reasons of philanthropy.

[1] ibid.
[2] *Annual Report of Co-operative Societies for 1907.*

The facility with which the urban castes could be organised into co-operative societies had been brought to the notice of the Government of Bombay even before 1904. In Sholapur, for instance, resided a community of 15,000 weavers, who were reduced to destitution in the 1890s by consecutive bad harvests which made deep inroads into the purchasing power of the *kunbis* who lived in the surrounding villages and purchased the products of these weavers. To alleviate the misery of the weavers of Sholapur a local philanthropist, Mr. Veerchand Deepchand, made a grant of Rs. 25,000. This grant was utilised by Mr. T. J. Pitre, an officer of the municipality of Sholapur, to advance sums of money to the weavers at low rates of interest to enable them to purchase yarn and other raw material which they required for their industry. The grants made by Mr. Pitre enabled the weavers of Sholapur, who had hitherto borrowed money from *vanis* at exorbitant rates of interest, to re-establish their business on a novel basis. Indeed, the experiment turned out to be so successful that Pitre proposed the institution of a 'Weavers' Co-operative Society managed by the panch of the Sholapur Weavers for the benefit of their community under the benevolent supervision of the State'.[1]

Since the sophistication of the urban castes enabled them to grasp the advantages of co-operation with great dispatch, and since they also possessed a strong sentiment of solidarity, it was natural for the first co-operatives in the cities to be organised on the basis of caste. A pioneering co-operative society in Bombay was the Shamrao Vithal Society of the saraswat brahmans, which was founded in 1907, and which acquired a membership of 371, and accumulated capital amounting to Rs. 14,000, within two years. The Shamrao Vithal Society was able to play a most creative role among the saraswat brahmans, and since the caste was widely scattered in the Presidency of Bombay, the society opened branches in remote little towns like Karwar, Hubli and Kumta within a remarkably short space of time. 'There is no knowing into what corner of the Presidency or activities of life the Society may not penetrate, on discovering a constituent through whom to preach a practical lesson of co-operation,' the Registrar of Co-operative Societies pointed out

[1] *BA:* A. Maconochie, Collector of Sholapur, to Bombay Government dated 11 August 1904: R.D., Vol. 22 of 1904.

in 1909.[1] Nor did the Registrar see any harm in the proliferation of societies which rested on the institution of caste. A particularly promising field of endeavour for the Registrars were castes like the *julahas* or the *chamars*, which were committed to a distinct profession. While such castes could be organised into co-operatives with the same facility as the saraswat brahmans, the benefits derived from organising them were far more substantial, since the advantages of co-operation could be focused directly on the means whereby they earned their livelihood. The Registrars of Co-operative Societies were quick in grasping the opportunity which the institution of caste offered to them. In 1907, for instance, twenty-two out of thirty societies in Bombay embraced castes like the *chamars*, the *julahas*, the *sutars*, the *khatiks* and the *mahars*.

Despite the success of caste co-operatives, such societies did not occupy the centre of the stage in co-operation, and their strength in numbers conveys a distorted impression of their significance for the movement as a whole. As we have already emphasised, while there was no dearth of capital in the cities, credit societies in the villages were starved of capital, and they could not make any progress so long as they relied exclusively upon the prosperous *kunbis* for their financial resources. More important for the co-operative movement than caste co-operatives, therefore, were associations called Central Unions, which sought to organise unutilised capital in the cities in order to finance rural societies. Immediately after McNeill was appointed Registrar of Co-operative Societies he met a group of *sowcars* from Bombay headed by a philanthropic financier, Sir Vithaldas D. Thackersey, whom he persuaded to launch a Central Union to help credit societies in the villages.[2] Thackersey's Central Union proposed to raise capital through fixed deposits bearing interest at the rate of 6 per cent. This capital was to be distributed to credit societies in the villages through the Registrar, who was expected to advise the Union on the solvency and the credit worthiness of the village societies. By 1909 five Central Unions had been launched in the Presidency of Bombay, each one of which enjoyed the patronage of a leading financier. Thus there existed besides Thackersey's Central Union the Broach

---

[1] *Annual Report of Co-operative Societies for 1909.*
[2] *Annual Report of Co-operative Societies for 1905.*

District Society of Rao Bahadur Motilal Chunilal; the Dhulia Society of Mr. K. N. Bhangaonkar; Mr Harlekar's Southern Maratha Society of Dharwar; and finally, the Surat Credit Union. The Bombay Central Union was the most substantial of these societies, and within two years of its inception it had loaned Rs. 14,000 to eight village societies, and it had also opened negotiations with the Government of Bombay for the institution of a Central Bank.[1]

For although the Central Unions were able to extend substantial support to village societies, they did not eliminate the need for an institution like the Central Bank, which could attract all the capital which lay unutilised in the cities, and channelise it to credit societies in villages which did not possess any resources of their own. Lalubhai Samaldas, a leading businessman of Bombay, focused on the need for such an institution as early as 1902, and he pointed to the 'growing . . . class of capitalists' which desired a higher return on its capital than the return given by government securities, but which lacked the acumen to enter into business on its own.[2] Samaldas' scheme for a bank which would draw its capital from the *sowcar* and the rich cultivator failed to arouse any enthusiasm when it was first proposed. But in 1908 he joined hands with Sir Vithaldas Thackersey to sponsor a proposal for a Central Bank in Bombay.[3] This bank was to commence business with a capital of Rs. 500,000, and with the authority to extend this capital to Rs. 2,500,000. It would also issue debentures at 4 per cent to be guaranteed by the government. Finally, the capital at the bank's disposal was to be used exclusively for advancing loans to credit societies in the villages.

When Thackersey expounded his scheme before a Conference on Co-operation held in Bombay in December 1908, he pointed out that a guarantee on debentures, and the management of funds on commercial principles, were vital to the success of the proposed Central Bank. The guarantee would inspire public confidence in the bank until it had justified itself as a viable

[1] *Annual Report of Co-operative Societies for 1909.*
[2] *BA:* L. Samaldas to J. Monteath, Revenue Member of the Bombay Council, dated 2 May 1902: R.D., Vol. 22 of 1902.
[3] *BA:* Vide 'Scheme for a Central Financing Society' presented by Sir Vithaldas Thackersey and L. Samaldas at a Co-operative Conference held in Bombay on 15–18 December 1905: R.D., Vol. 69 of 1909.

proposition, and its management on commercial principles would ensure the success of the project. Although Thackersey's scheme leaned heavily on an official guarantee, and exploited the profit motive, it received strong support from the Government of Bombay as a measure which would greatly strengthen the co-operative movement.[1] But the Government of India opposed the proposal on the ground that it violated the fundamental principles of co-operation. A guarantee, it pointed out, would foster dependence upon the State instead of encouraging habits of independence; and a guarantee was all the more objectionable when it was meant to support a credit institution based on the profit motive. Besides, assistance to an urban bank was wholly unnecessary. The Government of India was confident that co-operation had come to stay in the country, and the movement had aroused sufficient 'interest in commercial and banking circles that it is quite possible that in the early future capital may be forthcoming for its needs without the necessity of any Government guarantee. . . '.[2]

The objections advanced by the Government of India to a guarantee for the proposed Central Bank were refuted by J. McNeill and C. S. Campbell, the first two Registrars of Co-operative Societies in Bombay, on grounds which illustrate how the objectives of co-operation gradually changed in the eyes of those who were most intimately connected with the movement.[3] Campbell asserted that it was patently absurd to talk of the dangers of excessive interference by the State when co-operation owed its origin to an act of legislature, and when it had been promoted by officers who were specially appointed to organise credit societies in the villages. Equally pointless, so he believed, was the refusal to extend support to a Central Bank because it was based on the profit motive. While an emphasis on non-acquisitiveness would prove fatal for urban societies, an over-emphasis on such a principle could undermine credit societies even in the villages, for the *kunbis* who managed such societies could thereby be persuaded to be indulgent towards lazy or dis-

---

[1] *BA:* Minute by Sir George Clerk, Governor of Bombay, dated 13 December 1908 and 10 March 1909: R.D., Vol. 60 of 1911.
[2] *BA:* Government of India to Bombay Government dated 20 September 1909: R.D., Vol. 60 of 1911.
[3] *BA:* Memorandum by J. McNeill dated 24 October 1909 and C. S. Campbell dated 6 November 1909: R.D., Vol. 60 of 1911.

honest members. But irrespective of the considerations which were assumed to govern credit societies in the villages, to hold the profit motive against the Central Bank was nothing short of ridiculous. It mattered little to what extent the Bank offended abstract principles; it mattered only to what extent the Bank benefited co-operation, and how substantial were the advantages which it bestowed on the peasants:

> Turning from the abstract to the concrete [McNeill observed], I could cite the case of Hulkoti Village Society.... The society collected about Rs. 2,600 from members, borrowed Rs. 2,000 from the Bombay Society organised by Sir Vithaldas and others. After a little (more) experience was gained it borrowed Rs. 4,000 (more) from the same source to liquidate various debts. It was now flourishing, possessed a considerable reserve, and has done much to familiarise the people of several talukas with the benefits, both moral and material of co-operation. Its borrowing ... may be termed ... unhealthy. But I do not think that the only result was to teach the people of the village to rely on official aid or Bombay philanthropy. On the contrary, the main lesson learnt was the ease with which ordinary villagers could combine to help themselves and manage their own business without reference to officials. They have profited both morally and materially, and they are at the beginning of the lesson.[1]

With the support of the Government of Bombay, Sir Vithaldas Thackersey and Lalubhai Samaldas launched the Bombay Central Co-operative Bank in 1911, with a working capital of Rs. 700,000 which was subscribed by 911 *sowcars*. The launching of the Central Bank was an important landmark in the development of co-operation in Maharashtra. Because the bank possessed abundant resources of capital, and because it could channelise money to remote villages through a wide network of branches, credit societies in the villages were no longer starved of capital, provided they were able to demonstrate that they possessed leadership and enterprise in requisite quantities. The bank altered the market for money to such an extent that the Registrars had to guard against the dangers of facile credit, and to prevent the growth of societies which were not backed by thrifty and industrious *kunbis*, and therefore lacked any strength of their own. The financial resources of the Central Bank were

---

[1] Vide memo by J. McNeill quoted in footnote 3, on p. 260.

so extensive that besides supporting credit societies in the villages it sponsored schemes of debt redemption, and it also sponsored the cultivation of cash crops in Poona District. With the institution of the Central Bank, therefore, co-operation came into its own, and spread into the villages as fast as the enterprise of the *kunbis* permitted the spread of the movement.[1]

Yet the principles which actually sustained co-operation were a far cry from the principles through which pioneers like Nicholson and Dupernex had hoped to regenerate rural society in India. The emphasis they placed on credit societies organised on the principles advocated by Raiffeissen, and the importance they attached to the absence of the profit motive, indicates that the movement was launched to check the individualism, the rationality and the spirit of competition which had been disseminated in rural society by the utilitarians. It is equally obvious that the advocates of co-operation aimed at restoring that balance of power in the villages, and that dignity of the *kunbis'* style of life, which had been undermined by policies of reform which were sponsored by radical administrators. However, the *kunbis* of Maharashtra had acquired acquisitiveness and rationality to such an extent that the Government of Bombay found it impossible to organise credit societies in the villages which did not rest on the profit motive.

The abandonment of the profit motive as a guiding principle of co-operation had an important effect on gradations of wealth within the villages. In launching credit societies in Germany, Raiffeissen had laid a great emphasis on the organisation of the poor peasants, who comprised the most depressed class in rural society. Raiffeissen societies were meant primarily for the benefit of the poor peasants, and prosperous peasants were discouraged from joining them, because if they did so, they could easily acquire control over the movement, and exploit it for their own purposes. In the villages of Maharashtra, however, it was impossible to exclude the rich peasants from co-operative societies because the poor peasants were so utterly demoralised by poverty that it was impossible to float such societies exclusively on their resources and initiative. However, to encourage rich peasants to join the credit societies was to surrender to them a controlling interest in co-operation. The influence exercised by

[1] *Annual Reports of Co-operative Societies for 1912 and 1913.*

the *patil* and the dominant *kunbis* over the Hulkoti Society, of which we have had a glimpse earlier, was characteristic of credit societies throughout Maharashtra.[1] As a result of this, the credit societies supported the interests of the rich peasants rather than the interests of the poor peasants, thereby defeating the objectives of co-operation to the extent they devolved upon the moral and material salvation of the poor peasants.

But even if co-operative societies failed to improve the condition of the poor peasants, they none the less reinforced the position of the *kunbis* as a class *vis-à-vis* the *vanis*. Before the British conquest of Maharashtra the *kunbis* had borrowed capital from the *sowcars* through the village organised as a community, and since they confronted the *sowcars* with the authority of the community behind them the *sowcars* were unable to establish their dominance over the *kunbis*. By directing the flow of capital through the *vanis*, instead of the village community, the *ryotwari* system had deprived the *kunbis* of the strength they derived from association with their fellow-villagers. The creation of credit societies in the villages partially restored the old order of things, since the *kunbis* could once again borrow money through an institution which protected them from the designs of the *sowcars*. The spread of co-operation, therefore, reinforced the position of the *kunbis vis-à-vis* the *vanis*, despite the fact that co-operative societies mainly served the interests of the prosperous peasants and increased differences of wealth in rural society.

[1] Vide discussions in Poona with Dr Kakade of the Servants of India Society, and with a rich peasant who was the Vice-President of the Hadapsar Credit Society, the first Village Bank to be founded in Poona District.

VIII

Old Elites and New Horizons

The consequences of the policies pursued by administrators who subscribed to the principles of utilitarianism were on the whole destructive rather than creative. These administrators had attempted to stimulate a climate of competition and individualism in the villages on the assumption that the dissemination of such values would create the conditions for progress and prosperity in rural society. But in their zeal for reform the utilitarians merely succeeded in undermining the cohesion of rural society, and in heightening tension between different social groups in the villages of Maharashtra. The agrarian disturbances of 1875 were, as we have already seen, a direct consequence of the policies advocated by the utilitarians. But while the attempt of British administrators to remould rural society on the principles of competition and individualism proved abortive, they were far more successful in the intellectual development which they tried to foster in the community, and more particularly, in the values which they sought to propagate among the sophisticated classes. It is, indeed, in the dissemination of rational and liberal ideas in a section of the community that we must look for the enduring impact of British rule on Maharashtra.

To understand the changes in the intellectual climate of Maharashtra in the 19th century we must bear in mind the consensus which existed on the eve of the British conquest. This consensus was a result of the influence exercised by *advaitavada* over élite castes like the chitpavan brahmans, and by its hold

264

on the middle and lower castes through the literature of *bhakti* which expressed the philosophy of *advaita* in simple poetry comprehensible to the unsophisticated classes. The significance of the consensus which linked the brahmans and the *kunbis* to a common religious outlook was heightened by the support which Elphinstone extended to institutions like the Hindu College and the *dakshina*, in the first instance for the dissemination of traditional ideas, but with the ultimate purpose of introducing the brahmans to the rational and liberal values of the West. The policy initiated by Elphinstone to channelise the intellectual development of Maharashtra did not share the fate of his economic policy; instead, it was faithfully implemented by the utilitarians who assumed control of the Government of Bombay after his departure in 1827. The result of all this was the creation of a class of new brahmans who combined a commitment to liberal and rational ideas with a concern for the values which held together different classes and castes in allegiance to a common corpus of religious beliefs.

A commitment to Elphinstone's views on education was fully consistent with the periodic review, and the reform, of the institutions which he had created as the instruments of his policy. His successors, therefore, kept a close watch on the progress of the Hindu College, and the distribution of the *dakshina*. When in 1874 J. H. Baber, the Principal Collector of Poona, turned his attention to the Hindu College he discovered that the institution had drifted very far from the ideals for whose promotion it had been founded by Elphinstone. Instead of providing young brahmans of outstanding ability with a classical education in Sanskrit the College had become a refuge for idlers and drones 'having the appearance of men 25 to 30 years old, to whom . . . it was never intended that allowance should be continued'.[1] The apparent failure of the institution raised several important questions. The College had been established by Elphinstone in order to impress upon the Hindu community his concern for the religious traditions and the values to which the community was deeply attached. Elphinstone had also hoped that the College would encourage young men from respectable brahman families to enter into the service of the Government of Bombay. But

[1] *BA:* J. H. Baber, Collector of Poona, to the Secretary of the Government of Bombay dated 31 October, 1834: G.D., Vol. 8/303 of 1836.

neither of these expectations was realised. The College had provided only one candidate for the civil service; and the courses it offered were so unattractive that not a single brahman family of repute had deigned to send any member to it. In view of these circumstances, Baber raised the question whether the College was serving any useful purpose, and whether it deserved any support from the Government of Bombay.

Baber had presented so dismal a picture of the Hindu College that a Commission appointed in 1835 to investigate the institution, a Commission which had as its President a conservative like Thomas Williamson, the Commissioner of the Deccan, recommended the outright abolition of the College.[1] However, Robert Grant, the Governor of Bombay, refused to take so precipitate a step even when it concerned an institution which, as he put it, 'preserves and cherishes the old Brahmanical interest, which is anti-British in all its tendencies'.[2] To abolish the Hindu College, Grant argued, at a time when the Government of Bombay had established a school in Poona for imparting education in English would be highly offensive to the brahman community, even though the students of the English School did not receive any financial assistance from the State, unlike the drones who led a parasitic existence at the Hindu College. Since political considerations ruled out its abolition, so Grant believed, the only solution open to the government was to modify the courses offered in the Hindu College in keeping with its long-term objectives.

However political expediency was not the only reason which pointed to the need for assistance by the State to the Hindu College. It was left to the Reverend J. Stevenson, a Poona Missionary who was also a distinguished Sanskritist, to impress upon the Government of Bombay the role of a Sanskrit College, and the importance of some of the disciplines which formed part of a brahmanical education.[3] The existence of parasitic students in the Hindu College, Stevenson argued, could be ascribed to

[1] *BA:* Report submitted by the Committee for the Reorganisation of the Hindu College dated 29 October 1835: G.D., Vol. 17/349 of 1836.
[2] *BA:* Minute by Robert Grant, Governor of Bombay, dated 22 March 1835: G.D., Vol. 17/349 of 1836.
[3] *BA:* Report by the Reverend J. Stevenson dated 28 November 1836: G.D., Vol. 39/409 of 1837. Also see Memorandum by W. H. Wathen, Chief Secretary to the Government of Bombay dated December 1836: G.D., Vol. 39/409 of 1837.

the inefficiency of Narayan Shastri, who had succeeded Raghu Acharya Chintamum as the *Mukhya Shastri* (Principal) in the late 1820s, rather than to any inherent defect in the institution. Sanskrit, he continued, was the root of all the languages of India, and its study was therefore essential for the development of the regional languages, and for their transformation into media adequate to transmit modern ideas to the common people. In the words of Stevenson, while 'English is necessary to furnish ideas to the native mind, the SANSKRIT is equally necessary to enable the learned in European science to diffuse their knowledge among the masses of the community'. But although he argued for the retention of Sanskrit, Stevenson simultaneously proposed drastic alterations in the courses taught at the Hindu College. Instead of any encouragement being given to metaphysical speculation on the nature of the universe and the spiritual quality of man, he argued, emphasis ought to be placed entirely on practical fields of study. Stevenson listed among the 'pernicious' disciplines taught at the Hindu College subjects like *Advaita*, *Jyotish*, *Alankar*, *Nyaya* and the *Vedas*, and he recommended the abolition of the Chairs in these fields. Courses of instruction in disciplines like *Mayukh* (jurisprudence), *Vyakaran* (grammar) and the *Dharamshastra* would have to be continued, since proficiency in these spheres could equip a young brahman for a useful career in life.

The reconstitution of the Hindu College along the lines advocated by Stevenson in 1836 reflected the determination of the Government of Bombay to undermine gradually the hold of traditional values on young brahmans, and to expose them to the influence of western ideas. Similar motives inspired the changes which were introduced in the distribution of the *dakshina*. Of course, for the Hindu community in general, and for the brahmans in particular, the *dakshina* was far more important an institution than the Hindu College, since it not only supported a large number of impecunious *Shastris*, but it also identified the State with the values and traditions of Hinduism.

When Baber looked into the distribution of the *dakshina* in 1834 he discovered that the institution was being exploited in a way which defeated its objectives.[1] In recommending candidates

[1] *BA:* J. H. Baber, Collector of Poona, to the Government of Bombay dated 8 November 1834: G.D., Vol. 6/301 of 1835.

for the award of the *dakshina* the Committee of *Shastris* appointed for this purpose by the Government of Bombay was guided by caprice rather than by the merits of the applicants. But apart from the arbitrary principles which influenced its distribution, the *dakshina*, Baber argued, hardly promoted any of the objectives which had encouraged Elphinstone to support it. Instead of training the minds of the rising generation of brahmans 'in habits of respect and attachment to the British Government', it confirmed them in their allegiance to traditional values, and it was also instrumental in widening the gulf between the rulers and the ruled. Baber's appraisal led the Government of Bombay to appoint a Special Commission to investigate the distribution of the *dakshina*, and to suggest ways and means for its reform. On the advice of this Commission the old Committee of *Shastris* which had discredited itself through its arbitrary practices was dismissed, and the rules for admission to the *dakshina* were made much more rigorous than before. Also on the advice of the Commission, the Government of Bombay decided not to entertain any requests for admission to the *dakshina* after 1836.[1]

The reaction of the brahmans of Maharashtra to a decision which affected their interests so adversely was sharp and instantaneous. It was so because the *dakshina* not only provided the means of subsistence to impecunious but scholarly brahmans but it also represented the predominance of brahmanical values over the community, and the acquiescence by the State in this predominance. The brahmans, therefore, interpreted the decision to discontinue the *dakshina* as a challenge to their position in Hindu Society, and a bid to undermine the traditions of Hinduism. After debating the issue in their caste assemblies, the brahmans of Poona presented a petition to the Government of Bombay in November 1836. This petition was signed by 800 'Shastris, Pandits and Puraniks, etc.', and it stated in forthright language the serious consequences that were likely to flow from the discontinuation of the *dakshina*.[2] The study of the *Vedas* and the *Shastras*, the petition pointed out, was necessary to sustain a

[1] *BA:* Report submitted by the Committee for the Reorganisation of the *Dakshina* dated 20 September 1836: G.D., Vol. 17/349 of 1836.
[2] *BA:* Petition by the Brahmans of Poona to the Government of Bombay dated 4 November 1836: G.D., Vol. 15/385 of 1837.

creative relationship between the Hindu community and the values which gave it moral cohesion, and fashioned its secular and spiritual objectives. In keeping with their traditional role the brahmans of Maharashtra had taken upon themselves this responsibility, while the Peshwas on their part had promised to maintain them, and to encourage them in their labour, through the distribution of the *dakshina*. Such an alliance between the political and the intellectual leaders of the community had worked with the happiest of results in the past and it had protected the interests of the brahmans as well as the rulers of the land. Elphinstone, the petition argued, had recognised the benefits which the *dakshina* had bestowed on the State and on the community, and he had therefore refrained from abolishing it. To do this now, the brahmans of Poona stated in conclusion, would be to undermine the moral foundations of Hindu society, and to bring about social anarchy and political disintegration:

> We therefore entreat [ran the petition] that the Sircar will take the whole of these circumstances into consideration, and make such arrangements as to cause all such balances as will have remained in hand, after the distribution of the ensuing Dakshina, on account of the absent Brahmins, to be distributed to all new candidates, who may be admitted after passing the usual examination. This will be the means of disseminating the learning and the people will moreover be happy and it will greatly tend to the honour of the Government but should it be otherwise, both science and religion will be lost and ruined, and people will not act uprightly in their dealings, and every one will suffer extremely.[1]

But the Government of Bombay refused to be browbeaten into surrender by the spectre of anarchy and disintegration which was raised by the brahman community. Its confidence in its policies stemmed from the belief that the values disseminated in institutions like the Poona English School (which was founded in 1832) would, in the course of time, give rise to a new generation of brahmans who would sympathise with its political ideals and its social objectives. The orthodox brahmans who had petitioned against the decree which prohibited new individuals from presenting themselves as candidates for the *dakshina* were,

[1] ibid.

therefore, told that the government was unable to reconsider its decision.[1] It was, however, pointed out to them that the funds released through the discontinuation of the *dakshina* would 'continue to be made available to the general purposes of promoting education and rewarding acquisitions of science'. The government also committed itself to a *de novo* consideration of the problem after the number of brahmans who received the *dakshina* had fallen sufficiently low.

Since the Government of Bombay had refused to acquiesce in the demands of the brahmans of Poona, the agitation against the discontinuation of the *dakshina* persisted with unabated vigour and even spread in widening circles to embrace the brahmans of Satara, Wai, Pandharpur, Kurud, etc. Throughout the 1840s the authorities were made to feel the brunt of brahmanical disapproval through representations drawn along the lines of the Poona petition of 1836.[2] But the government did not retreat before this onslaught, since it was confident that the establishment of institutions like the English School was bound to exercise a liberalising influence over the community. Nor was it disappointed in its expectations. A series of representations received in 1850 from a group of Poona brahmans, and from some students of the English School, spoke in clear terms of a cleavage in the brahman caste, and of the emergence of a group of liberal brahmans who had disowned the values and traditions of their forefathers, and who were anxious to exploit the opportunities which British rule had opened up to them.

The liberal brahmans threw out a challenge to the orthodox *Shastris* the moment sufficient arrears had accumulated from the *dakshina* funds to oblige the government to consider ways and means to put these funds to some use. Their challenge took the form of a representation to Viscount Falkland, the Governor of Bombay, which contained suggestions seeking to extend the scope of the *dakshina* beyond the promotion of studies in Sanskrit, and the assistance of the *Shastris*. The liberal brahmans proposed the institution of sixteen prizes, of the total value of Rs. 1,000, in Sanskrit; and of a similar number of awards,

[1] *BA:* Bombay Government to the Collector of Poona dated 19 January 1837: G.D., Vol. 15/385 of 1837.
[2] *BA:* See Petition by the Brahmans of Poona, Wati, Satara, etc., dated 19 January 1838: G.D., Vol. 9/526 of 1840. Also see Petition by 300 Brahmans of Poona to Bombay Government dated 2 November 1849: G.D., Vol. 26 of 1850.

amounting to Rs. 2,000, in Marathi and English. These prizes were to be awarded to individuals of any caste on the submission each year before a competent body 'of an original useful composition in the Prakrit, or translation from some original works in the Sanskrit, English or any other language'.[1]

In stating the reasons which encouraged them to propose alterations in the distribution of the *dakshina*, the liberal brahmans defined their social vision and their political objectives with unmistakable clarity. Under the Peshwas, they pointed out, support of Sanskrit and the pretensions of the brahmans could be justified on the basis of the legitimacy which the brahmans conferred on the State. But for the British Government to desist from introducing changes in the distribution of the *dakshina* would be a pointless surrender to reaction. The ideals to which it subscribed were in no way related to the ideals of which the orthodox *Shastris* regarded themselves as the custodians; nor did it draw its sanctions from the political traditions which had sustained the Maratha Government. Indeed, with a little boldness and a little imagination the British Government could be instrumental in disseminating values that would widen the intellectual horizons of the community, and spread habits of thought and action conducive to progress and prosperity. It was incumbent on the Government of Bombay to adopt such policies for altruistic reasons, and on grounds of equity. Its revenues were largely drawn from a tax paid by the *kunbis*, and a policy which subordinated the *kunbis'* interests to the interests of the superior castes was morally reprehensible and politically inexpedient:

> The present system of the distribution of the Dukshunna Fund [the liberal brahmans of Poona stated in conclusion] has no tendency to promote learning among and extend its benefits to the great mass of the population. It is found (sic) on the old illiberal and barbarous prejudice of confining learning to the Brahmin caste and locking it up in stores which the great mass of the people can never be able or hope to open. . . . (The) present plan is calculated to civilise the nation in general and lay open for its benefit these stores of learning and wisdom . . . which have hitherto been inaccessible to the nation at large.

[1] *BA:* Petition by the liberal Brahmans of Poona to the Bombay Government dated September 1849: G.D., Vol. 16 of 1849.

Another striking characteristic of the old system of the institution of the Dukshunna is the confinement of its benefits to the caste of Brahmins. . . . The cultivator, the gardner (sic), the carpenter, the blacksmith, who are the most useful members of the society, and from whom the Dukshunna Fund is wrung, would not under the old system, share in its benefits nor can be civilised by it. . . . What the nation most wants is useful arts, science, and morals and they shall find them not certainly in the dead Sanskrit, but in the animated English literature. This essential reform must therefore be introduced and it cannot be commenced too soon.[1]

When the petition from the liberal brahmans calling for drastic changes in the distribution of the *dakshina* was followed by a representation, couched in identical language, from the 'students of Government English School and other English Schools in Poona',[2] J. G. Lumsden, the Secretary to the Government of Bombay, concluded that the time had come when the government could safely embark upon a policy of reform.[3] The support given by Elphinstone to the *dakshina* and to the study of Sanskrit, Lumsden argued, did not involve any permanent commitment to support the traditional order in Maharashtra. Elphinstone had yielded to no one in his anxiety to introduce liberal ideas among the brahmans. But with his Burkean concern for continuity in the processes of change he had visualised the liberalisation of the brahmans as a gradual process. Since a considerable number of brahmans were now clamouring for a liberal education, and a bold attitude towards the *dakshina*, it was clear that a policy of reform could be adopted without any fear of social disintegration. That reform would have to be initiated sooner or later, Lumsden argued, was inevitable. For to retain the institution of *dakshina* as it stood under the Peshwas was to deny the ideals and objectives for whose fulfilment British rule had been established over Maharashtra. Brahmanical values, with their emphasis on rank and order and status, conflicted with concepts like equality (in the eyes of the law) and progress and mobility. To submit to brahmanical

[1] ibid.
[2] *BA*: Petition by the students of the Government English School dated 23 October 1849: G.D., Vol. 26 of 1850.
[3] *BA*: Memorandum by J. G. Lumsden, Secretary to the Bombay Government dated January 1850: G.D., Vol. 26 of 1850.

values would prevent the British Government from embarking upon any scheme of improvement or reform:

> Are the recipients of the Duxxina [Lumsden asked] unable to comprehend that the system at work around them is directly at variance with the social system and the entire body of ethics which have formed the subjects of their studies and which they regard with a bigoted reverence? Or is it to be supposed that a single act of concession like the distribution of this Duxxina will conciliate the views of (those?) who receive it or render them less alive to the fact that the Government is pursuing a course which threatens eventually to deprive them of their cherished social supremacy?

> If there be justice in the above remarks the course which it is proper to pursue will not require much consideration. Unless Government are deterred by the apprehension of adding to the dissatisfaction of this class who in the present day are rather subjects for compassion than for admiration it should avoid all occasions of extending to them a direct and prominent support which places them in a false position equally in relation to ourselves and to the people.

> What encouragement Government can afford should rather be given to those among them who have come out from their camp and who have been educated under the auspices of Government in ideas more consonant with 'the progress of national education'. The time has arrived when without concern for the result, Government can afford to give a direct and unequivocal support to those men whose ideas it has helped to liberalise and whose minds it has endeavoured to advance beyond the prejudices of their nation and in so doing has placed them in the position of opponents to their own caste and to caste interests while they may unquestionably be regarded as more friendly and partial to ourselves.[1]

Since it focused on the contradiction between the values of the orthodox *Shastris* and the British Government, and because it recognised the liberal forces at work within the brahman community, the memorandum written by Lumsden was the signal for sweeping changes in the *dakshina* and in the Hindu College. The Government of Bombay did not admit any new candidates to the *dakshina* after 1836, and it reduced the sum of money distributed to the *Shastris* from Rs. 28,000 in 1839 to Rs.

[1] ibid.

12,000 in 1857.[1] In 1859 the *dakshina* fund was completely taken over by the Department of Education, and a number of Fellowships were instituted, which were awarded to candidates of all castes to enable them to recive a secular education in the schools and colleges of Bombay.[2] The Hindu College had in the meanwhile been transformed into an institution for imparting a modern as opposed to a classical education. Through reforms initiated in 1850 the College was thrown open to all castes, and its Professorships in Sanskrit were substituted by four Chairs: the first in Vernacular, the second in English, the third in Marathi and the fourth and last in the Sciences.[3] Students who sought admission to the College were required to possess a sound knowledge of the Vernacular. It was also obligatory for them to study Marathi, though Sanskrit was optional for candidates whose main interest centred on the English language, and *vice versa*. A second set of reforms introduced in 1856 heightened the importance of the Chairs of English and Science in the College, and stipulated that 'Sanskrit students should be made to learn also the other branches of a useful general education taught in the College. . . '.[4] Finally, in 1864 the Hindu College was renamed the Deccan College, and thereafter played a key role in the intellectual development of Maharashtra through giving a liberal education to young brahman students.

Despite the changes brought about in the intellectual climate of Maharashtra by a calculated policy of westernisation, the radical brahmans whom a liberal education, and the support of the government, had encouraged to challenge the position of their orthodox caste-fellows were still in a minority. The weakness in numbers of the radical brahmans is underscored by the fact that while the liberal petition seeking changes in the *dakshina* was supported by only twenty-two men, the orthodox faction could persuade 500 *Shastris* to endorse a counter-petition to the Government of Bombay.[5] However, while the orthodox brahmans had the strength of numbers on their side, the winds

[1] R. V. Parulekar, *Selections from the Records of the Bombay Government*, Education Pt. I, 1819–1852 (Bombay, 1953), pp. xx to xxv.
[2] *Report of the Director of Public Instruction in Bombay for 1857–1858.*
[3] *Report of the Board of Education of Bombay for 1850–1851.*
[4] Parulekar, *op. cit.*, p. xlviii.
[5] *BA:* Petition by 500 Brahmans of Poona, Satara, Wai, etc., dated 13 December 1849: J. D., Vol. 16 of 1849.

of change that were blowing across Maharashtra had created a climate that was favourable to the aspiration of the liberal brahmans for the leadership of the community. The power of the orthodox *Shastris*, we should remember, did not rest exclusively on their religious role. For besides regulating the spiritual life of the individual, the *Shastris* provided leadership to those caste assemblies which mediated between the castemen and the State, and protected the secular interests of the community. The *Shastris* could play such a role effectively only if the State subscribed to their values, and shared their social ideals and political objectives. Since the British Government was committed to social ideals and political objectives which were different from, and in some respects antagonistic to, the ideals and objectives of the *Shastris*, they were unable to perform their secular role adequately under the new dispensation. The stage was thus set for the emergence of new leaders and for the development of a new style in politics.

The inability of the orthodox *Shastris* to act creatively in the political climate engendered by British rule, and the consequent need for new leaders in the community, is brought into sharp focus by the riots which broke out in Surat in 1844.[1] The Surat riots of 1844 were no doubt connected with the depressed conditions which prevailed in the city ever since its displacement by Bombay as the entrepôt for the trade of western India.[2] But the immediate cause of the outbreak was a decree which raised the duty on salt to off-set the losses sustained by the government through the abolition of transit duties on commercial goods. In raising the duty on salt the Government of Bombay unwittingly imposed a new and heavy burden on broad sections of the community: on the cultivators, who were already staggering under the weight of a heavy land-tax; on the local brahmans, who were living on the wreck of fortunes of better times, and whose main diet consisted of vegetables cured in salt; and on the poor fishermen of the coast, who employed large quantities of salt in preserving the fish they caught. The increase in the duty

---

[1] I have drawn upon the Surat Riots of 1844 to illustrate my point in full knowledge of the fact that Surat lies outside Maharashtra proper. I would like to maintain, however, that the location of the city does not in any way invalidate the conclusions I have drawn from the entire episode.

[2] *BA:* Petition by 1180 Merchants of Surat to the Bombay Government dated 24 April 1827: J.D., Vol. 20/146 of 1827.

on salt was particularly ill-conceived since the classes it affected did not gain anything from the abolition of transit duties. Dr. Gibson, a missionary who was intimately acquainted with public opinion in Surat, pointed out how the measure had confirmed the citizens of Surat in their suspicion that the British Government would ultimately burden them with taxes just as arbitrary, and oppressive, as the taxes levied by the Peshwas:

> I have often conversed [Gibson observed] with natives who were ready to twit me with the philanthropy of the British Government in giving up transit duties, and in substituting this tax which brought in a huge sum. . . . It seems to me that one could not have hit on a measure better calculated to excite extreme discontent among the various classes who have suffered by our rule, and whose affection we have no opportunity of conciliating otherwise than by letting them alone. The different classes are numerous—they are influential.[1]

As pointed out by Gibson, and subsequently underscored by the riots, the intensity of feeling against the increase in the duty on salt afforded an excellent opportunity to the traditional leaders of Surat to acquaint the Government of Bombay with public reaction to the measure. But the traditional leaders were so divorced from the realities of power that they were unable to act to any purpose in the crisis precipitated by the British Government. In the absence of any initiative from their leaders, the citizens of Surat expressed their opposition to the increase in the duty on salt through spontaneous action. On 30 August 1844 an angry and excited mob of 30,000 men marched to the *adawlut* in Surat, and demanded a cancellation of the duty on salt from the Magistrate, Sir Robert Arbuthnot.[2] The march on the *adawlut* by a spontaneously organised mob brings into sharp focus the inadequacy of the traditional leaders in a situation which they could easily have turned to their advantage, by asserting their leadership over the citizens of Surat, and by demonstrating to the British Government their role as channels of communication between the State and the wider community. The spontaneity of the demonstration at Surat, and the extent to

[1] *BA:* Memorandum by Dr Gibson enclosed in letter from Sir R. K. Arbuthnot, Collector of Surat, to Bombay Government dated 31 August 1844: P. & S.D. (Political and Secret Department) Vol. 92/1625 of 1844.
[2] *BA:* Letters from A. Remington, Judge of Surat, to Bombay Government dated 30 August, 31 August and 2 September 1844: P. & S.D., Vol. 92/1625 of 1844.

which the traditional leaders were compelled to adopt a stance of belligerency under pressure from their followers, is all too clear from an account of the riots by Sheikh Sharif, the foremost Muslim divine in the city:

> In the hope of seeing you hereafter [Sheikh Sharif wrote to Arbuthnot] I beg now to repeat that since this morning, the whole men of this city have united and assembled at my house and urged me to proceed to the Sirdar (i.e., the British representative). But I have since morning till this time told them to have great patience and make no disturbance or tumult . . . and that those who have anything to say, should petition on the subject, and to agree to whatever a beneficient Government may desire, but in no way will they be satisfied. At length they have agreed to be satisfied in this manner: the Government to order . . . that an answer will be given to the petition in a few days and for the present, until a final order be given that all the ryots shall remain in their own homes . . . .[1]

That the dilemma which confronted the traditional leaders of Surat was genuine and not simulated is obvious from Arbuthnot's description of Sheikh Sharif as 'a very respectable and good man . . . whose followers are a discontented set . . . '.[2] But in the absence of any other channel of communication with the mob on the streets, Arbuthnot was obliged to turn to traditional leaders like Sheikh Sharif, and the Mullah of the Borahs, and the Goswamijee Maharaj of the Hindus, for assistance in bringing the situation under control.[3] However, since the traditional leaders were unable to adjust to the changing political values and institutions of Maharashtra, the future lay with the liberal brahmans, who were in a position to communicate the sentiments of the community to the new rulers, and who shared the values and the ideals of the British Government. Of course, the traditional leaders were by no means ignorant of their growing impotence, and of the changes which were undermining their predominance over the community. All this is clearly reflected in the retort of an embittered *Shastri* of the old school to

---

[1] *BA:* Letter from Sheikh Sharif to R. K. Arbuthnot dated 30 August 1844: P. & S. D., Vol. 92/1625 of 1844.
[2] *BA:* Letter from R. K. Arbuthnot to Bombay Government dated 3 September 1844: P. & S.D., Vol. 92/1625 of 1844.
[3] *BA:* Letter from R. K. Arbuthnot to Sheikh Sharif dated 30 August 1844: P. & S.D., Vol. 92/1625 of 1844.

a liberal brahman who tried to win him over to the cause of reform: 'We *Shastris* know that the tide is against us and it is no use opposing. You people should not consult us, but go your own way, and do the thing you think right; and we shall not come in your way. But if you ask us and want us to twist the *shastras* to your purpose and go with you, we must speak plainly and we must oppose. . . .'[1]

Who were these new brahmans who were seeking to deprive the orthodox *Shastris* of their role as the leaders of the community? What were the social and political values which sustained them? How wide was the gulf which separated them from the orthodox leaders, and how fundamental were the changes which they sought to bring about in Maharashtra? Were they an alienated group, or did their enthusiasm for reform stop short of a rupture of their ties with the more conservative sections of the community?

To answer these questions we sketch brief portraits of some representative new brahmans of Maharashtra.

Gopal Hari Deshmukh, also known as the *Lokhitwadi* (Advocate of the People's Welfare), was born in 1823 in a deshasth family which had served the Peshwas with unflinching loyalty, and whose estates were confiscated by the British Government for their faithfulness to the *ancien régime*. After completing his education in the Poona English School, the *Lokhitwadi* entered into the service of the Government of Bombay, and he rose from a humble position to be a judge in the District Court of Nasik. He was a pioneer of Marathi journalism, in which capacity he applied himself to social reform, and to the political education of the common people of Maharashtra. The '*Satapatren*', or the weekly letters which the *Lokhitwadi* contributed to a contemporary journal, are by no means the effusions of a very sophisticated mind, nor do they reveal any deep insight into social and political problems. But despite his limited vision, and notwithstanding his superficial acquaintance with western ideas, the *Lokhitwadi* was able to arrive at a shrewd assessment of the impact of British rule on Maharashtra. The British occupation, he pointed out, differed fundamentally from the Muslim occupation of India. While Islam had made very little impression on

[1] Quoted in 'The Mandlik School' by N. G. Chandavarkar: *The Speeches and Writings of Sir Narayan G. Chandavarkar* (Bombay, 1911), pp. 32–8.

the educated classes, British rule had opened their eyes to new and exciting social values and political objectives, and it had convinced them of the superiority of representative institutions and popular democracy. By creating such a climate, the British Government had cleared the way for the political emancipation of the country. After the people of Maharashtra had reformed the institution of caste, and reorganised their society on liberal and democratic principles, they would have no trouble in achieving political emancipation. The *Lokhitwadi* was more concerned with social reform than he was concerned with political power, but like many new brahmans of his generation, he did not look upon political and social problems as mutually exclusive, and he also believed that social progress would automatically result in political progress.[1]

Vishwanath Narayan Mandlik was born in 1823 in a distinguished chitpavan family which was connected with the Peshwas by ties of kinship, and which had provided the former rulers with many a high officer of State.[2] Mandlik was endowed with an intellectual stature and with qualities of leadership which would have assured him an outstanding political career anywhere. He received his education in the Elphinstone College, Bombay, and after a brief spell of government service he embarked upon a legal career which turned out to be highly successful. However, it was through his participation in public affairs, first in the Bombay Municipality, then in the Provincial Legislative Council, and finally in the Imperial Legislative Council, that he made his mark upon the contemporary scene. Mandlik was a Whig who saw no contradiction between the British connection and the increasing participation of his countrymen in the business of government, and he provided a striking contrast to those sycophantic leaders from whose ranks the British Government all too frequently packed the legislatures. Yet his commitment to conservative principles, and his regard for traditional values, alienated him from impetuous new

---

[1] I am indebted to Mrs. Indira Rothermund for a biographical note on Gopal Hari Deshmukh and for translations from the *Satapatren* on which this paragraph is based. Also see article entitled 'Pioneers of the Reform Movement in Maharashtra' from unpublished source material available with *Bombay State Committee for the History of the Freedom Movement in India*. (Henceforth referred to as *BSCHFM*.)

[2] Based on a biographical note on V. N. Mandlik by D. G. Padhye in *Writings and Speeches of Vishwanath Narayan Mandlik* (Bombay, 1911), pp. 32–8.

brahmans who were impatient of the pace at which power was flowing into their hands. Mandlik lives in history as an enlightened conservative who was outpaced by the growth of radical sentiment among the second generation of new brahmans; and although he initiated his public life as a liberal, towards the end of his career he was battling furiously on behalf of orthodoxy to protect Hindu society from schemes of reform which, so he believed, would have weakened its fabric by opening a wide gulf between its leading and its conservative elements.[1]

A new brahman with a difference, because of his political interests, was Ganesh Vasudev Joshi, who was born in Satara in 1828, and who came to Poona in 1848 in search of employment on completing his preliminary schooling in the city of his birth. After a brief spell of service with the government, Joshi applied himself to a legal career, and at the same time started taking an active interest in the politics of Poona. He was a founding member of the *Poona Sarvajanik Sabha*, and as its first secretary he was responsible (along with M. G. Ranade) for guiding its agitational activity, and for shaping its political style. Like other liberal brahmans of his generation, Joshi recognised the wide gulf which separated the traditional leaders from those who controlled political power, and he regarded the *Sarvajanik Sabha* as 'a mediatory body which may afford to the people facilities for knowing the real intentions and objectives of the government . . . (and provide them with means) for securing their rights by presenting timely representations to Government of the circumstances in which they are placed'.[1] Joshi's search for a creative political role encouraged him to extend the support of the *Poona Sarvajanik Sabha* to the *kunbis* of Indapur in their opposition to the rates proposed by Francis in 1867; it also encouraged him to organise protests against the repressive press legislation enacted by Lord Lytton. Neither of these agitations was marked by any conspicuous success. But Joshi did not have any illusions about the strength of entrenched interests, within the community, and in the ranks of the administration, which were pitted against him. Besides, he regarded participation in politics by the new brahmans not as a short cut to victory but

[1] Vide footnote 2 on p. 279.
[2] Vide article entitled 'Note on the Life and Work of G. V. Joshi' in unpublished source material available with *BSCHFM*.

as an experience which would strengthen their moral fibre and sharpen their intellectual faculties. Joshi's finest hour came in 1877, when he attended the Imperial Durbar as the representative of the *Sarvajanik Sabha*, and invoked a 'parliament' of the princes and feudal chiefs who had assembled there to expound for their benefit the ideals and objectives of liberalism.[1]

The most influential new brahman of his day was Vishnu Shastri Chiplunkar, a creative writer and a journalist who transformed Marathi into a language capable of expressing modern ideas. Besides being a prose stylist of distinction, Vishnu Shastri was also an iconoclast, a satirist and a visionary. Before he died a premature death in 1881, Vishnu Shastri had made a profound impression on the intellectuals of his generation, and in assessing the loss which Maharashtra had suffered through his demise, a contemporary compared him to 'Voltaire (who) made everyone from Stockholm to Rome, and St. Petersburg to Lisbon, tremble in his shoes when he took up his pen. . . . (So) did Shastribua make the Rao Sahebs, the Rao Bahadurs, the Reverends and the Saraswatis squirm and squeak under his literary lash'.[1] While he accepted western values with far more critical a mind than an intellectual with the limited vision of a *Lokhitwadi*, Vishnu Shastri's sympathies lay with the protagonists of change rather than with the orthodox *Shastris*, and he looked with optimism to a future in which Maharashtra would play a creative role after having reformed itself socially and regenerated itself politically. Vishnu Shastri's ideals were most clearly expressed in the New English School, which he founded in 1880 with a group of young intellectuals like Tilak, Agarkar and Apte, who were destined to play a leading part in the politics of Maharashtra.

I

Despite the influence exercised by Vishnu Shastri Chiplunkar on the new brahmans of his generation, the intellectual impact of the West on Maharashtra was most creatively reflected in Mahadev Govind Ranade, who was also the most sophisticated

[1] See *Source Material for A History of the Freedom Movement in India* (1885–1920), II (Bombay, 1958) pp. 1–10.
[2] Quoted in D. M. Limaye, *The History of the Deccan Education Society*, (Poona, 1935), p. 19.

thinker of his times. Ranade was born in a poor chitpavan family in 1842, and he received his early schooling in Poona. In 1859 he proceeded to the Elphinstone College in Bombay, where he was influenced by liberal teachers like Green and Wordsworth. Although Ranade's poverty obliged him to enter into the service of the Government of Bombay he did not permit his official commitments to restrict his interests or his activities. Ranade's interests encompassed a wide range of social activities, and once he had entered public life through the *Poona Sarvajanik Sabha* in the 1870s he continued to play an active role till his death in 1901. But despite the example which he set to the new brahmans, Ranade compels our attention for the insight which he possessed into the values and institutions of Hindu society, rather than for the leadership he provided to his generation. The intellectual qualities which raised Ranade head and shoulders above his contemporaries simultaneously restricted him as a man of action, and placed him at a disadvantage in the rough and tumble of politics. Ranade's melancholic cast of mind; his inability to compromise on matters of principle; and the sophistication of his intellect circumscribed the influence of his ideas and restricted his popularity as a leader.[1]

Besides reflecting his personality, Ranade's social vision was shaped by his membership of a caste whose values were also the values of the lower and middle castes of Maharashtra, and which retained, even after the lapse of half a century, vivid memories of the dominant position it had enjoyed under the Peshwas. The transfer of power in 1818 had shattered the hegemony of the chitpavan brahmans. But such was the strength of their traditions, and the hold which they had formerly exercised over the administration, that even after 1818 they remained the most influential social group in Maharashtra, flocking in great numbers to the schools and colleges opened by the British Government, and monopolising the junior ranks of the civil service. An examination of Table M reveals the extent to which they dominated the institutions of education, which provided the only means of access to the civil service, and to the liberal professions.[2] In the Deccan College in Poona, for in-

[1] J. Kellock, *Mahadev Govind Ranade* (Calcutta, 1926), Chaps. I and II, *passim*.
[2] Vide *Education Commission*, Bombay, Vol. I: Report of the Bombay Provincial Committee (Calcutta, 1884), p. 136.

stance, more than 97 per cent of the students were brahmans, although the caste constituted only 4 per cent of the total population of the region. Small wonder then that British officers viewed the preponderance of the chitpavans with alarm;

TABLE M

Caste Breakdown of Students in the Colleges of Bombay and Poona in 1884

Institution	Brahmans	Kshtriyas	Vanis
St. Elphinstone College, Bombay	59	10	38
Deccan College, Poona	107	1	1
Free General Assembly's Institution, Poona	34	1	6
St. Xavier's College, Bombay	15	1	5
Gujarat College, Ahmedabad	3	–	1
Rajaram College, Kohlapur	23	–	–
Total	241	13	51

small wonder also that such officers wondered what chitpavan memories of the past implied for the future of British rule in India:

Now the Chitpawun tribe [wrote Sir Richard Temple, the Governor of Bombay, to the Viceroy, Lord Lytton, in 1879] still stands in vigour and prosperity. They are inspired with national sentiment and with an ambition bounded only with the limits of India itself. . . . If you were to count heads among our best native employees all over the Deccan and the Concan, and even among our humble village accountants, you would be surprised to find what a *hold* this tribe of Chitpawuns has over the whole administrative machinery of the country. And this position is won over not by favour but by force of merit. For among prizemen and honours holders in the schools and graduates of the University the Chitpawuns are predominant. . . . But nothing that we do now, by way of education, emolument, or advancement in the public service, at all *satisfies* the Chitpawuns. They will never be satisfied till they

283

regain their ascendency in the country, as they had it in the last century.[1]

The social background of a new brahman like Ranade deserves special emphasis because of the light it throws on his commitments, and the significance it bestows upon the ideals and objectives he set before the community. It would be foolish to deny that Ranade's views reflected a temperament which encouraged him to look upon politics as the art of the possible, and to reject the utopian and the visionary for the concrete and the practical. But it would be equally foolish to deny that the values to which Ranade subscribed as a member of the 'Chit-pawun tribe', and the spiritual outlook which he shared with the *kunbis* through allegiance to a common corpus of religious ideas, inculcated in him a concern for social cohesion, and encouraged him to reject progress achieved at the cost of social alienation.

Ranade's concern for social cohesion as a member of a high caste which shared its values with the rest of the community was reinforced by the intellectual influences which shaped his views on politics and society. Like other new brahmans of his generation, he read extensively of the works of Adam Smith, Burke, Bentham and the Mills; also like his contemporaries, he was impressed by Burke's notion of tradition, and Mill's notion of liberty, despite the reservations voiced by the prophet of liberalism about societies which lacked political sophistication. But the social theories of Herbert Spencer, to whom Ranade once referred as 'the greatest living philosopher of the age',[2] made the most significant impact on his mind, and inculcated in him a belief in evolution, and a vision of progress, which saw social or economic or political activity as intimately related rather than as fragmented and isolated fields of human endeavour. Ranade and the new brahmans who came under his influence are frequently referred to as liberals. But this label is meaningful only to the extent that it distinguishes them from orthodox *Shastris* who were committed to traditional values, and from individuals who subscribed to activist theories of political action. The new brahmans who were influenced by Ranade did not subscribe to the principles of individualism which charac-

[1] Vide *The Hindustan Times* (New Delhi), 8 July 1962.
[2] Quoted from a speech given by M. G. Ranade in the Prarthana Samaj: *The Mahratta*, 11 December 1887.

terised liberalism in the 19th century, nor did they pin their faith on economic policies which relegated the State to the position of a watch-dog. Indeed, instead of being committed to *laissez-faire* values, Ranade held the economics of liberalism to be responsible for much of the poverty of India under British rule.

Despite the catholicity of Ranade's social vision, since the circumstances of India under British rule hinged upon a relationship of political superordination and subordination between two societies, he was obliged to place an emphasis on political progress which did some violence to the ideas of Herbert Spencer. The need for such an emphasis became all the more pressing when a group of conservative officers initiated a debate concerning the political objectives of British rule which (to Ranade) appeared to contradict the manifest principles of political progress, and to violate the basic assumptions which sustained the British connection with India. It is true that these officers were provoked into showing their hand by the liberal policies of Lord Ripon, and by the Ilbert Bill in particular. But since Ranade looked upon the devolution of power initiated by Ripon as a process to which the British Government was committed irretrievably, he regarded the conservative offensive as an attempt to give a novel interpretation to the connection between India and Great Britain.

The most distinguished exponent of the conservative standpoint was Sir Fitzjames Stephen, a utilitarian who was influenced by the authoritarian doctrine of Hobbes, and whose experience as the Law Member of the Government of India from 1869 to 1872 reinforced his contempt for popular democracy and representative institutions, and for the shibboleths of 'Liberty, Equality, and Fraternity'.[1] Stephen regarded Ripon's attempt to promote the progressive participation of Indians in the administration as a step which would undermine British authority, and he subjected the liberal vision of British rule over India to a scathing attack in an article which spelt out his view of 'The Foundations of the Government of India'.[2] At the root of liberal pusillanimity and liberal blunders in India, Stephen

[1] See E. Stokes, *The English Utilitarians and India* (Oxford, 1949), pp. 273–98. Also see J. F. Stephen, *Liberty, Equality, Fraternity* (London, 1874), for Stephen's attack on John Stuart Mill.
[2] J. F. Stephen, 'The True Foundations of the Government of India', in *Nineteenth Century*, Vol. XIV, 1883.

stated, lay the feelings of guilt which overwhelmed the disciples of John Stuart Mill when they found themselves upholding two different, and contradictory, political ideals in India and Great Britain. The policy to be pursued in a dependency which was also an oriental polity became clear once the principles of Mill were disavowed, and it was recognised that England was a 'belligerent' civilisation in India, and that she could achieve her political objectives in the subcontinent only by refusing to share power with any indigenous group. The Government of India, Stephen argued, was

> essentially absolute Government, founded not on consent, but on conquest. It does not represent the native principles of Government, nor can it do so unless it represents heathenism and barbarism. It represents a 'belligerent civilisation', and no anomaly can be so startling or so dangerous as its administration by men who, being at the head of a government founded on conquest, implying at every point the superiority of the conquering race, of their ideas, institutions, their opinions, and their principles, and having no justification for its existence except that superiority, shrink from the open, uncompromising, straightforward assertion of it, seek to apologise for their own position, and refused, for whatever cause, to uphold and support it.[1]

Stephen was convinced that British rule over India was based on principles which were quite different from the principles of government in Great Britain. These principles hinged on the assertion by the British Government of absolute power. Stephen further argued that the exercise of absolute power was legitimate in itself, and not as something leading to popular democracy, as was assumed by the liberals in India. In justifying British rule over India, the liberals argued that the exercise of absolute power could be justified only as a means to educate the people of India in popular democracy, and in the use of representative institutions. 'I do not think,' Stephen pontificated, 'that the *permanent existence* of such a government as ours in India need in itself be a bad thing; that we ought not to desire its permanence even if we can save it; and that the establishment of some kind of parliamentary system instead of it is an object which ought to be distinctly contemplated, and, as soon as it is practicable, carried out'.[2]

[1] ibid.   [2] ibid.

Ranade looked upon the authoritarian principles of Stephen as anathema, since they condemned India to permanent servitude and deprived the British Government of a moral argument which could justify its presence in the country. Since Stephen's principles were shared by influential officers in India, and by powerful politicians in Great Britian, their enunciation held implications that Ranade was quick to recognise. To neutralise the insidious influence exercised by Stephen's onslaught on the liberal position he outlined his view of 'The True Foundations of British Rule in India'[1] in an article which set forth a cogent exposition of the liberal conception of British rule, and which also prognosticated with remarkable foresight the process by which political power was transferred into Indian hands.

At the very outset Ranade attacked Stephen's doctrine of absolute power, and the practical inferences which Stephen drew from the application of this doctrine to the issues which confronted the British Government in India. Stephen had argued, Ranade observed, that since the British Government in India was founded on conquest, it should not hesitate to proclaim the superiority of the conquering race, and it ought not to permit the sentiments or the prejudices of its subjects to interfere with its freedom of action. Both the inferences drawn by by Stephen, however, were fallacious. If the culture of the ruling caste was superior to the culture of the subject race, then the ruling caste could quite legitimately assert its superiority over the latter, whether it had acquired power through conquest, or through the consent of the governed. But the superiority of the ruling caste did not invest it with the right to completely disregard the sentiments, or the prejudices, of the subject people. Instead, it imposed on the rulers the responsibility of raising their level of culture. For his own part, Ranade was ready to admit the superiority of western culture in some branches of human activity, and he proclaimed his willingness 'to receive, from our English rulers, the benefits of the new civilisation'. But the reasons which encouraged him to welcome 'the benefits

---

[1] M. G. Ranade, 'The True Foundations of the Government of India', *Quarterly Journal of the Poona Sarvajanik Sabha* (henceforth referred to as *JPSS*), April 1894. This article does not appear under Ranade's name but can be attributed to him on stylistic grounds.

of the new civilisation' also convinced him that British authority over India could never be absolute or unquestioned:

> (We) . . . have no objection [Ranade pointed out] to open and straightforward assertion of the superiority of Englishmen over us, in so far as such assertion is necessary for the spread amongst us of the higher civilisation of which Englishmen are the representatives. But on the other side, we say such assertion should not be uncompromising as Sir F. Stephen makes it—because it is essential to the spread of that civilisation that at many points it should proceed by way of compromise. . . .[1]

Ranade's opposition to the conservative position stemmed from his disapproval of the authoritarian principles which Stephen applied to the British Government in India, and from his dismay at Stephen's denial of any creative role to the new brahmans whom he represented. In focusing attention on the dangers of absolute government, Ranade leaned heavily on the classic liberal indictment of authoritarianism. Stephen, he argued, had made a plea for absolute government on grounds of its ability to initiate reform more effectively than was possible for a government that was subject to the popular will. But was this supposition at all justified? Government, whether absolute or otherwise, was run by individuals who were fallible, and who had, therefore, to appraise and to modify their policies according to the reactions of the enlightened sections of the community. For the British Government in India, so Ranade believed, the new brahmans constituted the one and only link with the native community. While the majority of Indians were ignorant and apathetic, a small but significant minority had developed a deep commitment to western values and institutions through the education it had received in the new schools and colleges. This minority was anxious to see representative institutions work in India, and it sought to apply rational principles to the development of the country. It could be accepted as a partner by the British Government in India with advantage both to the State and the community, and it would in course of time provide a base for the transfer of power into Indian hands. By embarking upon such a policy, Ranade argued, British rule in India would justify itself and successfully accomplish its civilising mission:

[1] ibid.

We dissent almost entirely [Ranade stated in conclusion] from the political principles which Mr. Justice Stephen wishes to be prevailing in the government of this country. We consider these principles to be erroneous and of evil tendency. Our general conclusion is, that while the shell and husk . . . which belong to the English constitution as it at present rests, may be and ought to be cast aside, the real kernel of it is as suitable in this country, as in the soil where it has had such beneficial growth. We agree, that even this essential portion of that constitution should not be introduced all of a sudden. Let each successive step that is taken be justified by the event before further progress is attempted. But however slowly we may move, however cautiously and circumspectly we may look about us at every step that we take, let our progress be towards the goal which is indicated by the constitution of the great kingdom with which we are now so closely associated as parts of the great empire in which the sun never sets. . . .[1]

The debate in which Ranade participated as an antagonist of Stephen, and the definition he gave to his political views, represented only one aspect of his activities as a public figure. Since he believed in an intimate interdependence between the political, the social, the religious and the economic facets of a society, Ranade was convinced that it would be futile to place an exaggerated emphasis on the achievement of political objectives, to the exclusion of progress in other directions. To be meaningful and enduring, he argued, progress had to embrace all the fields of social activity, and it had to proceed uniformly in all the branches of human endeavour.

Ranade's catholic vision of progress, and the importance he attached to the values which shaped the intellectual climate of a community, are seen clearly in an article in which he outlined 'The Exigencies of Progress in India'.[2] The first requirement for progress, he pointed out, was a belief in progress itself. For progress to be achieved, it had first to be desired. The revolution of rising expectations, and the commitment to social mobility and economic growth, were the two most fundamental changes which had taken place in India under British rule. Prior to the British conquest, social values had encouraged individuals to

---

[1] ibid.

[2] M. G. Ranade, 'The Exigencies of Progress in India', *JPSS*, April 1893. This article does not appear under Ranade's name but can be attributed to him on stylistic grounds.

acquiesce in the *status quo* rather than to attempt to improve their station in life:

> Satisfied with an ancient civilisation [Ranade pointed out] we have never, in recent history endeavoured to fall in line with modern progress; nor, but for our education, is it likely that even now we should cherish any new ideal. Our ruin is attributable to our national apathy, lethargy and torpor, the direct result of past isolation and foreign conquests. The active impediments to progress are the inquisitorial power of religion, and the overpowering influence of custom and tradition, which have associated the highest ideal of happiness in our minds with inactivity and ease. While the western nations have striven to develop human energies and powers and to secure a mastery over physical nature, we have stood before the world with folded hands, a picture of helplessness and despair, but in dutiful veneration of everything pertaining to the past, and yielding ourselves in placid contentment to the guidance of antiquated usages, and to rules of conduct which regulated social life before the dawn of modern civilisation.[1]

If a commitment to values which placed a premium on stability had retarded the development of India, how, Ranade posed the question, could the progress of the country be ensured? The most important attribute of a progressive society was a rational approach to economic activity. Reduced to its bare essentials, a progressive society was one in which every person was constantly striving to improve his position through rational effort. In the quest for self-improvement there was no place for sentimentality, and even if the irrational was not wholly eliminated, it was certainly subordinated to the achievement of practical ends. Science and rationalism were the foundations of progress, and they played the same role in modern society which faith and superstition had played in primitive societies.

Since the key to progress lay in the substitution of reason for sentiment, Ranade's attempt to effect a religious revival was designed to promote such changes in the intellectual climate of Maharashtra. Alone among the new brahmans of his generation he discerned the implications of the rise of protestantism in Europe; alone also among his contemporaries he recognized the creative energy which had invigorated the West through the

[1] ibid.

idea of individual responsibility to God, and through the belief that a commitment to a secular calling could bring about spiritual fulfilment. The spread of protestantism in Europe had prepared the ground for progress through creating a social and intellectual climate which had undermined the values and institutions of medieval society. The *bhakti* saints of Maharashtra, so Ranade believed, had attempted to stimulate similar changes, and they stood for ideals and objectives identical to the ideals and objectives which had inspired the religious reformers of medieval Europe:

> There is a curious parallel [Ranade pointed out] between the history of the Reformation movement in Western Europe, and the struggle represented by the lives and teachings and writings of these saints and prophets. . . . The European reformers of the sixteenth century protested strongly against the authority claimed by the priests and clergy with the Roman bishop at their head. . . . The Reformation in western India had its counterpart in this respect. Ancient authority and tradition had been petrified there, not in an ambitious Bishop and his clergy, but in the monopoly of the Brahmin caste, and it was against the exclusive spirit of this caste domination that the saints and prophets struggled most manfully to protest. They asserted the dignity of the human soul as residing in it quite independently of the accidents of its birth and social rank.[1]

Ranade's critique of the *bhakti* movement is more of an exposition of the religious values which he sought to disseminate in Maharashtra, than an appraisal of the social objectives which inspired popular saints like Jnaneshwar, Namadeva and Tukarama. In their attitude towards established religion, and towards spiritual privileges which were immoral and arbitrary, the protestant reformers of Europe resembled the *bhakti* saints of Maharashtra. But the emphasis laid by the protestant reformers on the worthiness of the secular life, and on the possibility of spiritual salvation through commitment to a secular profession, was conspicuous by its absence in the teachings of the *bhakti* saints. The leaders of the *bhakti* movement were primarily interested in disseminating the values of Hinduism (which had till then remained confined to the brahmans) among the lower

[1] M. G. Ranade, 'The Saints and Prophets of Maharashtra', in *Rise of the Maratha Power* (Bombay, 1901 reprinted in 1961), pp. 66–7.

and middle castes through expressing them in a language, and in an idiom, comprehensible to the common people. They sought to strengthen the fabric of society by directing the allegiance of different castes to a common corpus of religious values. Whether Ranade (like many a reformer before him) deliberately misinterpreted the objectives of the *bhakti* saints is difficult to say. What is unmistakable is his desire to disseminate in Maharashtra the religious values which, so he believed, had put western society on the path to progress and prosperity.

Such were the principles of the 'Hindu Protestantism'[1] which Ranade preached from the platform of the *Prarthana Samaj*, a religious society which he launched in association with men like Dadoba Pandurang and R. G. Bhandarkar. The *Prarthana Samaj* sought to reconcile Hinduism to the spirit of progress, and to transform it into a religion resting on spiritual enlightenment rather than on crude superstition. Ranade rejected the philosophy of Sankara as something whose arid intellectual quality left the emotional roots of the individual untouched; nevertheless, he acknowledged his indirect debt to *advaita* through attributing the creation of the universe, and the existence of man, to a single and omnipotent God. 'There are not many Gods, nor a hierarchy of Gods, nor deified good and bad powers, nor principles of light and darkness, of matter and spirit, of Prakriti or Maya and Purusha. God is One and without a second and not many persons—not a triad, nor a duality of persons,'[2] he asserted in *A Theist's Confession of Faith*. Ranade saw this divine person in the compassionate God of the *bhakti* saints, to whom Ekanatha, Namdeva and Tukarama had addressed their *abhangas*, and who could be reached more readily through devotion than through intellectual inquiry.

Because of the ideas which influenced Ranade's approach to social problems, and convinced him of the inevitability of progress, in reinterpreting Hinduism he saw himself rationalising trends within Hindu society, rather than inflicting alien values upon it. Nor was such a view unjustified, for all around him he saw changes stemming from the interaction between the traditional society of Maharashtra and the ideas which the new rulers

[1] The term 'Hindu Protestantism' is used by N. G. Chandavarkar to describe the teachings of the *Prarthana Samaj*.
[2] Quoted in Kellock, *op. cit.*, pp. 168—9.

had disseminated in the community. As early as 1821 the brahmans of Poona had split into two groups over the re-admission of a caste-fellow called Gangadhar Dixit Phadke, who had defied custom by residing for a period of time in Bombay. The conservative and the liberal brahmans had clashed even more violently when Shivprasad Seshadri, a convert to Christianity, had indicated a desire to be readmitted into his caste. In 1840, barely two decades after the British conquest, a group of brahmans launched a society on masonic principles to propagate the abolition of caste. A more important landmark in the spread of liberal values was the establishment in 1848 by some young students of a *Literary and Scientific Society* which served as a forum for the discussion and dissemination of radical ideas. The members of this society were associated with social reform and they tried to promote the emancipation of women. The liberal brahmans met with some initial success in reforming the institution of caste, and in promoting the education of women, and this success encouraged them to launch in the 1870s an attack on the interdict on the remarriage of widows. The habits of thought which the liberals encountered when they attempted to promote the remarriage of widows were far too deeply entrenched to be shaken by a single assault. But Vishnu Shastri Pandit, the leader of the liberal brahmans, had the satisfaction of drawing into the debate a person as eminent as Shri Shankaracharaya, the spiritual head of the *Advaitists*; and even though the Hindu pontiff decreed the marriage of widows to be against the letter and the spirit of the *Shastras*, his participation in the controversy reflected the deep concern of the orthodox community over the rapidly changing intellectual climate of Maharashtra.[1]

Yet Ranade did not permit his belief in evolution to blind him to the need for organised action, or to convert him to the view that the ferment at work within Hindu society would spontaneously ensure its development along liberal principles. He dismissed the conviction of some liberals in the spontaneity

[1] N. G. Chandavarkar, 'The Forces at Work (Within Hindu Society)' in *Times of India* (Bombay), 8 December 1887. Also see M. G. Ranade's speech before the *Prarthana Samaj* reprinted in *The Mahratta*, 11 September 1887. For a brief review of the social reform movement in Maharashtra, see speech by N. G. Chandavarkar before the Bombay Provincial Social Conference in 1901 reproduced in his *Speeches and Writings, etc.*, pp. 92–6.

of social change as something compounded in equal parts of apathy and intellectual sophistry; and he argued that change, if it was to be desirable, could come about only through the active assertion of their will by the liberal members of the community. Ranade's concept of a liberal élite in the role of a social catalyst was enunciated with great clarity by one of his most distinguished disciples:

> Though a state of transition [stated N. G. Chandavarkar] such as that through which our Hindu society is passing is inevitable under the present conditions . . . we should not delude ourselves with the belief that a period of mere scepticism. . . without any inward impetus or conviction must necessarily and unconditionally give way to a better period in the long run. When a society is being disintegrated . . . no hope of a better integration of it can be held unless there are found even in the midst of the forces that disintegrate it 'organic filaments' or forces which promise to bring the disturbed elements together, and reunite the different and dispersing elements of society on a better and higher principle of life. It is in the formation of those 'organic filaments' that the work and value of the social reformer lies; while the forces around us are slowly loosening our faith in the old . . ., the social reformer has to bring those very forces to his aid and show the way to the formation of a new faith, a new ideal, and a new bond, which shall enable society to enter into a higher and richer form of life, instead of being disorganised.[1]

Equally vital to social progress along desirable lines was Ranade's view of reform as a process which transformed values and institutions slowly and gradually.[2] Ranade's conservative cast of mind, and his commitment to social theories which preferred evolution to revolution, led him to believe that the advocates of drastic change only harmed the course of progress, and the community which they tried to serve. He was conscious of the obstacles in the path of cautious reform. But to assume a contrary course of action, he argued, could easily prove disastrous. The reformer had to 'accept the teachings of the evolutionary doctrine . . ., because they teach that growth is struc-

[1] From N. G. Chandavarkar's speech on Social Reform delivered on 28 November 1896: *Writings and Speeches, etc.*, pp. 62–3.
[2] From M. G. Ranade's speech on Social Evolution before the Indian Social Conference of 1892: *Miscellaneous Writings of Justice M. G. Ranade* (Bombay, 1895), pp. 114–21.

tural and organic, and must take slow effect in all parts of the organism. . . '.[1] The supreme illusion, Ranade pointed out, was the belief that the reformer had to write on a clean slate. Nothing could be farther from the truth; for his work was to 'complete the half-written sentence. . . , (and) to produce the ideal out of the actual, and by the help of the actual'. As it happened, for the Hindu reformer the task of retaining a link with tradition presented no serious difficulty. Hinduism had shown remarkable flexibility in the past, and there was no reason to believe that Hindu society had lost this quality in the 19th century.[2] Indeed, the liberal Hindu could actually turn to the past for guidance, just as it was possible for him to relate the present to the past in a spirit of true catholicity. The liberal Hindu could also proclaim his commitment to the spirit of the *Shastras* though he might on occasion violate their letter. Such was the spirit which inspired Ranade to ally himself with B. M. Malabari in the debate which the Parsi reformer initiated in 1886 through his *Notes on Infant Marriage and Enforced Widowhood*. A similar logic impelled him to seek in the *Shastras* support for the reforms proposed by Malabari.[3]

Ranade's desire to create a modern society in Maharashtra without weakening the ties of interest, and the bonds of sentiment, between different castes and classes provides the key to his social ideals and his political objectives. He realised that the *bhakti* movement had mitigated social tensions to such an extent that 'caste exclusiveness finds no place in the religious sphere of life, and is relegated solely to the social concerns of men, and even there its restrictiveness is much relaxed, as any one can judge who compares (the caste feelings of) Brahmins of South India . . . with the comparative indifference shown in such matters in the Deccan portion of Maharashtra'.[4] This realisation prompted him to reject the politics of extremism, and to oppose religious movements like the *Brahma Samaj*, whose members alienated themselves because of their radical views on

[1] ibid., p. 118.
[2] From M. G. Ranade's Speech on 'The Part History of Social Reform' before the Indian Social Conference of 1894: *Writings of Ranade, etc.*, pp. 133–43.
[3] M. G. Ranade, 'The Sutras and Smriti dicta on the Age of Hindu Marriage', in *JPSS*, April 1891.
[4] M. G. Ranade, 'The Saints and Prophets of Maharashtra', in *Rise of the Maratha Power, op. cit.*

religious and social reform.[1] The values which sustained the fabric of society in Maharashtra impressed themselves forcibly even on an alien like I. P. Minayeff, the Russian traveller who journeyed extensively in India in the 1880s, and who was struck by the intellectual climate of Poona and Bombay. Minayeff noticed how the brahman student of the Deccan College 'admire(d) Spencer and at the same time is devoted to spiritualism'; and how in any discussion on the state of society and the nature of politics with brahman young men, the problems of the *kunbis* occupied a prominence which they rarely occupied in other regions of India.[2]

Since Ranade was acutely conscious of the strength of the social fabric of Maharashtra, he wanted to modernise it without disrupting the ties of interest and sentiment which linked together different castes and classes in a close relationship. Ranade's policies did not reserve for the brahmans a dominant role in society; indeed, notions of caste exclusiveness and caste superiority had no place in Ranade's vision of the future. But because he wanted to usher Maharashtra into the age of rationality and progress without exposing the social fabric to any strain, and because the brahmans occupied a position of superiority in the community, he did not advocate a frontal attack on the institution of caste. Any attempt to undermine the position of the brahmans through a frontal attack would have struck Ranade as morally reprehensible and incompatible with orderly progress. When in 1884 the Government of Bombay attempted to stimulate education among the lower and middle castes by offering them scholarships on a preferential basis in the schools and colleges, the *Sarvajanik Sabha* launched a bitter campaign against what Ranade regarded an act of discrimination towards the brahman community.[3]

However, since Ranade's notions of progress and rationality challenged the traditional values of Hinduism, and the beliefs which sustained the institution of caste, they were designed to

[1] Address by M. G. Ranade to the Indian Social Conference of 1895: *Writings of Ranade, etc.*, p. 151.
[2] I. P. Minayeff, *Travels in and Diaries of India and Burma* (translated by S. Bhattacharya) (Calcutta?), pp. 49, 52–3.
[3] *The Mahratta* dated 20 September 1885; *The Kesari dated* 29 September 1885; *The Bombay Chronicle* dated 27 September 1885; *The Din Bandhu* dated 10 December 1885.

undermine the social and the intellectual preponderance of the brahmans. The implications of Ranade's ideas were clear to the orthodox *Shastris*, whose grip over positions of power was in any event being weakened by changes in the political scene. The *Shastris*, therefore, rejected Ranade's social ideals and political objectives as subversive of the values and institutions of Hindu society. Their reaction to liberalism was voiced by Rama Shastri Apte, the leader of a deputation of *Shastris* from Poona, who apprised Sir James Fergusson, the Governor of Bombay, of the strong disapproval with which the brahmans viewed interference in the social and religious life of the Hindu community along the lines suggested by the advocates of reform. 'According to the Hindu *Shastras* marriage was a religious institution regulated by strict rules and injunctions . . . ,' Rama Shastri told Fergusson, '(and no) good government has yet interfered with our religious laws and customs. . . . '[1]

Ranade's policies did not commend him to the majority of the brahmans of Maharashtra because of the implications of the changes he advocated in Hindu society. Indeed, despite the catholicity of his vision; the insight he possessed into contemporary society; and the rationality of his programme of social and economic reform, Ranade attracted support from only a small section of the brahman community whose dominance over society remained unshaken till the closing decades of the 19th century. But the tragedy of liberal brahmans like Ranade did not lie in their failure to influence the brahman rank and file. Their tragedy lay in their inability to influence the middle and lower castes of Hindu society. The *Sarvajanik Sabha*, which was created by the new brahmans to provide an institutional basis for their power, did make an attempt to lead the discontented *kunbis* against the Government of Bombay in the 1870s. But the agitation of the 1870s was an isolated attempt on their part to win the support of the *kunbis* for their policies; and apart from the 'no-tax' campaign which preceded the Deccan Riots of 1875 the new brahmans were unable to make any impression on the *kunbis* whose cause they supported with such integrity and such skill. Their failure to do so deprived them of the role of leadership which they were meant to fulfil by administrators like Mountstuart Elphinstone.

[1] *The Mahratta* dated 10 October 1886.

IX

The Poona Districts in 1918

Since the social values and the political institutions of Maharashtra in 1818 were overwhelmingly influenced by the organisation of rural society, and since the region retained its rural character in the 19th century, the social climate and the economy of the villages continued to exercise a dominating influence over Maharashtra in 1918. But precisely because the political life of the region was moulded by rural influences, the chitpavan brahmans who had dominated Maharashtra in 1818, and who continued to dominate it during the course of the 19th century, found their position increasingly under attack in the opening decades of the 20th century by a small class of *nouveaux-riches kunbis*. These *kunbis*, as we shall presently see, owed their rise to policies which sought to transform Maharashtra into a modern society, and to put her on the path to progress and prosperity.

The revenue policy of utilitarians like Pringle was designed to create in the villages a class of rich peasants whose prosperity would stimulate progress in rural society and provide a stable social base for British rule over Maharashtra. When Goldsmid and Wingate revised the revenue survey conducted by Pringle, the new rates which they proposed showed less consideration for the interests of the dominant *kunbis* than the scale proposed by Pringle. Nevertheless, the assessment levied by Goldsmid and Wingate still favoured the dominant *kunbis* in a way they had not been favoured under the Marathas, partly because the tax

298

levied by the former government was based upon what the cultivators actually produced rather than on the fertility of the land, and partly also because under the old dispensation they were often required to make up through large personal contributions the total demand on the village. The result of the Settlements conducted by Goldsmid and Wingate, therefore, was the accumulation of capital in the hands of dominant *kunbis* who had formerly been reduced to the level of subsistence through the irrational policies pursued by the Marathas, and whose dominance had been expressed before 1818 in social rather than in economic terms. These dominant *kunbis* are not to be confused with the traditional leaders of rural society like the Kowreys of Parner, who were delivered into the hands of the *vanis* through the policies pursued by the British Government, and whose resentment at their decline was responsible for the disturbances of 1875. These dominant *kunbis* comprised that section of the rural population whose prosperity enabled them to secure loans from the *vanis* even after the contraction of credit which followed the Deccan Agriculturists' Relief Act of 1879, and who provided the leadership and the money for co-operative societies in the villages after 1904.

The growth of a *nouveau-riche* class of *kunbis* in Maharashtra was a process which we can attribute to a number of factors like the absence of chronically unsettled conditions, the improvement in communications, the growth of markets and the general extension of commercial horizons, over and above the rates of land-tax levied by Goldsmid and Wingate. It was also a process which was vividly reflected in the capital spent by such *kunbis* to improve their holdings, or to heighten the social pretensions of their villages, though it was mistakenly interpreted by a number of Survey Officers to reflect an improvement in the conditions of all sections of rural society.

When J. Francis resurveyed the villages of Indapur in 1867, for instance, he was struck by the extent to which the rich *kunbis* had excavated wells to irrigate their fields and to convert them into holdings capable of producing superior food-grains like rice, or cash crops like sugar-cane. Thus in 1835–36, there existed in all 812 wells in Indapur, of which 366 were in an advanced state of disrepair, leaving only 446 wells which could be used to irrigate the fields. Between 1835–36 and 1865–66, however, the *kunbis* of the *taluka* had not only repaired 184 wells, but they had also excavated 625 new wells, providing a total of 1,255 wells. The capital required for all this amounted to a most substantial sum. The excavation of a new well called for an outlay of Rs. 400; and to repair an old well required anything from Rs. 150 to Rs. 175. The 625 new wells excavated in Indapur represented an investment of Rs. 250,000, while the repair of 184 old wells involved an expenditure of Rs. 50,000. All told, therefore, the rich *kunbis* of Indapur had spent Rs. 300,000 between the years 1835–36 and 1865–66 to irrigate their fields.[1]

To convey the impression that the rich *kunbis* of Indapur invested all their capital in irrigating their fields is to do them a serious injustice. While the *kunbis* were anxious to invest their capital in something which assured them of increasing returns, they were equally anxious to spend their new wealth in channels which heightened their social status, and the social status of the villages in which they lived. The *chowdis*, or the municipal halls where the *kunbis* debated their affairs; and the *dharamsalas*, or rest houses for weary travellers, were generally recognised as the most conspicuous signs of prosperity in a village. 'They are unremunerative works, it is true,' a British Survey Officer pointed out, 'but they add to the social comfort of the people, and in their ideas raise the general status of the village.'[2] During the thirty years of the Goldsmid Settlement the *kunbis* of Indapur constructed fifty-nine new *chowdis* and seventeen new *dharamsalas*. This activity represented a capital outlay of Rs. 26,268; and even though Rs. 4,546 of this sum was provided as assistance by the Department of Revenue, the *kunbis* had still made a substantial contribution of Rs. 21,762 towards the erection of new *chowdis* and new *dharamsalas* in the *taluka*.

An unmistakable index of an increase in rural wealth, and more particularly, of an increase in the wealth of those *kunbis* who produced a surplus for sale, was the dramatic rise in the number of bullock carts in Indapur during the course of the Goldsmid Settlement. When the rural districts around Poona were conquered by the British Government, bullock carts were

---

[1] Report by Colonel J. Francis on the *taluka* of Indapur dated 12 February 1867 in *Bombay Government Selections*, New Series, No. 151.
[2] ibid.

virtually unknown in the region. The few carts in existence were clumsy contrivances, with wheels which were mere discs of stone, and they required at least eight bullocks to pull them. However, Lt. Gaisford, an officer of the Survey Department, introduced a cart with wooden wheels to the region, and he also established a manufactory at Tamburni near Sholapur for the fabrication of such carts. Between 1835 and 1866 the number of carts in Indapur increased from 291 to 1,165. These carts were used to carry manure to the fields, and more importantly, to carry crops for sale to the *petahs*. The striking increase in the number of carts, therefore, clearly indicates the emergence in the *taluka* of Indapur of a class of *kunbis* who cultivated crops for sale in the markets rather than for subsistence.

The progress made by the rich *kunbis* of Indapur during the thirty years of the Goldsmid Settlement was sustained by them in the course of the next Settlement (see Table N). The population of the *taluka*, for instance, showed a steady increase during the six decades which intervened between 1835–36 and 1895–96. For capital-consuming items like wells and carts, however, the increase (both absolute and proportional) in the course of the first Settlement was far more striking than the increase in the course of the second Settlement. But this is to be attributed to the achievement of a condition of near saturation in the 1860s, rather than to any diminution in the rate at which the rich *kunbis* accumulated capital in the closing decades of the 19th century.

The rise of a *nouveau-riche* class of *kunbis* in Maharashtra becomes all the more obvious when we focus on individual villages instead of focusing on entire *talukas*. The changes which occurred in three villages, namely, Kalegaon, Ghoregaon and Golpoli in the *taluka* of Barsi in Sholapur District in the course of a settlement were nothing short of revolutionary. This was partly so because these villages were located on the banks of the river Bhagawati and, therefore, possessed a rich and fertile soil. It was also so because they were sandwiched between the *petahs* of Pangaon and Wyrag, on the highway from Barsi to Sholapur, which enabled the *kunbis* who lived in them to sell their surplus at very attractive prices. The result of all this is eloquently expressed in Table O. While the total area under cultivation in the three villages remained more or less constant during the

TABLE N

Table showing Economic Growth in the *Taluka* of Indapur
between 1835–36 and 1865–66 and 1865–66 and 1895–96

	1st Settlement [1835–36 to 1865–66]			
	1835–36	1865–66	Increase	Increase, %
Population	40,179	52,830*	12,651	31
Wells	446	1,255	809	281
Carts	291	1,165*	874	300
Ploughs	1,454	1,820	366	25
Cattle	27,002	24,565*	−3,303	−18

2nd Settlement [1865–66 to 1895–96]			
1865–66	1895–96	Increase	Increase, %
54,199*	67,684	13,485	25
1,255	2,181	926	74
1,187*	1,844	657	55·3
–	–	–	–
21,423*	23,231	1,808	8·4

*Discrepancies due to alteration in the boundaries of the *taluka*.

TABLE O

Table Showing Economic Growth in three Villages in Barsi *Taluka*,
Sholapur District, between the Years 1856–57 to 1889–90

	1856–57	1889–90	Difference	%
Population	1,922	2,655	733	38
Land Under Cultivation				
i. Dry crop	8,306	8,014	−292	−3·5
ii. Garden	174	481	307	177
iii. Unassessed	844	851	7	0·6
iv. Total	9,324	9,346	22	2
Houses				
i. Tiled	226	390	164	72·6
ii. Thatched	218	173	−45	−20·6
iii. Total	444	563	119	26·8
Carts	20	108	88	441
Wells	56	96	40	71
Cattle	823	936	113	14

twenty-five years of the settlement, the amount of garden land
increased from 174 to 481 acres, indicating a rise of 177 per
cent. This was made possible through the excavation of forty
new wells. As a result of the increase in the area of garden land,
and indeed, of a general improvement in the quality of cultivation, the rich *kunbis* of the three villages produced so much surplus for sale that they added eighty-eight carts to the stock of
twenty carts they possessed at the commencement of the settlement. The prosperity of the *kunbis* was also reflected in an
increase of 72·6 per cent in the number of 'tiled' cottages in the
villages, which required a larger outlay of capital than 'thatched'
cottages, and therefore conferred a superior status on those who
lived in them.[1]

[1] Report on the Resettlement of Three Villages in the *taluka* of Barsi, Sholapur
District, by the Superintendent of the Deccan Revenue Survey dated 6 October
1891: *Bombay Government Selections*, New Series, No. 257.

The growth of a class of rich peasants towards the opening decades of the 20th century held serious implications for the politics of Maharashtra. If the Government of Bombay had accepted the education policy of Elphinstone in its entirety, and if it had established schools in the villages for the dissemination of liberal and rational values among the cultivators at the same time as it had established the Hindu College, then the views of new brahmans like Ranade could possibly have acquired some popularity among the *nouveaux-riches kunbis*, if not in rural society as a whole. But since the field of popular education came to be dominated by the advocates of the theory of diffusion, and the education of the *kunbis* was entrusted to westernised brahmans who were unable and unwilling to educate them, the political values of the *kunbis* remained unchanged under British rule. Those *kunbis* who grew up in a traditional climate acquiesced readily in the institution of caste, and in the absence of opportunities for raising their standard of living. The extent of their subservience to the values of caste is indicated by their refusal to attack brahman *vanis* (of whom there were a goodly number) in 1875, despite the fact that such *vanis* were just as unscrupulous in their dealings with the peasants as *vanis* from other castes.[1]

Even before 1875, however, a small but articulate group of non-brahmans encouraged the *kunbis* to reject the institution of caste, and tried to instil among them an awareness of their true interests. Prominent in this group was Jyotiba Phule, who was born in 1827 in a *mali* (a *kunbi* subcaste) family, and whom the non-brahmans of Maharashtra came to revere as their Mahatma.[2] Phule possessed unusual courage and strength of character, but his intellect was more forceful than it was subtle. He was also endowed with the single-eyed vision of a fanatic. Phule was educated in a missionary school, and his association with the missionaries influenced his attitude towards the brahmans, and impressed upon him the need for improvement in the moral

---

[1] *Report of the Deccan Riots Commission* (Bombay, 1876), para. 76.
[2] Based on a biographical note on Jyotiba Phule available with the Bombay State Committee for the History of the Freedom Movement in India (henceforth referred to as *BSCHFM*).

and material condition of the non-brahmans. He first tried to achieve this objective through opening schools for low-caste children. But when his efforts in the field of education failed to make any significant impact, he committed himself to a programme of political activity, and created in the *Satya Shodak Samaj* (Association for the Propagation of Truth) a counterpoise to the *Sarvajanik Sabha* which was dominated by the new brahmans. He also wrote a number of polemical tracts like *Gulamgiri* (Slavery) which brought to light the extent and the iniquity of the dominance which the brahmans exercised over Hindu society.

Phule's *Gulamgiri*, which appeared in 1873, not only focused on the exploitation of the *kunbis* of Maharashtra by the brahmans but it also created a series of historical myths which subsequently inspired virulent anti-brahman movements in other parts of India. The brahmans, Phule argued, were not the original inhabitants of India. They were a people of Aryan stock who had been attracted to the country by its wealth and its fertility in a period of remote antiquity, and who had subjugated its original inhabitants, and referred to them subsequently in terms of opprobrium as the *shudras* (the insignificant). The sanguine conflicts which marked the Aryan invasion of India held a sacred place in the memory of the Aryans, and this memory found expression in legends like the story concerning the annihilation of the kshtriyas by the Aryan hero, Parashuram. To establish their superiority on a firm basis, the Aryans had

> devised that weird system of mythology, the institution of caste, and the code of cruel and inhuman laws, to which we can find no parallel amongst other nations. They founded a system of priestcraft so galling in its tendency and operation, the like of which we can hardly find anywhere since the times of the Druids. The institution of caste, which has been the main object of their laws, had existence among them originally. . . . The highest rights, the highest privileges and gifts, and everything that could make the life of the Brahmin easy . . . were inculcated and enjoined, whereas the shudras and the atishudras were regarded with supreme contempt, and the meanest rights of humanity were denied to them.[1]

According to *Gulamgiri* the history of India after the Aryan conquest revolved around a perennial struggle for power

[1] From translation of *Gulamgiri* available with *BSCHFM*.

between the brahmans and the non-brahmans. The dominance of kshtriya dynasties like the house of Shivaji in certain periods of history indicated that the non-brahmans had often held their own in this grand contest. But the hold which the brahmans possessed over the community through monopolising for themselves the function of priests assured them of a privileged position which they never hesitated to exploit for their selfish ends. Whenever their intellectual predominance was reinforced through the acquisition of political power, as it was reinforced under the Peshwas, the position of the non-brahmans became completely intolerable, and they were subjected to the most gross humiliation by the brahmans.

Since Phule identified the rule of the Peshwas with the tyranny of the brahmans, he looked upon the events of 1818 with approval, and he regarded the British conquest of Maharashtra as an act of deliverance for the non-brahmans from the brahmanical yoke. He admired the spiritual and secular values which inspired the new rulers of Maharashtra; and he singled out for special praise the notion of egalitarianism which inspired them to equate the bigoted brahman with the lowly shudra. But, Phule argued, although the British Government was inspired by noble ideals, its ignorance often led it to support policies which strengthened the hold of the brahmans over the rest of the community. Civil service and the liberal professions, particularly the former, were the two avenues to progress open to the people under British rule. Access to these avenues was gained through the schools and colleges set up under British aegis. Since the British Government was committed to the diffusionist theory of education, it had concentrated its efforts on a few schools and colleges in the hope that those who graduated through these institutions would take upon themselves the task of educating the masses. Such an assumption, so Phule believed, took no account of the selfishness of the brahmans. Instead of disseminating the new ideas they had acquired among the lower castes, the brahmans had exploited their position to monopolise the civil service and the liberal professions. The position of the *shudras* under British rule was, therefore, even worse than their position under the Peshwas:

> The Brahmin deceives the shudra [Phule pointed out] not only in his capacity of the priest, but does so in a variety of other ways.

... In the most insignificant village, as in the largest town, the Brahmin is all in all; the be all and end all of the ryot. He is the master, the ruler. The Patil of a village, the real head, is in fact a nonentity. The kulkarni, the hereditary Brahmin village accountant ... moulds the Patil according to his wishes. He is the temporal and spiritual advisor of the ryots, the sawkar in his necessities, and the general referee in all matters. . . . If we go up higher, to the court of a mamlatdar, we find the same thing. The first anxiety of a mamlatdar is to get around him, if not his own relations, his castemen to fill the various vacancies under him. . . . If a Shudra repairs to his court, the treatment which he receives is akin to what the meanest reptile receives. . . . If we go up higher still . . ., the same system is followed in a greater or smaller scale. The higher European officers generally view men and things through Brahmin spectacles, and hence the deplorable ignorance they exhibit in forming a correct estimate of them.[1]

Since the schools and colleges instituted under British aegis had reinforced the dominance of the brahmans over the rest of the community, Phule believed that it was incumbent on the British Government to drastically amend its policy in the field of education. The Government of India, he pointed out before the Education Commission of 1884, drew the bulk of its revenues from a tax paid by the peasants. It was, therefore, morally bound to focus its attention on the education of the *kunbis* rather than the brahmans, who constituted a small minority. This could be done most effectively by making primary education compulsory in the villages, and by teaching subjects of practical interest in the primary schools. At the same time, since secondary schools and colleges were important for the acquisition of intellectual skills of a high order, it would be wrong for the government to withdraw the support it had hitherto extended to such institutions. But to prevent them from being monopolised by the brahmans, the lower castes ought to be encouraged to join the institutions of higher learning through special incentives. 'The *shudras* are the life and the sinews of the country,' Phule told the Education Commission, 'and it is to them alone, and not to the Brahmins, that the Government must look to tide over the difficulties, financial as well as political. If the hearts

[1] ibid.

307

and the minds of the *shudras* are happy and contented, the British Government need have no fear for their loyalty in the future.'[1]

II

Although the anti-brahman crusade launched by Phule failed to make any immediate impact on the *kunbis* of Maharashtra, the implications of his movement were not lost on the brahman community. The orthodox *Shastris* and, indeed, a majority of the brahmans of Maharashtra opposed even the moderate policies of a liberal like Ranade, since they saw a threat to their position in any attempt to disseminate rational and liberal values in Hindu society. But while Ranade's ideas were characterised by restraint, and while he contemplated a gradual change in the values and structure of Hindu society, Phule sought to unleash a social revolution through launching a frontal attack on the dominance of the brahmans and on the institution of caste. Phule, therefore, presented a more serious threat than Ranade to the position of the brahmans.

When the brahmans of Maharashtra were confronted with non-brahmans like Phule who advocated revolution, and new brahmans like Ranade who preached reform, their first impulse was to turn to the orthodox *Shastris* who were their traditional leaders. The orthodox *Shastris*, on their part, concentrated their fire on reformers like Ranade who worked from within the brahman community, rather than on revolutionaries like Phule who were outside the brahmanical pale. The impassioned debate which took place in 1886 between Narayan Vishnu Bapat, the President of the liberal Hindu Union Club, and Bhima Shastri Zhalkikar, the Professor of Sanskrit at the Elphinstone College, on the secular implications of *advaitavada* illustrates the attempt of the traditional leaders to undermine rational ideas before they had a chance to influence the ordinary brahmans and to convert them to a new religious and secular outlook.[2] In tracing the development of the philosophy of *advaita*, Bapat made a strong plea for active involvement by the individual in the affairs of society, and he dismissed interpretations of

[1] Vide Evidence by Jyotiba Phule before the Education Commission: Report of the *Education Commission, Bombay*, Vol. II (Calcutta, 1884).
[2] *The Mahratta* dated 17 January 1886.

advaitavada which looked upon the world as illusion as interpretations which reflected the political subservience of Hindu society. Bapat's arguments were rejected by Bhima Shastri Zhalkikar, who held that 'the advait philosophy was sought only by those who were convinced of the *transient* nature of the universe, and the common herd of people generally were allured by objects which influence the passions. . . '.[1] Yet the *Shastris* were not always on the defensive, nor did they hesitate to adopt the agitational techniques of modern politics in order to secure their objectives. This is indicated by a meeting held at the Madhav Bagh in Bombay in September 1886, when a crowd of 10,000 drawn from high-caste Hindus congregated to protest against the reforms in Hindu marriage which were proposed by Malabari with the support of individuals like Ranade.[2] It is also reflected in the creation of organisations like the *Sanatama Dharma Parishad* (the Association for Preserving the Orthodox Religion), which enjoyed the patronage and support of Shri Sankaracharya, the spiritual leader of the *advaitins*, and Pandit Gattulalji Sharma, a distinguished Vaishnavite theologian, and which sought to revitalise Hindus society through the co-operation of the heads of different sects and denominations.[3]

But Zhalkikar Shastri's defence of *advaitavada* against the liberal attack was as futile as the attempt of the traditional leaders to reinvigorate Hinduism through organisations like the *Sanatama Dharma Parishad*. The basic, and indeed irremediable, weakness of the traditional leaders lay in the intellectual gulf which separated them from the new rulers of Maharashtra. This gulf made it impossible for the *Shastris* to lead the brahman community in its secular affairs. However, while the orthodox *Shastris* were unable to perform any secular role under the altered conditions of British rule, this was not true of those new brahmans who believed that the structure of Hindu society was perfectly compatible with social progress, and who looked forward to an age of improvement and prosperity in which orthodox values, and orthodox institutions, would flourish with regained vitality. The exponent of such a standpoint among the first generation of new brahmans was Vishnu Shastri Chiplunkar. Despite his vitriolic attacks on the upholders of Hindu

[1] ibid.　　[2] *The Mahratta* dated 5 September and 12 September 1886.
[3] From unpublished source material available with *BSCHFM*.

orthodoxy, and despite his belief in the desirability as distinct from the inevitability of social change, Vishnu Shastri did not subscribe to the liberal ideas of men like Ranade, and he was opposed to radical changes in the values and in the institutions of Hindu society.

The most forceful advocate of orthodoxy among the new brahmans was Bal Gangadhar Tilak, who combined a belief in *advaitavada* with a commitment to the spirit of progress, and who tried to reconcile the institution of caste with the modernisation of Hindu society. Tilak's vision of a dynamic as opposed to a static society, and his belief in economic progress along the lines of the West, committed him to objectives which were in conflict with the objectives of the orthodox *Shastris*. But unlike liberals like Ranade, he did not see any incompatibility between the social institutions of Hindu society, on the one hand, and the political and economic development of Maharashtra, on the other. In presenting his views on 'The Hindu Caste from an Industrial Point of View' before the Bombay State Industrial Conference of 1892, Tilak launched a scathing attack on those who

> held that any amelioration of the industrial classes of this land is impossible without a religious revival, or at any rate without a complete annihilation of the caste system, which they have been brought up to regard as the prime source of all evil in Hindu society. . . .[1]

He attribted the emergence of caste to the increasing complexity of production and the consequent multiplicity of roles in society, and he rejected the notion that distinctions of caste implied differences in status and rank. Caste, he pointed out, was 'a secular institution among the members of the Aryan race, for the propagation of hereditary institutions, and for purpose of mutual help and co-operation'. Like the guilds of medieval Europe, the institution of caste had formerly played an important role in the community. Caste *panchayats* had regulated the social behaviour of the members of different castes, and they had simultaneously upheld values which were essential for maintain-

[1] B. G. Tilak, 'The Hindu Caste from an Industrial Point of View', in *The Industrial Quarterly Review of Western India*, October 1892.

ing order in society. Could caste play a similar role in a modern and an industrial society? Tilak raised the question:

I think [he stated in answer] there can be no two opinions on this point. . . . The free competition of foreign countries has well nigh threatened the very existence of many industrial classes in the land, and the ignorance of the latter leaves them completely helpless in such a crisis. . . . Under these circumstances . . . our industrial classes badly want an organisation which will protect them from total ruin. The organisation of caste already prevails among them, and its history shows that it has saved them from similar crises in ancient times. . . . If we prudently attempt to build on the existing foundations there is every hope that the organisation of caste might again become a living force, and under the altered circumstances of the country protect the working classes in the same way as it did in ancient times. . . .[1]

Despite Tilak's allegiance to the institution of caste he recognised the need, indeed, the inevitability of social change. Where he differed from the liberal brahmans was in his belief that the political community was distinct from the social community, and that the former could progress independently of the latter. Since Tilak distinguished the social from the political, he believed that the advocates of social reform would delay the achievement of political objectives which were looked upon as desirable by all sections of opinion. These differences assumed an acrimonious note in 1895, when Tilak's followers prevented the Indian Social Conference, which was organised by Ranade to promote social reform, from holding its session jointly with the Indian National Congress.[2] In defence of his followers, Tilak disputed Ranade's vision of social progress as a process catalysed by a small group of liberal brahmans, and he stressed the advantages of change which was spontaneous and therefore carried along with it all the sections of the community. Hindu society, Tilak argued, was divided into castes and communities which differed from each other in their social development and in their intellectual sophistication. Whenever the question of social reform was raised these castes and communities were immediately transformed into antagonistic social groups, and the differences between them were heightened and brought into

[1] ibid.
[2] *The Mahratta* dated 24 November 1895.

the open. In the field of politics, however, the different sections of the community possessed the same objectives, and the demand for political autonomy united instead of dividing Hindu society.

Although Tilak opposed the social programme of the liberal brahmans on grounds of expediency, he cheerfully accepted the need and the inevitability of change. His differences with the liberals were not fundamental differences. Indeed, when Tilak examined the classical texts of Hinduism for the light they shed on the individual's role in the community, his conclusions were similar to the conclusions voiced by Narayan Vishnu Bapat, the President of the Hindu Union Club, during the controversy of 1886.[1] The distinction between the secular and the spiritual drawn by a conservative like Bhima Shastri Zhalkikar, he pointed out in the *Gita Rahasya*, was based on a mistaken reading of the religious texts:

> The conclusion I have come to [Tilak stated] is that the Gita advocates the performance of action in this world even after the actor has achieved the highest union with the Supreme Deity by *Gnyana* (knowledge) or *Bhakti* (devotion). This action must be done to keep the world going by the right path of evolution which the Creator has destined the world to follow. . . . This I hold is the lesson of the Gita. . . . Gnyanayoga (the path of knowledge) there is, yes. Bhaktiyoga (the path of devotion) there is, yes. Who says not? But they are both subservient to the Karmayoga (the path of action) prescribed in the Gita.[2]

Despite his differences with the orthodox *Shastris* on the meaning of the classical texts, and on questions of social change, Tilak's views gained considerable popularity in the brahman community. If the choice for the brahmans had rested between the orthodox *Shastris* and Tilak, their reaction to his ideas might well have been hostile. But the climate of British rule had undermined the power of the *Shastris* to such an extent that the only alternative to the acceptance of Tilak's views was acquiescence in the views of new brahmans like Ranade. When the brahman community was offered a choice between Tilak

[1] See *Srimad Bhagavadagita Rahasya or Karma-Yoga-Shastra*, by B. G. Tilak, trans. by R. S. Suthankar, 2 Vols. (Poona, 1936).
[2] See *Bal Gangadhar Tilak: His Speeches and Writings* (Madras, 1909), p. 233. Also see D. M. Brown, 'The Philosophy of Bal Gangadhar Tilak: Karma vs. Jnana in the Gita Rahasya', *Journal of Asian Studies*, February 1958, pp. 197–208.

and Ranade it showed little hesitation in selecting the former. Why it did so is easy to see. Ranade acknowledged the superiority of the political ideals and the social values of the West; Tilak advocated the revitalisation of Hinduism. Ranade wanted to introduce a new ethic in Hindu religion; Tilak regarded any such attempt as completely superfluous. Finally, Ranade regarded the institution of caste as opposed to progress and a rational organisation of society; Tilak, on the other hand, looked upon caste as an institution that could protect the individual from alienation and from *anomie* in a modern and an industrial society.

Tilak's attitude to the traditional institutions of Hindu society persuaded the brahman community to extend its support to him. The brahmans of Maharashtra believed that so long as the institution of caste survived, and so long as the values of orthodoxy claimed the allegiance of Hindu society, their privileged position would not be seriously challenged. They were equally convinced that the weakening of the sentiment of caste would put an end to their dominance. Since Ranade wanted to substitute traditional by rational values, and since he advocated a change in the structure of Hindu society, the policies which he recommended were designed to undermine the position which the brahmans had won for themselves under British rule. However, the brahmans were reluctant to abandon their privileges and they consequently preferred to follow the leadership of Tilak who proposed to leave their supremacy unchallenged.

III

The reasons which endeared Tilak to the brahmans at the same time alienated him from the non-brahmans, who were condemned to a position of permanent inferiority by orthodox Hinduism. The sentiment of caste was so strong, and the ties which linked the *kunbis* and the brahmans to a common corpus of religious values so powerful, that there was no immediate opposition to the ideals or the pretensions of the orthodox new brahmans. But the growth of a small and articulate class of educated non-brahmans who were greatly influenced by Phule, and the rise of rich *kunbis* who were anxious to enhance their status in society, introduced new social conflicts in Maharashtra. The educated non-brahmans saw in the devolution of power which lay ahead both an opportunity for, and a challenge to, the rich peasants whose interests they represented. If the brahmans were not challenged, they argued, and if they were permitted to acquire control over the machinery of government and politics, then the withdrawal of the British from India would result in caste tyranny and caste oppression of an unparalleled intensity. However, if the non-brahmans exploited the rights and prerogatives which they enjoyed under British rule, and if they played their role in representative institutions, then they could secure for themselves a fair share of political power. Indeed, the extent to which the non-brahmans flourished under conditions of popular democracy depended upon their capacity for organisation and their ability to respond creatively to western ideas.

Such arguments were presented to the *kunbis* of Maharashtra by Phule's lieutenants through the *Satya Shodak Samaj*. Prominent among these lieutenants was Krishnarao Pandurang Bhalekar, who hailed from the *mali* caste, and whose 'restlessness and serious sympathies for the poverty stricken masses . . . made him a staunch, fearless leader of the (non-brahman) movement'. Also prominent among Phule's lieutenants was V. R. Gholay, an eminent surgeon whose ancestors had despite their lowly status held high military office under the Peshwas, and who was one of the leading men of his times in Maharashtra. Representative of the agitational activity of the *Satya Shodak Samaj* were the meetings addressed by Phule and other non-brahman leaders in Junnar and in the villages around Junnar in the summer of 1874, which were attended by 'three thousand men of Sali, Mali, Sonar and other Hindu communities', and in which the speakers 'exposed the hypocrisy, cunning and evil deeds of Brahmins and explained how their activities and conduct were unjust'.[1] After Phule's death in 1890, the activities of the *Samaj* were conducted by obscure agitators like Narayan Pensai, who addressed a meeting of *kunbis* in the village of Kowli in Amraoti District in 1901, or by Dharmaji Ramaji, who travelled from village to village distributing pamphlets, which told the *kunbis* 'how we have all fallen victims to the religious tyranny of the Brahman', and which exhorted them to rise against this tyranny. Such activity kindled in the hearts of the

[1] Dhananjay Keer, *Mahatma Jyotirao Phooley* (Bombay, 1966), pp. 132–4, 196–9.

kunbis a desire for equality of status with other castes, and for a fair share of the profits of office and politics.[1]

But it would be a mistake to attribute the awakening of the *kunbis* of Maharashtra exclusively to the agitational activity of the *Satya Shodak Samaj.* The ferment among the *kunbis* was part of a wider process which affected all the castes and classes of Maharashtra. Behind this ferment lay the growing belief that progress and social mobility were both desirable and attainable; that castes of lowly status could improve their position through industriousness and through a rational approach to work; and that the key to improvement lay in education, and in careers in the administration or in the liberal professions, which had for so long been monopolised by the brahman castes. Consider, for instance, the advice given to his caste-fellows by the President of 'The Third Educational and Social Conference of the Reddies of Bombay Province' in 1910. The President welcomed the growth of an awareness of their identity among the Reddies 'with a view to uplift ourselves socially and to devise means for the spread of education amongst us', and he advised his caste-men to pursue the path of loyalty to the Government of India. In return for this loyalty he demanded of the British Government 'special facilities' for the Reddies in the institutions of education and in the administration. 'It is very easy to scoff at office seeking,' the President stated,

> but in the particular circumstances in which we are situated, the bestowal of office would, apart from the good it directly does to the recipient, give hope and infuse energy into other members of the community and make them strive their utmost, not only to get themselves educated, but to spread education among their clansmen.[2]

The intellectual climate which prevailed in Maharashtra under British aegis undermined the values which had formerly reconciled the lowly castes to a position of social inferiority. The erosion of caste values and the introduction of representative institutions unleashed a deadly conflict between different social groups, since every caste and community realised that to be

[1] Note on the Anti-Brahman Movement available with the *BSCHFM.*
[2] *BA:* Address before the Third Social Conference of the Reddies of Bombay dated 22 May 1910: R.D., Vol. 59 of 1910.

outmanoeuvred in the struggle for influence and power which lay ahead would condemn it to a position of total insignificance. So far as the peasants were concerned their desire for power was reinforced by the emergence of a class of rich *kunbis* through the economic policies pursued by the British Government. Since these *kunbis* had accumulated wealth by exploiting the opportunities open to them under British rule they sought for themselves a position in keeping with their newly acquired economic status. Their aspirations formed the driving force behind the movement which sought to wrest social and political control from the brahmans. All this is eloquently reflected in the demand of the Deccan Ryots' Association in 1918 for separate electorates for the agricultural classes in the legislatures which were to be instituted under the new constitution. While the Ryots' Association claimed to represent all sections of the cultivating community, its social base is obvious from its demand that the rural vote be limited to rich peasants 'who paid Rs. 48 or more as land revenue'.[1]

The *kunbis*' demand for separate electorates in 1918 represents a high water mark in the conflict between the brahmans and the non-brahmans of Maharashtra. Behind this demand lay the growth of a *nouveau-riche* class of *kunbis* which was anxious to transform its economic gains into political power; behind it also lay the conflict unleashed between the different sections of the community through the introduction of representative institutions in India. However, the consensus which characterised Maharashtra prevented the conflicts arising from the introduction of representative institutions from creating deep divisions in the community. What prevented any serious weakening of this consensus despite the changes we have described in the preceding pages was the enlightened conservatism of Elphinstone, and the cautious liberalism of Ranade, the two most creative men in Maharashtra in the 19th century. The strength of the sentiment of solidarity between different classes and castes in Maharashtra exercised a powerful influence on the development of the region in the 20th century. It also influenced the tone of the anti-brahman movement, and the success with which the *kunbis* were able to forge a creative political alliance with the

[1] Representation from the Deccan Ryots' Association to the Bombay Government dated 12 September 1918.

brahmans, on the one hand, and the lower castes, on the other. The political stability and the social harmony between different castes which characterise Maharashtra are unique in India. They are partly a tribute to the religious reformers who shaped her destiny during the time of troubles under the shadow of Islam. They are equally a tribute to men like Elphinstone and Ranade who handled with such consummate skill the heritage bequeathed to them by the Saints and Prophets of Maharashtra.

X

~~~~~~

Retrospect

~~~~~~

BETWEEN the downfall of Baji Rao Peshwa in 1818, and the *kunbis'* demand for an appropriate political status in the new constitution of 1919, there intervened a century of rapid social and political transformations in Maharashtra. We have attempted to focus on these changes; and we have also attempted to trace their connection with the social ideals and the political objectives which inspired the new rulers of Maharashtra, and shaped their administrative policy. Our attempt to look upon the transformation of Maharashtra in the 19th century as a result of the interaction between the institutions and the values which prevailed before 1818, and the policies implemented by the new rulers, has posed to us a series of questions: What were the factors of conflict and consensus in Maharashtra before 1818? What were the values which sustained the community and shaped its spiritual and secular outlook? How did the new rulers look upon this society? To what extent did they agree with its moral suppositions? and in what respect did they desire to modify these suppositions? Were there any conflicts of opinion within the Government of Bombay? If so, how were these conflicts resolved? How did the policies of the British Government affect the structure of society in Maharashtra? What were the new conflicts and cleavages it created in the community? How did it proceed to heal these cleavages? Did

British rule bring about any change in social values, and in the complexion of the dominant social groups? And finally, what were the characteristics of the new society which emerged out of a century of innovation and reform?

The two striking features of society in Maharashtra before 1818 were the consensus in religious values which tied different social groups in an intimate relationship, and the extent to which the brahmans in general, and the chitpavans in particular, dominated the rest of the community. The consensus between the high and the low castes stemmed from a religious movement which expressed the philosophy of *advaita* in devotional poetry of striking simplicity and emotive strength, and thereby gained the allegiance of social groups which were otherwise unaffected by the great tradition of Hinduism. The *bhakti* movement bound the lowly *kunbis* and the bigoted brahmans in a close bond of religious values, and it mitigated the tension which characterised the relationship between these social groups in regions (such as Tamil Nad) where brahmanical values and popular religion were based on different, and even conflicting, systems of philosophy. However, while the consensus between the high and low castes was deliberately fostered by the Saints and Prophets of Maharashtra in order to neutralise the threat which Islam posed to Hindu society, the dominance of the brahmans over the community flowed from the purely fortuitous seizure of power by the chitpavans in the person of their caste-fellow, Balaji Vishwanath. Since the brahmans monopolised the function of priesthood, and since they also looked upon themselves as the guardians of the traditions of Hindu society, they enjoyed a unique position all over the country. But by seizing political power in Maharashtra, the chitpavan brahmans heightened the dominance of their caste over the rest of the community. Since the Peshwas, in addition, created a new class of landed aristocrats who were recruited from their caste in order to buttress their position, the chitpavans enjoyed a position of unparalleled ascendency over Maharashtra before the events of 1818 transferred authority into the hands of the British Government.

The institution of caste and the consensus which linked the *kunbis* with the brahmans were both intimately connected with the stagnation which characterised Maharashtra before 1818.

But although economic progress and social mobility were conspicuous by their absence under the Peshwas, it would be wrong to assume that the relative position of different castes and classes within the community was incapable of alteration over long periods of time. Conflict between different castes was by no means unusual in Maharashtra, and the displacement of one social group by another in a position of dominance occurred quite frequently. The eclipse of the 'kshtriya' dynasty of Shivaji by the Peshwas, and the feud between the brahmans and the prabhus, support this assertion. But since these conflicts never questioned the values which sustained the community, the antagonism between different social groups reinforced, instead of weakening, the institutions of Hinduism and it contributed to the stability of society in Maharashtra.

The stagnation which characterised Maharashtra before 1818 stemmed from principles of social organisation which encouraged co-operation and mutual assistance between individuals, and which stifled that acquisitiveness and that spirit of competition which form the basis of progress and mobility. In the cities, caste organisations imposed a rigorous code of behaviour on the individual, and shaped his relations, on the one hand with the government, and on the other with his caste-fellows. The villages were similarly controlled by institutions like the *panchayat* and the *jatha*, which were interposed between the *kunbi* and the administration. The role of the village community in shielding the peasant from the arbitrary power of the *mamlatdar*, and in defining his fiscal obligations to the government, is well known. But it is not generally realised that caste organisations played a comparable role in the cities. The distribution of the *dakshina* by a few *Shastris* who were recognised as the leaders of the brahman community, and the payment of the *mohturfa* by the commercial and artisan castes collectively, focus attention on the secular functions of caste organisations. What requires to be emphasized is the premium put by such institutions on stability as against progress, and the extent to which they discouraged attempts at self-improvement. Both the village communities and the urban castes distributed the tax demanded by the State among their members on the basis of an individual's ability to contribute to the collective obligations, rather than on the basis of a proportional deduction from his gross income. As a result of this, the *kunbis* and the artisans were unable to accumulate the capital necessary for economic growth.

The notions of social equity which prevailed before 1818 sustained a system of taxation which was based on collective principles of social organisation, and which reduced inequalities in incomes to a minimum. This was particularly true of rural society, where accumulations of capital were rare, and where differences in status were reflected in social styles rather than in standards of living. Both the pitch of the land-tax and the manner in which it was distributed among the cultivators of a village reduced the majority of the *kunbis* to a level of bare subsistence, and precluded the possibility of any glaring contrasts in wealth in rural society. The absence of such contrasts in wealth reinforced the consensus which stemmed from the *bhakti* orders, and which linked the community in a texture of common religious values. These two factors interacted with and reinforced each other and they were responsible for the cohesion and stability which characterised Maharashtra before the British conquest.

I

The conservative administrators who took charge of Maharashtra after 1818 faced a task which was beset with serious difficulties. This was so because of the vision and the values which inspired their administrative policy. The conservatism of Elphinstone, who represented a powerful group of British administrators in Maharashtra, did not encourage him to defend indiscriminately the *status quo*, since he regarded innovation and change as an inevitable, indeed, a necessary part of the social process. But he also subscribed to the view that effective measures of reform were based on the enduring moral suppositions of a community, and sought to establish a creative relationship between the past which they were seeking to undo, and the future which they were attempting to build. Natural as opposed to artificial innovation, so Elphinstone believed, was based on the principle of continuity in the processes of change. Progress, he further believed, was an affirmation of the ideals and objectives which formed the moral basis of a community.

Elphinstone's view of social change, and his belief in an intimate relationship between the moral principles which sustained a community, on the one hand, and its social and political institutions, on the other, presented him with a serious dilemma in Maharashtra. The institution of caste which rested on gross inequalities in spiritual and secular status; an arbitrary administration which was not restrained by legal and rational principles; an economy which achieved stability through the simple expedient of preferring stagnation to progress, were all morally repugnant to Elphinstone and opposed to the values which he cherished. But he could not initiate reforms which he considered desirable and essential without violating the principles of natural innovation, and without forcing the pace of social progress.

To avoid alienating the brahmans Elphinstone extended his support to the *dakshina* and to the Hindu College, in the first instance to reinforce traditional values, but with the ultimate objective of disseminating liberal and rational ideas among the brahmans. Elphinstone's views on the intellectual development of Maharashtra stemmed from his conservative vision of progress, and his understanding of the role played by the brahmans in Hindu society. He believed that any attempt to undermine the position of the brahmans as the intellectual leaders of the community would alienate them from the Government of Bombay, and reinforce their affection for traditional values in a gesture of defiance towards the new rulers of Maharashtra. On the other hand, if the British Government recognised the position which the brahmans occupied in Hindu society, then they could be persuaded to support the social ideals and the political objectives to which it was committed. Such support could be trusted to put an end to that dominance of the brahmans which was an insurmountable obstacle in the way of progress. But since the support would come spontaneously from westernised brahmans who had rejected the traditional values of Hinduism, it would not breed any conflict between the British Government and the intellectual leaders of Hindu society, or between these leaders and the wider community.

Although the response of the brahmans to Elphinstone's policies differed in some respects from the reaction which he had anticipated, his success in converting a section of the caste to liberalism and rationality without alienating them, and without weakening the fabric of society, was quite remarkable. But while Elphinstone achieved considerable success in his policy towards the brahmans, precisely the reverse was true of his attempt to modernise the administration which he had inherited from the Marathas, and to reform the former system of land-revenue. His failure in these spheres was due to the instruments which he selected to implement his policies. The use of traditional institutions for creating a modern society was impossible because it involved their exploitation for objectives which were completely opposed to the objectives for which they were created. The government of the Marathas stood for prescriptive status and social stability; Elphinstone wanted to create a system of administration which promoted economic progress and social mobility. It was impossible, therefore, to utilise the institutions of the former government to achieve the objectives to which Elphinstone was committed.

The futility of Elphinstone's attempt to exploit traditional institutions is highlighted in his failure to preserve the status of hereditary officers like the *deshmukhs* and the *patils*, who had played an important part in the administration of the Peshwas. The position enjoyed by these officers was due partly to the personal dominance which they exercised over rural society, and partly also to the role which they played in the collection of land-revenue. Since the administration of the Marathas did not rest upon legal and rational principles, the *patils* and the *deshmukhs* were able to act simultaneously as spokesmen for the peasants and the administration, and to reconcile the interests of the former with the interests of the latter. But the Regulations of 1827 transformed them into the supine instruments of the new administration, and undermined their ties with the peasants, and alienated them from the rural communities which had formerly accepted them as their leaders. The creation of a modern administration weakened the authority of the traditional leaders of rural society, and in combination with other changes, it stimulated the rise of new social groups in the villages of Maharashtra.

Elphinstone attempted to modernise Maharashtra without introducing drastic changes in values and institutions. But his successors calculatedly undermined the sentiment of solidarity in the villages, and encouraged individualism and acquisitiveness among the *kunbis*, in the hope that such values would create progress and prosperity in Maharashtra. The conservatism of Elphinstone encouraged him to look upon society as something which embraced conflicting social groups in a condition of equipoise, an equipoise whose destruction would create *anomie* and social disintegration. The utilitarians who succeeded Elphinstone, however, possessed a mechanical and atomistic vision of society and they looked upon collective institutions like the village community and the *jatha* as obstacles in the way of progress. They consequently substituted a system of land-revenue which rested on the *jatha* and the village community by the *ryotwari* system which revolved around a direct relationship between the *kunbi* and the State without the interposition of any intermediaries. The utilitarians simultaneously substituted the arbitrary principles which had determined the pitch of the land-tax under the Marathas with criteria which rested upon the laws of political economy and which sought to promote economic growth in rural society.

The *ryotwari* system of land-revenue was the most important measure of utilitarian reform in Maharashtra. Its advocates sought to liberate the peasants from their obligations to the *jatha* and to the village community, since they believed that these obligations prevented the peasants from seeking gain for themselves, and discouraged them from working hard to improve their economic conditions. While the land-tax levied by the Marathas fell heavily on the prosperous peasants, the *ryotwari* system taxed rich and poor peasants on a uniform basis, and it sought to create a class of *kunbis* whose acquisitiveness and wealth would form the basis for a steady improvement in agricultural productivity. The utilitarians justified their revenue system both on theoretical and on practical grounds. The laws of political economy, so they believed, demonstrated that it was equitable that peasants who owned fertile land should enjoy higher returns than peasants whose fields were of a poor quality. Political expediency supported a similar course of action, since by protecting the interests of the rich peasants the Government of Bombay would secure the loyalty of a class whose dominance over rural society would ensure the stability of British rule over Maharashtra.

The objectives which had inspired the utilitarians were only partly realised by the *ryotwari* system of land-revenue, and by the legal and rational administration which they created in Maharashtra. Within half a century of the British conquest the village communities were divested of their cohesion and vitality, and they were fragmented into discrete, indeed, antagonistic social groups which had formerly enjoyed an intimate relationship of interdependence. True, the growth of a small class of rich peasants, whose acquisitiveness and ostentatiousness created the illusion of a general improvement in rural society, appeared to vindicate the policy of the utilitarians. But the advantages which accrued to the community from the rise of this class were completely eclipsed by the disadvantages which stemmed from the decline of the *patils* and the *deshmukhs*, who had formerly sustained the self-sufficiency and the creativity of the villages of Maharashtra.

The disastrous consequences of utilitarian policies are reflected most vividly in the decline of the traditional leaders of rural society. The condition of the villages was all the more depressed through the rise of a *nouveau-riche* class of *vanis* whose social values prevented them from participating directly in agriculture, and who therefore preferred to play a parasitical role in the rural economy. Even before 1818 the *vanis* had occupied an important position in rural society, since they provided the capital which enabled the *kunbis* to carry out their agricultural operations, and to pay their taxes to the State. But despite the important role they played in the rural economy the *vanis* were not a dominant class, partly because of the strength and cohesion of the *kunbis* in the villages, and partly also because the judicial institutions of the Marathas favoured the *kunbis* as against the *vanis*. The atomisation of the village community through the *ryotwari* system, and the establishment of judicial institutions which were based on *laissez-faire* principles, completely transformed the situation in rural society. Under the new dispensation the *kunbis* confronted the *vanis* as individuals rather than as members of a community, and they no longer controlled the judicial institutions which resolved conflicts in rural society. These changes resulted in a drastic redistribution of power in rural society, and the *vanis* replaced the *patils* and the *deshmukhs* as the dominating class in the villages of Maharashtra.

The transfer of dominance from the *kunbis* to the *vanis* created a serious antagonism in rural society, and it weakened the cohesion which had formerly held together different social groups in the villages. The *kunbis* communicated their resentment at the dominance of the *vanis* to the Government of Bombay through representations which protested against the iniquity of the new courts of law, and which denounced the oppression of the *vanis*. But the administrators who controlled power in the British Government were far too committed to utilitarian and *laissez-faire* principles to amend their policies. This, of course, was not true of District Officers whose intimate knowledge of the tensions breeding within rural society made them sceptical of the laws of political economy, and made them particularly sceptical of the relevance of these laws to the villages of Maharashtra. But the changes proposed by such District Officers led to nothing because of the doctrinaire commitments of the men who controlled power in the Government of Bombay.

The growth of tension within the villages of Maharashtra led to the disturbances of 1875, when the frustrated *kunbis* suddenly rose against the *vanis* in order to dispossess them of the title deeds and the mortgage bonds which they looked upon as the instruments of oppression. The conflict between the *kunbis* and the *vanis* was by no means the only factor behind the Deccan Riots of 1875. The depression which followed the all too brief stimulus given to the rural economy by the Civil War in America; a series of ill-conceived revenue surveys which raised the burden of tax on the poor cultivators; the agitation conducted by the westernised leaders of the *Poona Sarvajanik Sabha* with the support of the declining landed families, all contributed to the tension which erupted in 1875. But the participation of the *kunbis* and *vanis* in these disturbances to the exclusion of other social groups clearly reflects that these factors only heightened the fundamental antagonism in rural society.

III

The Deccan Riots of 1875 revealed the bankruptcy of the reforms inspired by utilitarianism. They simultaneously destroyed

the faith of the utilitarians in their social vision. True, their reforms had undermined the stagnation which had characterised
rural society before 1818, and they had stimulated the rise of a
small class of rich *kunbis*. But the utilitarians had not anticipated
the rise of the *nouveaux-riches vanis* who exploited the peasants
without contributing anything to agricultural productivity.
Instead of creating the conditions for stability and progress,
therefore, the policies inspired by utilitarianism had created a
rural society which was fragmented into antagonistic social
groups, and which was incapable of making any sustained effort
to raise agricultural productivity. The economic repercussions
of such policies were disquieting enough, but their political
implications were even more dangerous. The rich peasants who
owed their prosperity to the new dispensation were far too insignificant a social group to provide a firm base for British rule
over Maharashtra. The villages of Maharashtra were dominated instead by the *vanis* and the *sowcars*, but their dominance
bred antagonism instead of creating order, and it created conditions which could (vide 1875) precipitate conflicts, not only
between the *kunbis* and the *vanis*, but also between the *kunbis* and
the British Government whom the former partially blamed for
their misfortunes.

After the Riots of 1875, therefore, the Government of Bombay
tried to foster the interests of the *kunbis* whom the *ryotwari* system
of land-revenue, and the weakening of social cohesion in the
villages, had exposed to exploitation at the hands of the *vanis*
and the *sowcars*. The dissemination of new ideas of evolution and
change by men like Maine and West provided British administrators with a new insight into Hindu society, and helped them
to understand why the utilitarians had failed so disastrously.
According to Maine, social evolution was a process which involved the slow and orderly progress of a society from one epoch
to another epoch, and each of these epochs was characterised by
appropriate social values and political institutions. Because
Maine was committed to progress through evolution he looked
upon the attempt of the utilitarians to transform Hindu society
overnight from a community based on status and prescription
to a community resting on individualism and rationalism as an
attempt foredoomed to failure. The principles of utilitarianism,
so Maine believed, were relevant only to the sophisticated

societies of the West. Their application to primitive societies was bound to create *anomie* and to weaken the fabric of such societies.

Maine's vision of progress reinforced the arguments of British officers who were in favour of extending support to the *kunbis* of Maharashtra, and it encouraged the Government of Bombay to reform the institutions of justice in order to check the growing power of the *vanis*. The notion of freedom of contract, for instance, was a principle which formed the basis of the courts of law that were created after 1818. However, administrators who were influenced by Maine looked upon this principle as relevant only to the sophisticated societies of the West. The application of freedom of contract to Hindu society, they argued, could only result in chaos and confusion. Since their apprehensions were justified by the disturbances of 1875 the Government of Bombay accepted their recommendations, and it placed a partial interdict on the freedom of land sales through the Deccan Agriculturists' Relief Act of 1879, which simultaneously threw the weight of the administration in favour of the *kunbis* as opposed to the *vanis*.

But the Relief Act overlooked the question of credit which lay at the root of the *kunbis*' troubles. Although the *vanis* were an unscrupulous class, it is nevertheless true that they played an important role in rural society by providing the *kunbis* with the resources to finance their agricultural operations. Since the Relief Act imposed a partial interdict on the sale of land, it deprived the *kunbis* of the only possession which made it worth while for the *vanis* to advance them money. The Act, therefore, interfered with that flow of credit from the *vanis* to the *kunbis* which was necessary for the prosperity of rural society. Unfortunately, it restricted the credit of the poor peasants to a far greater extent than it restricted the credit of the rich peasants, since the goodwill of the latter depended upon their general prosperity, and enabled them to secure loans from the *vanis* even after 1879. Despite the protection which it extended to the *kunbis*, therefore, the Relief Act failed to improve the condition of those poor peasants whose welfare was the primary concern of the Government of Bombay.

The failure of the Relief Act to improve the condition of the poor *kunbis* turned the attention of the Government of Bombay to the problems of rural credit, and to the necessity of creating a new social climate and disseminating new values in the villages of Maharashtra. The officers of the Government of Bombay all agreed that the *kunbis* had to be protected from exploitation by the *vanis*, but they also agreed that legislative remedies in themselves would prove inadequate. Indeed, measures like the Relief Act which struck indiscriminately at the *vanis* created just as many problems as they solved, since the support they extended to the *kunbis* simultaneously deprived them of the resources of capital on which they depended for the cultivation of their fields. Conservatives like Nicholson and Dupernex believed that the analysis of the problems of rural society by Maine and West suffered from oversimplification, since it took no account of the difficulties which stemmed, on the one hand, from the weakening of social cohesion in the villages, and on the other, from the spread of acquisitiveness among the *kunbis* and other social groups in rural society. Formerly the *sowcars* had lent money to the village organised as a community instead of lending it to individual *kunbis*, and the strength of this community had prevented the *sowcars* from embarking upon a career of exploitation. Since the *ryotwari* system obliged the *kunbi* to borrow money directly from the *vani*, the latter was now in a position to establish his dominance over the former. The acquisitiveness fostered by the utilitarians further strengthened the *vanis*, since it discouraged the *kunbis* from assisting each other and weakened that spirit of co-operation which had sustained the villages in times of distress.

To weaken the dominance of the *vanis* Nicholson and Dupernex proposed the creation of credit societies in the villages on the principles advocated by Raiffeissen. The organisation of such societies, they argued, would not only provide the *kunbis* with capital but it would also revive that spirit of co-operation which had characterised rural society under the Marathas. The *kunbi* who was a member of a credit society would strengthen his position *vis-à-vis* the *vani*, and he would at the same time proclaim his preference for the principle of association to the principle of acquisition. Besides, credit societies which were based on the principles of Raiffeissen would revive the values which had flourished in the villages before 1818, and they would stimulate prosperity which rested on mutual assistance rather than on competition. However, the advocates of co-operation based their expectations on a mistaken notion of the extent to which the *kunbis* had acquired individualism and acquisitiveness. The credit societies established in the villages soon fell under the control of the prosperous peasants who exploited them for their personal gain rather than for the benefit of the community as a whole. Like the Relief Act, therefore, co-operation reduced the power of the *vanis* by organising the *kunbis* and by throwing open to them a new source of credit. But also like the Relief Act, the advantages which it offered reinforced the position of the prosperous rather than the poor peasants. By the opening decades of the 20th century, therefore, the villages of Maharashtra were dominated by a *nouveau-riche* class of *kunbis* who owed their prosperity to the policies pursued by the Government of Bombay, and who played an important part in the political life of the community.

IV

A social transformation comparable in its significance to the rise of the rich peasants was the growth of the new brahmans who gradually displaced the orthodox *Shastris* as the intellectual leaders of Hindu society, and who usurped the role which the *Shastris* had formerly played in the secular affairs of the community. The rise of the new brahmans did not produce a crisis comparable to the Deccan Riots of 1875, partly because of the consensus which characterised Maharashtra before 1818, and partly due to the new institutions of education which were created under British aegis. Elphinstone's policy in the field of education rested on the recognition of the intellectual predominance of the brahmans over the rest of the community, and on the gradual introduction of western science and philosophy in the schools and colleges which were created for them. Such a policy, so Elphinstone believed, would create a class of liberal brahmans who would subscribe to the social ideals and the political objectives of the British Government, and who would, therefore, play a creative role in bringing together the new rulers and the wider community. His policy was vindicated when within three decades of the British conquest the brahmans had split into liberal and orthodox factions, of which the former supported the Government of Bombay, and sought to transform

Maharashtra into a modern society resting on the principles of social equality and popular democracy.

Although the policy of Elphinstone was designed to foster liberal brahmans like Ranade, this does not mean that their rise to positions of leadership did not present the Government of Bombay with problems of stability and order, or that their dominance was not challenged by other sections of the Hindu community. Since the liberal brahmans looked upon themselves as the heirs of the Peshwas, and because they subscribed to the values which inspired the new rulers of Maharashtra, they expected the British Government to sympathise with their aspirations, and to transfer power into their hands as they increased in numbers and strengthened their hold over Hindu society. Elphinstone, to do him credit, had anticipated such a development, and he had pointed out that the growth of social groups which believed in representative institutions, and which were dedicated to social progress, would spell the fulfilment of British rule in India. But his views were most unpopular with a majority of British civil servants in India, and conservative politicians in England, who subscribed to the authoritarian principles of men like Fitzjames Stephen. Although the new brahmans were products of the western enlightenment, and although they subscribed to liberal values, they ran into conflict with the British Government on the important question of the devolution of power until the men who ruled India substituted the authoritarianism of Fitzjames Stephen for the liberalism of Elphinstone.

But conservative civil servants and authoritarian politicians were not the only source of opposition to the new brahmans. Since the concepts of social equality and popular democracy which they promoted were designed to undermine the institution of caste, and to destroy the supremacy of the brahmans, the brahman community looked upon their programme of social action with considerable hostility. The brahmans of Maharashtra, given the choice, would have preferred to follow the orthodox *Shastris*, who were committed to values which ensured brahmanical supremacy, and which rejected progress and social mobility. But the inability of the *Shastris* to perform their secular role adequately under the British Government compelled the brahman community to turn to a group of new brahmans who reconciled progress with brahmanical supremacy, and who saw

331

no contradiction between popular democracy and the institution of caste. The 'orthodox' new brahmans shared the political objectives of the 'liberal' new brahmans. But unlike the latter, they refused to countenance social action which was designed to weaken the traditional structure of Hindu society. Since the orthodox new brahmans did not attack brahmanical supremacy, and because they believed that political emancipation could be achieved independently of social reform, they enjoyed a popularity in the brahman community which was denied to their liberal antagonists like Ranade.

The values of the orthodox new brahmans set them in opposition to educated non-brahmans who looked upon the institutions of caste as the greatest obstacle in the progress of Hindu society, and who apprehended the transfer of power into the hands of the brahman community. But while a liberal education had destroyed the faith of educated non-brahmans in the institution of caste, the majority of the non-brahmans, of whom the *kunbis* comprised the largest group, were far too attached to traditional values to take any serious notice of their ideas. Phule's fulminations against the *joshis* and *kulkarnis*, for instance, made little immediate impact on the *kunbis*, who refused to attack brahmans *vanis* during the agrarian disturbances of 1875. The consideration extended by the *kunbis* to *vanis* who were also brahmans in 1875 is clear proof of their attachment to the institution of caste, and of their acquiescence in their prescriptive status. However, *kunbis* who had grown rich and prosperous by the opening decades of the 20th century refused to accept a position of social inferiority, and they sought to transform their wealth into political power. Their search for a place in the sun was reflected in the non-brahman movement of Maharashtra. But the religious ties between the brahmans and the *kunbis* prevented this movement from acquiring the virulence it acquired in regions like Tamil Nad. Consensus rather than conflict dominated the political life of Maharashtra, and it contributed to social stability and to harmony in relations between different social groups to an extent unknown in other parts of India.

BIBLIOGRAPHY

The various sources used in preparing this book are indicated under the following heads:

A   ARCHIVAL SOURCES

B   PRIVATE PAPERS

C   PUBLICATIONS OF THE GOVERNMENT OF INDIA

D   PUBLICATIONS OF THE GOVERNMENT OF BOMBAY

E   PARLIAMENTARY PAPERS

F   CONTEMPORARY BOOKS

G   NEWSPAPERS AND JOURNALS

H   THESES

I   SECONDARY BOOKS

A   ARCHIVAL SOURCES

1 National Archives of India:

The following series of records were consulted at the National Archives of India, New Delhi—

(i)   Home Department Proceedings from 1818 to 1914
(ii)   Finance Department Proceedings from 1811 to 1914
(iii)   Commerce Department Proceedings from 1872 to 1914
(iv)   Legislative Department Proceedings from 1818 to 1914
(v)   Survey of India from 1818 to 1914

Y

2 Bombay State Archives:

The following series of records were consulted at the Bombay State Archives for the years 1818–1914—

 (i) Proceedings of the Revenue Department
 (ii) Proceedings of the Judicial Department
 (iii) Proceedings of the Education Department
 (iv) Proceedings of the Secret and Political Department
 (v) Proceedings of the Public Works Department
 (vi) Proceedings of the Ecclesiastical Department

3 Peshwa's Daftar, Poona:

The administrative and judicial records available at the Peshwa's Daftar under the heading 'The Deccan Commissioner's Files'.

B PRIVATE PAPERS

 1 The private papers of G. K. Gokhale which I was permitted to see by the courtesy of Shri D. V. Ambekar of the Servants of India Society, Poona.

 2 The private papers of Sir F. J. Stephen of which a microfilm copy is available with the National Archives of India, New Delhi.

 3 The private papers of Lord Minto of which a microfilm copy is available with the National Archives of India, New Delhi.

C PUBLICATIONS OF THE GOVERNMENT OF INDIA

 1 Selections of Papers from the Records at the East India House, Relating to Revenue, Police and Civil and Criminal Justice, Under the Company's Government in India, Vol. IV (London, 1828).

 2 Papers Relating to Act X of 1904 (Co-operative Credit Societies Act), 2 Vols.

 3 Selections from Papers on Indebtedness and Land Transfers, 4 Vols.

 4 Papers relating to the Deccan Agriculturists' Relief Act of 1879, 2 Vols. Selections From the Records of the Government of India, Home Department. No. 342.

 5 F. A. Nicholson, Report Regarding the Possibility of Introducing Land and Agricultural Banks Into the Madras Presidency, 2 Vols. (Madras, 1895).

6 Report of the Education Commission of 1884 (Calcutta, 1885).

7 Census of India, 1931, Vol. VIII, Pt. I, Bombay Presidency: General Report (Bombay, 1933) by A. H. Dracup and H. J. Sorbey.

8 H. Sharp, Selections from Educational Records, Pt. I, 1789–1859 (Calcutta, 1920).

D PUBLICATIONS OF THE BOMBAY GOVERNMENT

1 Selections from the Records of the Bombay Government, No. 4: Report on the Village Communities of the Deccan by R. N. Goodine.

2 Selections from the Records of the Bombay Government, New Series, No. 39: Concealment of the Revenue Records of the former Government by Hereditary District Officers.

3 Selections from the Records of the Bombay Government, New Series, No. 47: Papers Relating to the Deccan Agriculturists' Relief Act of 1879.

4 Selections from the Records of the Bombay Government, New Series, No. 151: Report by Col. J. Francis on the taluka of Indapur.

5 Report of the Committee on the Riots in Poona and Ahmednagar, 1875 (Bombay, 1876), 2 Vols.

6 District Gazetteers of the Bombay Presidency.

7 R. V. Parulekar, Selections from the Education Records of the Bombay Government, 4 Vols.

8 G. W. Forrest, Selections from Letters, Despatches, and other State Papers in the Bombay Secretariat: Maratha Series, Vol. I, Pt. III (Bombay, 1885).

9 Reports of the Registrars of Co-operative Societies from 1905 to 1921.

10 Selections from the Records of the Peshwa's Daftar, 42 Vols.

11 Source Material for a History of the Freedom Movement in India (Published by the Bombay State Committee):

(i) Vol. I, 1818–1885 (Bombay, 1957).
(ii) Vol. II, 1885–1920 (Bombay, 1958).

BIBLIOGRAPHY

E PARLIAMENTARY PAPERS

1 House of Commons Vol. 62 of 1887. Correspondence Regarding Agricultural Banks in India.

F CONTEMPORARY BOOKS

1 H. Dupernex, *People's Banks for Northern India.*

2 G. W. Forrest, *Selections from the Minutes and other Official Writings of Mountstuart Elphinstone, Governor of Bombay* (London, 1884).

3 G. V. Joshi, *Writings and Speeches of the Honourable Rao Bahadur G. V. Joshi* (Poona, 1912).

4 Sir Henry Maine, *Lectures in the Early History of Institutions* (London, 1893).

5 B. M. Malabari, *Notes on Infant Marriage and Enforced Widowhood* (Bombay, 1884).

6 N. V. Mandlik, *Writings and Speeches of the late Honourable Vishwanath Narayan Mandlik* (Bombay, 1896).

7 I. P. Minayeff, *Travels in and Diaries of India and Burma* (translated by S. Bhattacharya) (Calcutta, n.d.).

8 M. G. Ranade: (i) *Essays in Indian Economics: A Collection of Essays and Speeches* (Bombay, 1895); (ii) *Rise of the Maratha Power* (Bombay, 1900); (iii) *Religious and Social Reform: A Collection of Essays and Speeches* (Bombay, 1902); (iv) *The Miscellaneous Writings of Justice M. G. Ranade* (Bombay, 1915).

9 A. Steele, *Summary of the Laws and Customs of the Hindoo Castes Within the Dekhun Provinces Subject to the Presidency of Bombay* (Bombay, 1827).

10 J. E. Stephen, *Liberty, Equality, Fraternity* (London, 1874).

11 B. G. Tilak: (i) *Srimad Bhagavadgita Rahasya* (translation by B. S. Suthankar), 2 Vols. (Poona, 1935); (ii) *His Writings and Speeches* (Madras, n.d.); (iii) *Speeches of Bal Banghadhar Tilak* (Fyzabad, 1913).

G NEWSPAPERS AND JOURNALS

1 *The Times of India.*

2 *The Mahratta.*

BIBLIOGRAPHY

3 *The Sudharak.*

4 *The Pioneer.*

5 *Digest of Native Newspapers for Bombay.*

1 *The Quarterly Journal of the Poona Sarvajanik Sabha.*

2 *The Industrial Quarterly Review of Western India.*

3 *The Bombay Co-operative Quarterly.*

4 *Transactions of the Literary Society of Bombay*, 3 Vols., 1820–23.

5 *The Nineteenth Century.*

6 *The Journal of Asian Studies.*

7 *Contemporary Studies in History and Society.*

8 *The Calcutta Review.*

9 *The Imperial and Asiatic Quarterly Review.*

10 *Journal of the Bombay Royal Asiatic Society.*

11 *The Artha-Vigyana.*

H THESES

1 D. K. Garde, 'Social and Political Thought of the Saints of Maharashtra,' Thesis submitted to the University of Allahabad for the degree of Doctor of Literature, 1956.

2 M. Patterson, 'A Preliminary Study of the non-Brahmin Problem in Maharashtra', M. A. Thesis at the University of Pennsylvania, 1952.

I SECONDARY BOOKS

1 D. V. Athalye, *The Life of Lokmanya Tilak* (Poona, 1929).

2 J. E. Abbott, *The Poet Saints of Maharashtra*, 12 Vols. (Poona, 1926–41).

3 K. Ballhatchet, *Social Policy and Social Change in Western India, 1817–30* (London, 1957).

4 R. G. Bhandarkar, *A Note on the Age of Remarriage and its Consummation According to Hindu Religious Law* (Poona, 1891).

5 G. G. Bhate, *History of Modern Marathi Literature, 1800–1938* (Poona, 1939).

337

6 H. Bhattacharya, *The Cultural History of India*, 4 Vols. (Calcutta, 1956).

7 G. L. Chandavarkar, *A Wrestling Soul: Story of the Life of Sir Narayan Chandavarkar* (Bombay, 1956).

8 *The Speeches and Writings of Sir Narayan G. Chandavarkar* (Bombay, 1911).

9 R. D. Choksey: (i) *The Aftermath* (Bombay, 1950); (ii) *Economic History of the Bombay Deccan* (Poona, 1956); (iii) *The Last Phase* (Bombay, 1948); (iv) *Selections from the Deccan Commissioner's Files* (Poona, 1945).

10 T. E. Colebrooke, *Life of Honourable Mountstuart Elphinstone*, 2 Vols. (London, 1884).

11 W. S. Demming, *Ramdas and the Ramdasis* (Calcutta, 1928).

12 R. E. Enthoven, *The Tribes and Castes of Bombay*, 3 Vols. (Bombay, 1921).

13 R. Gopal. *Lomkanya Tilak: A Biography* (Bombay, 1956).

14 J. Grant-Duff, *A History of the Marathas* (Oxford, 1921).

15 D. G. Karve, *Ranade: Prophet of Liberated India*.

16 I. Karve, *Hindu Society: An Interpretation* (Poona, 1961).

17 J. Kellock, *Mahadev Govind Ranade: Patriot and Social Servant* (Calcutta, 1926).

18 N. C. Kelkar, *Life and Times of Lokmanya Tilak* (translated by D. V. Divekar) (Madras, 1928).

19 P. M. Limaye, *The History of the Deccan Education Society* (Poona, 1935).

20 A. C. Lyall, *Asiatic Studies: Religious and Social*, 2 Vols. (London, 1907).

21 J. Martineau, *The Life and Correspondence of Sir Bartle Frere*, 2 Vols. (London, 1893).

22 J. Muccann, *Six Radical Thinkers* (London, 1903).

23 *Memorandum from the Samyakta Maharashtra Committee to the States Reorganisation Committee.*

24 A. Roger, *The Land-Revenue System of Bombay*, 2 Vols. (London, 1892).

25 G. S. Sardesai: (i) *New History of the Marathas*, 3 Vols. (Bombay, 1946–48); (ii) *The Main Currents of Maratha History* (Bombay, 1849).

26 E. Stokes, *The English Utilitarians and India* (Oxford, 1959).

27 B. H. Tahmankar, *Lokmanya Tilak* (London, 1956).

28 H. W. Wolff, *Co-operation in India* (London, 1925).

Index

abhangas, 11, 31, 32, 43, 292
administration, before 1818, 12–16, 318–21; by 1818, 16–43; of utilitarians and some conservatives, 85–155, 324–7; exercise of control over hereditary officers by, 128–50; effect of reforms in, on rural society, 151–90; attempt to restore balance of power in rural society by, 190–263; and the Deccan Agriculturists' Relief Act, 212–28; and co-operative societies, 236–63. Administration of the law, *see* judicial administration. Administration of education, *see* education
administrators, British, 112, 122, 137, 190; summary of their achievements in Maharashtra, 321–2. *Also see* Elphinstone; Chaplin; Dupernex; Goldsmid; Grant; Maine; Munro; Nicholson; Pringle; Robertson; Temple; Thornton; West; Williamson; Wingate; and Wodehouse
advaita, and Sankara, 7–8; influence of, 43; and the intellectual climate of Maharashtra, 265, 292, 308, 319; Bhima Shastri Zhalkikar's debate of 1886 on, 308–12
advaitavada, 264; the debate of 1886 on, 308–12
advaitin, 9
advaitists, 293
Agricultural Banks, 228–36; *sowcars'* proposal regarding, 228; attitude of Government of Bombay to, 231–3; India Office rejects proposal for, 234–5; disadvantages of, 236, 238, 239
Agriculture, cultivation, 17–30; and land revenue surveys, 57–71, 178, 298–304, 321, 324–30
Ahmednagar (District), 25, 53, 57, 90, 138, 158

Baber, J. H., report on the Hindu College, 265–6
bakhar, 17
Bentham, Jeremy, influence on Elphinstone, 74, 75, 81; influence on Pringle, 128; influence on J. S. Mill, 196; and the utilitarians, 195, 197; and the principle of efficiency, 212; and M. G. Ranade, 284
bhagwata (cult), 9
bhatri, *see* footnotes on 8, 9; Jnaneshwar and, 9; the movement and its principal exponents in Maharashtra, 9–11, 12, 31, 43, 312; initiation into, 31–2; its effect on elite castes, 264–5; its effects on society, 42, 319, 321
bhayachara, 113, 246, 250
bhowbund, 138–47
Bombay Education Society, 53; its branch called Native Education Society 52–5
Brahma Samaj, 295
brahmans, 7–9, 14; position in society, 30–1, 37–44; chitpavan, 37, 38, 39, 43–4, 48–9, 282, 283–4; and *dakshina*, 48–9; the education of, 50–6, 322–3, 330–2; and the Poona Association, 174–6; the rise of liberal, 264–7; position of orthodox, 274–81; M. G. Ranade and western education, 281–97; the rich *kunbis* threaten position of, 298, 313–17; Jyotiba Phule's criticism of, 304–8, 313–15; attitude of orthodox, towards modernisation, 308–10; and B. G. Tilak, 310–13
Briggs, John, 60–3
bullotedars, 29–30, 184, 185, 187

caste co-operatives, 257–9
caste institutions, their role, 37, 40–1, 320–1: their merits and demerits, 72–3

341

42317